ESSENTIAL FOR LIVING

A Communication, Behavior
and Functional Skills
Assessment, Curriculum
and Teaching Manual

For Children and Adults
with Moderate-to-Severe
Disabilities

Patrick McGreevy
Troy Fry and Colleen Cornwall

Essential for Living
A Communication, Behavior, and Functional Skills
Assessment, Curriculum, and Teaching Manual

© 2012 by Patrick McGreevy

Published by: Patrick McGreevy, Ph.D., P.A.
               1035 South Semoran, Suite 1031
               Winter Park, FL 32792   USA
               (01) 407-415-5241
               essential4living@me.com
               www.behaviorchange.com

All rights reserved. No part of this publication can be reproduced in any manner or shared digitally without written permission from the publisher.

Copies of this book can be ordered from www.behaviorchange.com.

Printed in the United States of America

August, 2012

ISBN: 978-0-9855605-0-8

Acknowledgments

Throughout the development of this instrument, we have invited and received suggestions from many colleagues and parents. We once envisioned keeping an accurate list of these contributions, but have failed to keep up with this task. There are, however, individuals whose contributions have been substantial and whom we wish to acknowledge: Carl Sundberg, Vince Carbone, Mark Sundberg, Ernie Vargas, Merrill Winston, Bob Ryan, and Eb Blakely.

We are grateful for the assistance of Janine Shapiro, who co authored chapter 6, and A. Hunter Williams, who edited each chapter and helped us produce the *ARP* manual.

We gratefully acknowledge our teachers: Ogden Lindsley, Jack Michael, and Don Baer, and those who influenced us, B. F. Skinner and Stephen Jay Gould. Standing on their shoulders has permitted us to see more and to see further...

Finally, and most importantly, we wish to acknowledge some of our best teachers -- the many hundreds of children and adults with disabilities with whom we have worked, along with their instructors, care providers, and parents. From Glenda in 1968 to Hector in 2012, from one continent to another, they have significantly shaped the content of this instrument.

Patrick McGreevy, Ph.D., BCBA-D
Winter Park, FL

Troy Fry, M.S., BCBA
Chaska, MN

Colleen Cornwall, Ed.D., BCBA-D
Naples, FL

Dedication

To Kristin, Phyllis, and Hunter

and

to all those children and adults with moderate-to-severe disabilities,
especially those with limited communication skills...

ESSENTIAL FOR LIVING
Table of Contents

Chapter 1.	What You Need to Know	1
Chapter 2.	Intellectual Capacity and Other Fallacies: Much Ado About Nothing	9
Chapter 3.	Scope and Sequence Summary Assessment and Record of Progress and Sample IEPs and ISPs	11
Chapter 4.	Conducting an Assessment and Recording Progress	25
Chapter 5.	The Quick Assessment	39
Chapter 6.	Methods of Speaking	45
Chapter 7.	Speaking and Listening Skills	113
	7a. Requests and Related Listener Responses	113
	7b. Listener Responses, Names, and Descriptions	145
	7c. Answers to Questions and Conversations	167
Chapter 8.	Doing Skills	187
	8a. Daily Living and Related Skills	187
	8b. Functional Academic Skills	205
	8b1. Responding to Text as a Listener and Reading	205
	8b2. Schedules, Lists, and Time	211
	8b3. Math Skills	221
	8b4. Writing or Typing Skills	227
Chapter 9.	Tolerating Skills and Eggshells	231
Chapter 10.	Problem Behavior	241
Chapter 11.	Tool Skills and Component Skills	257
Chapter 12.	Teaching Protocols	265
Chapter 13.	References	279
Appendix		287

Chapter 1. What You Need to Know

What *Essential for Living* is and What It is not

Essential for Living is a communication, behavior, and functional skills assessment, curriculum, and skill-tracking instrument for both children and adults with moderate-to-severe disabilities. It is especially useful for learners with limited communication repertoires, minimal daily living skills, or severe problem behavior. This instrument is based on concepts, principles, and empirically-validated procedures from Applied Behavior Analysis (ABA) and from B. F. Skinner's ground-breaking analysis of verbal behavior (Skinner, 1957).

Other functional skills assessments and curriculums, such as, *A Functional Curriculum for Teaching Students with Disabilities* (Valletutti et al., 2008), have been helpful for children and adults with moderate-to-severe disabilities. *Essential for Living*, however, is the first instrument of its kind that is based on concepts, principles, and procedures from Applied Behavior Analysis and that includes speaking and listening skills based on B. F. Skinner's analysis of verbal behavior (Skinner, 1957).

Essential for Living is both an assessment and a curriculum. It is used to determine the current performance level of each child or adult with respect to skills that are part of the instrument, in other words, to conduct a curriculum-based assessment. This instrument is also used to develop appropriate goals and objectives for individual education or support plans and to track skill acquisition and problem behavior.

Essential for Living is not a developmental instrument and it is neither age, nor grade-referenced. That is, it does not include skills arranged in an order in which they are often acquired by typically developing children, and sets of skills within in this order are not categorized by age or grade. By contrast, *The Verbal Behavior Milestones Assessment and Placement Program: The VB-MAPP* (Sundberg, 2008) is an excellent example of a developmental assessment, curriculum, skill-tracking instrument, and IEP development guide, which is also based on concepts, principles, and empirically-validated procedures from Applied Behavior Analysis (ABA) and B. F. Skinner's analysis of verbal behavior (Skinner, 1957). The developmental levels in the *VB-MAPP* are also age-referenced.

Essential for Living is composed of functional skills and behaviors, which are essential for effective daily living and which result in an improved quality of life for children and adults. Specifically, this instrument includes skills and behaviors, or components thereof:

- which are required in other settings,
- which are taught in circumstances similar to those which occur in those settings,
- in the absence of which, learners would require the assistance of other persons, or
- which result in increased access to preferred items, activities, places, and people.

By contrast, *The VB-MAPP* is composed of skills arranged in a sequence in which typically-developing learners generally acquire them and that, if acquired, tend to result in typical or nearly typical language, social, and academic skills, and partial or full mainstreaming with peers of the same or nearly the same age. Table 1 provides examples of developmental skills from *The VB-MAPP* and functional skills from *Essential for* Living.

Table 1
Developmental Skills from *The VB-MAPP* and Functional Skills from *Essential for Living*

Developmental Skills from The VB-MAPP	Functional Skills from Essential for Living
Makes requests with three different carrier phrases	Makes a request for assistance with menstruation or locating a restroom
Looks for an item that has fallen out of sight	Retrieves a wash cloth from a linen closet
Matches identical items or pictures in a neat array of three	Takes clothes out of a dryer, *matches socks*, and folds socks
Touches one of two body parts when directed to do so	Retrieves items and participates in activities that are part of snack or break time (e.g., plate, napkin, pouring juice, table, trash can, and throwing away trash)
Completes out of context fill-in-the blank phrases	Provides name and address when asked to do so
Uses irregular plurals correctly	Makes requests that include two of the same item, two items, or an item with a feature (e.g., two cookies, juice and crackers, or strawberry yogurt)

As shown in Table 2, *Essential for Living* is divided into five categories of skills describing how children and adults interact with the world around them, seven skill domains, and one domain on problem behavior. Speaking and listening, in other words, how we use language to communicate with others and how we respond to their use of language, includes three domains: (1) making requests, (2) responding as a listener to the requests of others, along with naming and describing items, activities, people, and places, and (3) answering the questions of others and participating in conversations. Doing, in other words, completing activities when situations occur which require these activities, includes two skill domains: (4) daily living and related skills, which includes leisure and vocational skills, along with (5) functional academic and related skills, which includes responding to text as a listener, reading, math skills, schedules, lists, and time, and functional writing skills. Tolerating, in other words, remaining in unpleasant situations without resisting or exhibiting problem behavior until these situations have changed, is incorporated in a single skill domain: (6) tolerating skills and eggshells. These skills are seldom included in assessment instruments. Tool movements are basic motor movements, along with matching and imitation, that, when taught until they occur without prompts and without hesitation, sometimes result in a more rapid acquisition of [occur at a fluent level] complex skills that include these movements. These movements are incorporated in a single skill domain: (7) tool skills and component skills. Inappropriate behavior occurs in many situations and becomes problem behavior when it results in harmful or disruptive outcomes for learners exhibiting the behavior, for their environment, or for those around them. Social skills are included in all domains except tool skills and component skills.

Table 2.
The Structure and Content of *Essential for Living*

Facilitating and Teaching Spoken-word Communication Selecting, Confirming, and Maintaining an Alternative Method of Speaking	
The Essential Eight and The Essential for Living Quick Assessment	
How Children and Adults Interact with the World Around Them	The Domains of *Essential for Living*
Speaking and Listening	1. Requests and Related Listener Responses 2. Listener Responses, Names, and Descriptions 3. Answers to Questions and Conversations

Doing	4. Daily Living and Related Skills
	5. Functional Academic Skills
	  • Responding to Text as a Listener and Reading
	  • Schedules, Lists, and Time
	  • Math Skills
	  • Writing or Typing Skills

Tolerating	6. Tolerating Skills and Eggshells
Tool Movements	7. Tool Skills and Component Skills
Inappropriate Behavior	Problem Behavior
Teaching Protocols	

Skills within each of the seven skill domains are sequenced from less to more difficult and more to less functional and designated as *must-have, should-have, good-to-have, and nice-to-have*. Assessment and teaching begin with *must-have skills*. A suggested assessment and teaching sequence within and across domains is provided in chapter 3.

Essential for Living includes an extensive array of skills in each domain. It does not include, nor could it possibly include, all of the skills that might be functional for specific children and adults with moderate-to-severe disabilities. It does provide, however, opportunities for instructors and care providers to add skills to each domain for children and adults with whom they work. Skills from *A Functional Curriculum for Teaching Students with Disabilities* (Valletutti et al., 2008) and task analyses from *The Murdoch Center Program Library*[1] (Wheeler et al., 1987) can be used in conjunction with *Essential for Living*.

---

[1] Available from The Murdoch Foundation -- http://www.murdochfoundation.org/programlibrary.htm

The skills in *Essential for Living* are taught *in context*, in other words, in situations nearly the same as those in which they will be expected to occur. This often precludes or minimizes the necessity for generalization. When instructors, care providers, and parents inquire about the importance of context, we often respond by saying "*context is everything*".

Essential for Living also includes discriminations that are required in everyday living. For example, while having lunch, setting the table, or unloading the dishwasher, children or adults may learn to retrieve and relocate spoons and forks. While this discrimination may be more difficult than pointing to a spoon and a picture of a giraffe during discrete-trial instruction at a table, it is arguably more functional.

As shown in Table 2, *Essential for Living* includes two sections not found in other instruments. The first of these provides specific guidelines and procedures for (1) facilitating and teaching spoken-word communication, and (2) selecting, confirming, and maintaining alternative methods of speaking for children and adults who have limited or no effective use of spoken words. The second section provides an array of protocols for teaching the skills included in this instrument.

The Essential Eight

Essential for Living includes eight skills that are absolutely essential for a happy, fulfilling, and productive life as a child or an adult. These skills have been designated as *The Essential Eight* (see Table 3) and are the central focus of *Essential for Living*. Without these skills, children and adults with disabilities will almost certainly exhibit forms of problem behavior, will have limited access to preferred items, activities, places, and people, and will have limited contact and interaction with the community in which they live. These skills, their skill domain, and their skill numbers are specified in Table 3.

Table 3.
The Essential Eight

	Skill	Domain	Skill Number(s)
One.	Making Requests	Requests and Related...	R1-5, R6, R7-8, R14, R17-21
Two.	Waiting	Requests and Related...	R9
Three.	Accepting Removals, Making Transitions, Sharing, and Taking Turns	Requests and Related...	R10, R12, R13
Four.	Completing 10 Consecutive, Brief, Previously Acquired Tasks	Requests and Related...	R11
Five.	Accepting "No"	Requests and Related...	R15-16
Six.	Following Directions Related to Health and Safety	Listener Responses, Names, and Descriptions	LR1-11
Seven.	Completing Daily Living Skills Related to Health and Safety	Daily Living and Related Skills	DLS-EDF1-9, DLS-Slp1-2, DLS-MT1-5, DLS-AHS1-15, DLS-HS1-8
Eight.	Tolerating Situations Related to Health and Safety	Tolerating Skills and Eggshells	T-BHI-5, T-EDF1-11, T-DM1-9, T-Slp1-5, T-Toil1-5, T-PRM1-6 T-PTA1-11, T-PEMR1-10, T-BPH1-8, T-DD1

How Performance is Measured

The collection of daily probe data is recommended and self-graphing data sheets similar to those that are part of the Murdoch Center Program Library (Wheeler et al., 1987) are provided in chapter 12 for that purpose. Performance is measured by:

- the presence or absence of problem behavior,
- the presence or absence of resistance to prompts,
- the presence or absence of inappropriate responses,
- the extent to which prompts are required or hesitation occurs,
- the extent to which permanent, partial assistance is required,
- the extent to which an environmental adaptation or prosthetic device is required,

- additional situations in which the skill occurs, and
- any deterioration in performance after skill acquisition.

The assessment of problem behavior includes the extent to which specific forms occur, the intensity of those forms, and the supports that are provided because of those forms. These supports may include:

- protective equipment or mechanical restraint,
- crisis stabilization procedures,
- psychoactive medications,
- and self-restraint.

How Often should *Essential for Living* be Administered

Essential for Living should be administered when you first begin working with a specific child or adult. This instrument includes skills that are functional and occur frequently in learners' everyday lives. And, these skills are considered acquired only when they occur in at least one appropriate situation without prompts and without hesitation (at a fluent level). As a result, maintenance, the extent to which acquired skills continue to occur, is not assessed directly (i.e., maintenance checks are not conducted). Once skills occur at a fluent level, frequent opportunities to practice should insure maintenance. If acquired skills no longer occur in specific situations, this performance deterioration is recorded. And, it is obvious to instructors and care providers that re-teaching or rearranging management procedures is necessary. Assessing and teaching frequently occurring skills and recording performance deterioration, rather than maintenance, virtually insures that *Essential for Living* is always up-to-date and that learners should not require periodic reassessments.

The *Essential for Living* Quick Assessment

The initial administration of *Essential for Living* may require several weeks. With some learners, especially those with no method of speaking and severe problem behavior, *The Essential for Living Quick Assessment* may be useful. This assessment can be conducted by interviewing one or more instructors or care providers and can generally be completed within 1-2 hours. Then, teaching skills and managing problem behavior can begin almost immediately. *The Essential for Living Quick Assessment*, which is described in chapter 5, includes the following skills and skill domains, including *The Essential Eight*:

- Spoken Words,
- Alternative Method of Speaking,
- Making Requests,   ⎫
- Waiting,   ⎪
- Accepting Removals, Making Transitions, Sharing, and Taking Turns, ⎪
- Completing 10 Consecutive, Brief, Previously Acquired Tasks, ⎬ **The Essential Eight**
- Accepting 'No',   ⎪
- Following Directions Related to Health and Safety, ⎪
- Completing Daily Living Skills Related to Health and Safety, ⎪
- Tolerating Unpleasant Situations Related to Health and Safety ⎭
- Matching,
- Motor Imitation,
- Other Daily Living Skills,
- Tolerating Other Situations,
- Naming and Describing,
- Recognizing and Retrieving,
- Answering Questions, and
- Problem Behavior.

How We Came to Where We Are

Essential for Living is a product of many years of experience with children and adults who, when first referred to us, exhibited severe disruptive, destructive, aggressive, or self-injurious behaviors, used few if any spoken words to communicate, had no other formal method of speaking, and functioned almost exclusively as listeners. Many, but not all, of these problem behaviors were followed and maintained by specific forms of attention, avoidance or escape from specific types of demands, or access to preferred items or activities. were socially-mediated

In the absence of a formal method, problem behaviors functioned as a form of speaking. In our early years, after conducting functional assessments, we targeted appropriate listening skills (e.g., completing assigned tasks) as replacement behaviors. Then, if children or adults exhibited these listening skills without exhibiting problem behaviors for brief, but gradually increasing, periods of time, we provided access to attention, preferred items or activities, or removed demands briefly. *In other words, in children and adults with few to no speaking skills, we replaced problem behaviors equivalent to speaking with listening skills.*

Functional Communication Training (Carr and Durand, 1985) helped us become aware of the error of our ways. In what represented a huge step forward, these behavior analysts were replacing problem behaviors maintained by attention, escape from demands, or access to tangible items and activities, with vocal, sign, or picture-selection requests for the same type of item or activity. They were teaching children and adults with severe developmental disabilities and limited communication skills to function, for the first time, as effective speakers. In the footsteps of Carr and Durand (1985) and their colleagues, we began replacing socially-mediated problem behaviors with generalized requests for attention, escape, or access to a category of items or activities (e.g., 'an arm tap', or a sign or picture card for 'eat', 'play', or 'break') until these requests replaced the problem behaviors. *became functionally equivalent to*

Then, after several years of teaching generalized requests, we re-examined B. F. Skinner's *generalized mands* analysis of speaker behavior and audience control (Skinner, 1957) and became more familiar with the pioneering work of Jack Michael (Michael, 1982a, 1982b, 1983, 1984, 1985, 1988, 1993), Mark Sundberg (Sundberg, 1979, 1980, 1983, 1987, 1993, 1998; Sundberg & Partington, 1998; Partington and Sundberg, 1999) and their colleagues (Spradlin, 1963, 1985; Catania, 1973a, 1973b; Hall and Sundberg, 1987; Braam and Sundberg, 1991; Shafer, 1993, 1994; Brady, Saunders & Spradlin, 1994; to name a few). As a result of this work, and that of our colleague, Vince Carbone, we began teaching vocal, sign, and picture-selection requests for specific, preferred items and activities (e.g., 'cookies' [chocolate chip cookies], 'music' [a small musical toy], and 'jump [jumping on a trampoline]'), rather than the more generalized requests we had been teaching.

By capturing and contriving motivation, prompting errorlessly (Carbone, 1999; McGreevy, 2003), and fading prompts rapidly (Touchette, 1971; Sundberg & Partington, 1998), we began building repertoires of requests in children with autism, including those who began with no requests and no method of communication. As each child acquired a repertoire of requests for specific *no communication* items and activities, we began using *The ABLLS* (Partington & Sundberg, 1998) and teach- *response form* ing (1) cooperation and receptive skills, (2) names and descriptions of items, proper-ties of items, and activities, (3) advanced requests, (4) answers to questions, and (5) conversational skills. Later we replaced *The ABLLS* (Partington & Sundberg, 1998) with *The VB-MAPP* (Sundberg, 2008), which provided a sequence of skills that coincided more closely with language acquisition in typically-developing children. This approach has been described as Applied *We prefer ABA-Verbal Behavior* Verbal Behavior, the Verbal Behavior Approach (Barbera, 2008; Carr & Firth, *(or EAB-Verbal Behavior) because* 2005), or ABA-Verbal Behavior (McGreevy, 2009). *this term suggests, as should be the case, that B. F. Skinner's analysis of verbal behavior is an orientation within the field of Applied Behavior Analysis (or the Experimental Analysis of Behavior).*

Soon we began using this approach with older children and adults with autism and other moderate-to-severe disabilities, including those with very limited sensory or motor skills. Using *The VB-MAPP*, we began teaching requests, motor imitation, matching, and listening skills. Many of these learners struggled to acquire developmentally appropriate skills, especially those skills that required complex discriminations. These experiences and our long history *conditional discriminations* with this population of learners suggested that a developmental assessment and curriculum designed to result in typical or nearly typical language and academic skills did not address the most important challenge facing these children and adults -- communicating and functioning effectively in the world around them -- and that this outcome would be more likely to occur with a functional assessment and curriculum.

As a result, we began modifying programs for specific children and adults that were based on the VB-MAPP. We revised and added speaking, listening, and tool skills, added tolerating skills, emphasized the management of problem behavior in the context of skill development, and added daily living and some functional academic skills using the *Murdoch Center Library* (Wheeler et al., 1987) and *A Functional Curriculum for Teaching Students with Disabilities* (Valletutti et al., 2008).

For some of these children and many of these adults, functional skills leading to effective daily living were already being taught or, at least, being considered for inclusion in their instructional program. And, since a functional skills assessment, curriculum, and skill-tracking instrument based on B. F. Skinner's analysis of speaker behavior was not available, we set about the task of developing one. Since there were no available guidelines for selecting alternative methods of speaking for learners with limited to no vocal skills, we also set about this task. And, we decided to include in this instrument teaching protocols with empirically-validated teaching procedures.

Our decision to develop this instrument was also influenced by the emergence of state-mandated alternative assessment instruments in the United States, an outgrowth of *The No Child Left Behind Act of 2001*, which emphasize 'academic, graded-referenced skills', almost to the exclusion of functional skills, even for learners with moderate-to-severe developmental disabilities. Some states, who have developed these instruments, have suggested that teachers abandon the term *functional* in favor of *relevant*. The first author has observed the conduct of state alternative assessments and the teaching of these 'so called' relevant skills. The following examples have been selected from these observations:

- a 12-year-old girl with severe developmental disabilities and no method of speaking, who was presented with drawings of a square and a triangle and asked "which one is a triangle"; and,
- students in a middle school with moderate developmental disabilities were expected to use a calculator to solve double-digit addition problems when they could not count and retrieve items, recognize or identify coins, make purchases, or use a vending machine; when one of the students was asked to read one of her answers, she pointed to 83 and replied "8 and 3".

These assessment instruments and academic standards for students with moderate-to-severe disabilities have placed teachers in an untenable position -- teach to non-functional standards or risk losing your job.

With Whom Should *Essential for Living* be Used

Essential for Living was designed for -- *children and adults of all ages* -- with:

- neurological disorders,
- chromosomal disorders,
- congenital or acquired conditions, or
- global developmental delays (sometimes inaccurately referred to as intellectual disabilities or mental retardation)

which result in moderate-to-severe disabilities. As part of their disabilities, these learners may also experience:

- a hearing impairment,
- a visual impairment,
- a hearing and a visual impairment (deaf and blind),
- a severe orthopedic impairment or medical condition limiting arm and hand movements,
- a medical condition that requires suction and ventilation or other forms of continuous care,
- a medical condition that poses a continuous risk of injury,
- a medical condition that requires frequent hospitalization, or
- a terminal medical condition.

These children and adults may be diagnosed with:

- Down Syndrome,
- Autism,
- Pervasive Developmental Disorder or PDD-NOS,
- Cerebral Palsy,
- Fragile-X Syndrome,
- Landau-Kleffner Syndrome,
- Hydrocephalus,
- Microcephaly,
- Spina Bifida,
- Angelman Syndrome,
- Microcephaly,
- Cornelia de Lange Syndrome,
- Lesch-Nyhan Syndrome,
- Tay-Sachs Syndrome,
- Hunter Syndrome,

- Hurler Syndrome,
- Williams Syndrome,
- Prader-Willi Syndrome,
- Rett Syndrome,
- a form of apraxia,
- a stroke,
- a closed head injury,
- a form of aphasia,

or another condition or syndrome resulting in moderate-to-severe disabilities. Or, they may be among the majority of children and adults with moderate-to-severe developmental disabilities, who have not been diagnosed with any specific condition or syndrome.

Essential for Living was designed for children and adults who use spoken words to communicate and those who do not, especially those:

- who have not acquired an effective, alternative method of speaking, or
- from whom expressive communication (i.e., functioning as a speaker) is no longer expected.

And, last but not least, *Essential for Living* was designed for learners who exhibit moderate-to-severe forms of non-compliant, aggressive, self-injurious, or destructive behavior.

Choosing Which Instrument to Use

The VB-MAPP and *Essential for Living* are complementary instruments based on the same concepts, principles, and procedures, but each with a different purpose: the former to guide the instruction of young children as instructors try to help them 'catch up' with typically-developing peers with respect to language and social skills, and the latter to provide children and adults with speaking, listening, and other skills that are essential for effective daily living.

Many young children from 2-6 years of age with developmental disabilities, including autism, appear to experience delays primarily in language and social skills. With these children, we strongly recommend that *The VB-MAPP* be used to determine their current language and social skills and to guide the development of a program of instruction and behavior management. Some of these children will acquire nearly typical language and social skills and will be placed for academic instruction in inclusion settings with typically-developing peers. Many others will experience improved language and social skills, resulting in more effective interaction with adults and peers, and placement for instruction in special education programs, with opportunities for inclusion with typically-developing peers in social situations.

Many other children two years of age and older appear to experience significant global developmental delays or specific syndromes which typically result in limited language development, abstract concepts, and discrimination skills. These children may also experience severe hearing, visual, or orthopedic impairments, or compelling medical conditions. With these children, we suggest that *Essential for Living* be used to: (1) determine the extent to which they communicate with understandable spoken words, (2) select an alternative method of speaking, if understandable spoken words are limited, (3) determine the extent of their speaking and listening repertoires, (4) determine the extent of their basic motor movements, matching and imitation skills, daily living skills, functional academic skills, and tolerating skills, (5) determine the extent to which they exhibit problem behavior, (6) guide the development of a program of instruction and behavior management, and (7) select and implement teaching procedures designed specifically for identified skill deficits. Some of these children will acquire many skills, while others will acquire a core set of skills, that are immediately functional for them, that will help them benefit from instruction in special education programs and from inclusion in social situations, and that will remain functional over the span of their lives.

For children from 7-8 years of age, who are making steady progress on *The VB-MAPP*, we recommend continuing with this assessment and curriculum. For children within this age range who are making very little progress, we strongly recommend securing the assistance of an individual with *considerable training and experience* teaching language and social skills using B. F. Skinner's analysis of verbal behavior. If progress does not begin to occur, despite multiple adjustments in teaching procedures, consider changing from a developmental to a functional curriculum and beginning to use *Essential for Living* or using both instruments for a period of time while that decision is being made.

For most children 9-10 years of age and older, who experience difficulty answering questions or participating in conversations and who have not acquired academic skills at a first or second grade level, we suggest *Essential for Living*.

For some children, *Essential for Living* can function as a companion to *The VB-MAPP*, helping instructors and care providers: (1) determine the extent to which children exhibit understandable spoken words and select teaching procedures designed to improve this repertoire, (2) select an alternative method of speaking, for children whose repertoire of understandable spoken words is limited, (3) assess and teach functional skills along with the developmental ones they are currently teaching, and (4) determine the extent to which children exhibit problem behavior and learn to manage these behaviors in the context of teaching the *Essential Eight*.

For adults with moderate-to-severe disabilities, developmental or acquired, we suggest *Essential for Living*.

Essential for Living: A Product of Empirically-validated Concepts, Principles, and Procedures

Essential for Living is based on a vast body of scientific knowledge, most of which has accumulated over the past 50 years. It is based primarily on B. F. Skinner's analysis of verbal behavior (Skinner, 1957) and the research and writing of Jack Michael (Michael, 1982, 1984, 1985, 1988, 2000), A. Charles Catania (Catania, 2007), Ernest Vargas (Vargas, 1982, 1986), Mark Sundberg (Sundberg, 1993, 2007, 2008; Sundberg & Michael, 2001; Sundberg & Partington, 1998), Esther Shafer (1993, 1994), R. Douglas Greer (Greer and Ross, 2007), Barry Lowenkron (Lowenkron, 2004, 2006), Vince Carbone (Carbone, 2004; Carbone, Morgenstern, Zecchin-Tirri, & Kolberg, 2007), the first author (McGreevy, 2009), their colleagues, and many others (Terrace, 1963; Moore & Goldiamond, 1964; Touchette, 1971; Etzel & LeBlanc, 1979; Brownjohn, 1988; Graff & Green, 2004; to name a few). Specific citations are provided throughout this instrument and an extensive reference list is provided in chapter 13.

A Note About the Format

This instrument was written in language familiar to most professionals in the fields of special education, developmental disabilities, and rehabilitation. As you will notice, sections of the text are printed in blue. These sections describe specific concepts, principles, and procedures from Applied Behavior Analysis, B. F. Skinner's analysis of verbal behavior, and Speech and Language Pathology. Just to the right of these sections, printed in red, are corresponding descriptions written in technical language familiar to most speech-language pathologists and behavior analysts. These translations will help professionals guide and supervise the use of this instrument and will assist students of speech and language pathology and applied behavior analysis acquire these fundamental concepts, principles, and procedures.

Chapter 2. Intellectual Capacity and Other Fallacies: Much Ado About Nothing

Intellectual Capacity

When a child or an adult has a tested IQ of 50 or less *and* exhibits little-to-no communication or language skills, some psychologists and speech-language pathologists conclude that these skills are commensurate with the learner's limited intellectual capacity and that the learner may be cognitively incapable of acquiring communication or expressive language skills.[1] incapable of functioning as an effective speaker

A number of years ago, Drs. Vince Carbone and Patrick McGreevy were providing consultation to a large residential facility for adults with moderate-to-severe developmental disabilities. One afternoon, they were called to a unit, where a young man was exhibiting intense aggressive behavior. Upon their arrival, they learned that the young man was ambulatory, 37 years old, and non-verbal (i.e., did not use spoken words to communicate), and that episodes of intense not vocal-verbal aggressive behavior occurred several times per month. They also learned that he displayed good fine motor skills, but did not imitate spoken words or motor movements.

When Dr. Carbone asked if the young man had acquired an alternative method of speaking, the staff produced a report based on an assessment by a speech-language pathologist, indicating that he was *incapable of benefitting from a formal system of communication*. Upon learning from a staff member that the young man liked coffee, Dr. Carbone obtained a pot of coffee and began errorlessly prompting a sign for coffee. Within *seven* minutes, the young man was requesting coffee with a two-step sign, *pour coffee*, without prompts.

Several years ago, a teacher, a behavior analyst and Dr. McGreevy worked with a 19-year-old young man with severe developmental disabilities. He was ambulatory and did not use spoken words to communicate. He exhibited limited fine motor skills and did not imitate spoken words or motor movements. He did not point or lead others to preferred items or exhibit any other method of speaking. His most recent IQ score was reported as 18 and he was not receiving speaker response form speech and language services. They taught him to request the only food he could consume orally -- small pieces of soft bread with butter and cinnamon -- with an idiosyncratic sign (i.e., a gesture that is understandable only to a familiar audience). By the end of the third week of instruction, he was requesting the bread without prompts.

Recently, Dr. McGreevy was asked to provide consultation for a seven-year-old girl with severe developmental disabilities. She had no method of speaking and was mobile by wheelchair. She experienced spastic movements, both flexion and extension. She displayed very limited fine motor movement and range of motion, and only with her right arm and right hand. Her communication was limited to looking toward an item in her immediate environment or smiling when asked if she wanted a specific item or activity. Dr. McGreevy taught her to request yogurt and a toy with idiosyncratic signs. She learned to exhibit both signs without prompts in one 20-minute session. Many hundreds of cases like these have prompted us to conclude that *very few children and adults are cognitively incapable of functioning as effective speakers*.

Pre-speaking Stages and Skills

Many children and adults with moderate-to-severe developmental disabilities have not 'reached' one or more of the following developmental stages:

1. cause and effect,
2. communicative intent, or
3. object permanence,

or acquired either or both of the following skills:

4. eye contact, or
5. joint attention.

Some psychologists and speech-language pathologists have been taught that all of these stages and skills are *prerequisites to functioning as an effective speaker*. As a result, they often try to teach eye contact and joint attention, but tend to wait for skills that are said to be indicative of cause and effect, communicative intent, and object permanence to 'emerge'.

---

[1] For an eloquent account of the fallacies inherent in biological determinism, the concept of intelligence, and the resulting injustices, see *The Mismeasure of Man* by Stephen Jay Gould (included in the Reference List).

With many children and adults, these skills are not easily acquired and don't often emerge. As a result, communication and expressive language are not taught for months and often years, and, with many older children and adults, *never acquired*. We have taught hundreds of children and adults to be effective speakers who have not 'reached' any of these stages or acquired either of these skills. These experiences have led us to conclude that these stages and skills, while helpful in acquiring speaking skills, *are not prerequisites to functioning as an effective speaker*.

speaker behavior

In conclusion, most children and adults are capable of functioning as effective speakers and can learn to do so without 'reaching' specific, developmental stages or without acquiring pre-speaking skills. Our experience suggests that functioning as an effective speaker requires (1) *a specific motor movement or collection of movements that can function effectively as the learner's method of speaking*, (2) *some indication that the learner wants specific, preferred items or activities*, and (3) *scientifically-validated teaching procedures from Applied Behavior Analysis and B. F. Skinner's analysis of verbal behavior*.

(1) an effective speaker response form;
(2) some indication that motivating operations have occurred or are occurring; and,
(3) a set of empirically-validated, behavior analytic teaching procedures.

Chapter 3. Scope and Sequence
Summary Assessment and Record of Progress
Sample IEPs and ISPs

As indicated in chapter 1, *Essential for Living* includes seven skill domains. Skills are designated as must-have, should-have, good-to-have, and nice-to-have *within* each domain. *Must-have* skills are generally more functional and less difficult and should be taught first, followed by *should-have, good-to-have,* and *nice-to-have* skills that are progressively less functional and more difficult. Table 1 describes the scope and sequence of *Essential for Living*, that is, the skills in each domain from *must-have* to *good-to-have* or *nice-to-have* and their skill numbers. Skills that are part of the *Essential Eight* are printed in bold. As described in chapter 4, *Essential for Living also* provides spaces for instructors, care providers, and parents to add skills for individual learners.

Table 1.
The Scope and Sequence of *Essential for Living* within Skill Domains

Chapter 7. Speaking and Listening Skills

7a. Requests and Related Listener Responses R1-90

   Must-have Skills R1-21

      Making Requests R1-5, R6, R7-8, R14, R17-21
      Waiting R9
      **Accepting Removals, Making Transitions,
      Sharing, and Taking Turns R10, R12-13**
      **Completing 10 Consecutive,
      Brief, Previously Acquired Tasks R11**
      Accepting 'No' R15-16

   Should-have Skills R22-48

      Making Requests R22-24, R27-28, R30-31,
                                                                    R33-39, R41, R43-45, R47-48
      Waiting R25
      Accepting Removals from Peers R46
      Completing 20 Consecutive,
      Previously Acquired Tasks R29
      Accepting 'No' R26, R32, R40, R42

   Good-to-have Skills R49-79

      Making Special Requests R49-70
      Making Requests that Require
      2-4 Words, Signs, or Pictures R71-79

   Nice-to-have Skills R80-90

      Making Advanced Requests R80-83
      Requesting Information R84-88
      Other Advanced Requests R89-90

7b. Listener Responses, Names, and Descriptions LR1-17, LREv1-15, NDEv1-15

   Must-have Skills

      Following Directions Related to Health and Safety LR1-11

   Should-have Skills

      Following Directions to Complete Routine Activities LR12-17

Table 1. (cont.)
The Scope and Sequence of *Essential for Living* within Skill Domains

7b. Listener Responses, Names, and Descriptions (cont.)

    Good-to-have Skills

        Recognizing, Retrieving, and Relocating Items,
Completing Activities, and Naming Items and
Describing Activities that are Part of Routine Events............... LRND1-13

            Routine Events 1-3 the First Time Around............................. LRND1-3.1 rec ret rel
                                                                                          LRND1-3.1 nd
            Routine Events 4-6 the First Time Around............................. LRND4-6.1 rec ret rel
                                                                                          LRND4-6.1 nd
            Routine Events 1-3 the Second Time Around....................... LRND1-3.2 rec ret rel
                                                                                          LRND1-3.2 nd
            Routine Events 7-13... LRND7-13 rec ret rel
                                                                                          LRND7-13 nd
            Routine Events 1-3 the Third Time Around........................... LRND1-3.3 rec ret rel
                                                                                         LRND1-3.3 nd
            Routine Events 4-6 the Second Time Around...................... LRND4-6.2 rec ret rel
                                                                                        LRND4-6.2 nd

    Nice-to-have Skills

        Recognizing, Naming and Describing
Physical Sensations or Emotions.. LRND14-15

            Event 14 -- Pain or Discomfort.. LRND14rec
                                                                                                     LRND14nd
            Event 15 -- Sadness, Happiness, or Anger........................... LRND15rec
                                                                                                     LRND15nd

7c. Answers to Questions and Conversations

    Good-to-have Skills

        Answering Questions that are Part of Routine Events............. AQ1-13
            Routine Events 1-3 the First Time Around............................. AQ1-3.1
            Routine Events 4-6 the First Time Around............................. AQ4-6.1
            Routine Events 1-3 the Second Time Around....................... AQ1-3.2
            Routine Events 7-13... AQ7-13
            Routine Events 1-3 the Third Time Around........................... AQ1-3.3
            Routine Events 4-6 the Second Time Around...................... AQ4-6.2

        Participating in Conversations that are Part
of Routine Events... C1-13

            Routine Events 1-3 the First Time Around............................. C1-3.1
            Routine Events 4-6 the First Time Around............................. C4-6.1
            Routine Events 1-3 the Second Time Around....................... C1-3.2
            Routine Events 7-13... C7-13
            Routine Events 1-3 the Third Time Around........................... C1-3.3
            Routine Events 4-6 the Second Time Around...................... C4-6.2

    Nice-to-have Skills

        Answering Questions about
Physical Sensations or Emotions.. AQ14-15

            Event 14 -- Pain or Discomfort.. AQ14
            Event 15 -- Sadness, Happiness, or Anger........................... AQ15

Table 1. (cont.)
The Scope and Sequence of *Essential for Living* within Skill Domains

- Chapter 8. Doing Skills
  - 8a. Daily Living and Related Skills
    - **Must-have Skills**
      - **Eating, Drinking, and Feeding** **DLS-EDF1-9**
      - **Sleeping** **DLS-Slp1-2**
      - **Mobility and Transportation** **DLS-MT1-5**
      - **Avoiding Harmful Items, Substances, and Situations** **DLS-AHS1-15**
      - **Other Activities Related to Health and Safety** **DLS-HS1-8**
    - Should-have Skills
      - Eating, Drinking, and Feeding DLS-EDF10-28
      - Medical Procedures and Medication Administration DLS-MM1-9
      - Sleeping DLS-Slp3-6
      - Mobility and Transportation DLS-MT6-16
      - Avoiding Harmful Items, Substances, and Situations DLS-AHS16-19
      - Toileting DLS-Toil1-11
      - Bathing and Personal Hygiene DLS-BPH1-21
      - Dressing DLS-D1-39
      - Leisure Activities at Home DLS-LAH1-13
      - School, Instruction, and Therapy DLS-SIT1-25
      - Day Activity Skills DLS-DAS1-6
      - Vocational Skills DLS-V1-47
    - Good-to-have Skills
      - Other Routine, Daily Activities DLS-RDA1-9
      - Leisure Activities in the Community DLS-LAC1-12
      - Laundry DLS-L1-14
      - Cleaning DLS-C1-16
      - Using a Telephone DLS-TC1-7
      - Preparing Food DLS-PF1-25
  - 8b. Functional Academic Skills
    - 8b1. Responding to Text as a Listener and Reading RTL1-14, Rdg1-14
      - Good-to-have Skills
        - Responding to Text as a Listener RTL1-14
        - Reading Rdg1-14
    - 8b2. Schedules, Lists, and Time SLT1-17
      - Good-to-have Skills
        - Schedules and Lists SLT1-10
      - Nice-to-have Skills
        - Time Skills SLT11-17
    - 8b3. Math Skills
      - Good-to-have Skills
        - Math Skills Num1-16
    - 8b4. Writing or Typing Skills WT1-12
      - Good-to-have Skills
        - Writing or Typing WT1-6
      - Nice-to-have Skills
        - Writing or Typing WT7-12

Table 1. (cont.)
The Scope and Sequence of *Essential for Living* within Skill Domains

Chapter 9. Tolerating Skills

Must-have Skills

Basic Human Interaction	T-BHI1-5
Eating, Drinking, and Feeding	T-EDF1-11
Daily Medical Procedures and Medication Administration	T-DM1-9
Sleeping	T-Slp1-5
Toileting	T-Toil1-5
Positioning and Range of Motion	T-PRM1-6
Prosthetic, Therapeutic, and Adapted Equipment	T-PTA1-11
Protective Equipment and Mechanical Restraints	T-PEMR1-10
Bathing and Personal Hygiene	T-BPH1-8
Daily Dental Procedures	T-DD1

Should-have Skills

Clothing and Accessories	T-C1-15
Transportation	T-Trp1-9
Sleeping	T-Slp6-8
Daily Dental Procedures	T-DD2-4
Bathing and Personal Hygiene	T-BPH9-13
School, Instruction, and Therapy	T-SIT1-9
Eating, Drinking, and Feeding	T-EDF13-18
Basic Human Interaction	T-BHI6-12
Basic Daily Activities	T-BDA1-10
Toileting	T-Toil7-9
Occasional, Routine Medical Procedures	T-ORM1-10
Occasional, Routine Dental Procedures	T-ORD1-4
Home and Community	T-HC1-11

Chapter 11. Tool Skills and Component Skills

Should-have Skills

Basic Motor Movements	MM1-11

Good-to-have Skills

Matching Skills	M1-11
Imitation Skills	Im1-2

Nice-to-have Skills

Matching Skills	M12-13
Imitation Skills	Im3

A recommended teaching sequence must also take into account skills *across* domains so that learners have 'balanced' skill repertoires, rather than 'splinter' skills. The First Things First diagram, shown in Table 2, provides a recommended teaching sequence across skill domains. The first two columns include primarily speaking and listening skills, while the other columns include problem behavior, doing skills, and tolerating skills, respectively. Cells with solid borders and bold type include skills that are part of the *Essential* Eight and problem behaviors, and are located at the bottom of the diagram. Cells with dashed borders and italic type include academic skills and are located primarily in the upper right hand corner. Skills near the bottom are generally more functional and less difficult, and, as you proceed upward, skills become less functional and more difficult. As shown in Table 2, with children and adults who have learned to perform independently many examples of *must-have requests and related listener responses* (**R1-21**), but only a few *must-have daily living and tolerating skills* (**DLS-EDF1-9** and **T-BHI1-5**), achieving a balanced repertoire would suggest teaching additional *must-have* daily living and tolerating skills (e.g., **DLS-Slp1-2** and **T-DM1-5**), rather than beginning to teach *should-have requests and related listener responses* (**R22-48**).

As shown in Table 3, the *First Things First* diagram also provides a one-page summary of the assessment and subsequent progress of each learner. During the assessment, a learner's performance on each item is recorded in the *Assessment and Record of Progress (ARP)* manual using specific performance criteria (see chapter 4). As shown in Table 3, when an initial assessment has been completed, a yellow highlighter can be used to indicate the skills in which all of the performance criteria were achieved. If problem behaviors are occurring and have been defined, the yellow highlighter can be used to indicate the intensity of these behaviors, the extent of occurrence, and the extent to which psychoactive medications, mechanical restraint, protective equipment, crisis stabilization procedures, and self-restraint are occurring. Then, skills can be selected for instruction, along with protocols for teaching these skills and managing the problem behaviors.

As indicated in Table 2, begin by selecting skills for inclusion in a learner's individual education or support plan, which are included in the first cell at the lower left hand corner and for which the learner has yet to achieve all of the performance criteria. Then, move to the right and select several skills from each of the other three cells. When a learner exhibits independently most of the skills in a specific cell, select new skills by first moving to the right or the left and then moving upward. Since some skills can influence the acquisition of other skills, it is generally not advisable to skip cells. Three sample Individual Education or Support Plans (IEPs or ISPs) are included in Table 4. Program 1 is based on the assessment and record of progress shown in Table 3.

Periodically use the *First Things First diagram to update each learner's overall progress and to select new skills*. As shown in Table 3, when all of the performance criteria for specific skills are achieved by a learner, indicate that this has occurred using a highlighter of a different color. The *First Things First* diagram is included in the first few pages of the *Assessment and Record of Progress (ARP) manual*.

Table 2.
ESSENTIAL FOR LIVING
First Things First: The Scope and Sequence Across Skill Domains

Less Functional ↑ / More Functional ↓ (left axis)
More Difficult ↑ / Less Difficult ↓ (right axis)

Nice-to-have Answers to Questions: AQ14-15	Good-to-have Conversations: C1-3.3 & C4-6.2	Nice-to-have Time Skills: SLT11-17	Nice-to-have Writing or Typing Skills: WT7-12
Nice-to-have Requests for Information and Other Advanced Requests: R84-90	Good-to-have Conversations: C1-3.2 & C7-13	Good-to-have Reading Skills: Rdg1-14	Good-to-have Writing or Typing Skills: WT1-6
Nice-to-have Listener Responses, Names, and Descriptions: LRND14-15			Nice-to-have Imitation Skills: Im3
	Good-to-have Conversations: C1-3.1 & C4-6.1	Good-to-have Schedules and Lists: SLT6-10	Good-to-have Math Skills: Mth8-16
Nice-to-have Advanced Requests: R80-83	Good-to-have Answers to Questions: AQ1-3.3 & AQ4-6.2	Good-to-have Daily Living Skills: DLS-RDA1-9, DLS-LAC1-12, DLS-L1-14, DLS-C1-16, DLS-TC1-7, DLS-PF1-25	
Good-to-have Requests with 2-4 Words, Signs, or Pictures: R71-79	Good-to-have Answers to Questions: AQ1-3.2 & AQ7-13	Good-to-have Responses to Text as a Listener: RTL1-14	Good-to-have Math Skills: Mth1-7
		Nice-to-have Matching Skills: M12-13	Should-have Daily Living Skills: DLS-EDF10-28, DLS-MM1-9, DLS-Slp3-6, DLS-MT6-16, DLS-AHS16-19, DLS-Toil1-11, DLS-BPH1-21, DLS-D1-39, DLS-LAH1-13, DLS-SIT1-25, DLS-DAS1-6, DLS-V1-47
Good-to-have Special Requests: R49-70	Good-to-have Answers to Questions: AQ1-3.1 & AQ4-6.1	Should-have Tolerating Skills: T-C1-15, T-Trp1-9, T-Slp6-8, T-DD2-4, T-BPH9-13, T-SIT1-9, T-EDF13-18, T-BHI6-12, T-BDA1-10, T-Toil7-9, T-ORM1-10, T-ORD1-4, T-HC1-11	
	Good-to-have Listener Responses, Names, and Descriptions: LRND1-3.3 & LRND4-6.2		
Should-have Requests and Related Listener Responses: Making Requests, Waiting, Accepting Removals, Completing Previously Acquired Tasks, and Accepting 'No' R22-48	Good-to-have Listener Responses, Names, and Descriptions: LRND1-3.2 & LRND7-13		
	Good-to-have Listener Responses, Names, and Descriptions: LRND1-3.1 & LRND4-6.1	Good-to-have Schedules and Lists: SLT1-5	Good-to-have Imitation Skills: Im1-2
	Should-have Listener Responses: Following Directions to Complete Routine Activities LR12-17	Good-to-have Matching Skills: M1-11	Should-have Basic Motor Movements: MM1-11

Problem Behaviors: Self-injurious, Aggressive, Destructive, Disruptive, or Repetitive • Severe, Moderate, or Mild The Extent to which • Psychoactive Medications, • Protective Equipment, • Mechanical Restraints, and • Crisis Stabilization Procedures are used. The Extent to which • Self-restraint Occurs and the Extent to which • the Problem Behaviors Occur.

| Must-have Requests and Related Listener Responses: Making Requests, Waiting, Accepting Removals, Making Transitions, Sharing, and Taking Turns, Completing 10 Consecutive, Brief, Previously Acquired Tasks, and Accepting 'No' R1-21 | Must-have Listener Responses Related to Health and Safety: LR1-L11 | Must-have Tolerating Skills: T-BHI1-5, T-EDF1-11, T-DM1-9, T-Slp1-5, T-Toil1-5, T-PRM1-6, T-PTA1-11, T-PEMR1-10, T-BPH1-8, T-DD1 | Must-have Daily Living Skills: DLS-EDF1-9 DLS-Slp1-2 DLS-MT1-5 DLS-AHS1-15 DLS-HS1-8 |

Start **here**

Table 3.
ESSENTIAL FOR LIVING
First Things First: A Summary of a Learner's Assessment and Subsequent Progress

AQ14 15	C5.2 2 3 4 5 6 C6.2 2 3 4 5 6 C3.3 2 3 4 5 6 C4.2 2 3 4 5 6 C1.3 2 3 4 5 6 C2.3 2 3 4 5 6	SLT15 16 17 SLT11 12 13 14	WT7 8 9 10 11 12
R89 90 R84 85 86 87 88	C12 2 3 4 5 6 C13 2 3 4 5 6 C10 2 3 4 5 6 C11 2 3 4 5 6 C8 2 3 4 5 6 C9 2 3 4 5 6 C3.2 2 3 4 5 6 C7 2 3 4 5 6 C1.2 2 3 4 5 6 C2.2 2 3 4 5 6	Rdg9 10 11 12 13 14 Rdg1 2 3 4 5 6 7 8	WT1 2 3 4 5 6 Im3
LRND15nd LRND15rec LRND14nd LRND14rec	C5.1 2 3 4 5 6 C6.1 2 3 4 5 6 C3.1 2 3 4 5 6 C4.1 2 3 4 5 6 C1.1 2 3 4 5 6 C2.1 2 3 4 5 6	SLT6 7 8 9 10 DLS-TC1 2 3 4 5 6 7 DLS-L1 x x x x x 14 DLS-RDA1 x x x x x 9	Mth13 14 15 16 Mth8 9 10 11 12 DLS-PF1 x x x x x 25 DLS-C1 x x x x x 16 DLS-LAC1 x x x x x 12
R80 81 82 83	AQ4.2 5.2 6.2 AQ1.3 2.3 3.3	RTL9 10 11 12 13 14 RTL1 2 3 4 5 6 7 8	Mth5 6 7 Mth1 2 3 4
R76 77 78 79 R71 72 73 74 75	AQ7 8 9 10 11 12 AQ1.2 2.2 3.2	M12 13	DLS-V34 x x x x x 47 DLS-V17 x x x x x 33
R69 70 R68 R61 62 63 64 65 66 67 R60 R57 58 59 R49 50 51 52 53 54 55 56	AQ4.1 5.1 6.1 AQ1.1 2.1 3.1 LRND4.2 5.2 6.2 nd LRND4.2 5.2 6.2 rec ret rel LRND1.3 2.3 3.3 nd LRND1.3 2.3 3.3 rec ret rel	T-HC4 5 6 7 8 9 10 11 T-ORD3 4 T-HC1 2 3 T-ORM9 10 T- ORD1 2 T-ORM1 2 3 4 5 6 7 8 T-BDA9 10 T-Toil7 8 9 T-BDA1 2 3 4 5 6 7 8 T-BHI6 7 8 9 10 11 12 T-EDF13 14 15 16 17 18 T-SIT1 2 3 4 5 6 7 8 9 T-BPH9 10 11 12 13	DLS-V1 x x x x x 16 DLS-DAS1 2 3 4 5 6 DLS-SIT14 x x x x x 25 DLS-SIT1 x x x x x 13 DLS-LAH1 x x x x x 13 DLS-D27 x x x x x 39 DLS-D14 x x x x x 26 DLS-D1 x x x x x 13 DLS-BPH11 x x x x x 21 DLS-BPH1 x x x x x 10
R46 R47 48 R43 R44 45 R40 R41 R42 R33 34 35 36 37 38 39 R30 31 R32 R27 28 R29 R25 R26 R22 23 24	LRND7 8 9 10 11 12 13 nd LRND7 8 9 10 11 12 13 rec ret rel LRND1.2 2.2 2.3 nd LRND1.2 2.2 3.2 rec ret rel LRND4.1 5.1 6.1 nd LRND4.1 5.1 6.1 rec ret rel LRND1.1 2.1 3.1 nd LRND1.1 2.1 3.1 rec ret rel LR15 16 17 LR12 13 14	T-Slp6 7 8 T-DD2 3 4 T-Trp1 2 3 4 5 6 7 8 9 T-C10 11 12 13 14 15 T-C1 2 3 4 5 6 7 8 9 SLT1 2 3 4 5 M7 8 9 10 11 M1 2 3 4 5 6	DLS-Toil1 x x x x x 11 DLS-AHS16 17 18 19 DLS-MT6 x x x x x 16 DLS-Slp3 4 5 6 DLS-MM1 x x x x x 9 DLS-EDF20 x x x x x 28 DLS-EDF10 x x x x x 19 Im1 2 MM6 7 8 9 10 11 MM1 2 3 4 5

SIB Agg Des Dis Rep ● Sev Mod Mild ● Med3+> Med3+ Med3+< Med2> Med2 Med2< Med1> Med1 Med1< -Med				
● PE>2 PE>1 PE PE<1 PE<2 PE<3 -PE ● MR>2 MR>1 MR MR<1 MR<2 MR<3 -MR				
● CS>5hW CS2-5hW CS1-2hW CS30m-1hW CS<30mW -CS ● SR>2 SR>1 SR SR<1 SR<2 SR<3 -SR				
● >100D 50-100D 20-50D 10-20D 1-10D <1D <1W <1M <1Y				
R16 R17 18 19 20 21 R14 R15-1 2 3 4 5 6 7 8 9 10 R13-1 2 3 4 5 6 7 8 9 10 R12-1 2 3 4 5 6 7 8 9 10 R11-1 2 3 4 5 6 7 8 9 10 R10-1 2 3 4 5 6 7 8 9 10 R8-1 2 R9-1 2 3 4 5 6 7 8 9 10 R1 2 3 4 5 R6 R7-1 2 3 4 5 6 7 8 9 10		LR10 LR11 LR7 LR8 LR9 LR4 LR5 LR6 LR1 LR2 LR3	T-BPH1 2 3 4 5 6 7 8 T-DD1 T-PEMR1 2 3 4 5 6 7 8 9 10 T-PTA1 2 3 4 5 6 7 8 9 10 11 T-PRM1 2 3 4 5 6 T-Slp1 2 3 4 5 T-Toil1 2 3 4 5 T-DM1 2 3 4 5 6 7 8 9 T-EDF1 2 3 4 5 6 7 8 9 10 11 T-BHI1 2 3 4 5	DLS-HS5 6 7 8 DLS-HS1 2 3 4 DLS-AHS11 12 13 14 15 DLS-AHS6 7 8 9 10 DLS-AHS1 2 3 4 5 DLS-MT1 2 3 4 5 DLS-EDF8 9 DLS-Slp1 2 DLS-EDF1 2 3 4 5 6 7

Table 4.
Sample Individual Education or Support Plans (IEPs or ISPs)

Program 1: An individual education or support plan for a **non-ambulatory, non-vocal child or adult with multiple, severe disabilities**, including...

- no effective, alternative method of speaking,
- orthopedic impairments that permit only very limited motor movement,
- a significant visual impairment, and
- significant deficits in most or all of the *Essential Eight* skills, and in many Daily Living and Tolerating Skills,

who requires frequent, daily, medical procedures, may include the following components:

Must-have Requests and Related Listener Responses

R6. Exhibits a reliable motor movement that permits a learner to use an alternative method of speaking which includes selecting photographs, pic-symbols, printed words, or letters

When R6 has been acquired, an alternative method of speaking should be selected for the learner...

AMS ___. _____

Other Must-have Requests and Related Listener Responses

R7. Makes requests for highly preferred snack foods, drinks, non-food items, or activities that can be made frequently and immediately available

R9. Waits after requesting each of the items and activities in R7 and R8 for gradually increasing periods of time

R10. Accepts the removal of access to 10 items or activities from R7 and R8 by a person in authority

Must-have Listener Responses

LR1. Holds and maintains contact with the hand of an instructor, care provider, or parent when directed to do so

LR4. Waits within arms length of an instructor, care provider, or parent

LR10. Turns toward others when her/his name is called and makes two consecutive listener responses from LR1-9

Must-have Tolerating Skills

T-BHI5.	Touch, physical guidance, or physical prompts
T-EDF7.	Soft foods
T-EDF8.	Mashed foods
T-DM2.	Liquid medication from an oral syringe
T-DM9.	Ventilation and suction
T-Toil3.	Potty chair or adapted toilet
T-PRM2.	A side lyer
T-PRM3.	A corner chair
T-PTA3.	A wheelchair
T-PTA7.	A MOVE device
T-BPH1.	Someone washing your hands
T-BPH2.	Someone washing your face
T-DD1.	Someone brushing your teeth

Should-have Tolerating Skills

T-Slp6.	Own bed
T-ORM1.	Touching and tapping parts of the body during a physical examination
T-ORM2.	A heart and lung examination with a stethoscope
T-ORM3.	An ear examination with an otoscope
T-SIT1.	Physical therapy sessions
T-SIT2.	Occupational therapy sessions
T-SIT3.	Specific therapeutic exercises or stretching

Essential for Living

Table 4 (cont.).
Sample Individual Education or Support Plans (IEPs or ISPs)

Program 1 (cont.)

Must-have Daily Living Skills

DLS-EDF4.	Chews three soft foods
DLS-EDF9.	Drinks from a cup or glass
DLS-Slp2.	Sleeps through the night until morning
DLS-MT5.	Transported in a wheelchair
DLS-HS5.	Attends medical appointments
DLS-HS7.	Attends therapy sessions

Should-have Daily Living Skills

DLS-SIT1.   Attends a school or therapy program
DLS-SIT2.   Participates in 1:1 guidance, instruction, and therapy
DLS-D1.   **MR**   Extends parts of the body toward someone who is removing or putting on his/her clothes

Should-have Basic Motor Movements

MM5.   Gently grasps items (grasps an adapted spoon)

Program 2: An individual education or support plan for **an older ambulatory child or adult with a moderate-to-severe disability, limited vocal skills, and severe problem behavior** including...

- only a few understandable spoken words,
- no effective method of speaking,
- significant deficits in most or all of the *Essential Eight* skills, and in many Speaking, Academic, Listening, Daily Living, and Tolerating Skills,

who has not made significant progress on a developmental curriculum, such as the ABLLS or the VB-MAPP, may include the following components:

An alternative method of speaking should be selected for the learner...

    AMS ___. _____

Other Must-have Requests and Related Listener Responses

R7.   Makes requests for highly preferred snack foods, drinks, non-food items, or activities that can be made frequently and immediately available
R9.   Waits after requesting each of the items and activities in R7 and R8 for gradually increasing periods of time
R10.   Accepts the removal of access to 10 items or activities from R7 and R8 by a person in authority
R11.   Completes 10 consecutive, brief, previously acquired tasks
R12.   Shares or takes turns obtaining access to each of the items and activities in R7 and R8 with an instructor, care provider, parent, or peer
R13.   Makes transitions from preferred items and activities to required tasks
R15.   'Accepts no' after making requests for items and activities that were taught and are often honored (R7, R8, and R14)

Must-have Listener Responses

LR1.   Holds and maintains contact with the hand of an instructor, care provider, or parent when directed to do so
LR2.   Moves toward and stands or sits next to an instructor, care provider, or parent when directed to do so
LR3.   Moves toward and stands or remains in a line when directed to do so
LR4.   Waits within arms length of an instructor, care provider, or parent, or waits in line when directed to do so

Table 4 (cont.).
Sample Individual Education or Support Plans (IEPs or ISPs)

Program 2 (cont.)

Must-have Listener Responses (cont.)

LR5. Stands up, sits down, folds hands, lies down, or sits up when directed to do so
LR8. Moves to and remains in a designated area when directed to do so
LR10. Turns toward others when her/his name is called and makes two consecutive listener responses from LR1-9

Should-have Listener Responses

LR13. Places items in designated locations when directed to do so
LR14. 'Cleans up' after making a mess when directed to do so

Good-to-have Listener Responses

LRND1.1rec ret rel recognizes, retrieves, and relocates items and recognizes activities that are part of Event 1, the first time around

Problem Behavior

SIB Episodes of self-injurious behavior: brings fist forcefully to left temporal lobe area

This behavior occurs in the absence of **R7, R9, R10, R11, R12**, and some must-have tolerating skills

Sev	Intensity: Severe
Med2	Psychoactive medications: 2
-MR	Mechanical restraints: not required
PEA	Protective equipment at the time of the initial assessment: a soft, karate helmet worn continuously
CS>5hW	Crisis stabilization procedures: used more than 5 hours per week
-SR	Self-restraint: does not occur
20-50D	Frequency: 20-50 episodes occur each day

Must-have Tolerating Skills

T-BHI5. Touch, physical guidance, or physical prompts
T-Slp3. Own bed
T-BPH7. A tub bath
T-DD1. Someone brushing your teeth

Should-have Tolerating Skills

T-BPH9. A shower at home
T-BPH10. Deodorant
T-BHI7. The word "no" or other indications of disapproval or incorrect responding
T-Trp8. Escalator
T-EDF14. Vegetables
T-SIT8. Small group instruction

Must-have Daily Living Skills

DLS-HS2. Looks both ways, waits for traffic to clear, and crosses the street quickly
DLS-HS4. Fastens and remains in a seat belt for the duration of specific trips

Good-to-have Matching Skills

M2. Matches essential items to other items that are part of an activity
M10. Matches items, activities, people, places, or locations to corresponding photographs
M11. Matches photographs to corresponding items, activities, people, places, or locations

Good-to-have Imitation Skills

Im2. Imitates motor movements with items

Table 4 (cont.).
Sample Individual Education or Support Plans (IEPs or ISPs)

Program 2 (cont.)

Should-have Daily Living Skills

DLS-EDF10.		Drinks from a can or bottle
DLS-EDF15.		Drinks with a straw
DLS-Slp4.		Goes to bed at a designated time
DLS-AHS16.		Does not use a stove, oven, or microwave without supervision
DLS-Toil11.	**MR**	Locates, enters, and uses the appropriate public restroom
DLS-BPH1.	**MR**	Washes hands
DLS-BPH2.	**MR**	Washes face
DLS-BPH3.	**MR**	Washes hair
DLS-BPH4.	**MR**	Takes a shower or bath
DLS-LAH2.		Puts puzzles together
DLS-LAH3.	**MR**	Plays card games
DLS-D34.	**MR**	Puts on a sweater, coat, or jacket with snaps, a zipper, or velcro
DLS-D35.	**MR**	Puts on a sweater, coat, or jacket with buttons
DLS-RDA5.	**MR**	Cleans own room
DLS-RDA6.	**MR**	Retrieves dishes, glasses, utensils, and napkins, and sets the table

if the learner is school-age...

- **DLS-SIT1.** Attends a school or therapy program
- **DLS-SIT2.** Participates in 1:1 guidance, instruction, and therapy
- **DLS-SIT3.** Completes single-response tasks during 1:1 instruction and therapy
- **DLS-SIT4.** Completes 2 consecutive, single-response tasks during 1:1 instruction and therapy
- **DLS-SIT5.** Completes 3 consecutive, single-response tasks during 1:1 instruction and therapy
- **DLS-SIT6.** Completes 5 consecutive, single-response tasks during 1:1 instruction and therapy

if the learner is an adult...

- **DLS-V1.** Attends a sheltered work program
- **DLS-V2.** Participates in a sheltered work program
- **DLS-V5.** Completes a single-response assembly or packaging task
- **DLS-V6.** Completes 2 or more single-response assembly or packaging tasks

Good-to-have Schedules and Lists

- **SLT1.** Participates in events and activities slated to occur later that same day using a personal, daily, picture or tactile schedule

Program 3: An individual education or support plan for **an older, ambulatory child or adult with a moderate disability, vocal skills,** and significant deficits in some speaking, listening, and daily living skills, and in many academic skills,

who has great difficulty answering questions in social or academic contexts, may include the following components:

Should-have Requests and Related Listener Responses

- **R22.** Makes requests for highly preferred foods, drinks, non-food items, or activities that cannot be made either frequently or immediately available -- makes requests for McDonald's french fries, a merry-go-round, or the swings
- **R23.** Makes requests for highly preferred foods, drinks, non-food items, or activities that cannot be made either frequently or immediately available
- **R26.** 'Accepts no' after making requests for items and activities that were taught and are often honored as part of R22 and R23
- **R29.** Completes 20 consecutive, brief, previously acquired tasks
- **R34.** Makes a generalized request for affection
- **R39.** Makes a generalized request for a 'break' in required activities
- **R59.** Makes a request to perform an activity without assistance

Table 4 (cont.).
Sample Individual Education or Support Plans (IEPs or ISPs)

Program 3 (cont.)

Good-to-have Listener Responses, Names, and Descriptions

- **LRND4.1rec-ret-rel**   recognizes, retrieves, and relocates, items, activities, familiar persons, and places that are part of Event 4, the first time around
- **LRND4.1nd**   names and describes items, activities, familiar persons, and places that are part of Event 4, the first time around
- **LRND5.1rec-ret-rel**   recognizes, retrieves, and relocates, items, activities, familiar persons, and places that are part of Event 5, the first time around
- **LRND5.1nd**   names and describes items, activities, familiar persons, and places that are part of Event 5, the first time around

Good-to-have Answers to Questions

- **AQ4.1**   answers to questions that are part of Event 4, the first time around
- **AQ5.1**   answers to questions that are part of Event 5, the first time around

Good-to-have Conversations

- **C4.1**   conversations that are part of Event 4, the first time around
- **C5.1**   conversations that are part of Event 5, the first time around

Good-to-have Matching Skills

- **M2.**   Matches essential items to other items that are part of an activity
- **M3.**   Matches items to containers or other locations
- **M4.**   Matches containers or other locations to items

Good-to-have Imitation Skills

- **Im2.**   Imitates motor movements with items

Should-have Daily Living Skills

DLS-MM3.		Administers own pills or vitamins using a one-day pill sorter
DLS-Slp4.		Goes to bed at a designated time
DLS-Slp5.		Remains in own bed throughout the night
DLS-AHS16.		Does not use a stove, oven, or microwave without supervision
DLS-AHS17.		Does not touch or turn on a fan or space heater without supervision or training
DLS-Toil7.		Uses a urinal (for males)
DLS-Toil11.	**MR**	Locates, enters, and uses the appropriate public restroom
DLS-BPH7.	**MR**	Shaves face or legs and underarms
DLS-BPH11.		Uses mouthwash
DLS-BPH12.		Combs or brushes hair
DLS-LAH5.		Watches movies or videos
DLS-LAH6.		Colors, draws, or paints pictures
DLS-D31.	**MR**	Ties shoes with laces
DLS-MT16.	**MR**	Rides a train, bus, or taxi to 5 specific locations

if the learner is school-age...

DLS-SIT12.	**MR**	Completes two-response tasks while working alone
DLS-SIT13.	**MR**	Completes three-response tasks while working alone
DLS-SIT14.	**MR**	Completes five-response tasks while working alone
DLS-SIT15.		Returns to tasks after significant interruptions
DLS-SIT18.	**MR**	Completes two-response tasks during instruction with 2-4 peers

Table 4 (cont.).
...ation or Support Plans (IEPs or ISPs)

...e learner is an adult...

		...s 2 or more two-response tasks that include inventory control or
		Completes 2 or more two-response tasks that include folding, cutting, using a stapler, using a hole punch, or glue
		Completes 2 or more two-response tasks that include washing, cleaning, or laundry
....	MR	Completes 2 or more two-response tasks that include property maintenance
...-V28.	MR	Completes 2 or more two-response tasks that include food preparation or clean-up
DLS-V35.		Works continuously for 10 minutes
DLS-V36.		Works for 20 minutes with one or two pauses of less than one minute

Chapter 4. Conducting an Assessment and Recording Progress

This chapter describes how to score items, to conduct an assessment, and to record progress using the *Assessment and Record of Progress (ARP) manual*. The completion of an initial assessment often requires a few minutes per day for 10-15 days. The *Essential for Living Quick Assessment*, which can be completed in 2-3 hours, is often temporarily helpful with children or adults with no method of speaking, a limited speaking repertoire, or severe problem behavior. Once The Quick Assessment is completed, you can begin teaching a few skills and managing problem behaviors while completing the remainder of the assessment. The Quick Assessment is described in chapter 5 and included in the first few pages of the *ARP*.

Scoring Items

Essential for Living includes eight skill domains:

> Requests and Related Listener Responses
> Listener Responses, Names, and Descriptions
> Answers to Questions and Conversation
> Daily Living and Related Skills
> Academic and Related Skills
> Tolerating Skills and Eggshells
> Tool Skills and Component Skills

Skills within each domain are sequenced from less to more difficult and more to less functional and designated as:

> **Must-have,**
> **Should-have,**
> **Good-to-have**, and
> **Nice-to-have.**

Must-have skills are generally assessed and taught first, while other skills are assessed and taught as indicated in the instrument.

The performance of a learner on each skill is assessed using a set of performance levels which specify:

IA	[the initial assessment of this skill has been completed]
IM	[instruction or management has begun]
-SA	the absence of self-injurious, aggressive or destructive behavior
-DC	the absence of disruptive behavior or complaints
-RP	the absence of resistance to prompts
FP	when a full physical, full demonstration, or full echoic prompt is required or when there is contact with a specific item or activity
PP	when a partial physical, partial demonstration, or partial echoic prompt is required or when there is brief contact with a specific item or activity
MP	when a minimal physical, minimal demonstration, or minimal echoic prompt is required or when there is very brief contact with a specific item or activity
Ind	when no prompts are required and the skill occurs without hesitation
_s, _m	the extent to which 'waiting', 'tolerating' or another specific skill continues to occur without problem behavior for designated periods of time (seconds, minutes)
PPA	[some or all of the responses (steps) that are part of this skill require permanent partial assistance]
APD	[some or all of the responses (steps) that are part of this skill require an environmental adaptation or prosthetic device]
CO	the critical outcome of this skill has occurred
?F	the occurrence of this skill with two or more examples of the same item or activity
2S	the occurrence of this skill in two or more settings
2P	the occurrence of this skill with either of two persons
<M	when motivating events have occurred, but are weak
>M	when motivating events have occurred and are strong
NI	the occurrence of 'a request' when the learner does not have sensory contact with the requested item or activity
Det	[this skill is no longer occurring consistently]

These levels range from exhibiting problem behavior or resistance to prompts (**-SA**, **-DC**, **-RP**), to exhibiting the skill with prompts (**FP**, **PP**, **MP**), to exhibiting the skill independently (i.e., without prompts and without hesitation) (**Ind**), to exhibiting the skill for specific periods of time (**_s**, **_m**), to **PPA**, which occurs when learners, because of physical limitations, cannot perform a specific skill or one or more responses that are part of that skill without assistance, to **APD**, which occurs when learners require an environmental adaptation or prosthetic device to perform the skill, to **CO**, which occurs when the critical outcome of a skill has occurred, and to exhibiting the skill in situations other than those in which it was originally taught (**2E, 2S, 2P, <M, >M, NI**). There is no level which specifies the repeated occurrence of a skill in appropriate situations after prompts are no longer required (often called maintenance). Instead, there is a level that indicates that the skill is no longer occurring consistently (**Det**).

Essential for Living also includes one domain on problem behavior. The performance of each learner is assessed according to the form, type, and intensity of each behavior, along with the extent to which psychoactive medications, mechanical restraints, protective equipment, and crisis stabilization procedures are used, the extent to which self restraint occurs, and the frequency with which each behavior occurs.

The form of a problem behavior is defined by a precise description of the movements a learner makes from the start to the end of an instance. For example, an instance of 'head hitting' may be defined as:

makes a fist with his right hand and makes contact with his head just above his right ear.

If several instances of the same behavior occur within a few seconds, it may be advisable to define and record episodes, rather than instances. In this case, the end of an episode will need to be defined by a specific period of time during which no instance of the problem behavior occurs. For example, an episode of 'head hitting' may be defined as:

makes a fist with his right hand and makes repeated contact with his head just above his right ear and does not make any of these movements for one minute.

Sometimes more than one problem behavior can occur within a few seconds, in which case defining and recording episodes, rather than instances is also advisable. For example, an episode of 'head hitting and arm biting' may be defined as:

makes a fist with his right hand and makes contact with his head just above his right ear; and brings his teeth toward and makes contact with his right forearm and does not make any of these movements for 30 seconds.

The type of problem behavior is defined by its probable outcome:

SIB	Self-injurious	physical harm to that child or adult
Agg	Aggressive	physical harm to another person
Des	Destructive	property damage or destruction
Dis	Disruptive	interruption in the ongoing activities of other children or adults
Cpl	Complaining	interruption in the ongoing activities of that child or adult

The intensity of specific types and forms of problem behavior is defined by a more detailed description of the probable outcome of these behaviors:

Sev	Severe	movements of a learner that have resulted or could result in serious injuries to that learner or others requiring medical attention, and, in some cases, resulting in a permanent impairment
Mod	Moderate	movements of a learner that have resulted or could result in minor injuries to that learner or others
Mild	Mild	movements of a learner that have not resulted in injuries to that learner or others; if, however, these movements became more forceful or occurred over an extended period of time, minor or serious injuries could begin to occur

The form and intensity of some problem behaviors may lead to the use of one or more psychoactive medications (**Med**). The extent to which this occurs is defined by the number of such medications currently taken daily by a learner and any recent increases or reductions in dosage:

Med 3+>	Three or more psychoactive medications with some increases in dosage
Med 3+	Three or more psychoactive medications
Med 3+<	Three or more psychoactive medications with some reductions in dosage
Med 2>	Two psychoactive medications with some increases in dosage

Med 2	Two psychoactive medications
Med 2<	Two psychoactive medications with some reductions in dosage
Med 1>	One psychoactive medication with some increase in dosage
Med 1	One psychoactive medication
Med 1<	One psychoactive medication with some reductions in dosage
-Med	No psychoactive medications

The form and intensity of some problem behaviors may require the use of protective equipment (**PE**) or mechanical restraint (**MR**) in order to protect the learner. Protective equipment is designed to prevent injuries, but does not limit the movements learners can make. Mechanical restraints, while also designed to protect the learner, limit movements learners can make. A padded helmet is an example of protective equipment, while an arm split is an example of mechanical restraint. Protective equipment and mechanical restraints can be applied *continuously*, that is, throughout the day, or *contingently*, that is, from the beginning to the end of episodes of problem behavior. The extent to which continuous protective equipment (**PEA**) or mechanical restraints (**MRA**) are used is defined across two dimensions: form and duration. In other words, **PEA** and **MRC** can be increased or faded in terms of their appearance or the length of time each is applied. The use of contingent protective equipment (**PEC**) or mechanical restraints (**MRC**) is defined by form only, that is, **PEC** and **MRC** are applied until the learner is calm and are increased or faded in appearance only:

MR>2	Mechanical restraint(s) have been increased twice
MR>1	Mechanical restraint(s) have been increased once
MR	Mechanical restraint(s) at the time of the initial assessment
MR<1	Mechanical restraint has been partially faded once
MR<2	Mechanical restraint has been partially faded twice
MR<3	Mechanical restraint has been partially faded three times
-MR	Mechanical restraint are not required
PE>2	Protective equipment has been increased twice
PE>1	Protective equipment has been increased once
PE	Protective equipment at the time of the initial assessment
PE<1	Protective equipment has been partially faded once
PE<2	Protective equipment has been partially faded twice
PE<3	Protective equipment has been partially faded three times
-PE	Protective equipment is not required

The form and intensity of some problem behaviors requires the use of crisis stabilization procedures[1]. These procedures include physically assisted transportation and temporary immobilization. The extent to which crisis stabilization procedures are used is defined by the total duration of these procedures per week:

CS>5hW	Crisis stabilization procedures are used for more than 5 hours per week
CS2-5hW	Crisis stabilization procedures are used for 2-5 hours per week
CS1-2hW	Crisis stabilization procedures are used for 1-2 hours per week
CS30m-1hW	Crisis stabilization procedures are used for 30 minutes to hour per week
CS<30mW	Crisis stabilization procedures are used for less than 30 minutes per week
-CS	Crisis stabilization procedures are not required

Some learners exhibit what is often called 'self-restraint'. Examples include:

Placing their hands under their shirt, or
Carrying small toys or other items in both hands.

These activities temporarily limit movements they can make or provide a form of protection. Unlike mechanical restraint or protective equipment, learners can discontinue these activities at any time. The extent to which self-restraint occurs is defined by its form and how that form has increased or been faded across time:

SR>2	Self-restraints have been increased twice
SR>1	Self-restraints have been increased once
SR	Self-restraints at the time of the initial assessment
SR<1	Self-restraints have been partially faded once
SR<2	Self-restraints have been partially faded twice
SR<3	Self-restraints have been partially faded three times
-SR	Self-restraints are not occurring

---

[1] We strongly recommend Professional Crisis Management (PCM). Information is available from http://www.pcma.com .

And, the frequency with which instances or episodes of problem behavior occur is specified by the following performance levels:

>100D	this problem behavior occurs 100 or more times per day
50-100D	this problem behavior occurs 51-100 times per day
20-50D	this problem behavior occurs 21-50 times per day
10-20D	this problem behavior occurs 11-20 times per day
1-10D	this problem behavior occurs 1-10 times per day
<1D	this problem behavior consistently occurs less than once per day
<1W	this problem behavior consistently occurs less than once per week
<1M	this problem behavior consistently occurs less than once per month
<1Y	this problem behavior has not occurred for one year

Conducting an Assessment

Assessing Skills. Secure a copy of the *ARP* and begin conducting an initial assessment for each learner in your care. Whenever possible, an assessment should be based on direct observation and should include the steps described in Table 2. There are circumstances, however, that necessitate obtaining information by interviewing parents, instructors, or care providers using *The Essential for Living Quick* Assessment. An assessment should include all *must-have skills* in each domain, and should continue with *should-have skills*, followed by *good-to-have* and, finally, *nice-to-have skills*. Within each of these sections, there are places to add skills for each learner. In each skill domain, the assessment should continue until the learner requires full physical, full demonstration, or full echoic prompts with three consecutive skills or examples of three consecutive skills, or exhibits severe or moderate problem behavior when these skills are assessed.

Table 2.
Assessing Skills in *Essential for Living*

Step 1.	Provide an opportunity for a learner to exhibit each skill or example thereof by presenting a cue to which you want the learner to respond or capturing or contriving motivating events to which you think the learner will respond
Step 2.	Wait for the learner to respond, without providing prompts
Step 3.	If the learner does not exhibit self-injurious, aggressive, or destructive behavior, fill in the **-SA** box as shown in Table 3; if the learner does not exhibit disruptive behavior or complaining, mark the **-DC** box; if the learner does not resist prompts, mark the **-RP** box
Step 4.	If the learner does not respond within three seconds or responds incorrectly or inappropriately, repeat step 1 and provide a minimal physical, minimal demonstration, or minimal echoic prompt, or very brief contact with a specific item or activty (**MP**); if the learner does not respond, repeat step 1 and provide a partial physical, partial demonstration, or partial echoic prompt, or brief contact with a specific item or activity (**PP**); if the learner still does not respond, repeat step 1 and provide a full physical, full demonstration, or full echoic prompt, or contact with a specific item or activity (**FP**); as shown in Table 4, mark all of the boxes from FP to the box that corresponds to the least amount of prompt that resulted in a correct or appropriate response
Step 5.	As shown in Table 5, if the learner responds correctly or appropriately without a prompt, mark all of the boxes from **FP** to **Ind** OR with some skills, as shown in Table 6, if the learner responds correctly or appropriately and maintains that response for specific periods of time, mark all of the boxes from **1s** to the box indicating the longest period of time during which the response was maintained (**1s, 2s, 5s, 10s, 20s, 1m, 2m, 5m, 10m, or 20m**)
Step 6.	As shown in Table 7, if the learner, because of physical limitations, cannot perform part or all a specific skill without assistance, mark **PPA**; if the learner requires an environmental adaptation or prosthetic device to perform part or all the skill, mark **APD**; and when the critical outcome of a skill has occurred (see the next section), mark **CO**
Step 7.	As shown in Table 8, if the learner responds correctly or appropriately without a prompt, repeat step 1 with a second example of an item or activity (**2E**), in a different setting (**2S**), with a different person (**2P**), with weak or strong motivation (**<M** or **>M**), or in the absence of a requested item (**NI**), and mark each of the boxes that indicate the situations in which the learner responded correctly or appropriately
Step 8.	Mark the **IA** box on the ARP to indicate that the assessment of a specific skill has been completed
Step 9.	As shown in Table 9, if the learner does not respond correctly or appropriately after having done so without prompts in the past, mark the **Det** box and re-teach this skill

Table 3.
If a Learner Responds without Self-injurious, Aggressive, or Destructive Behavior, Mark -SA,
without Disruptive Behavior or Complaining, Mark -DC, without Resisting Prompts, Mark -RP

R7. Requests 10 highly preferred snack foods, drinks, non-food items, or activities that can be made frequently and immediately available

1 cookies | IA | IM | -SA | -DC | -RP | FP | PP | MP | Ind | 2S | 2P | <M | NI | Det |

R13. Makes transitions from preferred items and activities to required tasks

1 from computer to washing hands | IA | IM | -SA | -DC | -RP | FP | PP | MP | Ind | 2S | 2P | >M | Det |

Table 4.
If a Learner Responds without Problem Behavior and Makes a Correct
or Appropriate Response but Requires a Prompt, Mark All of the Boxes from FP to the Box
that Corresponds to the Least Amount of Prompt that Resulted in a Correct Response

R7. Requests 10 highly preferred snack foods, drinks, non-food items, or activities that can be made frequently and immediately available

1 cookies | IA | IM | -SA | -DC | -RP | FP | PP | MP | Ind | 2S | 2P | <M | NI | Det |

Table 5.
If a Learner Responds without Problem Behavior and Makes a Correct or Appropriate Response
Without Prompts, Mark FP, PP, MP, and Ind

R7. Requests 10 highly preferred snack foods, drinks, non-food items, or activities that can be made frequently and immediately available

1 cookies | IA | IM | -SA | -DC | -RP | FP | PP | MP | Ind | 2S | 2P | <M | NI | Det |

Table 6.
If a Learner Responds without Problem Behavior, Makes a Correct or Appropriate Response Without
Prompts, and Maintains that Response for Specific Periods of Time, Mark All of the Boxes from 1s
to the box indicating the longest period of time during which the response was maintained

R9. Waits after requesting each of the items and activities in R7 and R8 for gradually increasing periods of time

1 cookies | IA | IM | 1s | 2s | 5s | 10s | 20s | 1m | 2m | 5m | 10m | 20m | Det |

Table 7.
If a Learner Cannot Perform Part or All a Specific Skill Without Assistance, Mark PPA;
or if the Learner Requires an Environmental Adaptation or Prosthetic Device, Mark APD;
and When the Critical Outcome of a Skill Has Occurred, Mark CO

DLS-BPH-01. Washes hands   **MR**   CO: clean hands

| IA | IM | 1st | 1/4 | 1/2 | 3/4 | Ind | 2m | PPA | APD | CO | 2S | 2P | Det |

Table 8.
If a Learner Makes a Correct Response with Another Example of an Item, in Another Setting,
in the Presence of Another Person, in the Absence of a Requested Item, Activity, or Person, or when
Motivation is Weak or Strong, Mark 2E, 2S, 2P, NI, <M, or >M

LRND1.1rec Recognizes items

1 cup | IA | IM | -SA | -DC | -RP | FP | PP | MP | Ind | 2E | 2P | Det |

R7. Requests 10 highly preferred snack foods, drinks, non-food items, or activities that can be made frequently and immediately available

1 cookies | IA | IM | -SA | -DC | -RP | FP | PP | MP | Ind | 2S | 2P | <M | NI | Det |

R12. Shares or takes turns obtaining access to each of the items and activities in R7 and R8 with an instructor, care provider, parent, or peer

1 cookies | IA | IM | -SA | -DC | -RP | FP | PP | MP | Ind | 2S | 2P | >M | Det |

Table 9.
If a Learner Does Not Respond Correctly or Appropriately After Having Done So
Without Prompts in the Past, Mark Det

R11. Completes 10 consecutive, previously acquired brief tasks between opportunities to make requests

2	putting his book bag in his locker	IA	IM	-SA	-DC	2S	2P	>M (**Det**)

Assessing Problem Behavior. When assessing problem behavior, begin by observing each learner in at least two different environments (e.g., home and school, or group home and work site). If observation is not feasible, interview a parent or group home manager and an instructor, care provider, or work supervisor. If a learner is exhibiting one or more behaviors that have resulted or could result in physical harm to that learner or others, significant property damage or destruction, or a significant interruption in the ongoing activities of that learner or others, define instances or episodes of these problem behaviors and designate each as self-injurious (**SIB**), aggressive (**Agg**), destructive (**Des**), disruptive (**Dis**), or (**Cpl**) complaining. Record this information, along with the extent to which a learner takes psychoactive medications (**Med**), on the *Problem Behavior Direct Observation and Interview Form*. In the example shown in Table 9, the learner is exhibiting one form of self-injurious behavior (**SIB**) defined as an episode (**PB1**), and one form of aggressive behavior defined as an instance (**PB2**), and is currently taking two psychoactive medications.

As shown in Table 9, record instances or episodes as defined for a fixed amount of time each day (e.g., 5 hours). Continue recording for 6-10 days using this form. If more than 20 instances or episodes occur during the recording period, you should consider decreasing the duration of this period. If less than 5 instances or episodes occur, you should consider increasing the duration. As shown in Table 10 with data from **PB1**, transfer the total number of instances or episodes each day to the Adapted Daily Standard Celeration Chart[2] or the Daily Standard Celeration Chart[3]. While hand-drawn or computer-generated graphs can be used, parents, instructors, and care providers will find the standard charts more informative and more useful. As shown in Table 9, also record the intensity of each instance or episode as severe (**Sev**), moderate (**Mod**), or mild (**Mild**), according to criteria previously specified. Also record the form and the extent to which protective equipment (**PE**) or mechanical restraints (**MR**) are used and specify whether either is continuous (**PEA** or **MRA**) or contingent (**PEC** or **MRC**). And, finally, record the extent to which crisis stabilization procedures (**CS**) are used, and the extent, if any, to which the learner exhibits self-restraint (**SR**).

As shown in Table 9, the learner exhibited nine episodes of **PB1** in one day, six of which were moderate in intensity and all of which required a form of protective equipment -- a soft, karate helmet, which was worn continuously. Four of the episodes required crisis stabilization procedures and from 14-22 minutes were required to achieve calm. None of the episodes required mechanical restraints. The learner also exhibited four instances of **PB2** on the same day, three of which were severe in intensity and all of which were preceded and followed by a form of self-restraint -- tucking his hands under his shirt. Three of the instances required crisis stabilization procedures and from 4-8 minutes were required to achieve calm. None of the instances required mechanical restraints or protective equipment. As also shown in Table 9, an estimate of this information can be obtained by interviewing an individual who is extremely familiar with the learner. The accuracy of this estimate will depend on the amount of time this individual has spent with the learner and the extent to which they are accustomed to reporting exactly what they have observed. Then, as shown in Table 11 with data on **PB1** from *Problem Behavior Direct Observation and Interview Form* and the Adapted Daily Standard Celeration Chart, transfer this information to the **Assessment and Record of Progress (ARP)**.

If the problem behaviors are extremely intense and restraints and/or protective equipment are necessary to maintain safety, or learners are exhibiting forms of self-restraint, as may be the case with boys with Lesch-Nyhan disorder or children with Cornelia de Lange syndrome, it is highly advisable to retain the services of a behavior analyst or comparable professional 'with considerable experience with severe problem behavior'.

Annual Assessments. Once the assessment of *performance* with respect to skills and problem behaviors has been completed, the task of teaching begins and the *ARP* should be used to record progress with respect to these same skills and problem behaviors. If there are frequent opportunities for these skills and problem behaviors to occur, it is not necessary to assess maintenance or conduct annual assessments. If skills are no longer occurring or problem behaviors begin occurring again, and you indicate these situations (Det or 1-10D) on the *ARP*, the assessment will always be current and may suggest re-teaching specific skills.

---

[2] available from http://www.behaviorchange.com .

[3] available from http://www.behaviorresearchcompany.com .

Table 9.
Entering Information and Data on the Problem Behavior
Direct Observation and Interview Form

ESSENTIAL FOR LIVING

Problem Behavior Direct Observation and Interview Form

Learner: _____ Environment(s): _____

Date: _____ Observer or Person Interviewed: _____ Counting Period: **5 hours**

Definition of Problem Behavior(s) 1 -- **PB1**: *Makes a fist with his right hand and makes repeated contact with his head just above his right ear and does not make any of these movements for one minute*	Definition of Problem Behavior(s) 2 -- **PB2**: *Raises his arm and, with an open hand, slaps others*
Instance (**Episode**) (**SIB**) Agg Des Dis Rep	(**Instance**) Episode SIB (**Agg**) Des Dis Rep

Medications:	Risperdal, Clonidine

Direct Observation

PB1	Intensity	MRA	MRC	PEA	PEC	CS (min)	SR	PB2	Intensity	MRA	MRC	PEA	PEC	CS (min)	SR
①	Sev-**Mod**-Mild			PE: sk hlmt				①	**Sev**-Mod-Mild						X
②	Sev-**Mod**-Mild				PE	22		②	**Sev**-Mod-Mild					8	X
③	Sev-Mod-**Mild**				PE			③	**Sev**-Mod-Mild					4	X
④	Sev-**Mod**-Mild				PE	14		④	**Sev**-Mod-Mild					5	X
⑤	Sev-Mod-**Mild**				PE			5							
⑥	Sev-**Mod**-Mild				PE			6							
⑦	Sev-**Mod**-Mild				PE	17		7							
⑧	Sev-Mod-**Mild**				PE			8							
⑨	Sev-**Mod**-Mild				PE	20		9							
10								10							
11								11							
12								12							
13								13							
14								14							
15								15							
16								16							
17								17							
18								18							
19								19							
20								20							

Interview

| This behavior occurs **10** per day ___ per week ___ per month ___ per year and the intensity is: ___ sev **X** mod ___ mild The learner wears, requires, or exhibits: **MRA** or **MRC**: *none* (**PEA**) or **PEC**: *soft, karate helmet* **CS**: ___ minutes per day **3** hours per week **SR**: *none* | This behavior occurs **3-4** per day ___ per week ___ per month ___ per year and the intensity is: **X** sev ___ mod ___ mild The learner wears, requires, or exhibits: **MRA** or **MRC**: *none* **PEA** or **PEC**: *none* **CS**: ___ minutes per day ___ hours per week **SR**: *tucks his hands under his t-shirt* |

Table 10.
Recording the Total Number of Instances or Episodes of
Problem Behavior Each Day for 6-7 Days and Transferring These Data
to the Adapted Standard Celeration Chart

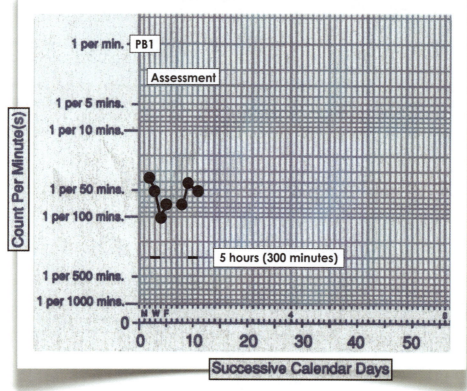

Table 11. Transferring Information from
the Problem Behavior Direct Observation and Interview Form
to the Assessment and Record of Progress (ARP)

ESSENTIAL FOR LIVING
Assessment and Record of Progress (ARP)

Problem Behavior

PB1. Makes a fist with his right hand, repeatedly and rapidly brings his hand toward and makes contact with his head just above his right ear and does not make any of these movements for one minute

IA	IM		Instance	Episode		SIB	Agg	Des	Dis	Rep
								Sev	Mod	Mild
Med3+>	Med3+	Med3+<	Med2>	Med2	Med2<	Med1>	Med1	Med1<	-Med
MRA	MRC		MR2>	MR1>	MR	MR1<	MR2<	MR3<	-MR
PEA	PEC		PE2>	PE1>	PE	PE1<	PE2<	PE3<	-PE
			CS>5hW	CS 2-5hW	CS 1-2hW	CS 30m-1hW	CS<30mW	-CS
			SR2>	SR1>	SR	SR1<	SR2<	SR3<	-SR
		>100D	50-100D	20-50D	10-20D	1-10D	<1D	<1W	<1M	<1Y

Recording Progress

Recording Progress on Skill Acquisition. When you begin teaching a specific skill, mark the **IM** box on the *ARP* to indicate that a program of instruction or behavior management has begun. As you are teaching skills targeted for instruction, collect data several days each week, or daily, if possible. We strongly recommend 'first opportunity of the day' probe data, the collection of which is described in Tables 12, 13, and 14.

Table 12.
Collecting 'First Opportunity of the Day' Probe Data

Step 1.	On the first opportunity of the day for a learner to exhibit a targeted skill or example thereof, present a cue to which you want the learner to respond OR capture or contrive motivating events to which you think the learner will respond
Step 2.	Wait for the learner to respond, without providing prompts
Step 3.	If the learner exhibits intense problem behavior or resistance to prompts or no performance level can be achieved, circle **0** on one of the *Skill Acquisition Self-graphing Data Recording Forms* shown in Table 13; If the learner does not exhibit self-injurious, aggressive, or destructive behavior, circle **-SA**; if the learner does not exhibit disruptive behavior or complaining, circle **-DC**; if the learner does not resist prompts, circle **-RP**
Step 3.	If the learner does not respond within 3-5 seconds or responds incorrectly or inappropriately, repeat step 1 and provide a minimal physical, minimal demonstration, or minimal echoic prompt, or very brief contact with a specific item or activity (**MP**); if the learner does not respond, repeat step 1 and provide a partial physical, partial demonstration, or partial echoic prompt, or brief contact with a specific item or activity (**PP**); if the learner still does not respond, repeat step 1 and provide a full physical, full demonstration, or full echoic prompt, or contact with a specific item or activity (**FP**); on the self-graphing data sheet, circle the type of prompt required for the learner to respond correctly or appropriately (see Table 13)
Step 4.	If the learner responds correctly or appropriately without a prompt, circle **Ind** OR with some skills, as shown in Table 14, responds correctly or appropriately and maintains that response for specific periods of time, circle the period of time during which the response was maintained (**1s, 2s, 5s, 10s, 20s, 1m, 2m, 5m, 10m, 20m,** or **1h, 2h, 5h, 2d**)
Step 5.	If the learner responds correctly or appropriately without a prompt, repeat step 1 with a different example of an item or activity (**2E**), in a different setting (**2S**), with a different person (**2P**), with weak or strong motivation (**<M** or **>M**), or in the absence of a requested item (**NI**), and circle the situations in which the learner responded correctly or appropriately (see Table 13)
Step 6.	Do not collect data the remainder of the day
Step 7.	If the learner does not respond correctly or appropriately after having done so without prompts in the past, circle **Det** and re-teach this skill

Table 13.
Tracking Daily Progress on Skills that were Assessed and Selected for Instruction

ESSENTIAL FOR LIVING

Self-graphing, First Opportunity of the Day, Probe Data Recording Form: Requests

Item or Activity Requested	Day/Date and First Opportunity of the Day Probe
	S | M | T | W | T | F | S | S | M | T | W | T | F | S | S | M | T
R7. 1- cookies	Det Det Det Det Det Det Det Det Det Det Det Det Det Det Det Det Det NI NI NI NI NI NI NI NI NI NI NI NI NI NI NI NI NI <M <M <M <M <M <M <M <M <M <M <M <M <M <M <M <M <M 2P 2P 2P 2P 2P 2P 2P 2P 2P 2P 2P 2P 2P 2P 2P 2P 2P 2S 2S 2S 2S 2S 2S 2S 2S 2S 2S 2S 2S 2S 2S 2S 2S 2S Ind Ind Ind Ind Ind Ind Ind Ind Ind Ind Ind (Ind) Ind Ind (Ind) (Ind) MP MP MP MP (MP) MP MP MP MP (MP) MP MP MP MP MP PP PP (PP) (PP) (PP) PP PP (PP) (PP) PP PP PP PP PP PP FP FP (FP) (FP) (FP) FP FP FP FP FP FP FP FP FP FP FP FP -RP -RP -RP -RP -RP -RP -RP -RP -RP -RP -RP -RP -RP -RP -RP -RP -RP -DC (-DC) -DC -DC -DC -DC -DC -DC -DC -DC -DC -DC -DC -DC -DC -DC -DC -SA -SA -SA -SA -SA -SA -SA -SA -SA -SA -SA -SA -SA -SA -SA -SA -SA 0 0 0 0 0 0 0 0 0 0 0 0 0 0 0 0 0

Table 14.
Tracking Daily Progress on Skills that were Assessed and Selected for Instruction
ESSENTIAL FOR LIVING
Self-graphing, First Opportunity of the Day, Probe Data Recording Form: Waiting

Item or Activity Requested and Waiting for	Day/Date and First Opportunity of the Day Probe															
	13	14	15	16	17	18	19	20	21	22	23	24	25	26	27	28	29
	S	M	T	W	T	F	S	S	M	T	W	T	F	S	S	M	T
R9. 1- cookies	20m 10m 5m 2m 1m 20s 10s 5s 2s 1s 0	20m 10m 5m 2m 1m 20s 10s 5s 2s 1s 0	20m 10m 5m 2m 1m 20s 10s 5s 2s 1s 0	20m 10m 5m 2m 1m 20s 10s 5s 2s 1s 0	20m 10m 5m 2m 1m 20s 10s 5s 2s 1s 0	20m 10m 5m 2m 1m 20s 10s 5s 2s 1s 0	20m 10m 5m 2m 1m 20s 10s 5s 2s 1s 0	20m 10m 5m 2m 1m 20s 10s 5s 2s 1s 0	20m 10m 5m 2m 1m 20s 10s 5s 2s 1s 0	20m 10m 5m 2m 1m 20s 10s 5s 2s 1s 0	20m 10m 5m 2m 1m 20s 10s 5s 2s 1s 0	20m 10m 5m 2m 1m 20s 10s 5s 2s 1s 0	20m 10m 5m 2m 1m 20s 10s 5s 2s 1s 0	20m 10m 5m 2m 1m 20s 10s 5s 2s 1s 0	20m 10m 5m 2m 1m 20s 10s 5s 2s 1s 0	20m 10m 5m 2m 1m 20s 10s 5s 2s 1s 0	20m 10m 5m 2m 1m 20s 10s 5s 2s 1s 0

In the examples in Tables 13 and 14, an individual was learning to request cookies and wait for this request to be honored. During the initial assessment of this request, the learner did not exhibit problem behavior, but did resist prompts, such that even a full physical prompt could not be provided. During the initial assessment of waiting, the learner did not wait without exhibiting problem behavior for even one second. After instruction, the learner experienced improvement in both skills. As shown in Tables 13-15, as learners reach new performance levels on three consecutive occasions, transfer this information to the *ARP*.

Table 15.
Transferring Information from Self-graphing Data Recording Forms
to the *Assessment and Record of Progress* (*ARP*)

R7. Requests 10 highly preferred snack foods, drinks, non-food items, or activities that can be made frequently and immediately available

1 cookies | IA | IM | -SA | -DC | -RP | FP | PP | MP | Ind | 2S | 2P | <M | Ni | Det |

R9. Waits after requesting each of the items and activities in R7 and R8 for gradually increasing periods of time

1 cookies | IA | IM | 1s | 2s | 5s | 10s | 20s | 1m | 2m | 5m | 10m | 20m | Det |

As shown in Tables 16 and 17, we recommend using a color-coding or symbol system, with one color or symbol for each one-year period of time. This makes tracking yearly progress on Individual Education Plans (IEPs) and Individual Support Plans (ISPs) a very easy task. As shown in Table 17, when an opportunity to exhibit R7, item 4, that is, requesting juice, was provided during the initial assessment, the learner did not exhibit problem behavior, but did resist prompts. After instruction the learner began to cooperate with prompts and respond correctly, that is, request juice with prompts. Eventually the learner began to respond correctly without prompts and without hesitation. Then, during the second year of instruction, the learner began to respond correctly in one additional setting, with one additional person, when motivation for juice was weak, and in the absence of the juice. During the second year, instruction was begun on R22 item 6, *requesting ice cream*. Before the end of the year, the learner was requesting ice cream without prompts and without hesitation, in two settings, in the presence of two people, when motivation was weak, and in the absence of ice cream. During the second year, R37 item 2, *making generalized requests for help*, which was not part of the original assessment, was introduced and began occurring without prompts and without hesitation in the presence of two people. Later during that same year, however, instructors noticed that the learner was exhibiting disruptive behavior when items were misplaced, rather than requesting help. The **Det** box was circled in pencil. After additional teaching, when the skill was occurring consistently, the circle was erased.

Table 16.
Tracking An Initial Assessment and Subsequent Yearly Progress using a Color-coding or Symbol System

Initial Assessment	Date:	yellow	O
Year 1	January 1, 20__ to December 31, 20__	green	X
Year 2	January 1, 20__ to December 31, 20__	red	+

Table 17.
Examples of Tracking An Initial Assessment and Subsequent
Yearly Progress using a Color-coding System

R7. Requests 10 highly preferred snack foods, drinks, non-food items, or activities that can be made frequently and immediately available

4 juice | IA | IM | -SA | -DC | -RP | FP | PP | MP | Ind | 2S | 2P | <M | Ni | Det |

R22. Makes requests for highly preferred foods, drinks, non-food items, or activities that can be made immediately, but not frequently, available

6 ice cream | IA | IM | -SA | -DC | -RP | FP | PP | MP | Ind | 2S | 2P | <M | Ni | Det |

R37. Makes a generalized request for 'help', followed by gestures, leading others, or completing related activities, in 6 specific situations that are not dangerous

2 (situation 2) an item has been misplaced | IA | IM | -SA | -DC | -RP | FP | PP | MP | Ind | 2S | 2P | <M | (Det) |

R37. Makes a generalized request for 'help', followed by gestures, leading others, or completing related activities, in 6 specific situations that are not dangerous

2 (situation 2) an item has been misplaced | IA | IM | -SA | -DC | -RP | FP | PP | MP | Ind | 2S | 2P | <M | Det |

Recording Progress on the Reduction of Problem Behavior. As shown in Tables 18 and 19 with information and data from PB1 and PB2, continue recording instances or episodes of problem behavior using the *Direct Observation and Interview Recording Form* and transfer this information to the the *Adapted Daily Standard Celeration Chart*, the *Daily Standard Celeration Chart*, or a hand-drawn or computer-generated graph. Also, continue recording any changes in form or type (**SIB**, **Agg**, **Des**, **Dis**, or **Rep**) and any changes in medication (**Med**), along with the intensity of each instance or episode (**Sev**, **Mod**, or **Mild**), the extent to which protective equipment (**PE**), mechanical restraints (**MR**), or crisis stabilization procedures (**CS**) are used, and the extent, if any, to which the learner exhibits self-restraint (**SR**). Then, as shown in Table 20 with information from PB1, periodically transfer all of this information to the *ARP*.

Table 18.
Entering Information and Data on the Problem Behavior
Direct Observation and Interview Form

ESSENTIAL FOR LIVING
Problem Behavior Direct Observation and Interview Form

Learner: _____   Environment(s): _____

Date: _____ Observer or Person Interviewed: _____ Counting Period: **5 hours**

Definition of Problem Behavior(s) 1 -- **PB1**: *Makes a fist with his right hand, repeatedly brings his hand rapidly toward and makes repeated contact with his head just above his right ear and does not make any of these movements for one minute*	Definition of Problem Behavior(s) 2 -- **PB2**: *Raises his arm and, with an open hand, slaps others*
Instance (Episode) (SIB) Agg Des Dis Cpl	(Instance) Episode SIB (Agg) Des Dis Cpl

Medications:	~~Risperdal~~, Clonidine

Direct Observation

PB1	Intensity	MRA	MRC	PEA	PEC	CS (min)	SR		PB2	Intensity	MRA	MRC	PEA	PEC	CS (min)	SR
(1)	Sev-(Mod)-Mild			PE1</-15mH		5			(1)	Sev-(Mod)-Mild						X
(2)	Sev-Mod-(Mild)			PE1<					(2)	Sev-(Mod)-Mild						X
(3)	Sev-Mod-(Mild)			PE1<					(3)	Sev-(Mod)-Mild						X
(4)	Sev-Mod-(Mild)			PE1<					4	Sev-Mod-Mild						
(5)	Sev-Mod-(Mild)			PE1<					5	Sev-Mod-Mild						
6	Sev-Mod-Mild								6	Sev-Mod-Mild						

Table 19.
Continuing to Record the Total Number of Instances or Episodes of
Problem Behavior Each Day and Transferring These Data
to the Adapted Standard Celeration Chart

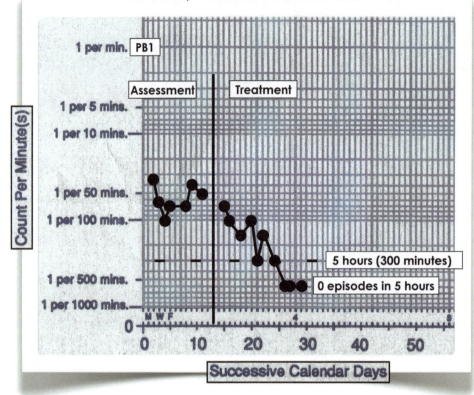

As shown in Table 20, during the first year of instruction, the frequency of episodes of **PB1** decreased from 1-10 per day to less than one per day, the intensity decreased from moderate to mild, and the padded helmet was partially faded, that is, taken off every hour for 15 minutes. Psychoactive medication was reduced from Risperdal and Clonidine to Clonidine only and crisis stabilization procedures were required less than 30 minutes per week. As shown in Table 21, during the second year of instruction), the frequency of episodes decreased to less than one per month, the intensity remained mild, the helmet was completely faded, psychoactive medication was eliminated, and crisis stabilization procedures were no longer required.

Table 20.
Transferring Information from the Data Recording Form and the Adapted Standard
Celeration Chart to the Assessment and Record of Progress (ARP)

ESSENTIAL FOR LIVING

Assessment and Record of Progress (ARP): Problem Behavior

PB1. Makes a fist with his right hand, repeatedly and rapidly brings his hand toward and makes contact with his head just above his right ear and does not make any of these movements for one minute

IA	IM		Instance	Episode		SIB	Agg	Des	Dis	Rep
							Sev	Mod	Mild	
Med3+>	Med3+	Med3+<	Med2>	Med2		Med2<	Med1>	Med1	Med1<	-Med
MRA	MRC		MR2>	MR1>		MR	MR1<	MR2<	MR3<	-MR
PEA	PEC		PE2>	PE1>		PE	PE!<	PE2<	PE3<	-PE
				CS>5hW		CS 2-5hW	CS 1-2hW	CS 30m-1hW	CS<30mW	-CS
				SR2>		SR1>	SR	SR1<	SR2<	SR3<	-SR
			>100D	50-100D		20-50D	10-20D	1-10D	<1D	<1W	<1M	<1Y

Table 21.
Tracking Yearly Progress on Problem Behaviors Specified in IEPs and IPPs

ESSENTIAL FOR LIVING
Assessment and Record of Progress (ARP): Problem Behavior

PB1. Makes a fist with his right hand, repeatedly and rapidly brings his hand toward and makes contact with his head just above his right ear and does not make any of these movements for one minute

IA	IM		Instance	Episode		SIB	Agg	Des	Dis	Rep
								Sev	Mod	Mild
Med3+>	Med3+	Med3+<	Med2>	Med2	Med2<	Med1>	Med1	Med1<	-Med
MRA	MRC		MR2>	MR1>	MR	MR1<	MR2<	MR3<	-MR
PEA	PEC		PE2>	PE1>	PE	PE!<	PE2<	PE3<	-PE
				CS>5hW	CS 2-5hW	CS 1-2hW	CS 30m-1hW	CS<30mW	-CS
			SR2>	SR1>	SR	SR1<	SR2<	SR3<	-SR
		>100D	50-100D	20-50D	10-20D	1-10D	<1D	<1W	<1M	<1Y

Chapter 5. The Quick Assessment

The initial administration of *Essential for Living* often requires a few minutes per day for 4-5 days. With children or adults with no method of speaking, a limited speaking repertoire, or severe problem behavior, *The Essential for Living Quick Assessment* can be temporarily helpful. *The Quick Assessment*, which is shown in Table 1 and provided in the *ARP manual*, can often be completed in about two hours. Then, teaching skills and managing problem behavior can begin immediately and administration of the entire instrument can be completed as time permits.

Table 1.
The Essential for Living Quick Assessment

THE ESSENTIAL FOR LIVING QUICK ASSESSMENT

Learner:_____   Date: _____

THE ESSENTIAL EIGHT

Spoken Words	Alternative Method of Speaking	Making Requests	Waiting	Accepting Removals, Making Transitions, Sharing, Taking Turns	Completing 10 Consecutive, Brief, Previously Acquired Tasks	Accepting 'No'	Following Directions: Health and Safety	Completing Daily Living Skills: Health and Safety	Tolerating Situations: Health and Safety	Matching	Imitation	Other Daily Living Skills	Tolerating Other Situations	Naming and Describing	Following Directions, Recognizing, Retrieving	Answering Questions	Problem Behavior
4	4	4	4	4	4	4	4	4	4	4	4	4	4	4	4	4	4
3	3	3	3	3	3	3	3	3	3	3	3	3	3	3	3	3	3
2	2	2	2	2	2	2	2	2	2	2	2	2	2	2	2	2	2
1	1	1	1	1	1	1	1	1	1	1	1	1	1	1	1	1	1

Spoken Words: the extent to which a learner exhibits spontaneous, understandable spoken words and the conditions under which spoken-word repetitions occur

4   Exhibits many spontaneous, spoken-words, nearly typical spoken-word interactions, and spoken-word repetitions when asked to do so, all of which are understandable **6. MS-Profile 1**

3   Exhibits a few spontaneous spoken words and spoken-word repetitions, both of which are understandable **6. MS-Profiles 2/3**

2   Exhibits occasional words or spoken-word repetitions, but neither are understandable **6. MS-Profiles 4/5**

1   Exhibits only noises and a few sounds **6. MS-Profile 6**

Alternative Method of Speaking: a method of speaking used by learners, who do not exhibit understandable spoken words or spoken-word repetitions

4   has been using an effective, alternative method of speaking for more than 6 months

3   has been using an effective, alternative method of speaking for 1-6 months

2   a new alternative method of speaking is being tested **6. MS-Tables 15 and 16**

1   Has no formal method of speaking or is using one or more ineffective methods **6. MS-AMS1-46**

------------------------ **THE ESSENTIAL EIGHT** ------------------------

One. Making Requests – the tendency to make requests for highly preferred items and activities

4   Makes requests for 10 or more preferred items or activities without prompts using an effective method of speaking **7a. R14, R17-21, R22-24, R27-28, R30-31**

3   Makes requests for 1-3 preferred items or activities with or without prompts **7a. R7-8**

2   Makes requests by leading others to items **7a. R1-5, R6, R7-8**

1   Makes requests by exhibiting problem behavior **7a. R1-5, R6, R7-8**

Two. Waiting -- the tendency to wait when access to items or activities is delayed after a request

4   Waits for 20 minutes without complaints

3   Waits for 5 minutes without complaints **7a. R9**

2   Waits for 1 minute with complaints or other minor disruptions **7a. R9**

1   Exhibits problem behavior when access is delayed for a few seconds **7a. R9**

Table 1. (cont.)
The Essential for Living Quick Assessment

Three. **Accepting Removals, Making Transitions, Sharing, and Taking Turns** -- the tendency to accept the removal of preferred items and activities by persons in authority or peers, to make transitions from preferred activities to non-preferred ones, and to share and take turns with preferred ones

- 4   Accepts the removal of items and activities, transitions, shares, and takes turns without complaints
- 3   Makes complaints when preferred items or activities are removed, during transitions, or during required sharing or taking turns, but only when motivating events are strong   **7a. R10, R12-13**
- 2   Makes complaints when preferred items or activities are removed, during transitions, or during required sharing or taking turns   **7a. R10, R12-13**
- 1   Exhibits problem behavior when preferred items or activities are removed, during transitions, or during required sharing or taking turns   **7a. R10, R12-13**

Four. **Completing 10 Consecutive, Brief, Previously Acquired Tasks** – the tendency to complete previously acquired tasks between opportunities to make requests

- 4   Completes 10 or more consecutive, brief, previously acquired tasks of varying durations and requiring varying degrees of effort without complaints
- 3   Completes 4-6 consecutive, brief, previously acquired tasks without complaints   **7a. R11**
- 2   Completes 1-3 consecutive, brief, previously acquired tasks without disruptive behavior   **7a. R11**
- 1   Exhibits problem behavior when directed to complete a brief, previously acquired task   **7a. R11**

Five. **Accepting 'No'** - the tendency to accept 'no' when access to items or activities is denied following requests that were taught and requests for dangerous items and activities that were not taught

- 4   Readily accepts "no" by continuing with ongoing activities
- 3   Complains only when motivation related to the requested item or activity is strong   **7a. R15-16**
- 2   Complains when told "no"   **7a. R15-16**
- 1   Exhibits problem behavior when told "no"   **7a. R15-16**

Six. **Following Directions Related to Health and Safety** – the tendency to follow directions from others that insure safety and that permit safe movement throughout the community

- 4   Follows all directions that involve matters of health and safety and can be taken anywhere with minimal supervision
- 3   Follows many directions related to safety and can be taken most places in a group of three with one supervisor   **7b. LR1-11**
- 2   Follows only a few directions and requires "hands on" supervision at all times   **7b. LR1-11**
- 1   Does not follow any directions that involve matters of safety and cannot be taken most places within the community without problem behavior or risking safety   **7b. LR1-11**

Seven. **Completing Daily Living Skills Related to Health and Safety** – the tendency to perform daily living skills which have an immediate impact on the health and safety of the learner

- 4   Completes most daily living skills related to health and safety
- 3   Completes 4-6 daily living skills related to health and safety   **8a. DLS-EDF1-9, Slp1-2, MT1-5, AHS1-15, HS1-8**
- 2   Completes 1-3 daily living skills related to health and safety with complaints, some resistance to prompts, or some problem behavior   **8a. DLS-EDF1-9, Slp1-2, MT1-5, AHS1-15, HS1-8**
- 1   Does not complete any daily living skills related to health and safety without prompts, resistance to prompts, or problem behavior   **8a. DLS-EDF1-9, Slp1-2, MT1-5, AHS1-15, HS1-8**

Eight. **Tolerating Situations Related to Health and Safety** – the tendency to tolerate unpleasant situations which have an immediate impact on the health and safety of the learner

- 4   Tolerates most routine activities related to health and safety without problem behavior
- 3   Tolerates 4-6 routine activities related to health and safety   **9. T-BHI-5, T-EDF1-11, T-DM1-9, T-Slp1-5, T-Toil1-5, T-PRM1-6, T-PTA1-11, T-PEMR1-10, T-BPH1-8, T-DD1**
- 2   Tolerates 1-3 routine activities related to health and safety with some complaints or problem behavior   **9. T-BHI-5, T-EDF1-11, T-DM1-9, T-Slp1-5, T-Toil1-5, T-PRM1-6, T-PTA1-11, T-PEMR1-10, T-BPH1-8, T-DD1**
- 1   Because of intense episodes of problem behavior, instructors and care providers occasionally avoid routine activities related to health and safety   **9. T-BHI-5, T-EDF1-11, T-DM1-9, T-Slp1-5, T-Toil1-5, T-PRM1-6, T-PTA1-11, T-PEMR1-10, T-BPH1-8, T-DD1**

Table 1. (cont.)
The Essential for Living Quick Assessment

Matching: the tendency to match items-to-items, photographs-to-items, and text-to-items

- 4 Matches photographs or miniature items, but not text, with items or activities and vice versa **11. M12-13**
- 3 Matches a few photographs or miniature items with items or activities and vice versa **11. M6-11**
- 2 Matches only identical items **11. M2-11**
- 1 Does not match identical items **11. M1**

Imitation: the tendency to imitate motor movements made by others

- 4 Imitates finger, hand, and arm movements and motor movements with items, but does copy words that have been written, typed, or Braille-written **11. Im3**
- 3 Imitates many finger, hand, arm movements and a few motor movements with items **11. Im2**
- 2 Imitates some finger, hand, arm movements, but not motor movements with items **11. Im1-2**
- 1 Does not imitate any movements **11. Im1**

Other Daily Living Skills: the tendency to perform daily living skills that do not have an immediate impact on the health and safety of the learner

- 4 Completes most daily living skills not related to health and safety
- 3 Completes 4-6 daily living skills not related to health and safety **8a. DLS-___**
- 2 Completes 1-3 daily living skills not related to health and safety with complaints, some resistance to prompts, or some problem behavior **8a. DLS-___**
- 1 Does not complete any daily living skills not related to health and safety without prompts, resistance to prompts, or problem behavior **8a. DLS-___**

Tolerating Other Situations – the tendency to tolerate unpleasant situations which do not have an immediate impact on the health and safety of the learner

- 4 Tolerates most routine activities not related to health and safety without problem behavior
- 3 Tolerates 4-6 routine activities not related to health and safety **9. T-___**
- 2 Tolerates 1-3 routine activities not related to health and safety with some complaints or problem behavior **9. T-___**
- 1 Because of intense episodes of problem behavior, instructors and care providers occasionally avoid routine activities not related to health and safety **9. T-___**

Naming and Describing: the tendency to name and describe items, activities, people, places, locations, and items with features that are part of routine events

- 4 Names or describes many items, activities, familiar people, places, locations, and items with features that are part of 7 or more routine events **7b. LRND11-13** or **LRND14-15**
- 3 Names many items, activities, familiar people, and places that are part of 4-6 routine events **7b. LRND7-13**
- 2 Names some items and activities that are part of 1-3 routine events **7b. LRND1-3.1, 1-3.2,** and **1-3.3**
- 1 Does not exhibit any names or descriptions **7b. LRND1-3.1, 1-3.2,** and **1-3.3**

Following Directions, Recognizing, and Retrieving: the tendency to follow directions, to recognize items, activities, people, places, locations, and items with features, and to retrieve items, people, and items with features that are part of routine events

- 4 Recognizes and retrieves many items, activities, familiar people, places, locations, and items with features that are part of 7 or more routine events **7b. LRND11-13** or **LRND14-15**
- 3 Recognizes and retrieves many items, activities, familiar people, and places that are part of 4-6 routine events **7b. LRND7-13**
- 2 Follows directions to complete routine activities, and recognizes and retrieves some items that are part of 1-3 routine events **7b. LRND1-3.1, 1-3.2, and 1-3.3**
- 1 Does not follow directions to complete routine activities and does not recognize or retrieve any item that is part of a routine activity **7b. LR1-11, LR12-17, LRND1-3.1, 1-3.2, and 1-3.3**

Table 1. (cont.)
The Essential for Living Quick Assessment

Answering Questions: the tendency to answer questions that occur before, during, or after routine events

4   Answers many questions like "What are you going to do after lunch?", "Where did you put your blue pants?", and "Who is driving you to the movies?" that are a part of 7 or more routine events **7c. AQ11-13** or **AQ14-15**

3   Answers many questions like "Where are the napkins?", "Who is that?", "What are you going to do?", "What are you going to get at the mall?", "Who is helping you?", "Where are you going?", and "When do you want your cigar?" that are a part of 4-6 routine events **7c. AQ7-13**

2   Answers some questions like "Do you want juice?", "Can you help me?", "What do you want?", or "Which one do you want?" that are part of 1- 3 routine events **7c. AQ1-3.1, 1-3.2**, and **1-3.3**

1   Cannot answer any commonly occurring questions   **7c. AQ1-3.1, 1-3.2**, and **1-3.3**

Problem Behavior: the tendency for the learner to exhibit problem behavior

4   Does not exhibit problem behavior
3   Exhibits disruptive behavior or frequent complaining that presents a problem **10**
2   Exhibits infrequent and less intense self-injurious, aggressive, or destructive behavior **10**
1   Exhibits frequent and intense self-injurious, aggressive, or destructive behavior **10**

Secure a copy of the *ARP* and begin conducting The Essential for Living Quick Assessment by interviewing an instructor or care provider who has known the learner for several years, or by interviewing one or both parents. Begin with 'Spoken Words' by asking "which one of the following statements most closely describes the learner?". Read statements '1-4'. As shown in Table 2, circle the number that corresponds with the statement each interviewee selects. Continue until all sections of the *Quick Assessment* have been completed. Then, mark the boxes in the diagram corresponding to the statements that were circled.

Table 2.
Conducting *The Essential for Living Quick Assessment*

THE ESSENTIAL EIGHT

Spoken Words	Alternative Method of Speaking	Making Requests	Waiting	Accepting Removals, Making Transitions, Sharing, Taking Turns	Completing 10 Consecutive, Brief, Previously Acquired Tasks	Accepting 'No'	Following Directions: Health and Safety	Completing Daily Living Skills: Health and Safety	Tolerating Situations: Health and Safety	Matching	Imitation	Other Daily Living Skills	Tolerating Other Situations	Naming and Describing	Following Directions, Recognizing, Retrieving	Answering Questions	Problem Behavior
2	**1**	**2**			**2**	**1**	**1**		**1**	**2**		**1**	**2**		**1**	**1**	**1**

Spoken Words – the extent to which a learner exhibits spontaneous, understandable spoken words and the conditions under which spoken-word repetitions occur

4   Exhibits many spontaneous, spoken-words, nearly typical spoken-word interactions, and spoken-word repetitions only when asked to do so, all of which are understandable   **6. MS-Profile 1**

3   Exhibits a few spontaneous spoken words and spoken-word repetitions, both of which are understandable   **6. MS-Profiles 2/3**

(2)   Exhibits occasional words or spoken-word repetitions, but neither are understandable **6. MS-Profiles 4/5**

1   Exhibits only noises and a few sounds   **6. MS-Profile 6**

Alternative Method of Speaking – the manner in which a learner functions as a speaker if understandable spoken words are not occurring

4   has been using an effective, alternative method of speaking for more than 6 months
3   has been using an effective, alternative method of speaking for 1-6 months
2   a new alternative method of speaking is being tested   **6. MS-Tables 15 and 16**
(1)   Has no formal method of speaking or is using one or more ineffective methods   **6. MS-AMS1-46**

Table 2. (cont.)
Conducting *The Essential for Living Quick Assessment*

One. Making Requests – the tendency to make requests for highly preferred items and activities

    4   Makes requests for 10 or more preferred items or activities without prompts using an effective method of speaking **7a. R14, R17-21, R22-24, R27-28, R30-31**

    3   Makes requests for 1-3 preferred items or activities with or without prompts **7a. R7-8**

    (2)   Makes requests by leading others to items **7a. R1-5, R6, R7-8**

    (1)   Makes requests by exhibiting problem behavior **7a. R1-5, R6, R7-8**

Problem Behavior -- the tendency to exhibit problem behavior

    4   Does not exhibit problem behavior

    3   Exhibits disruptive or repetitive behavior, or frequent complaining **10**

    2   Exhibits infrequent and less intense self-injurious, aggressive, or destructive behavior **10**

    (1)   Exhibits frequent and intense self-injurious, aggressive, or destructive behavior **10**

With each section of the *Quick Assessment*, note the chapter and skill numbers (in bold print) that correspond to the estimated performance levels and begin teaching. For example, with respect to Spoken Words, both interviewees selected performance level 2. As indicated next to this level (**6. Vocal Profiles 4-5**), vocal profiles 4 and 5 in chapter 6 provide guidelines for teaching learners who exhibit occasional words or spoken-word repetitions that are not understandable. Proceed to this section of the instrument and begin teaching. With respect to an alternative method of speaking, both interviewees indicated that the learner had no effective method of speaking. As indicated next to this performance level (**6. AMS1-46**), chapter 6 provides procedures for selecting 1 of 46 alternative methods. Proceed to this section and begin this task. With respect to making requests, one interviewee selected performance level 1, while the other selected performance level 2. As indicated next to these levels (**7a. R1-5, R6, R7-8**), skills R1-5, R6, and R7-8 in chapter 7a should be selected for teaching. Proceed to this section of the instrument, conduct an assessment of skills **R1-R8** as described in chapter 4 and begin teaching. With respect to problem behavior, both interviewees indicated frequent and intense episodes. As indicated next to this level (**10**), chapter 10 provides procedures for determining which of the *Essential Eight Skills* fails to occur when problem behaviors occur, along with protocols designed to teach these skills and reduce the frequency of problem behaviors. Proceed to this section and begin implementing these procedures and protocols.

Then, as time permits, administer the entire instrument.

Chapter 6. Methods of Speaking

Co-authored by: Janine Shapiro, M.S., CCC-SLP, BCBA

Most of us communicate by '*saying words*', '*writing words*', and '*typing words*'. '*Saying words*' is our primary method of speaking, as we use it frequently to converse with others, while '*writing words, typing words, and texting*' are secondary methods, which we use less frequently to convey messages to those who are not within the sound of our voice.

function as a speaker
primary speaker
response form

'Saying Words'. This method of speaking has more advantages than any other method. It permits us to easily make contact with an audience, to convey an almost unlimited number of messages quickly and without environmental supports, and to achieve a wide variety of outcomes with a very large audience. Many children and adults with developmental disabilities use this method effectively or can be taught to do so.

forms of verbal behavior across verbal operants

Alternative Methods of Speaking. Many children and adults with developmental disabilities, however, cannot effectively communicate by '*saying words*'. In order to function as effective speakers, these individuals require an alternative, primary method of speaking and, in many cases, one or more concurrent or secondary methods. Some of these individuals, whose primary method is understood by a small audience (e.g., methods that include '*signs*'), may also require a back-up method to increase the size of that audience. Many alternative methods of speaking also require a separate method of contacting an audience.

This section contains a list of 46 alternative methods of speaking. The first part of the list contains methods that include specific response forms that correspond to words or letters conveyed (Michael, 1985). For example, '*forming signs*' includes specific signs for '*ball*', '*cookie*', and '*juice*' and '*writing words*' includes specific letter combinations for each of the same words. The second part of the list contains methods that include non-specific response forms, such as, pointing, touching, activating an electronic switch or device, or depressing a key, which are used to select photographs, pic-symbols, printed words, or letters that correspond to '*ball*', '*cookie*', and '*juice*', or parts thereof (Michael, 1985). Each part of the list begins with alternative methods that tend to be effective with a greater number of learners and tend to result in more extensive communication. The advantages of each method are described later in this chapter.

Alternative Methods of Speaking

Alternative Methods that Include Specific Responses that Correspond to Words or Letters Conveyed

Topography-based Response Forms

- **AMS 1:** Using the sign language of the deaf community
- **AMS 2:** Forming standard signs (Signed English[1])
- **AMS 3:** Forming a repertoire of standard, adapted, and idiosyncratic signs
- **AMS 4:** Forming a repertoire of standard and adapted signs used with tactile signing
- **AMS 5:** Forming a repertoire of standard signs, iconic signs and iconic gestures
- **AMS 6:** Writing words or drawing diagrams on a small notepad
- **AMS 7:** Saying word approximations that are understood and discriminated only by a familiar audience
- **AMS 8:** Making distinguishable noises or sounds that are understood and discriminated only by a familiar audience

Alternative Methods that Include Non-specific Responses Which are Used to Select Photographs, Pic-symbols, Printed words, Letters, or Spoken Words

Selection-based Response Forms

- **AMS 9:** Visually scanning and pointing to or exchanging photographs using a small book worn by the learner
- **AMS 10:** Visually scanning and pointing to or exchanging pic-symbols with printed words using a small book worn by the learner
- **AMS 11:** Visually scanning and pointing to or exchanging printed words using a small book worn by the learner
- **AMS 12:** Visually scanning and touching photographs on a screen using a small speech-generating device (SGD) worn by the learner or attached to the learner's mobility or positioning device
- **AMS 13:** Visually scanning and touching pic-symbols with printed words on a screen using a small SGD worn by the learner or attached to the learner's mobility or positioning device

---

[1] Signs from the sign language of the deaf community exhibited in the order of the spoken language of the region.

Alternative Methods that Include Non-specific Responses Which are Used to Select Photographs, Pic-symbols, Printed words, Letters, or Spoken Words (cont.)

AMS 14: Visually scanning and touching printed words on a screen using a small speech-generating device (SGD) worn by the learner or attached to the learner's mobility or positioning device

AMS 15: Visually scanning and exchanging photographs using the Picture Exchange Communication System[2] and a PECS Binder

AMS 16: Visually scanning and exchanging pic-symbols with printed words using the Picture Exchange Communication System and a PECS Binder

AMS 17: Visually scanning and exchanging printed words using the Picture Exchange Communication System and a PECS Binder

AMS 18: Scanning by touch and selecting items or miniature items attached to an object board

AMS 19: Visually scanning and touching photographs using a large SGD that contains 20 or fewer messages or requires another person to change templates

AMS 20: Visually scanning and touching pic-symbols with printed words using a large SGD that contains 20 or fewer messages or requires another person to change templates

AMS 21: Visually scanning and touching printed words using a large SGD that contains 20 or fewer messages or requires another person to change templates

AMS 22: Visually scanning and selecting photographs on a large SGD by touching the screen, or by using one or two switches or eye-tracking

AMS 23: Visually scanning and selecting pic-symbols with printed words on a large SGD by touching the screen, or by using one or two switches or eye-tracking

AMS 24: Visually scanning and selecting printed words on a large SGD by touching the screen, or by using one or two switches, or eye-tracking

AMS 25: Typing words (Texting) with a small, electronic device

AMS 26: Typing words with a large, electronic or SGD

AMS 27: Typing words with a Braille Writer

AMS 28: Typing words with a switch or eye-tracking and a large SGD

AMS 29: Scanning by listening and selecting spoken words on a large SGD by touching the screen, or by using one or two switches

AMS 30: Scanning by touch and selecting locations on a large, adapted SGD

AMS 31: Visually scanning and pointing to large photographs using a binder

AMS 32: Visually scanning and pointing to large printed words using a binder

AMS 33: Visually scanning and selecting photographs presented two at a time

AMS 34: Visually scanning and selecting items presented two at a time

AMS 35: Scanning by touch and selecting items presented two at a time

AMS 36: Looking at and selecting photographs presented one at a time

AMS 37: Looking at and selecting items presented one at a time

AMS 38: Touching and selecting items presented one at a time

AMS 39: Scanning by listening and selecting spoken words presented two at a time

AMS 40: Listening and selecting spoken words presented one at a time

AMS 41: Listening to "do you want ___?" and gesturing to indicate 'yes' or 'no'

AMS 42: Listening to "do you want ___?" and activating a switch to indicate 'yes' or one of two switches to indicate 'yes' or 'no'

AMS 43: Reaching, pointing, gesturing, or gazing toward items or familiar locations for items

AMS 44: Leading others to items or to familiar locations for items

AMS 45: Selecting items or completing activities in the presence of another person that are typically paired with or precede preferred items or activities

AMS 46: Touching a photograph or printed words using a speech-generating device that contains only one message

This chapter describes when to select '*saying words*' as a learner's primary method of speaking, when to confirm this selection, and when and how to select and confirm an alternative primary method, a concurrent method, a back-up method, and secondary method. While communication also includes listening, this chapter will focus on learners functioning as effective speakers.

---

[2] *The Picture Exchange Communication System* (*PECS*) was developed by Lori Frost and Andrew Bondy and is a product of Pyramid Educational Consultants, Inc.

Selecting, Confirming, and Maintaining a Primary Method of Speaking

When to Select 'Saying Words" or an Alternative Primary Method of Speaking. Children and adults with moderate-to-severe developmental disabilities exhibit noises, sounds, and spoken words with varying degrees of understandability and functionality. Based on the extent of their spoken-word repertoires, these learners can be described using six profiles displayed in Table 1 and summarized in Table 2. Aligning specific learners with one of these profiles will help instructors, speech-language pathologists, and care providers determine (1) whether to select *saying words* as a learner's primary method of speaking or to select an alternative method, and (2) realistic goals for each learner, (3) a plan of action for meeting those goals, and (4) a recommended allocation of resources relative to *saying words* and/or an alternative method of speaking. Read each of the six profiles and select the one which best describes your learner. Then, review the recommendations for that profile described in Table 3.

Table 1.
Six Profiles of Learners with Moderate-to-severe Developmental Disabilities
Based on the Extent of their Spoken-word Repertoires

Vocal Profile 1: Typical Spoken-word Interactions and Controlled Spoken-word Repetitions

Many children with moderate-to-severe developmental disabilities, at a very young age, acquire 'saying words' as a method of speaking and communicate easily and effectively with a large number of listeners. They exhibit many understandable words, phrases, and sentences that function as requests. Some of these learners also name or describe items, activities, and people, answer questions, and participate in conversations regarding familiar topics. While their utterances may include a few errors in sound production, they are understood by both familiar and unfamiliar listeners. These learners also exhibit controlled repetitions, that is, they repeat words or phrases when directed to do so without repeating the direction, making it easy to teach them new words and phrases. For example, if an instructor says "say, car", these learners tend to say "car". [exhibit mands, tacts, and intraverbals] [exhibit controlled echoic responses]

Vocal Profile 2: Uncontrolled or Controlled Spoken-word Repetitions

A small, but distinctive number of children and adults with developmental disabilities, including autism, exhibit a variety of understandable words or phrases, but only immediately after hearing those same words or phrases. For example, if an instructor says "what's that" or "what do you want", the learner says "what's that" or "what do you want". Some learners with a limited length of utterance may say "that" or "you want". When directed to repeat words, many of these children and adults also tend to repeat the direction to do so. For example, if an instructor says "say, car", many of these learners will say "say, car". These reliable, but uncontrolled repetitions, are often described as *echolalia*. Some of these learners exhibit controlled repetitions, that is, they repeat words or phrases when directed to do so without repeating the direction. For example, if an instructor says "say, car", some of these learners will say "car". While occasional articulation errors may occur, the repetitions of learners aligned with this profile are generally understandable to both familiar and unfamiliar listeners. [only as echoic responses] [exhibit uncontrolled echoic responses] [exhibit controlled echoic responses]

Vocal Profile 3: Occasional Words

Learners aligned with this profile do not consistently exhibit controlled or uncontrolled repetitions. They do, however, occasionally say words or phrases that may include errors in sound production, but are generally understandable even to unfamiliar listeners. Examples include (1) seeing a dog and saying "doggie", (2) hearing someone say "where are your socks" and saying "socks on", or (3) riding in a car and saying "kitty cat" without seeing a cat or hearing someone say "cat". Some of these children also exhibit what is often called 'scripting'. For example, a learner may watch a video and hear 'Swiper, no swiping' and several hours later, while doing something else, is heard to say "Swiper, no swiping". These spoken words or phrases tend to occur inconsistently, even given the same or similar situations, and are not considered repetitions. [are not considered delayed echoic responses]

Table 1. (cont.)
Six Profiles of Learners with Moderate-to-severe Developmental Disabilities
Based on the Extent of their Spoken-word Repertoires

Vocal Profile 4: Uncontrolled or Controlled Repetitions that are Not Understandable

Learners aligned with this profile exhibit uncontrolled and controlled repetitions, but, because of errors in sound production, these repetitions are understandable to only a few familiar listeners. Some of these learners exhibit frequent sound substitutions, deletions, and distortions. Others repeat only a limited number of individual sounds; and, still others repeat most of the individual sounds from their native language, but have difficulty combining sounds into syllables and words.

Vocal Profile 5: Occasional Words that are Not Understandable

Learners aligned with this profile exhibit words infrequently as described in Profile 3 and with significant errors in sound production as described in Profile 4. These infrequent word approximations are understandable to only a few familiar listeners. They are often met with uncertainty as to whether a word or a fortuitous sound combination was uttered.

Vocal Profile 6: Noises, a Few Sounds, and Syllables

Learners aligned with this profile exhibit a very limited repertoire of sounds and syllables from their native language. They do not exhibit understandable words or distant word approximations. These vocal utterances may include 'noises', 'grunts', 'whines', or 'squeals'.

Table 2.
A Summary of Six Profiles of Learners with Moderate-to-Severe Developmental Disabilities
Based on the Extent of their Spoken-word Repertoires

Vocal Profiles	Spoken Words			Spoken-word Repetitions		
	Frequent	Spontaneous	Understandable	Controlled	Uncontrolled	Understandable
Profile 1: Typical Spoken-word Interactions and Controlled Repetitions	●	●	●	●		●
Profile 2: Uncontrolled and Controlled Repetitions	●			●	●	●
Profile 3: Occasional Words and Phrases		●	●			
Profile 4: Uncontrolled or Controlled Repetitions that are not Understandable	●			●	●	
Profile 5: Occasional Words that are not Understandable		●				
Profile 6: Noises, a Few Sounds, and Syllables						

Table 3.
Recommendations for Learners Aligned with Each of the Six Profiles of Spoken Words

Vocal Profile 1: Typical Spoken-word Interactions and Controlled Spoken-word Repetitions

Goal: Learners aligned with this profile exhibit spontaneous and understandable spoken words in contextually appropriate situations. These situations may include some or all of the following: making requests, naming and describing items, activities, places, and persons, answering questions, and participating in conversations [mands, tacts, intraverbals, mixed verbal behavior, and controlled echoic responses]. Learners aligned with this profile also exhibit controlled spoken-word repetitions. The primary goal for these learners is to increase their repertoire of requests, names and descriptions, and answers to questions within functional contexts, while teaching them to participate in conversations.

Action Plan: In order to reach this goal, we must convert their controlled repetitions into requests, names, and descriptions, and convert those names and descriptions into answers to questions. These conversions require capturing or contriving specific situations and using Teaching Protocols 1, 9, and 10, which are described in chapter 12, and which include specific teaching procedures developed by Sundberg and Partington (1998) and Greer and Ross (2007) [stimulus control transfer procedures, including the echoic-to-mand, echoic-to-tact, and tact-to-intraverbal transfer procedures].

Resource Allocation: Commit all available resources toward achieving the goal and make certain that all those who work with these learners are familiar with these protocols and procedures.

Vocal Profile 2: Uncontrolled and Controlled Spoken-word Repetitions

Goal: The spoken-word repertoires of learners aligned with this profile consist primarily of uncontrolled, but understandable, repetitions of words and phrases. The goal for these learners is to acquire a repertoire of requests, along with some names or descriptions, while acquiring controlled repetitions (i.e., become aligned with Profile 1).

Action Plan: In order to reach this goal, we must first convert their uncontrolled repetitions into requests and then convert these same uncontrolled repetitions into controlled ones as we teach additional requests, names or descriptions, and answers to questions. These conversions again require capturing or contriving specific situations and using Teaching Protocols 1, 9, and 10, which are described in chapter 12, and which include specific teaching procedures developed by Sundberg and Partington (1998) and Greer and Ross (2007).

No other teaching protocols or procedures will permit learners to reach this goal.

Resource Allocation: Commit all available resources toward achieving the goal and make certain that all those who work with these learners are familiar with these protocols and procedures.

Special Note: Many instructors, speech-language pathologists, and behavior analysts are not familiar with these teaching protocols. As a result, they have difficulty making these conversions and may recommend alternative methods of speaking. *For these learners, however, 'saying words' should almost always be selected and confirmed as their primary method of speaking.*

Vocal Profile 3: Occasional Words and Phrases

Goal: Learners aligned with this profile exhibit a limited number of spoken words and phrases, which are understandable to both familiar and unfamiliar listeners, but which occur infrequently across situations, inconsistently within the same situation, and rarely as spoken-word repetitions.

Scripts, which are exhibited by some learners aligned with this profile, are often described as 'delayed repetitions' or 'delayed echolalia'. These responses, however, do not occur within a few seconds of similar spoken words or phrases, should not be described in this manner, and cannot be converted to requests, names or descriptions using the procedures described in Profile 2. As a result, learners who exhibit scripts are aligned with this profile and cannot be aligned with Profile 2.

The goal for these learners is to exhibit words more frequently, along with repetitions of the same (i.e., become aligned with Profile 2). These repetitions can then be converted to spontaneous requests. If this goal is not achieved within six months, it should be revised to include selecting an alternative primary method of speaking, teaching requests (**R7, R8, R14, R17-21, R22-23,** and **R27**), confirming this selection, and maintaining this method of speaking.

Table 3. (cont.)
Recommendations for Learners Aligned with Each of the Six Profiles of Spoken-words

Vocal Profile 3: Occasional Words and Phrases (cont.)

Action Plan: Unfortunately, unless learners already exhibit at least some tendency to repeat what they hear, there is no consistently effective way to prompt them to say sounds or words. In other words, there is no way to ensure that sounds or words occur in response to prompts. In addition to gestural prompts sometimes used by speech-language pathologists, there are three teaching procedures which 'may' indirectly result in sounds or words, and *sometimes* in repetitions of the same:

1. Rewarding Spoken Words -- In this procedure, any sounds or spoken words result in the immediate delivery of a preferred item or activity;
2. Pairing and Rewarding Spoken-word Requests -- In this procedure, new sounds and spoken words are paired with preferred items and activities. Sometimes, but not often, this pairing results in the emergence of sounds or words that quickly begin to function as requests (Yoon & Bennett, 2000; Esch, Carr, & Michael, 2005; Greer & Ross, 2007) and result in the delivery of these preferred items and activities. If this occurs, the third procedure can be implemented;

    The stimulus-stimulus pairing procedure, sometimes referred to as the automatic reinforcement procedure.

3. Rewarding Requests and Providing Opportunities for Repetitions -- In this procedure, as learners are making requests with 'their new sounds or words', opportunities for repetitions are provided; if repetitions begin to occur, learners are provided with additional amounts of requested items or additional durations of requested activities.

These procedures, which are combined into Protocol 1a and described in chapter 12, should be implemented often throughout the day. *Sometimes* these procedures result in an increase in spoken words and repetitions of the same.

If selecting, confirming, and maintaining an alternative primary method of speaking becomes part of the goal, complete the following steps, which are described in this chapter:

1. selecting an alternative method of speaking for this learner,
2. teaching requests (**R7, R8, R14, R17-21, R22-23,** and **R27**), and
3. confirming and maintaining the selection of this method.

Then, use Teaching Protocol 1, which is described in chapter 12, and which includes teaching procedures developed by Sundberg and Partington (1998) and Greer and Ross (2007).

Resource Allocation: We strongly recommend using the first three procedures exclusively and intensively for 2-3 months. If an increase in the repertoire and frequency of spoken words occurs, continue using these procedures for 2-3 additional months. If repetitions begin to occur, continue with these procedures. If repetitions are occurring frequently, the learner should be aligned with Profile 2 and spoken-word communication should be pursued accordingly.

If the frequency of spoken words does not increase after 2-3 months, select an alternative method of speaking and begin teaching requests (see **R7, R8, R14, R17-21, R22-23,** and **R27**). Continue 'rewarding spoken words', but use 'pairing and rewarding spoken-word requests' and 'rewarding requests and providing opportunities for repetitions' only as part of teaching requests using an alternative method of speaking and Teaching Protocol 1. In other words, do not abandon the quest for spoken-word communication; simply spend more time and resources teaching an alternative method of speaking. Alternative methods, along with the aforementioned teaching procedures, sometimes result in an increase in the frequency of spoken words and the size of the spoken-word repertoire.

Table 3. (cont.)
Recommendations for Learners Aligned with Each of the Six Profiles of Spoken-words

Vocal Profile 4: Uncontrolled or Controlled Repetitions that are Not Understandable

Goal: Learners aligned with this profile repeat spoken words, but their repetitions are typically not understandable, especially when listeners are unfamiliar with the learner or the context. The goal for these learners is to improve the extent to which their repetitions are understandable (i.e., become aligned with Profile 2). If this does not occur within six months or is not projected to occur by a speech-language pathologist, this goal should also include selecting an alternative primary method of speaking, teaching requests (**R7, R8, R14, R17-21, R22-23,** and **R27**), confirming this selection, and maintaining this method of speaking.

Action Plan: Secure the services of a speech-language pathologist to:

1. assess the extent to which a learner aligned with this profile is understandable, and
2. estimate the extent to which this learner's production of sounds and words could be improved with intensive speech-language therapy. [a dynamic assessment]

If selecting, confirming, and maintaining an alternative primary method of speaking becomes part of the goal, complete the following steps, which are described in this chapter:

1. selecting an alternative method of speaking for this learner,
2. teaching requests,
3. confirming the selection of this method, and
4. maintaining this method of speaking.

Use Teaching Protocol 1, which is described in chapter 12, to teach requests using the selected alternative method of speaking.

Resource Allocation: If the speech-language pathologist indicates that the learner's sound and word production could be significantly improved with intensive speech therapy, regardless of the extent to which repetitions are currently understandable, allocate all available resources toward intensive speech therapy and evaluate progress after six months. If significantly more sounds and words are understandable to unfamiliar listeners, continue to allocate all available resources toward improving spoken-word communication. If improvement does not occur, continue with speech therapy, but also select an alternative method of speaking, teach requests, confirm this selection, and maintain this method of speaking using the steps described in this chapter.

Special Note: Some learners, who initially exhibit repetitions which are not understandable, demonstrate rapid improvement when provided with visual, tactile, or physical prompting. This frequently occurs with specific patterns of speech errors, such as, omitting final consonants. [phonological processes]

The speech-language pathologist may indicate that the learner's repertoire of understandable sounds and words is very limited and that sound and word production may not be significantly improved, even with speech therapy. If this occurs, allocate the majority of available resources toward establishing an alternative method of speaking using the steps described in this chapter, teaching requests, confirming the selection of this method, and maintaining this method of speaking. A small portion of these resources can continue to be devoted to speech therapy.

Special Note: Some speech errors are very resistant to therapeutic interventions. When learners experience great difficulty producing speech and their sounds and words are not understandable, allocating the majority of available resources to improving spoken-word communication may restrict the extent to which they can function as a speaker. It is not uncommon to meet learners, who have been restricted to a few requests because of poor speech, rapidly acquire a variety of requests using an alternative method of speaking (**AMS 2-46**).

Special Note: Some speech-language pathologists use 'oral-motor therapy' to treat speech disorders. This 'therapy' typically consists of non-speech exercises (e.g., pursing lips repeatedly or holding small pieces of cereal on the roof of the mouth using the tongue) and frequently includes props (e.g., horns, straws, or whistles). This form of 'therapy', however, has been shown in the scientific literature to be ineffective in improving speech. *Exercises to improve speech should always be conducted in the context of speech.*

Table 3. (cont.)
Recommendations for Learners Aligned with Each of the Six Profiles of Spoken-words

Vocal Profile 5: Occasional Words that are Not Understandable

Goal: Learners aligned with this profile infrequently exhibit a limited number of word approximations that are not undertstandable to unfamiliar listeners. In order to eventually use spoken words as their primary method of speaking, learners aligned with this profile must begin to:

1. produce many sounds and word approximations frequently,
2. repeat these sounds and word approximations,
3. produce words that are understandable to unfamiliar listeners, and
4. repeat understandable words.

In view of the enormity of this task, we strongly recommend that the goal for these learners be to select, confirm, and maintain an alternative primary method of speaking, and to use this method to teach requests (**R7, R8, R14, R17-21, R22-23,** and **R27**). The goal may also include 'exhibiting word approximations frequently' (i.e., becoming aligned with Profile 4).

Action Plan: Select, confirm, and maintain an alternative primary method of speaking by completing the following steps, which are described in this chapter:

1. selecting an alternative method of speaking for this learner,
2. teaching requests (**R7, R8, R14, R17-21, R22-23,** and **R27**),
3. confirming the selection of this method, and
4. maintaining this method of speaking.

Use Teaching Protocol 1, which is described in chapter 12, to teach requests using the selected alternative method of speaking. This protocol, which is described in chapter 12, includes procedures (see the action plan in Profile 3) which *sometimes* result in an increase in word approximations. In order to establish an effective alternative method of speaking and maximize the opportunity for word approximations to occur, make certain that you implement these protocols exactly as they are described.

Resource Allocation: Allocate nearly all available resources toward establishing an alternative primary method of speaking using the steps described in this chapter, teaching requests (**R7, R8, R14, R17-21, R22-23,** and **R27**), confirming this selection, and maintaining this method of speaking. The protocols used to teach requests using an alternative method of speaking will ensure that a small portion of these resources will continue to be allocated to increasing spoken word approximations.

Vocal Profile 6: Noises, a Few Sounds, and Syllables

Goal: Learners aligned with this profile exhibit noises, and often a few sounds and syllables from their native language. In order to eventually use spoken words as their primary method of speaking, learners aligned with this profile must begin to:

1. produce many sounds and word approximations frequently,
2. repeat these sounds and word approximations,
3. produce words that are understandable to unfamiliar listeners, and
4. repeat understandable words.

In view of the enormity of this task, we strongly recommend that the goal for these learners be to select, confirm, and maintain an alternative primary method of speaking, and to use this method to teach requests (**R7, R8, R14, R17-21, R22-23,** and **R27**).

Table 3. (cont.)
Recommendations for Learners Aligned with Each of the Six Profiles of Spoken-words

Vocal Profile 6: Noises, a Few Sounds, and Syllables (cont.)

Action Plan: Select, confirm, and maintain an alternative primary method of speaking by completing the following steps, which are described in this chapter:

1. selecting an alternative method of speaking for this learner,
2. teaching requests (**R7, R8, R14, R17-21, R22-23,** and **R27**),
3. confirming the selection of this method, and
4. maintaining this method of speaking.

Use Teaching Protocol 1, which is described in chapter 12, to teach requests using the selected alternative method of speaking. This protocol, which is described in chapter 12, includes procedures (see the action plan in Profile 3) which *sometimes* result in an increase in word approximations. In order to establish an effective alternative method of speaking and maximize the opportunity for word approximations to occur, make certain that you implement these protocols exactly as they are described.

Resource Allocation: Allocate nearly all available resources toward establishing an alternative primary method of speaking using the steps described in this chapter, teaching requests (**R7, R8, R14, R17-21, R22-23,** and **R27**), confirming this selection, and maintaining this method of speaking. The procedures used to teach requests will ensure that a small portion of these resources will continue to be allocated to increasing sounds, syllables, and word approximations.

A Message about Pursuing Alternative Methods of Speaking. All children and adults with disabilities, who, after a reasonable period of time, have not become aligned with Profiles 1 or 2, should be provided with an alternative method of speaking as soon as possible. Many children with moderate-to-severe disabilities, even if they have been exposed to early, intensive intervention that includes the teaching procedures previously described, will require an alternative method of speaking for their entire life.

It is important to remember that, no matter how much you as a parent, instructor, or care provider, may want 'saying words' to be a learner's primary method of speaking, one cannot 'make' this happen by simply selecting this method, demonstrating words over and over (e.g., "Tommy, say ball"), and providing opportunities for words to occur (e.g., "Tommy, tell me what you want"). We have known many families and professionals who have done this, only to find that they and their children become increasingly frustrated, and they are eventually compelled to select an alternative method.

There is a long standing myth that alternative methods that include 'signs' or 'pictures' make it more difficult for children or adults to begin 'saying words'. *This is just that, a myth.* The scientific literature supports the use of alternative methods and suggests that these methods, when accompanied by procedures that are included in the procedures described in this chapter (Carbone, Lewis, et al., 2006; Tincani, 2004), sometimes result in the emergence of 'spoken words'. In fact, there is evidence to suggest that teaching a non-vocal communication method may lead to more vocal communication than direct vocal communication training (Carbone, Lewis, et al., 2006; Tincani, 2004).

A note to parents -- When instructors who are using this manual suggest an alternative, primary method of speaking for your child, it does not mean that they are 'giving up' on 'saying words' as a potential, primary method. It does mean that (1) effectively prompting spoken words is not possible at the moment and (2) your child needs a way to communicate (i.e., function as an effective speaker). If these instructors are using procedures and following guidelines described in this chapter and elsewhere (Sundberg & Partington, 1998), they are continuing to encourage your child to exhibit 'sounds', 'word approximations', and 'spoken words'. If, as your child is using an alternative method of speaking, word approximations or spoken words begin to occur, do not discontinue using this alternative method until your child exhibits spoken words that include a wide variety of sounds, reliably repeats those words, and until those words are understandable to familiar and unfamiliar listeners. Finally, the importance of acquiring an effective method of speaking cannot be overstated. Without an effective method, the only responses available to children and adults with disabilities, which might achieve the same outcomes, are forms of non-compliant, disruptive, destructive, aggressive, or self-injurious behaviors.

How to Select an Alternative, Primary Method of Speaking. As consultants to public and private schools, along with residential, vocational, and hospital programs, the authors have met many children and adults with no effective method of speaking and we continue to meet these individuals every week. It is particularly distressing to meet older children and adults *who have spent their entire lives responding almost exclusively as listeners*.

Typically, in these settings, the selection of an alternative method of speaking is based on one or more of the following:

1- the physical skills of the learner,
2- the size of the audience for specific methods,
3- the ease with which specific methods can be implemented by instructors, care providers, and parents, or
4- the potential, which specific methods seem to offer, for the teaching of advanced language.

For many of these learners, an alternative method is selected, followed by another method a year or two later, followed by another method or a return to the original method several years later, only to reach their eighteenth or thirtieth birthday with no effective method of speaking at all. Many schools and residential facilities who serve older students and adults with very limited speaking skills, have a closet filled with boards, books, and electronic devices that were used for brief periods of time and are no longer used by anyone. To avoid situations in which one or more alternative methods have been ineffective or have not endured, we have developed a systematic approach to the selection of an alternative method of speaking (AMS), which is described in this section. Before proceeding further, readers should be aware that selecting an alternative method of speaking is a complex task that may require considerable time and effort, but that the benefit, spontaneous speaking, is well worth that time and effort.

As shown in Table 3, we begin the process of selecting alternative methods of speaking by defining an effective method of speaking as one that results in an increase in the size and frequency of specific communication repertoires and a decrease in the frequency of non-compliant, disruptive, destructive, aggressive, and self-injurious behaviors.

Table 3.
Evaluating the Effectiveness of Specific Methods of Speaking

In learners with limited communication repertoires, a primary method of speaking is effective...
if their requesting repertoire is improving rapidly, continuing to improve gradually, or includes most of their preferred items, activities, and people
if their audience responds appropriately to their requests,
if they make frequent, spontaneous requests often throughout the day, and
if the frequency of destructive, aggressive and self-injurious behavior is decreasing or has decreased significantly.
In learners with more extensive communication repertoires, a primary, secondary, or back-up method of speaking is effective...
if requests that include questions are beginning to occur or are occurring often throughout the day,
if the audience is responding appropriately to their questions,
if their naming and describing repertoire is improving rapidly, continuing to improve gradually, or includes many common items, and commonly occurring activities,
if they are beginning to answer questions or are answering questions frequently throughout the day,
if they are beginning to participate in conversations, and
if the frequency of non-compliant and disruptive behavior is decreasing or has decreased significantly.

As shown in Table 4, our experience suggests that alternative methods of speaking tend to be more effective when learners exhibit specific sensory, skill, and behavioral repertoires. For example, some methods tend to be more effective for children and adults who are sighted and hearing, while others are more effective for those with limited or no hearing, limited or no vision, or both. Some methods tend to be more effective with learners who are ambulatory and active, while other methods tend to be more effective with those who are inactive or those who are mobile by wheelchair or MOVE device. Some methods permit the rapid acquisition of communication skills when fine motor coordination, motor imitation, or matching are part of the learner's skill repertoire. Others are more effective when these repertoires are absent. And, finally, the effectiveness of some methods is a function of the presence or absence of destructive, aggressive, or self-injurious behavior. The presence or absence of these sensory, skill, and behavioral repertoires in a specific learner will suggest several methods of speaking for consideration and help us select a specific method that may be more effective for that learner.

Table 4.
Alternative Methods of Speaking Tend to be More Effective When
Learners Exhibit Specific Sensory, Skill, and Behavioral Repertoires

	Specific Sensory, Skill, and Behavioral Repertoires
H	Hearing
S	Sighted
HI	Hearing impaired
VI	Visually impaired
HVI	Hearing and visually impaired
Am	Ambulatory
NAm	Non-ambulatory
A	Active
I	Inactive
FM	Fine motor coordination
<FM	Limited or no fine motor coordination
MI	Motor imitation
<MI	Limited or no fine motor imitation
M	Matching
<M	Limited or no matching
PB	Moderate or severe problem behavior
-PB	No moderate or severe problem behavior

We have also found that specific, alternative methods which retain more advantages of 'saying words' with respect to behaving as a speaker and with respect to being understood by an audience tend to result in more effective speakers. As shown in Table 5, 'saying words' provides ten advantages with respect to functioning effectively as a speaker and one advantage with respect to being understood by an audience. While no alternative method provides all of these advantages, a method that retains more of these advantages tends to be more effective. The advantages of 'saying words' provide a second frame of reference, which will suggest several methods of speaking for consideration for a specific learner and help us select a specific method that may be more effective for that learner.

As a result of our experience, and in the absence of empirical evidence to the contrary, we strongly suggest that the selection of a method of speaking be based on: (1) the extent to which the learner's current sensory, skill, and behavioral repertoires correspond with those repertoires which tend to occur when specific, alternative methods of speaking under consideration are effective, and (2) the extent to which methods under consideration retain the advantages of 'saying words' with respect to functioning as a speaker and being understood by an audience. The extent to which repertoires correspond and proposed alternative methods of speaking retain the advantages of '*saying* words' can be displayed in a diagram shown in Table 6.

Table 5.
The Advantages of '*Saying words*' as a Method of Speaking

	The Speaker Advantages of 'Saying words'
Portability	
P	Children and adults can convey messages at any place and time without need for environmental supports;
Effort	
E	Information can be conveyed with very little effort.
Complexity	
1S	In the beginning, only one-step (i.e., single-word) responses are required.
-CD	In the beginning, complex discriminations are not required. conditional discriminations are not required
Communication Skills	
Rq	Many requests can be easily conveyed. many mands can be expressed
ND	Many items, activities, people, and places can be clearly named or described. tacts can be taught
AQ	Answers to questions can clearly and easily occur. intraverbals can occur
Con	Conversation can easily occur.
Rd	Reading can be taught. textual behavior can be taught
RA	Requests can be conveyed in the absence of what is being requested.
	The Audience Advantage of 'Saying words'
LA	The speaker can be understood by a large audience of instructors, care providers, parents, and peers with and without disabilities who do not require training.

Table 6.
Comparing a Learner's Current Sensory, Skill, and Behavioral Repertoires with Those Repertoires that Tend to Occur When a Proposed Method of Speaking is Effective and Displaying the Extent to Which a Proposed Method of Speaking Retains the Advantages of 'Saying Words'

The Learner's Current Sensory, Skill, and Behavioral Repertoires														
H	S	HI	VI	HVI	Am	NAm	A	I	FM	<FM	MI	<MI	M	<M	PB	-PB

Alternative Method of Speaking	

The Repertoires that Tend to Occur When This Method of Speaking is Effective														
H	S	HI	VI	HVI	Am	NAm	A	I	FM	<FM	MI	<MI	M	<M	PB	-PB

The Advantages of 'Saying Words' Retained by This Method of Speaking											
Speaker	P	E	1S	-CD	Rq	ND	AQ	Con	Rd	RA	Large Audience	LA

In the latter part of this chapter, 46 specific alternative methods of speaking are described. At the end of the description of each method, a diagram composed of the bottom three sections of Table 6 is provided, depicting the repertoires that tend to occur when this alternative method of speaking is effective and the extent to which this method retains advantages of '*saying words*'. The diagram for Alternative Method 2 (**AMS 2**), '*forming standard signs*', is depicted in Table 7.

Table 7.
'Forming Standard Signs': The Repertoires that Tend to Occur When This Method is Effective and the Extent to Which This Method Retains Advantages of *'Saying Words'*

Alternative Method of Speaking	AMS 2: Forming standard signs														
The Repertoires that Tend to Occur When AMS 2 is Effective															
H	S	HI	VI	HVI	Am	NAm	A	I	FM	<FM	MI	<MI	M	<M	PB	-PB
The Advantages of 'Saying Words' Retained by AMS 2															
Speaker	P	E	1S	-CD	Rq	ND	AQ	Con	Rd	RA	Large Audience				LA

A diagram made of mylar, hereafter referred to as *The Selection Diagram*, is composed of the top section of Table 6 and is included with this instrument. As shown in Table 8, an instructor or care provider should indicate a learner's current sensory, skill, and behavioral repertoires on this diagram, using a washable felt tip marker. Then, in order to select an alternative method of speaking that is likely to be effective for that learner, *The Selection Diagram* should be superimposed on each of the diagrams for the 46 alternative methods of speaking described in this chapter.

Table 8.
Using The Selection Diagram to Depict a Learner's Sensory, Skill, and Behavioral Repertoires

The Learner's Current Sensory, Skill, and Behavioral Repertoires																
H	S	HI	VI	HVI	Am	NAm	A	I	FM	<FM	MI	<MI	M	<M	PB	-PB

As shown in Table 9, when *The Selection Diagram* from Table 8 is superimposed on the diagram for *'standard signs'*, there are seven repertoire matches, indicating that the learner's repertoire closely corresponds with the repertoire that tends to occur when this method is effective.

Table 9.
Using The Selection Diagram to Compare a Learner's Current Sensory, Skill, and Behavioral Repertoires with Those Repertoires that Tend to Occur When *'Forming Standard Signs'* is Effective

The Learner's Current Sensory, Skill, and Behavioral Repertoires																
H	S	HI	VI	HVI	Am	NAm	A	I	FM	<FM	MI	<MI	M	<M	PB	-PB
Alternative Method of Speaking	AMS 2: Forming standard signs															
The Repertoires that Tend to Occur When AMS 2 is Effective																
H	S	HI	VI	HVI	Am	NAm	A	I	FM	<FM	MI	<MI	M	<M	PB	-PB
The Advantages of 'Saying Words' Retained by AMS 2																
Speaker	P	E	1S	-CD	Rq	ND	AQ	Con	Rd	RA	Large Audience				LA	

Also, as depicted in Table 10, *'forming standard signs'* retains all ten speaker advantages of *'saying words'*, but does not retain the audience advantage. This analysis suggests that, for this specific learner, *'forming standard signs'* should be set aside for further consideration as an alternative, primary method of speaking.

Table 10.
Using The Selection Diagram to Examine the Extent to Which 'Forming Standard Signs'
Retains the Advantages of 'Saying Words'

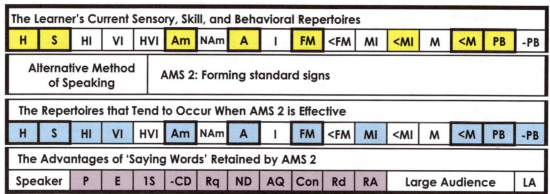

This procedure should be repeated with each of the 46 alternative methods of speaking. Then, select a method of speaking from the those that were set aside for further consideration, that closely corresponds to the learner's sensory, skill, and behavioral repertoires and that, at the same time, retains the most advantages of *'saying words'*.

Four examples will further illustrate how these comparisons and the *Selecting Diagram* can help you select an alternative method of speaking that is more likely to be effective for each of your learners. Example 1 includes a four-year-old boy with autism, who has been attending an early intervention program for six months. He exhibits a few spoken words, which are understandable to both familiar and unfamiliar listeners, but which occur infrequently across situations inconsistently within the same situation, and never as spoken-word repetitions. In other words, in terms of *'saying words'*, he is aligned with *Vocal Profile 3*. His current sensory, skill, and behavioral repertoires can be described as follows:

- ☑ is hearing and sighted,
- ☑ is ambulatory and active,
- ☑ exhibits excellent fine motor coordination,
- ☑ does not exhibit motor imitation skills,
- ☑ does not match identical items, or photographs to corresponding items, and
- ☑ exhibits only mild forms of disruptive behavior when he 'wants something' and when 'you ask him to come to the table to work'; these forms -- *leaving his assigned area and screaming* -- can be ignored or physically interrupted.

After two months, using protocols previously described, there was no improvement in the number and frequency of spoken words or spoken-word repetitions. The staff suggested to his mother that they select and begin to use an alternative method of speaking. Initially she resisted, but later granted permission when the staff assured her that (1) they were not 'giving up' on her son using spoken words, (2) an alternative method does not discourage learners from 'saying words', and, (3) research indicates that an alternative method may assist in the emergence of spoken words (Carbone, Lewis, et al., 2006; Tincani, 2004).

After the program staff compared the sensory, skill, and behavioral repertoires of this learner with those repertoires that tend to occur when the 46 alternative methods of speaking described in this instrument are effective and noted the number of advantages of *'saying words'* retained by each method, three methods were set aside for further consideration: *'forming standard signs'* (**AMS 2**), *'visually scanning and exchanging pic-symbols using the Picture Exchange Communication System* (**AMS 16**), and *'visually scanning and exchanging photographs using a small book worn by the learner'* (**AMS 9**) (see Table 11). With *'forming standard signs'* (**AMS 2**) seven repertoires coincided, all ten speaker advantages of *'saying words'* were retained, but the audience advantage was not retained. With *'visually scanning and exchanging pic-symbols using the Picture Exchange Communication System* (**AMS 16**) and *'visually scanning and exchanging photographs using a small book worn by the learner'* (**AMS 9**) four and six repertoires coincided, two and three speaker advantages were retained, and a partial audience and full audience advantage were retained, respectively.

Table 11.
Example 1: Using The Selection Diagram to Compare a Learner's Current Sensory, Skill, and Behavioral Repertoires with Those Repertoires that Tend to Occur When Specific Alternative Methods of Speaking are Effective and Displaying the Extent to Which These Methods Retain the Advantages of 'Saying Words'

The Learner's Current Sensory, Skill, and Behavioral Repertoires														
H	S	HI	VI	HVI	Am	NAm	A	I	FM	<FM	MI	<MI	M	<M	PB	-PB

Alternative Method of Speaking	AMS 2: Forming standard signs

The Repertoires that Tend to Occur When AMS 2 is Effective														
H	S	HI	VI	HVI	Am	NAm	A	I	FM	<FM	MI	<MI	M	<M	PB	-PB

The Advantages of 'Saying Words' Retained by AMS 2											
Speaker	P	E	1S	-CD	Rq	ND	AQ	Con	Rd	RA	Large Audience	LA

The Learner's Current Sensory, Skill, and Behavioral Repertoires														
H	S	HI	VI	HVI	Am	NAm	A	I	FM	<FM	MI	<MI	M	<M	PB	-PB

Alternative Method of Speaking	AMS 16: Visually scanning and exchanging pic-symbols with printed words using the Picture Exchange Communication System [PECS] and a PECS Binder

The Repertoires that Tend to Occur When AMS 16 is Effective														
H	S	HI	VI	HVI	Am	NAm	A	I	FM	<FM	MI	<MI	M	<M	PB	-PB

The Advantages of 'Saying Words' Retained by AMS 16											
Speaker	P	E	1S	-CD	Rq	ND	AQ	Con	Rd	RA	Large Audience	LA

The Learner's Current Sensory, Skill, and Behavioral Repertoires														
H	S	HI	VI	HVI	Am	NAm	A	I	FM	<FM	MI	<MI	M	<M	PB	-PB

Alternative Method of Speaking	AMS 9: Visually scanning and pointing to or exchanging photographs using a small book worn by the learner

The Repertoires that Tend to Occur When AMS 9 is Effective														
H	S	HI	VI	HVI	Am	NAm	A	I	FM	<FM	MI	<MI	M	<M	PB	-PB

The Advantages of 'Saying Words' Retained by AMS 9											
Speaker	P	E	1S	-CD	Rq	ND	AQ	Con	Rd	RA	Large Audience	LA

The staff indicated to the mother that, in view of the additional advantages for her son as a speaker, they were prepared to recommend *'standard signs'* as his primary method of speaking. They indicated that this selection would result in a smaller audience for her son, but that the entire staff were prepared to learn his signs and be part of that audience. The staff also indicated that, in order for this method to be effective, she and the other members of her family would need to learn his signs and become part of his audience. They also indicated that, if she and her family felt like they could not learn his signs, they would need to change their recommendation to *'visually scanning and pointing to or exchanging photographs using a small book worn by the learner'*. And, while this method has less advantages for her son as speaker, he would have access to a large audience that did not require training. His mother accepted the challenge and concurred with the original recommendation. The staff and his mother began teaching him to make requests (**R7**) with '*standard signs*' using teaching protocols described in chapter 12.

Our second example includes an eight-year-old girl with a non-specific developmental disability, who is non-ambulatory and mobile by both wheelchair and MOVE device. She is a student in a self-contained special education classroom in a public school. She uses the toilet when directed to do so, but does not initiate. With respect to toileting, eating, dressing, and other self-care skills, she participates partially, that is, she completes some steps of these tasks with or without assistance, and other steps must be completed for her (see **PPA** in *Daily Living Skills*).

She repeats spoken words, but most of these repetitions are not understandable, even to familiar persons. In other words, in terms of '*saying* words', she is aligned with *Vocal Profile 4*. Her current sensory, skill, and behavioral repertoires can be described as follows:

- ☑ is hearing and sighted,
- ☑ is non-ambulatory and somewhat passive,
- ☑ exhibits poor fine motor coordination,
- ☑ does not exhibit motor imitation skills,
- ☑ matches items to corresponding photographs, but does not match items to pic-symbols or printed words, and
- ☑ does not exhibit problem behavior.

When she was six years old, she was provided with a Dynavox with Mayer-Johnson pic-symbols (**AMS 23**). The professionals who provided this device programmed it with pic-symbol messages that permitted her to comment, appeared to permit her to answer questions, but did not permit her to make requests. She responded to the Dynavox as if it were a toy to play with, rather than a method of speaking. Her special education teacher and the school's new speech-language pathologist had recently attended a workshop on ABA-Verbal Behavior and recommended to her parents that a re-evaluation of her method of speaking be conducted, to which her parents consented.

After the school staff compared the sensory, skill, and behavioral repertoires of this learner with those repertoires that tend to occur when the 46 alternative methods of speaking described in this instrument are effective and noted the number of advantages of '*saying words*' retained by each method, three methods were set aside for further consideration (see Table 12): '*visually scanning and selecting photographs on a large SGD by touching the screen or by using one or two switches or eye-tracking*' (**AMS 22**), '*visually scanning and selecting printed words on a large SGD by touching the screen or by using one or two switches or eye-tracking*' (**AMS 24**), and '*forming standard signs*' (**AMS 2**). With '*visually scanning and selecting photographs on a large SGD*' (**AMS 22**), eight repertoires coincided, only three speaker advantages of '*saying words*' were retained, but the audience advantage was retained. With '*visually scanning and selecting printed words on a large SGD by touching the screen or by using one or two switches or eye-tracking*' (**AMS 24**), seven repertoires coincided, six speaker advantages of '*saying words*' were retained, but the audience advantage was only partially retained, that is, peers with similar disabilities would not be able to understand printed words. With '*forming standard signs*' (**AMS 2**), three repertoires coincided, all ten speaker advantages of '*saying words*' were retained, but the audience ad-vantage was not retained.

Table 12.
Example 2: Using The Selection Diagram to Compare a Learner's Current Sensory, Skill, and Behavioral Repertoires with Those Repertoires that Tend to Occur When Specific Alternative Methods of Speaking are Effective and Displaying the Extent to Which These Methods Retain the Advantages of 'Saying Words'

The Learner's Current Sensory, Skill, and Behavioral Repertoires															
H	S	HI	VI	HVI	Am	NAm	A	I	FM	<FM	MI	<MI	M	<M	PB	-PB

Alternative Method of Speaking	AMS 22: Visually scanning and selecting photographs on a large SGD by touching the screen, or by using one or two switches or an eye-tracking system

The Repertoires that Tend to Occur When AMS 22 is Effective															
H	S	HI	VI	HVI	Am	NAm	A	I	FM	<FM	MI	<MI	M	<M	PB	-PB

The Advantages of 'Saying Words' Retained by AMS 22										
Speaker	P	E	1S	-CD	Rq	ND	AQ	Con	Rd	RA	Large Audience	LA

Table 12. (cont.)
Example 2: Using The Selection Diagram to Compare a Learner's Current Sensory, Skill, and Behavioral Repertoires with Those Repertoires that Tend to Occur When Specific Alternative Methods of Speaking are Effective and Displaying the Extent to Which These Methods Retain the Advantages of 'Saying Words'

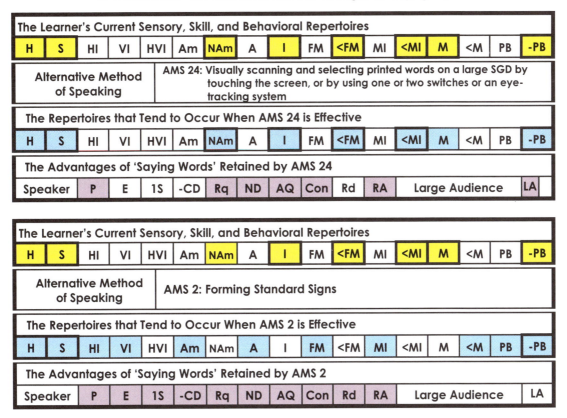

Since significantly more repertoires coincided for **AMS 22** and **AMS 24** than **AMS 2**, and **AMS 22** retained the audience advantage, the school staff recommended that 'visually scanning and selecting photographs on a large SGD' (**AMS 22**) be selected as her primary method of speaking. This method will ensure a large audience of adults and children with and without similar disabilities. The school staff also recommended that our learner be taught to match items to printed words, and, if she began to learn to make requests using printed words, that 'visually scanning and selecting printed words on a large speech-generating device' (**AMS 24**) be selected as a secondary method of speaking. This method would permit her to more clearly name and describe items, activities, and people, and answer related questions, but would slightly limit the size of her audience. Few, if any, peers with similar disabilities would be able to understand and respond effectively to 'printed words'. Her parents agreed with the recommendations, and staff and parents began teaching her to make requests (**R7**) by selecting photographs on an iPad with software that generates speech.

Our third example is a 15-year-old boy with a significant visual impairment (little to no functional vision) and a non-specific developmental disability, who attends a special school. He is ambulatory and, after an extended period of resistance, is beginning to use a cane effectively. He drinks from a cup and uses a spoon to eat, but requires soft foods, as his chewing skills are limited. He wears a pull-up, but will use the toilet when prompted to do so. He brushes his teeth with assistance and partial participation. He requires almost total assistance with all other self-care skills. He exhibits only noises and a few sounds and is aligned with *Profile* 6. Several years of speech therapy yielded only a few new sounds, no sound combinations, and no word approximations. He has never had an effective method of speaking.

His current sensory, skill, and behavioral repertoires can be described as follows:

- ☑ is hearing, but visually impaired,
- ☑ is ambulatory, but somewhat passive,
- ☑ exhibits poor fine motor coordination,
- ☑ tactile motor imitation skills have been difficult to acquire,
- ☑ although his visual impairment limits his matching skills, he has begun to match identical items by touch, and
- ☑ does not exhibit any significant form of problem behavior.

After the school staff compared the sensory, skill, and behavioral repertoires of this learner with those repertoires that tend to occur when the 46 alternative methods of speaking described in this instrument are effective and noted the number of advantages of 'saying words' retained by each method, three methods were set aside for further consideration: 'forming a repertoire of standard and adapted signs used with tactile signing' (**AMS 4**), a method of speaking commonly used with learners with both visual and hearing impairments (i.e., deaf and blind), 'scanning by touch and selecting items or miniature items attached to an object board' (**AMS 18**), and 'scanning by touch and selecting locations on a large, adapted, speech-generating device' (**AMS 30**).

With 'forming a repertoire of standard and adapted signs used with tactile signing' (**AMS 4**), a method of speaking commonly used with learners with both visual and hearing impairments (i.e., deaf and blind), three repertoires coincided, nine of the ten speaker advantages of 'saying words' were retained, but the audience advantage was not retained. With 'scanning by touch and selecting items or miniature items attached to an object board' (**AMS 18**), four repertoires coincided. With the recent emergence of tactile, item-to-item matching, a fifth repertoire partially coincided. While only two of the speaker advantages of 'saying words' were retained, the audience advantage was retained. With 'scanning by touch and selecting locations on a large, adapted, speech-generating device' (**AMS 30**), five repertoires and part of a sixth repertoire coincided. Again, only two of the speaker advantages of 'saying words' were retained, but the audience advantage was retained.

Table 13.
Example 3: Using The Selection Diagram to Compare a Learner's Current Sensory, Skill, and Behavioral Repertoires with Those Repertoires that Tend to Occur When Specific Alternative Methods of Speaking are Effective and Displaying the Extent to Which These Methods Retain the Advantages of 'Saying Words'

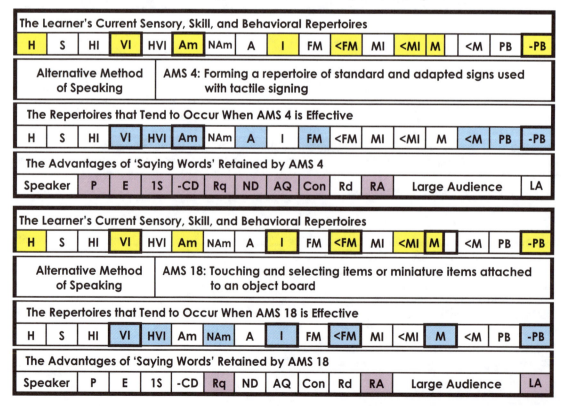

Table 13. (cont.)
Example 3: Using The Selection Diagram to Compare a Learner's Current Sensory, Skill, and Behavioral Repertoires with Those Repertoires that Tend to Occur When Specific Alternative Methods of Speaking are Effective and Displaying the Extent to Which These Methods Retain the Advantages of 'Saying Words'

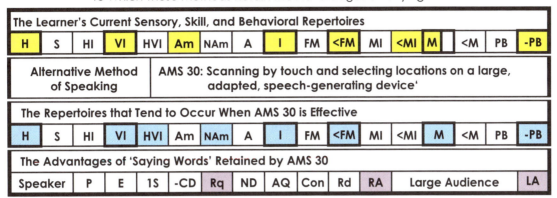

Since our learner was just beginning to exhibit item-to-item tactile matching, an important skill for *'touching and selecting items or miniature items attached to an object board'* (**AMS 18**) and a more advanced form of arbitrary matching, item-to-location, was important for *'scanning by touch and selecting locations on a large, adapted, speech-generating device'* (**AMS 30**), the first of these two was selected as our learner's primary method of speaking. His parents concurred with this selection. Staff and parents agreed that, if his skill repertoire began to include the arbitrary matching of items to locations, the second of these methods would be considered for selection as a secondary or concurrent method of speaking.

Our fourth example includes a 26-year-old woman with Down Syndrome, who recently came to live in a group home and who is beginning to participate in supported employment services. She feeds herself independently and completes many personal hygiene and self-care skills with little to no assistance. She is independent with respect to all aspects of toileting and menstruation. She exhibits spoken-word approximations infrequently across situations and inconsistently within the same situation. Most of these approximations are not understandable, even to familiar audiences. She does not repeat these approximations. In other words, in terms of *'saying words'*, she is aligned with *Profile 5*. Her current sensory, skill, and behavioral repertoires can be described as follows:

- ☑ is hearing and sighted,
- ☑ is ambulatory and active,
- ☑ exhibits good fine motor coordination,
- ☑ exhibits some motor imitation skills,
- ☑ matches identical items, but does not match items to corresponding photographs or pic-symbols, and
- ☑ exhibits a severe form of self-injurious behavior when she 'wants something or someone'; this form -- *hitting the temporal lobe area of both sides of her head with her fists* -- requires the continuous application of a protective helmet and a behavior improvement plan.

She makes occasional requests by *'leading others to items or to familiar locations for Items'* (**AMS 44**), which does not permit her to make requests in the absence of items she wants. For the first 22 years of her life she has had no other formal method of speaking and has responded almost exclusively as a listener.

Shortly after coming to live in the group home, her new support coordinator, group home manager, and speech-language pathologist met and decided to provide her with a formal method of speaking. They selected *'visually scanning and selecting pic-symbols on a large speech-generating device by touching the screen'* (**AMS 23**) as her primary method. The selection of this alternative method was based on the following:

- ☑ the young woman is physically capable of operating the electronic device;
- ☑ the young woman would have access to a large audience;
- ☑ after the device was initially programmed, instructors, care providers, and parents would find this method easy to implement; and,
- ☑ the device and this method would appear to provide the potential for advanced language in the future.

The staff began teaching her to use this method of speaking and to evaluate its effectiveness. They began by trying to teach her to name or describe items in her environment and to comment about events she experienced. They soon realized that the task they called 'naming' was actually 'matching', but they were not sure what to do about that. After two months, our learner had not begun to exhibit a single name, description, or comment without prompts. Meanwhile, she continued to exhibit episodes of self-injurious behavior over 20 times per day. The staff then attended a workshop on ABA-Verbal Behavior and became familiar with this manual. They soon realized that, in order for a new primary method of speaking to be effective, learners should first be taught to make requests for highly preferred items, activities, mand and persons, particularly those that can be made available immediately and frequently. The staff began teaching her to make these requests (see **R7**) using errorless teaching, which they also learned from the workshop. For the next two months, in spite of these changes, she continued to have difficulty learning to make these requests using the pic-symbols. Also, she often wanted to make requests but found herself some distance from the device, which could not be transported easily. After two additional months, she still required prompts to request any of several highly preferred items and continued to exhibit episodes of self-injurious behavior 20-25 times per day. Based on the definitions provided in Table 3, this method was clearly ineffective, that is, it was not permitting our learner to function effectively as a speaker.

A behavior analyst with considerable experience in B. F. Skinner's analysis of verbal behavior and the treatment of self-injurious behavior was contacted. This individual recommended that other alternative methods of speaking be considered. To begin this consideration, the behavior analyst compared the sensory, skill, and behavioral repertoires of this learner with those repertoires that tend to occur when the 46 alternative methods of speaking described in this instrument are effective and noted the number of advantages of 'saying words' retained by each method. As these comparisons were made, two methods were set aside for further consideration: 'visually scanning and pointing to or exchanging photographs using a small book worn by the learner' (**AMS 9**) and 'forming standard signs' (**AMS 2**). As shown in Table 14, these two methods were examined further and compared with the two methods with which this learner had previous experience: 'leading others to items or to familiar locations for Items' (**AMS 44**), the only effective method of speaking she had even known, and 'visually scanning and selecting pic-symbols on a large speech-generating device' (**AMS 23**), the alternative method of speaking selected for her four months ago.

With 'visually scanning and pointing to or exchanging photographs using a small book worn by the learner' (**AMS 9**), four repertoires and part of a fifth coincided, only three of the ten speaker advantages of 'saying words' were retained, but the audience advantage was retained. With 'standard signs' (**AMS 2**), however, six repertoires and part of a seventh coincided, all ten speaker advantages of 'saying words' were retained, but the audience advantage was not retained. On the other hand, with 'leading others to items or to familiar locations for Items' (**AMS 44**), four repertoires coincided, only one of the ten speaker advantages of 'saying words' were retained, but the audience advantage was retained. And, with 'visually scanning and selecting pic-symbols on a large speech-generating device' (**AMS 23**), only two repertoires and part of a third coincided, only two of the ten speaker advantages of 'saying words' were retained, but the audience advantage was retained.

Table 14.
Example 4: Using The Selection Diagram to Compare a Learner's Current Sensory, Skill, and Behavioral Repertoires with Those Repertoires that Tend to Occur When Specific Alternative Methods of Speaking are Effective and Displaying the Extent to Which These Methods Retain the Advantages of 'Saying Words'

The Learner's Current Sensory, Skill, and Behavioral Repertoires															
H	S	HI	VI	HVI	Am	NAm	A	I	FM	<FM	MI	<MI	M	<M	PB	-PB

Alternative Method of Speaking	AMS 9: visually scanning and pointing to or exchanging photographs using a small book worn by the learner

The Repertoires that Tend to Occur When AMS 9 is Effective															
H	S	HI	VI	HVI	Am	NAm	A	I	FM	<FM	MI	<MI	M	<M	PB	-PB

The Advantages of 'Saying Words' Retained by AMS 9										
Speaker	P	E	1S	-CD	Rq	ND	AQ	Con	Rd	RA	Large Audience	LA

Table 14. (cont.)
Example 4: Using The Selection Diagram to Compare a Learner's Current Sensory, Skill, and Behavioral Repertoires with Those Repertoires that Tend to Occur When Specific Alternative Methods of Speaking are Effective and Displaying the Extent to Which These Methods Retain the Advantages of 'Saying Words'

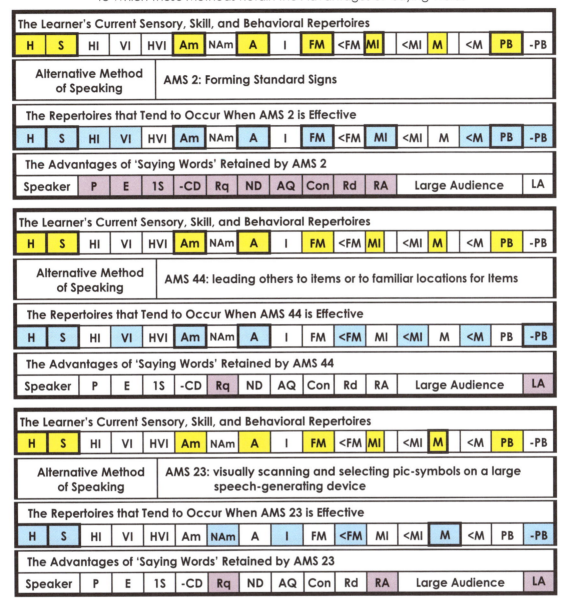

These comparisons, along with this learner's previous experiences with **AMS 44** and **AMS 23**, suggest that 'standard signs' be selected as our learner's primary method of speaking. The behavior analyst reviewed the issues related to 'standard signs' described in Example 1 with the support coordinator, group home manager, and speech-language pathologist, who eagerly accepted the challenge.

How to Confirm an Alternative, Primary Method of Speaking. The selection of an alternative method of speaking should always be considered tentative. The effectiveness of the selected method for a specific learner must always be tested to confirm or reject this selection. We strongly recommend that this testing include the steps described Table 15.

Table 15.
Testing the Effectiveness of an Alternative, Primary Method of Speaking

> Testing the effectiveness of an alternative method of speaking should include the following components:
> - ☐ providing a minimum of 2-3 months of daily instruction;
> - ☐ teaching a learner to '*make requests*' for specific, highly preferred items, activities, and persons, NOT to '*name or describe*' items or persons, NOT '*to comment*' on experiences, and NOT to '*answer questions*';
> - ☐ teaching requests for specific items, activities, and persons (see **R6**, **R19**, **R20**, and, for some learners, **R13**, **R15**, **R16**, **R17**, and **R18**); NOT requests for '*more*' or '*food*', and NOT requests with '*please*', '*yes*', or '*no*';
> - ☐ teaching 2-5 targeted requests at a time; when requests are exhibited consistently without prompts, add requests for new items and activities;
> - ☐ providing 200-300 opportunities to make targeted requests per day;
> - ☐ empirically-validated teaching procedures, such as errorless teaching and the teaching procedures described in chapter 11;
> - ☐ collecting data to determine the extent and frequency of occurrence of the targeted requests;
> - ☐ recording and displaying the extent to which the learner requires prompts to make targeted requests -- collect first opportunity of the day probe data using self-graphing data sheets as provided in chapter 11; when the learner makes a request without prompts on three consecutive days, add this re-quest to a cumulative count of requests the learner makes consistently with-out prompts;
> - ☐ displaying the weekly cumulative number of targeted requests the learner makes consistently without prompts on a graph provided in chapter 11;
> - ☐ recording the number of requests for any of the targeted items and activities that occur with and without prompts per day and displaying these data on an equal-interval, plain paper graph or the Adapted Daily Standard Celeration Chart (see chapter 11).

When data have been collected for 2-3 months, begin to estimate the effectiveness of a selected method of speaking using the criteria specified in Table 3, and more specifically in Table 21. If the selected method has been effective, confirm this selection and establish this method as *the learner's alternative, primary method of speaking*. If this method has been ineffective, reject this selection and begin the steps of selecting a new method.

Some learners, as shown in Example 4, already have an alternative, primary method of speaking in-place when we first encounter them. If a review of the criteria in Table 15 suggests that this method may be ineffective, it should be tested.

Most of the time, if a learner has alternative, primary method of speaking, it is well known to their instructors, speech-language pathologists, and care providers. Some learners, however, begin attending a school, living in a residence, or participating in a sheltered work or supported employment program *without any apparent, alternative method*. Staff may learn months later that a method was in-place in a previous setting, but did not '*make the move*' with the learner. They must then try to re-establish this method and, if necessary, test its effectiveness,

Now let's return to Example 4. After '*standard signs*' was selected as our learner's alternative, primary method of speaking, the staff began to test the effectiveness of this method. They used the testing and data collection procedures previously described, including the motor imitation-to-request and errorless teaching procedures, and first opportunity of the day probe data.

Her parents and the staff of her residence and employment program together provided over 250 opportunities per day for her to exhibit targeted requests. Within the first three months, she learned to request 15 of her favorite items activities without prompts. Her parents and the staff learned to recognize her signs and to respond appropriately to her requests. By the end of the third month, she was making over 100 spontaneous requests per day. And, the frequency of episodes of self-injurious behavior decreased from 20-25 per day to less than 3 per week. Our learner met all four effectiveness criteria specified in Table 16. As a result, the selection of '*standard signs*' was confirmed as her *alternative, primary method of speaking*.

Table 16.
Determining the Effectiveness of an Alternative, Primary Method of Speaking
and Confirming or Rejecting this Method

An alternative method of speaking should be considered effective and should confirmed as a learner's primary method, if the learner has a limited speaking repertoire and the following four criteria are met:

- ☐ the requesting repertoire...is improving rapidly (8-10 requests for new items or activities per month)...or...is continuing to improve gradually (1-2 requests for new items or activities per month)...or...includes most of the learner's preferred items and activities (20 items and activities);
- ☐ the audience responds appropriately to the learner's requests (i.e. provides what the learner requests);
- ☐ the learner makes frequent, spontaneous requests throughout the day (a minimum of 40-50 per day); and
- ☐ the frequency of self-injurious, aggressive, destructive, or disruptive behavior has decreased significantly.

If any of these criteria are not met, *this method should be rejected and a new method should be selected.*

An alternative method should be considered effective and should confirmed as a learner's primary method of speaking, if the learner has an extensive speaking repertoire and four of the following five criteria are met:

- ☐ requests that include questions are beginning to occur (3-4 per day) or are occurring frequently throughout the day (a minimum of 10-20 per day);
- ☐ the audience responds appropriately to the learner's questions (i.e. provides the learner with answers to her questions);
- ☐ the naming and describing repertoire...is improving rapidly (names or descriptions of 10-20 new items, activities, or persons per month)...or...is continuing to improve gradually (names or descriptions of 4-5 new items, activities, or persons per month)...or... includes many common items, commonly occurring activities, and familiar persons (names or descriptions of a minimum of 200 items, activities, or persons);
- ☐ the learner is beginning to answer questions (3-4 answers per day) or is answering questions frequently throughout the day (a minimum of 40-50 answers per day); and
- ☐ the learner is beginning to participate in conversations (2-3 per day).

If any of these criteria are not met, *this method should be rejected and a new method should be selected.*

Maintaining, Expanding, and Extending the Use of an Alternative, Primary Method of Speaking. Once an alternative method of speaking has been selected and confirmed as effective, instructors, care providers, work supervisors, and parents must become involved in achieving three goals: (1) maintaining the selected method of speaking, (2) expanding the learner's speaking repertoire, and (3) extending the use of this method to the learner's school, home or residential, and day activity or work environments. These goals, which are straight forward and require very little explanation, can be accomplished by:

1. making certain that the learner's method of speaking is as portable as possible, insuring frequent responding as a speaker (beginning with requests),
2. capturing and contriving many opportunities each day for the learner to respond as a speaker,
3. learning to understand and respond as an effective listener to what the learner 'says', providing others who respond in the same manner, and, if necessary, training others to respond accordingly,
4. learning to prompt the learner to exhibit new speaker responses and fade prompts, and
5. completing tasks 1-4 in the learner's school, home or residence, and day activity or work setting.

These goals and tasks, however, are often ignored, resulting in a deterioration in the extent to which the learner responds as a speaker and, often, a corresponding increase in the frequency of problem behavior. We meet many older children and adults, who, at an earlier time, learned to respond as a speaker in the presence of an instructor, speech-language pathologist, or care provider. This individual selected a method of speaking for them and taught them to name items and activities or make requests for the same. And now, that this individual no longer works with them, they are not responding effectively as a speaker, because one or more of the aforementioned tasks was not accomplished.

Alternative Methods of Making Contact with an Audience. Some methods of speaking require a separate method of making contact with or requesting an audience. For example, learners who *'form standard, adapted, idiosyncratic, or iconic signs or gestures'* (AMS 2, 3, 4, or 5) or who *'visually scan and point to or exchange, photographs, pic-symbols, or printed words using a small book worn by the learner or the Picture Exchange Communication System'* (AMS 9, 10, 11, 15, 16, or 17) might make a request for an item or activity and a potential audience would be unaware of their request. Also, some methods of speaking require specific responses from an audience before speaking can occur. For example, learners who 'visually scan and select photographs presented one at a time' (AMS 36) cannot begin to scan and select photographs until another person presents them. In either case, the learner needs to make contact with or request an audience before effective speaking can occur. A complete list of the methods of speaking which require a separate method of requesting an audience is provided below:

AMS 1: Using the sign language of the deaf community
AMS 2: Forming standard signs (Signed English)
AMS 3: Forming a repertoire of standard, adapted, and idiosyncratic signs
AMS 4: Forming a repertoire of standard and adapted signs used with tactile signing
AMS 5: Forming a repertoire of standard signs, iconic signs and iconic gestures
AMS 6: Writing words or drawing diagrams on a small notepad
AMS 9: Visually scanning and pointing to or exchanging photographs using a small book worn by the learner
AMS 10: Visually scanning and pointing to or exchanging pic-symbols with printed words using a small book worn by the learner
AMS 11: Visually scanning and pointing to or exchanging printed words using a small book worn by the learner
AMS 15: Visually scanning and exchanging photographs using the Picture Exchange Communication System and a PECS Binder
AMS 16: Visually scanning and exchanging pic-symbols with printed words using the Picture Exchange Communication System and a PECS Binder
AMS 17: Visually scanning and exchanging printed words using the Picture Exchange Communication System and a PECS Binder
AMS 18: Scanning by touch and selecting items or miniature items attached to an object board
AMS 25: Typing words with a small, electronic device
AMS 27: Typing words with a Braille Writer
AMS 31: Visually scanning and pointing to large photographs using a binder
AMS 32: Visually scanning and pointing to large printed words using a binder
AMS 33: Visually scanning and selecting photographs presented two at a time
AMS 34: Visually scanning and selecting items presented two at a time
AMS 35: Scanning by touch and selecting items presented two at a time
AMS 36: Looking at and selecting photographs presented one at a time
AMS 37: Looking at and selecting items presented one at a time
AMS 38: Touch and selecting items presented one at a time
AMS 39: Scanning by listening and selecting spoken words presented two at a time
AMS 40: Listening and selecting spoken words presented one at a time
AMS 41: Listening to "do you want ___?" and gesturing to indicate 'yes' or 'no'
AMS 42: Listening to "do you want ___?" and activating a switch to indicate 'yes' or one of two switches to indicate 'yes' or 'no'
AMS 43: Pointing, gesturing, or gazing toward items or familiar locations for items
AMS 46: Touching a photograph or printed words using a speech-generating device that contains only one message

Children and adults who use one of these methods of speaking should be taught to make contact with or request an audience using one of the following methods:

    AMCA 1 -- tapping someone on the shoulder or arm,
    AMCA 2 -- exhibiting a distinguishable vocalization (e.g., "ooo"),
    AMCA 3 -- making a loud sound (e.g., clapping, pounding on a tray, ringing a bell),
    AMCA 4 -- activating a blinking light, or
    AMCA 5 -- activating a speech-generating device that contains only one message

These learners can then make subsequent requests for items and activities, and the audience will be able to respond in an appropriate manner.

Selecting, Confirming, and Maintaining Concurrent, Back-up, and Secondary Methods of Speaking

Up to this point, we have been talking about selecting a single, primary method of speaking for each of our learners, that is, a method each of them will use most of the time. There are, however, three situations in which learners who already exhibit an effective primary method, would also benefit from an additional method of speaking. These situations are described in Table 17.

Table 17.
Three Situations in Which An Additional Method of Speaking May be Helpful to a Learner

Additional Method of Speaking	Situations in Which An Additional Method of Speaking May be Helpful to a Learner
Concurrent	When a child or an adult has been taught to request many preferred items and activities using two or more methods of speaking, both of which are effective, and which result in two, sizable, non-overlapping repertoires.
Back-up	When a learner's primary method of speaking limits the size of their audience, as it does with '*standard, adapted, or idiosyncratic signs*' (AMS 1-4)
Secondary	When a primary method of speaking limits what a learner can say, as '*visually scanning and exchanging photographs using the Picture Exchange Communication System [PECS] and one of the PECS Communication Binders*' limits a learner to requests

When to Select and Confirm Concurrent Methods of Speaking. Our experience suggests that most learners who require an alternative, primary method of speaking should begin and continue with a single method. Two or more concurrent methods tend to result in practice which is distributed among methods, making it difficult for some learners to achieve proficiency with any one method. Also, learners may experience problems discriminating when and with whom to use each method.

When we first encounter some learners, however, they are already using two or more concurrent methods of speaking. A common example is an older child or an adult who has been taught to make some requests by '*forming standard signs*', and others by '*visually scanning and exchanging pic-symbols using the Picture Exchange Communication System [PECS]*'. When this situation occurs, we strongly recommend testing the effectiveness of both methods as previously described. If one of the two methods is effective, establish it as the learner's primary method of speaking and teach the learner to use only this method. If both methods are effective, but one includes a much larger repertoire of *requests*, establish this method as the learner's alternative, primary method of speaking and, as described in the next section, consider using the other as a secondary method of speaking. If both methods are effective and include overlapping requesting repertoires of nearly the same size, select one of these methods as the learner's alternative, primary method of speaking.

If both methods are effective and both include sizable non-overlapping repertoires of requests, establish both as *the learner's concurrent methods of speaking*. While it is generally better for a learner to use one method, selecting one of these two would significantly reduce the learner's total speaking repertoire and, hence, would not be advisable. When one or two methods have been selected, the effectiveness of each method should be tested and determined as described in Tables 15 and 16.

When to Select and Confirm a Back-up Method of Speaking. When the primary method of speaking limits the size of the learner's audience, a back-up method of speaking should be considered. For example, when a learner's primary method includes *'forming standard, adapted, or idiosyncratic signs'* (**AMS 2** and **AMS 3**), her audience will include only those people who 'understand these signs'. If a second method of speaking is added that includes 'selecting photographs or printed words', which are easily understood, many more people can become part of her audience.

A similar situation occurs in the deaf community. Most individuals who are deaf or who have a significant hearing impairment use *'the sign language of the deaf community'* as their primary method of speaking and 'writing notes or drawing diagrams on a small notepad' as their back-up method.

The next section of this chapter, which describes the advantages and disadvantages of 46 alternative methods of speaking, includes (1) an indication of which methods, when serving as a primary method of speaking, may require a back-up method in order to increase the size of the audience, and (2) which back-up methods that should be considered. A back-up method should be selected using procedures previously described *only after*:

- a primary method has been selected and confirmed,
- the learner has acquired a requesting repertoire that includes most of her preferred items, activities, and people (**R7-8**, **R14**, **R17-21**, **R22-23**, and **R27**)
- the learner exhibits **R9-13**, **R15-16**, and **LR1-LR10**, and
- the learner exhibits little to no disruptive, destructive, aggressive, or self-injurious behavior.

Then, the effectiveness of the selected back-up method should be tested and determined using the steps previously described in Tables 15 and 16 and then this method should be confirmed or rejected.

Some older children and adults whose primary method of speaking includes *'standard, adapted, or idiosyncratic signs'* or *'iconic signs or gestures'* may acquire a few understandable 'spoken words' *and* 'word approximations', which increase the size of their audience and indicate that *'saying words' is beginning to* function as an additional back-up method of speaking.

When to Select and Confirm a Secondary Method of Speaking. When the primary method of speaking begins to limit the extent to which the speaking repertoire can be expanded, one or more secondary methods should be considered. For example, when a learner's primary method includes '*visually scanning and selecting photographs*', he can easily make requests, as he might otherwise do in a restaurant with a menu that includes photographs. He cannot, however, name or describe items or activities by selecting a photograph. That is, he cannot indicate "that's a cup" by selecting a photograph of a cup when he sees a cup. All he can do is indicate that a photograph of a cup matches a cup or looks nearly the same as a cup. If a second method is added that includes '*selecting printed words*', '*writing words*', or '*typing words*', the learner can easily name or describe items or activities. That is, he can indicate "that's a cup" by selecting the word 'cup', or writing or typing the word 'cup' when he sees a cup. He can also answer questions and participate in conversations using the word 'cup', and thereby greatly expand his speaking repertoire. If understandable 'word approximations' or 'spoken words' begin to emerge, '*saying words*' may begin to function as an additional secondary method.

A similar situation occurs in the deaf community. Young children begin functioning as speakers '*using the sign language of the deaf community*', which has its own unique grammar and syntax. When they begin attending school, they must learn a secondary method, '*forming standard signs*', in order to acquire academic skills, which are taught using the grammar and syntax of the dominant spoken and written language of the region.

Secondary methods may also have other functions. For example, 'typing or writing words' is used when an individual is communicating with someone who is not in the same location and when other people need a record of their communication.

A secondary method of speaking, while not initially suitable as a primary method, may later become a concurrent primary method or may replace the original, primary method altogether. For example, a learner's secondary method might include '*visually scanning and selecting printed words*', when the primary method includes '*visually scanning and selecting photographs*'. Over a period of time, the learner could acquire either sizable non-overlapping repertoires of '*photographs*' and '*printed words*' or a large repertoire of *'printed words'* which overlaps and eventually replaces the previous repertoire of *'photographs'*. In another example, *'saying words'* might begin as a child's secondary method of speaking when the primary method includes *'forming standard signs'* or *'visually scanning and exchanging pic-symbols'*. Over a period of time, it *may* be possible for the child to acquire a repertoire of *'sounds'* and *'word approximations'*, which could be shaped into understandable *'words'* and later into understandable repetitions of words. If so, with the help of specific teaching procedures like the echoic-to-request procedure, *'saying words'* could replace *'signs'* or *'pic-symbols'* as the child's primary method of speaking. *Most secondary methods, however, continue functioning as such for an indefinite period of time.*

The next section of this chapter, which describes the advantages and disadvantages of 46 alternative methods of speaking, includes (1) an indication of which methods, when serving as a primary method of speaking, may require a secondary method in order to expand the size of the speaking repertoire, and (2) which methods should be considered. In most cases, a secondary method should be selected using procedures previously described *only after*:

- a primary method has been selected and confirmed,
- the learner has acquired a requesting repertoire that includes most of her preferred items, activities, and people (**R7-8**, **R14**, **R17-21**, **R22-23**, and **R27**)
- the learner exhibits **R9**-**13**, **R15**-**16**, and **LR1**-**LR10**, and
- the learner exhibits little to no disruptive, destructive, aggressive, or self-injurious behavior.

Then, the effectiveness of the selected secondary method should be tested and determined using the steps previously described in Tables 15 and 16 and then this method should be confirmed or rejected.

The Advantages of '*Saying* Words' and 46 Alternative Methods of Speaking (*AMS*)

This section describes specific advantages and disadvantages of each alternative method of speaking, along with the sensory, skill, and behavioral repertoires that tend to occur when each method is effective. It also describes the extent to which each method retains the advantages of *'saying words'* with respect to behaving as a speaker and being understood by an audience. And, finally, when specific methods are selected as alternative, primary methods of speaking, it provides (1) an indication of which methods may require a back-up method in order to increase the size of the audience or a secondary method in order to expand a learner's speaking repertoire, and (2) which back-up or secondary methods that should be considered.

Use this section, along with procedures described in two previous sections of this chapter, to select primary, concurrent, back-up, and secondary methods of speaking for individual learners.

To serve as a point of reference, we will begin with a description of the sensory, skill, and behavioral repertoires that tend to occur when *'saying words'* is effective, and the advantages of this method of speaking with respect to behaving as a speaker and being understood by an audience, Then, we will begin with methods that include specific response forms and that retain more advantages of *'saying words'* and proceed to methods which include selecting photographs, pic-symbols, printed words, letters, locations, or items and which retain fewer advantages of *'saying words'*.

Saying Words

- is the primary method of speaking used by most children and adults.
- is effective with any combination of sensory, skill, and behavioral repertoires
- provides many advantages with respect to behaving as a speaker and with respect to being understood by an audience. As shown in Table 5, these advantages include: (P) portability -- children and adults can convey messages at any place and time without need for environmental supports; (E) minimum effort -- learners can convey a considerable amount of information with little to no effort; (1S) in the beginning, only one-step (i.e., single-word) responses are required to express needs and wants; (-CD) again, in the beginning, complex discriminations are not required; (Rq) requests are easily conveyed; (ND) many items, activities, people, and places can be easily named and described; (AQ) questions can clearly and easily be answered; (Con) conversations can easily occur; (Rd) reading can be taught; (RA) requests can be conveyed in the absence of what is being requested; and, (LA) spoken words are understood by a large audience without the need for training. The first ten advantages can be described as speaker advantages and the last as the audience advantage.

- should be selected as a learner's primary method of speaking *only when many spontaneous spoken words are already occurring* or when the learner reliably exhibits *understandable, repetitions of spoken words or phrases* (see Profiles 1 and 2 earlier in this chapter). If these repetitions are occurring, *no other sensory, skill, or behavioral repertoires are relevant or necessary*. If these repetitions are frequent and pervasive, many speech and language pathologists and behavior analysts recommend that '*saying words*' be set aside and replaced with an alternative method of speaking that includes '*scanning and selecting pic-symbols, photographs, or printed words*'. If you encounter such a recommendation, cite this book as a reference and suggest that '*saying words*' be retained as the method of speaking and that requests for highly preferred items and activities be taught using Teaching Protocol 1, which includes *the echoic-to-request teaching procedure* (see chapter 12). Follow this procedure *exactly as it is written*. Failure to do so will generally result in a continuation of the repetitions and a slow rate of acquisition of spontaneous requests. If repetitions, however, are not occurring reliably, it will be virtually impossible to prompt spoken words and will be very frustrating for the learner. As a result, '*saying words*' should be set aside as a primary method of speaking and replaced by an alternative primary method. This selection of an alternative method does not mean that '*saying words*' has been abandoned as a primary method of speaking. With the alternative method, you should begin teaching requests, modeling the corresponding spoken words, and providing additional amounts of requested items and extended durations of requested activities when spoken words or word approximations occur (this procedure is part of Teaching Protocol 1, which is described in chapter 12).

single or multiple-word echoic responses

echoic-to-mand transfer procedure

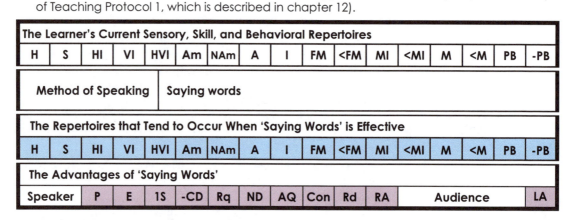

Alternative Methods that Include Specific Responses that Correspond to Words or Letters Conveyed

AMS 1: Using the Sign Language of the Deaf Community

'*Sign* language' is the primary method used in conversation by most sighted children and adults who are deaf or who have a hearing impairment that has interfered with the acquisition of understandable spoken words. In most regions of the world, there is a sign language developed by the deaf community of that region or adopted from another region. In the United States, there is American Sign Language (ASL). In the United Kingdom, there is British Sign Language (BSL), while in Quebec, Canada, there is Langue des Signes Québécois (LSQ). There are over 250 other sign languages, dialects, and sign systems used on planet earth.

'*Using the sign language of the deaf community*':

- requires learning a unique grammar and syntax, which does not correspond to that which is part of the dominant spoken language in that region. As a result, this method is not recommended for children or adults with a hearing impairment and moderate-to-severe disabilities.

- retains all of the speaker advantages of '*saying words*', except reading, which can only be accomplished with spoken words, Braille, or *AMS 2, Forming Standard Signs*; children with a hearing impairment generally use '*AMS2: Forming Standard Signs*' as a secondary method so that they can read and acquire academic skills and '*AMS 6: Writing words or drawing diagrams on a small notepad*' as a back-up method so that they can communicate with individuals who do not use ASL.

- does not retain the audience advantage of 'saying words'; that is, 'sign language' requires an audience of instructors or care providers, and later peers with deafness or significant hearing impairments, who understand and respond to this language, or an audience of hearing instructors or care providers and later peers who have been trained to do so.

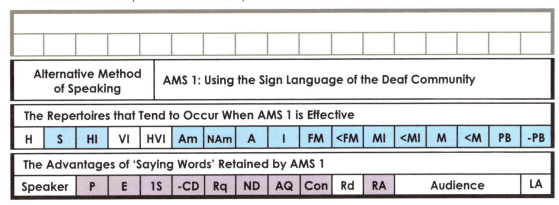

Alternative Method of Speaking	AMS 1: Using the Sign Language of the Deaf Community													
The Repertoires that Tend to Occur When AMS 1 is Effective														
H	S	HI	VI	HVI	Am	NAm	A	I	FM	<FM	MI	<MI	M	<M	PB	-PB
The Advantages of 'Saying Words' Retained by AMS 1														
Speaker	P	E	1S	-CD	Rq	ND	AQ	Con	Rd	RA	Audience			LA

AMS 2: Forming Standard Signs (Signed English)

'Forming standard signs' is a secondary method of speaking used by children who are deaf or hearing impaired when they are asked to perform academic tasks in school. In the United States, this method, which is often described as *Signed English*, is composed of signs from *American Sign Language (ASL)* with the grammar, syntax, and word order of English. In the UK, this method is composed of signs from *Makaton, Sign Along*, or *British Sign Language (BSL)* with the grammar, syntax, and word order of Queen's English. In other parts of the world, this method is composed of signs from the sign language used by the deaf community in that region with the grammar, syntax, and word order of the dominant spoken language.

'Forming standard signs' should also be seriously considered as a primary method of speaking for many sighted, hearing children and adults and some learners with a significant visual impairment, who exhibit only a limited repertoire of requests or no requests at all, or who have had difficulty learning to 'scan and select items, photographs, pic-symbols, or printed words', especially those who are ambulatory, active, and demonstrate some fine motor coordination, and those who have a history of exhibiting severe aggressive or self-injurious behavior.

'Forming standard signs' is especially useful as a temporary, primary method of speaking for nonverbal children and adults who have acquired and then lost part or all of their spoken-word repertoire due to closed head injury or a stroke.

'Forming Standard signs':

- retains all of the speaker advantages of 'saying words'.
- provides the advantage of portability not found in some methods that include scanning and selecting. *This advantage cannot be overstated.*
- often results in frequent, spontaneous, and interactive language, which includes requests, names, descriptions, answers to questions, and conversations.
- requires, in the beginning, only one-step responses and simple, rather than complex discriminations; some learners will find this method easier to learn than methods which include 'scanning and selecting items, pic-symbols, photographs, or printed words'.
- may facilitate the emergence or re-emergence of spoken words or word approximations in children or the re-emergence of spoken words in adults. If spoken words emerge or re-emerge while signing, and the words are exhibited reliably as understandable repetitions, 'standard signs' should be gradually discontinued and 'saying words' should be established as the learner's primary method of speaking; if not, 'standard signs' should be seriously considered as a permanent, primary method of speaking.

- permits sighted learners to read, that is, to *see words and form signs*. Learners cannot make responses that correspond to oral or sign reading with methods that include '*scanning and selecting pic-symbols, photographs, or printed words*', or methods that include '*writing or typing words*'. '*Standard signs*' also permit reading comprehension, especially when that includes answering questions.
- does not retain the audience advantage of '*saying words*'; requires an audience of instructors or care providers, and later peers with and without disabilities, that understands and can respond to '*standard signs*' or is willing to learn to do so. If an audience cannot be arranged or maintained, a method of speaking which includes '*scanning and selecting items, pic-symbols, photographs, or printed words*' should be selected.
- is sometimes ruled out as a method of speaking because of the perceived effort involved in arranging and maintaining an audience. We have, however, worked with hundreds of families, schools, hospitals, and residential facilities who have arranged and maintained an audience for one or more child or adult signers. They have indicated that the effort was well worth the *frequent, spontaneous, and interactive communication* that resulted.
- requires very specific teaching procedures, including errorless prompting and rapid prompt-fading (see chapter 12, Teaching Protocol 1); if these procedures are used *as they are described*, without additions or modifications, and data indicate that this method is ineffective for a specific child or adult, consider selecting a method that includes '*scanning and selecting items, pic-symbols, photographs, or printed words*'.
- a back-up method which includes '*scanning and selecting photographs or printed words*' enables learners to communicate with people who do not understand signs, in other words, increase the size of their audience.

If you would like to talk with the authors about using standard signs and arranging and maintaining audiences, or if you would like one of us to present a workshop on teaching signs, please contact us through our website or email address provided inside the front cover.

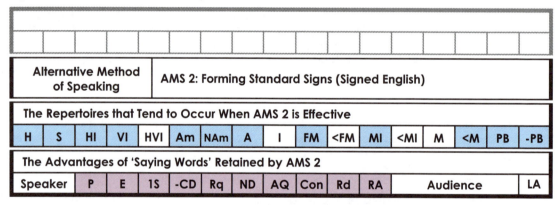

Alternative Method of Speaking	AMS 2: Forming Standard Signs (Signed English)													
The Repertoires that Tend to Occur When AMS 2 is Effective														
H	S	HI	VI	HVI	Am	NAm	A	I	FM	<FM	MI	<MI	M	<M	PB	-PB
The Advantages of 'Saying Words' Retained by AMS 2														
Speaker	P	E	1S	-CD	Rq	ND	AQ	Con	Rd	RA	Audience			LA

AMS 3: Forming a Repertoire of Standard, Adapted, and Idiosyncratic Signs

Adapted signs are standard signs that have been modified. For example, the standard sign in ASL for 'cookie' includes twisting one hand while touching the palm of the opposite hand, mimicking the motion a cook would use with a cookie cutter. An adapted sign might be touching the index finger to the palm of the opposite hand. Idiosyncratic signs are gestures specific to a learner that have been designated as signs. For example, a learner might touch her nose with the index finger of her right hand to designate 'yogurt'.[3]

'*A repertoire of standard, adapted, and idiosyncratic signs*' should be considered for sighted and hearing learners, or those with a visual or hearing impairment, who are active and ambulatory, who demonstrate limited fine motor coordination or resistance to prompting, and who have had difficulty acquiring '*standard signs*'. This alternative method can easily be combined with 'AMS5: *Forming a repertoire of standard, iconic signs and iconic gestures*' to function as alternative, concurrent methods of speaking.

---

[3] These are actual examples of adapted and idiosyncratic signs currently in use by learners with severe disabilities.

This alternative method is especially useful as a temporary, primary method of speaking for non-verbal children and adults who exhibit severe aggressive or self-injurious behavior or who have acquired and then lost part or all of their spoken-word repertoire.

'*A repertoire of standard, adapted, and idiosyncratic signs*':

- retains six of the ten speaker advantages of 'saying words'; with this method, however, it is difficult to expand a learner's speaking repertoire beyond requests; may result in a limited number of names and descriptions, if any, and a limited number of answers to questions; generally precludes reading.

- may facilitate the emergence or re-emergence of spoken words or word approximations in children or the re-emergence of spoken words in adults. If spoken words emerge or re-emerge while signing, and the words are exhibited reliably as understandable repetitions, '*standard, adapted, and idiosyncratic signs*' should be gradually discontinued and '*saying words*' should be established as the learner's primary method of speaking; if not, '*standard, adapted, and idiosyncratic signs*' should be established as the permanent, primary method of speaking.

- does not retain the audience advantage of '*saying words*'; requires an audience of instructors or care providers, and later peers with and without disabilities, that understands and responds to these signs.

- requires very specific teaching procedures, including errorless prompting and rapid prompt-fading (see chapter 12, Teaching Protocol 1); if these procedures are used *as they are described*, without additions or modifications, and data indicate that this method is ineffective for a specific child or adult, consider selecting a method that includes '*scanning and selecting items, pic-symbols, photographs, or printed words*'.

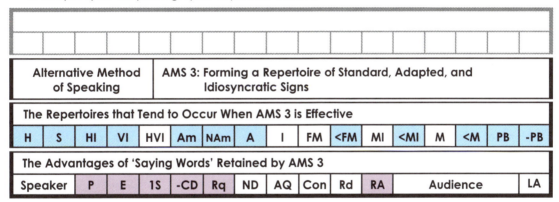

Alternative Method of Speaking	AMS 3: Forming a Repertoire of Standard, Adapted, and Idiosyncratic Signs												
The Repertoires that Tend to Occur When AMS 3 is Effective													
H	S	HI	VI	HVI	Am	NAm	A	I	FM	<FM	MI	<MI	M	<M	PB	-PB
The Advantages of 'Saying Words' Retained by AMS 3													
Speaker	P	E	1S	-CD	Rq	ND	AQ	Con	Rd	RA	Audience		LA

AMS 4: Forming a Repertoire of Standard and Adapted Signs Used with Tactile Signing

Adapted signs are standard signs that have been modified. For example, the standard sign in ASL for 'cookie' includes twisting one hand while touching the palm of the opposite hand, mimicking the motion a cook would use with a cookie cutter. An adapted sign might be touching the index finger to the palm of the opposite hand.

Tactile signs are standard and adapted signs used primarily by children and adults with a significant impairment in both vision and hearing. As speakers, these individuals form the signs with their hands and arms; as listeners, they understand messages by wrapping their hands around signs that are made by other speakers. For the convenience of listeners, tactile signs are often confined to movements of the hands making contact with the hands or arms.

'*A repertoire of standard and adapted signs used with tactile signing*' should also be considered for ambulatory and active children and adults with a significant visual impairment.

'*A repertoire of standard and adapted signs used with tactile signing*':

- retains all of the speaker advantages of '*saying words*'.

- does not retain the audience advantage of 'saying words'; requires a sighted audience of instructors or care providers and an audience of instructors or care providers and peers with a significant impairment in vision or in both vision and hearing, who understands and responds as listeners by touching their signs and who responds as speakers by signing 'into their hands'. If an audience cannot be arranged or maintained, 'scanning by touch and selecting items or miniature items attached to an object board' (**AMS 18**) or 'scanning by touch and selecting locations on a large, adapted, speech-generating device' (**AMS 30**) should be selected as the primary method of speaking.
- requires very specific teaching procedures, including errorless prompting and rapid prompt-fading (see chapter 12, Teaching Protocol 1). Demonstration prompts can often be adapted for learners with visual impairments. If these teaching procedures are used *as they are described*, without additions or modifications, and this alternative method has been shown to be ineffective for a specific child or adult, consider selecting 'scanning by touch and selecting items or miniature items attached to an object board' (**AMS 18**) or 'scanning by touch and selecting locations on a large, adapted, speech-generating device' (**AMS 30**).

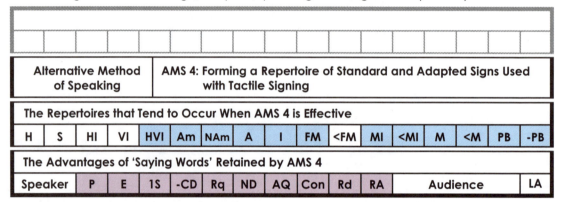

AMS 5: Forming a Repertoire of Standard, Iconic Signs and Iconic Gestures

Standard, iconic signs are signs from the sign language used by the deaf community that closely resemble the appearance of specific items or activities. For example, in *ASL*, a standard iconic sign for 'hot dog' involves placing an extended index finger into the curled palm of the other hand to resemble the appearance of a hot dog in a bun. Iconic gestures are physical movements that also resemble the appearance of specific items or activities, but are not part of sign language. For example, an iconic gesture for 'soda pop' might be a movement resembling opening a can or a bottle.

'Forming a repertoire of standard, iconic signs and iconic gestures' should be considered for older hearing, sighted children and adults, and those with a significant hearing impairment, who are ambulatory, active, and demonstrate some fine motor coordination, but who do not have access to an audience who understands and can respond to standard, adapted, or idiosyncratic signs or is willing to learn to do so. This method can easily be combined with 'AMS3: *Forming a repertoire of standard, adapted and idiosyncratic signs*' to function as concurrent methods of speaking.

'Forming a repertoire of standard, iconic signs and iconic gestures' is especially useful as a temporary, primary method of speaking for non-verbal children and adults who exhibit severe aggressive or self-injurious behavior or who have acquired and then lost part or all of their spoken-word repertoire.

'*A repertoire of standard, iconic signs and iconic gestures*':

- retains six of the ten speaker advantages of '*saying words*'; it is difficult to expand a learner's speaking repertoire beyond requests, as many items and activities do not have a standard, iconic sign and would be difficult to designate with an iconic gesture.
- may facilitate the emergence or re-emergence of spoken words or word approximations in children or the re-emergence of spoken words in adults. If spoken words emerge or re-emerge while signing, and the words are exhibited reliably as understandable repetitions, '*standard, iconic signs and iconic gestures*' should be gradually discontinued and '*saying words*' should be established as the learner's primary method of speaking; if not, '*standard, iconic signs and iconic gestures*' should be established as the permanent, primary method of speaking.

- does not retain the audience advantage of '*saying words*'; requires an audience of instructors or care providers and later an audience of peers with and without disabilities that understands and responds to these signs.

- requires very specific teaching procedures, including errorless prompting and rapid prompt-fading (see chapter 12, Teaching Protocol 1); if these procedures are used *as they are described,* without additions or modifications, and data indicate that this method is ineffective for a specific child or adult, consider selecting a method that includes '*scanning and selecting items, pic-symbols, photographs, or printed words*'.

Alternative Method of Speaking	AMS 5: Forming a Repertoire of Standard, Iconic Signs and Iconic Gestures													
The Repertoires that Tend to Occur When AMS 5 is Effective														
H	S	HI	VI	HVI	Am	NAm	A	I	FM	<FM	MI	<MI	M	<M	PB	-PB
The Advantages of 'Saying Words' Retained by AMS 5														
Speaker	P	E	1S	-CD	Rq	ND	AQ	Con	Rd	RA	Audience			LA

AMS 6: Writing words or drawing diagrams on a small notepad

'*Writing words and drawing diagrams on a small notepad*' is used by many children and adults with hearing impairments as a secondary method of speaking. '*Writing words and drawing diagrams*' is seldom useful as a primary method for children or adults with moderate-to-severe disabilities, because it requires writing and spelling skills that result in identifiable words or word approximations. There are, however, some non-verbal adult learners who have acquired these skills and use this method effectively. '*Writing words and drawing diagrams*' can be useful as a temporary, and sometimes permanent, primary method of speaking for non-verbal children and adults who have acquired and then lost part or all of their spoken-word repertoire due to closed head injury, stroke, or other traumatic event.

'*Writing words and drawing diagrams*':

- retains seven of the ten speaker advantages of '*saying words*'.
- requires a repertoire of written words, which are spelled correctly or can easily be identified.
- requires a considerable amount of effort to convey even simple messages.
- retains part of the audience advantage of '*saying words*'; when words are spelled correctly or can easily be identified, instructors, care providers, and peers without disabilities will understand what was 'said', but most peers with similar disabilities will not.

Alternative Method of Speaking	AMS 6: Writing words or drawing diagrams on a small notepad													
The Repertoires that Tend to Occur When AMS 6 is Effective														
H	S	HI	VI	HVI	Am	NAm	A	I	FM	<FM	MI	<MI	M	<M	PB	-PB
The Advantages of 'Saying Words' Retained by AMS 6														
Speaker	P	E	1S	-CD	Rq	ND	AQ	Con	Rd	RA	Audience			LA

AMS 7: Saying word approximations that are understood and discriminated only by a familiar audience

'Saying word approximations that are understood and discriminated only by a familiar audience' is a method of speaking used by older children and adults, who have not had the opportunity to learn a more effective method or who have had difficulty acquiring any other method.

'Saying word approximations that are understood and discriminated only by a familiar audience':

- retains four of the ten speaker advantages of 'saying words'.
- generally results in only a very limited repertoire of requests.
- does not retain the audience advantage of 'saying words'; utterances are understood only by a very small number of instructors, care providers, and peers with and without disabilities.
- *should almost always be replaced with a more effective method; reasons given for not doing so tend to invoke fallacies, such as intellectual capacity and pre-speaking skills described in chapter 2, or to emphasize the convenience of care providers, instructors, or family members, rather than the needs of our learners; these reasons are absolutely and completely unacceptable.*

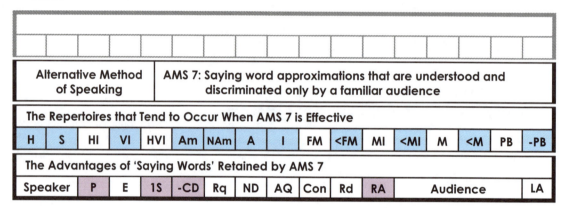

Alternative Method of Speaking	AMS 7: Saying word approximations that are understood and discriminated only by a familiar audience													
The Repertoires that Tend to Occur When AMS 7 is Effective														
H	S	HI	VI	HVI	Am	NAm	A	I	FM	<FM	MI	<MI	M	<M	PB	-PB
The Advantages of 'Saying Words' Retained by AMS 7														
Speaker	P	E	1S	-CD	Rq	ND	AQ	Con	Rd	RA	Audience			LA

AMS 8: Making distinguishable noises or sounds that are understood and discriminated only by a familiar audience

'Making distinguishable noises or sounds that are understood and discriminated only by a familiar audience' is a method of speaking used by older children and adults, who have extremely limited motor skills, who have not had the opportunity to learn a more effective method, or who have had difficulty acquiring any other method.

'Making distinguishable noises or sounds':

- permits learners with extremely limited motor skills to function as speakers.
- retains four of the ten speaker advantages of 'saying words'.
- generally results in only a very limited repertoire of requests.
- does not retain the audience advantage of 'saying words'; utterances are understood only by a very small number of instructors or care providers and peers with and without disabilities.
- *should almost always be replaced with a more effective method; reasons given for not doing so tend to invoke fallacies, such as intellectual capacity and pre-speaking skills described in chapter 2, or to emphasize the convenience of instructors, care providers, or family members, rather than the needs of our learners; these reasons are absolutely and completely unacceptable.*

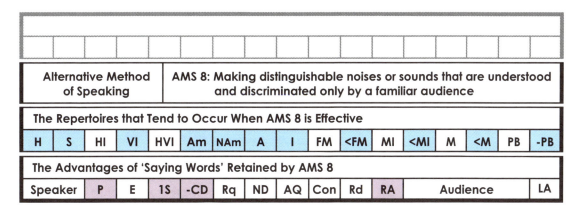

AMS 9: Visually scanning and pointing to or exchanging photographs using a small book worn by the learner[4]

'Visually scanning and pointing to or exchanging photographs using a small book worn by the learner' should be considered for some hearing, sighted learners who exhibit a limited repertoire of requests or no requests at all, especially those who are ambulatory and active, those who can readily match photographs to items (i.e., make complex discriminations), those with limited, but some fine motor coordination, those for whom an audience who understands and responds to signs is not available, or those who have had difficulty acquiring *'standard signs'* or *'standard, adapted, and idiosyncratic signs'*.

conditional discriminations

'Visually scanning and pointing to or exchanging photographs using a small book':

- retains three of the ten speaker advantages of 'saying words'.
- provides the advantage of portability not found in some other methods that include scanning and selecting. *This advantage cannot be overstated.*
- often results in spontaneous requests; as discussed in chapter 6, *Listener Responses, Names, and Descriptions,* this method does not permit learners to clearly name or describe items, activities, persons, or places, answer questions, or participate in conversations.
- some effort is involved in conveying requests, especially as more photographs are included in the book.
- requires two-step responses, even in the beginning, along with complex discriminations; photographs, rather than pic-symbols, may result in more rapid discriminations; many learners will find this method more difficult to learn than methods which include *'signs'*.
- may facilitate the emergence or re-emergence of spoken words or word approximations in children or the re-emergence of spoken words in adults. If spoken words emerge or re-emerge while pointing to or exchanging photographs, and the words are exhibited reliably as understandable repetitions, this method should be gradually discontinued and *'saying words'* should be established as the learner's primary method of speaking; if not, *'visually scanning and pointing to or exchanging photographs using a small book'* should be seriously considered as a permanent, primary method of speaking.
- does not permit sighted learners to read; it may, however, provide some indication of comprehension if it follows exposure to printed words.
- retains the audience advantage of *'saying words'*; in other words, a large audience of children and adults with and without disabilities can respond effectively to *'requests with photographs'* without training.

---

[4] Small communication books that can be worn by the learner are available from <augresources.com>.

- *in sum, with this method of speaking, many of the speaker advantages of 'saying words' are lost, while the audience advantage is retained. In other words, it may be somewhat more difficult for a child or adult to learn to make requests, more effortful to make them, and their repertoire may be limited to requests, but when these requests are conveyed, children and adults with and without disabilities will have no trouble understanding and responding to them.*
- requires very specific teaching procedures, including errorless prompting and rapid prompt-fading (see chapter 12, Teaching Protocol 1); if these procedures are used *as they are described*, without additions or modifications, and data indicate that this method is ineffective for a specific child or adult, consider selecting a method **AMS 12** or a method that includes '*signs*'.
- for learners who have been using this method effectively and who have acquired a large repertoire of requests, you may want to expand their speaking repertoire to include naming or describing items, activities, persons, or places, answering questions, and participating in conversations, you can do this by gradually replacing photographs with printed words and making '*visually scanning and pointing to or exchanging printed words using a small book worn by the learner*' (**AMS 11**) their primary or concurrent method of speaking.

Alternative Method of Speaking	AMS 9: Visually scanning and pointing to or exchanging photographs using a small book worn by the learner													
The Repertoires that Tend to Occur When AMS 9 is Effective													
H	S	HI	VI	HVI	Am	NAm	A	I	FM	<FM	MI	<MI	M	<M	PB	-PB
The Advantages of 'Saying Words' Retained by AMS 9													
Speaker	P	E	1S	-CD	Rq	ND	AQ	Con	Rd	RA	Audience			LA

AMS 10: Visually scanning and pointing to or exchanging pic-symbols with printed words using a small book worn by the learner[5]

'*Visually scanning and pointing to or exchanging pic-symbols with printed words using a small book worn by the learner*' should be considered for some hearing, sighted learners who exhibit a limited repertoire of requests or no requests at all, especially those who are ambulatory and active, those who can readily match pic-symbols to items, those with limited, but some fine motor coordination, those for whom an audience who understands and responds to signs is not available, or those who have had difficulty acquiring '*standard signs*' or '*standard, adapted, and idiosyncratic signs*'.

'*Visually scanning and pointing to or exchanging pic-symbols with printed words using a small book*':

- retains three of the ten speaker advantages of 'saying words'.
- provides the advantage of portability not found in some other methods that include scanning and selecting. *This advantage cannot be overstated.*
- often results in spontaneous requests; learners are generally taught to discriminate the more prominent pic-symbols, rather than the smaller printed words directly below them; as a result, this method does not permit learners to clearly name or describe items, activities, persons, or places, answer questions, or participate in conversations; the printed words help the audience identify the pic-symbol. — more salient stimuli
- some effort is involved in conveying requests, especially as more pic-symbols are included in the book.
- requires two-step responses, even in the beginning, along with complex discriminations; pic-symbols may require more time to make discriminations than photographs; many learners will find this method more difficult to learn than methods which include '*photographs*' or '*signs*'.

---

[5] Small communication books that can be worn by the learner are available from <augresources.com>.

- may facilitate the emergence or re-emergence of spoken words or word approximations in children or the re-emergence of spoken words in adults. If spoken words emerge or re-emerge while pointing to or exchanging pic-symbols, and the words are exhibited reliably as understandable repetitions, this method should be gradually discontinued and *'saying words'* should be established as the learner's primary method of speaking; if not, *'visually scanning and pointing to or exchanging pic-symbols using a small book'* should be seriously considered as a permanent, primary method of speaking.

- does not permit sighted learners to read; it may, however, indicate provide some indication of comprehension if it follows exposure to printed words.

- retains only part of the audience advantage of *'saying words'*; in other words, a large audience of children and adults without disabilities can respond effectively to *'requests with pic-symbols and printed words'*; an audience of peers with disabilities, however, may not be able to respond effectively to these requests.

- is often selected as a method of speaking, because of the audience advantage, and without regard to a learner's skill repertoire.

- *in sum, with this method of speaking, many of the speaker advantages of 'saying words' are lost and only part of the audience advantage is retained. In other words, it may be somewhat more difficult for a child or adult to learn to make requests, more effortful to make them, and their repertoire may be limited to requests, and when these requests are conveyed, only children and adults without disabilities will be able to understand and respond to them.*

- requires very specific teaching procedures, including errorless prompting and rapid prompt-fading (see chapter 12, Teaching Protocol 1); if these procedures are used *as they are described*, without additions or modifications, and data indicate that this method is ineffective for a specific child or adult, consider selecting **AMS 9**, **AMS 12**, or a method that includes *'signs'*.

- for learners who have been using this method effectively and who have acquired a large repertoire of requests, you may want to expand their speaking repertoire to include naming or describing items, activities, persons, or places, answering questions, and participating in conversations, you can do this by gradually replacing the pic-symbols with printed words, and making *'visually scanning and pointing to or exchanging printed words using a small book worn by the learner'* (**AMS 11**) their primary or concurrent method of speaking.

Alternative Method of Speaking	AMS 10: Visually scanning and pointing to or exchanging pic-symbols using a small book worn by the learner												
The Repertoires that Tend to Occur When AMS 10 is Effective													
H	S	HI	VI	HVI	Am	NAm	A	I	FM	<FM	MI	<MI	M	<M	PB	-PB
The Advantages of 'Saying Words' Retained by AMS 10													
Speaker	P	E	1S	-CD	Rq	ND	AQ	Con	Rd	RA	Audience	LA

AMS 11: Visually scanning and pointing to or exchanging printed words using a small book worn by the learner[6]

'Visually scanning and pointing to or exchanging printed words using a small book worn by the learner' should be considered for some hearing, sighted learners who have already acquired requests using **AMS 9** or **AMS 10**, especially those who are ambulatory and active, those who can readily match printed words to items, those with limited, but some fine motor coordination, those for whom an audience who understands and responds to signs is not available, or those who have had difficulty acquiring *'standard signs'* or *'standard, adapted, and idiosyncratic signs'*.

'Visually scanning and pointing to or exchanging printed words using a small book':

- retains six of the ten speaker advantages of *'saying words'*.
- provides the advantage of portability not found in some other methods that include scanning and selecting. *This advantage cannot be overstated.*
- often results in spontaneous requests; unlike **AMS 9** and **AMS 10**, this method permits learners to clearly name or describe items, activities, persons, or places, answer questions, and participate in conversations.
- some effort is involved in conveying requests, especially as more printed words are included in the book,
- requires two-step responses, even in the beginning, along with complex discriminations; printed words may require more time to make discriminations than photographs; many learners will find this method more difficult to learn than methods which include *'photographs'* or *'signs'*.
- may facilitate the emergence or re-emergence of spoken words or word approximations in children or the re-emergence of spoken words in adults. If spoken words emerge or re-emerge while pointing to or exchanging printed words, and the words are exhibited reliably as understandable repetitions, this method should be gradually discontinued and *'saying words'* should be established as the learner's primary method of speaking; if not, *'visually scanning and pointing to or exchanging printed words using a small book'* should be seriously considered as a permanent, primary method of speaking.
- does not permit sighted learners to read; it may, however, indicate provide some indication of comprehension if it follows exposure to printed words.
- retains only part of the audience advantage of *'saying words'*; in other words, a large audience of children and adults without disabilities can respond effectively to *'requests with printed words'*; an audience of peers with disabilities, however, may not be able to respond effectively to these requests.
- *in sum, with this method of speaking, many of the speaker advantages of 'saying words' are lost and only part of the audience advantage is retained. In other words, it may be somewhat more difficult for a child or adult to learn to make requests, more effortful to make them, and their repertoire may be limited to requests, and when these requests are conveyed, only children and adults without disabilities will be able to understand and respond to them.*
- requires very specific teaching procedures, including errorless prompting and rapid prompt-fading (see chapter 12, Teaching Protocol 1). if these procedures are used *as they are described*, without additions or modifications, and data indicate that this method is ineffective for a specific child or adult, consider selecting a method that includes **AMS 9**, **AMS 12**, or a method that includes *'signs'*.

---

[6] Small communication books that can be worn by the learner are available from <augresources.com>.

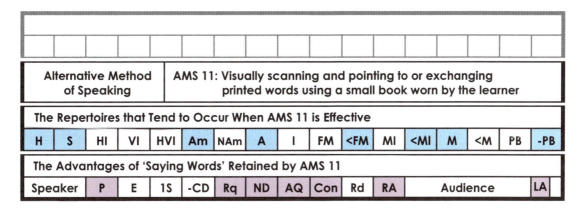

AMS 12: Visually scanning and touching photographs on a screen using a small speech-generating device (SGD) worn by the learner or attached to the learner's mobility or positioning device

'Visually scanning and touching photographs on a screen using a small speech-generating device (SGD) worn by the learner or attached to the learner's mobility or positioning device' should be considered for some hearing, sighted learners who exhibit a limited repertoire of requests or no requests at all, especially those who are ambulatory and active, those who can readily match photographs to items, those with limited, but some fine motor coordination, those for whom an audience who understands and responds to signs is not available, or those who have had difficulty acquiring *'standard signs'* or *'standard, adapted, and idiosyncratic signs'*.

'Visually scanning and touching photographs on a screen using a small speech-generating device (SGD) worn by the learner or attached to the learner's mobility or positioning device':

- retains three of the ten speaker advantages of *'saying words'*.
- provides the advantage of portability not found in some other methods that include scanning and selecting. *This advantage cannot be overstated.*
- often results in spontaneous requests; as discussed in chapter 6, *Listener Responses, Names, and Descriptions,* however, this method does not permit learners to clearly name or describe items, activities, persons, or places, answer questions, or participate in conversations.
- some effort is involved in conveying requests, especially as more photographs are included in the device,
- requires two-step responses, even in the beginning, along with complex discriminations; photographs, rather than pic-symbols, may result in more rapid discriminations; many learners will find this method more difficult to learn than methods which include *'signs'*;
- may facilitate the emergence or re-emergence of spoken words or word approximations in children or the re-emergence of spoken words in adults. If spoken words emerge or re-emerge while touching photographs, and the words are exhibited reliably as understandable repetitions, this method should be gradually discontinued and *'saying words'* should be established as the learner's primary method of speaking; if not, *'visually scanning and touching photographs on a screen using a small speech-generating device (SGD) worn by the learner or attached to the learner's mobility or positioning device'* should be seriously considered as a permanent, primary method of speaking.
- does not permit sighted learners to read; it may, however, indicate provide some indication of comprehension if it follows exposure to printed words.
- retains the audience advantage of *'saying words'*; in other words, a large audience of children and adults can respond effectively to *'requests with photographs'* without training.
- is often selected as a method of speaking, because of the audience advantage, and without regard to a learner's skill repertoire.

- *in sum, with this method of speaking, many of the speaker advantages of 'saying words' are lost, while the audience advantage is retained. In other words, it may be somewhat more difficult for a child or adult to learn to make requests, more effortful to make them, and their repertoire may be limited to requests, but when these requests are conveyed, children and adults with and without disabilities will have no trouble understanding and responding to them.*
- requires very specific teaching procedures, including errorless prompting and rapid prompt-fading (see chapter 12, Teaching Protocol 1); if these procedures are used *as they are described*, without additions or modifications, and data indicate that this method is ineffective for a specific child or adult, consider selecting **AMS 9** or a method that includes '*signs*'.
- for learners who have been using this method effectively and who have acquired a large repertoire of requests, you may want to expand their speaking repertoire to include naming or describing items, activities, persons, or places, answering questions, and participating in conversations; you can do this by gradually replacing photographs with printed words and making '*visually scanning and touching printed words on a screen using a small speech-generating device (SGD) worn by the learner or attached to the learner's mobility or positioning device*' (**AMS 14**) their primary or concurrent method of speaking

Alternative Method of Speaking	AMS 12: Visually scanning and touching photographs on a screen using a small speech-generating device (SGD) worn by the learner or attached to the learner's mobility or positioning device												
The Repertoires that Tend to Occur When AMS 12 is Effective													
H	S	HI	VI	HVI	Am	NAm	A	I	FM	<FM	MI	<MI	M	<M	PB	-PB
The Advantages of 'Saying Words' Retained by AMS 12													
Speaker	P	E	1S	-CD	Rq	ND	AQ	Con	Rd	RA	Audience		LA

AMS 13: Visually scanning and touching pic-symbols on a screen using a small speech-generating device (SGD) worn by the learner or attached to the learner's mobility or positioning device

'*Visually scanning and touching pic-symbols on a screen using a small speech-generating device (SGD) worn by the learner or attached to the learner's mobility or positioning device*' should be considered for some hearing, sighted learners who exhibit a limited repertoire of requests or no requests at all, especially those who are ambulatory and active, those who can readily match pic-symbols to items, those with limited, but some fine motor coordination, those for whom an audience who understands and responds to signs is not available, or those who have had difficulty acquiring '*standard signs*' or '*standard, adapted, and idiosyncratic signs*'.

'*Visually scanning and touching pic-symbols on a screen using a small speech-generating device (SGD) worn by the learner or attached to the learner's mobility or positioning device*':

- retains three of the ten speaker advantages of '*saying words*'.
- provides the advantage of portability not found in some other methods that include scanning and selecting. *This advantage cannot be overstated.*
- often results in spontaneous requests; learners are generally taught to discriminate the more prominent pic-symbols, rather than the smaller printed words directly below them; as a result, this method does not permit learners to clearly name or describe items, activities, persons, or places, answer questions, or participate in conversations; the printed words help the audience identify the pic-symbol.
- some effort is involved in conveying requests, especially as more pic-symbols are included in the device,
- requires two-step responses, even in the beginning, along with complex discriminations; pic-symbols may require more time to make discriminations than photographs; many learners will find this method more difficult to learn than methods which include '*photographs*' or '*signs*'.

- may facilitate the emergence or re-emergence of spoken words or word approximations in children or the re-emergence of spoken words in adults. If spoken words emerge or re-emerge while touching pic-symbols, and the words are exhibited reliably as understandable repetitions, this method should be gradually discontinued and 'saying words' should be established as the learner's primary method of speaking; if not, 'visually scanning and touching pic-symbols on a screen using a small speech-generating device (SGD) worn by the learner or attached to the learner's mobility or positioning device' should be seriously considered as a permanent, primary method of speaking.

- does not permit sighted learners to read; it may, however, indicate provide some indication of comprehension if it follows exposure to printed words.

- retains only part of the audience advantage of 'saying words'; in other words, a large audience of children and adults without disabilities can respond effectively to 'requests with pic-symbols and printed words'; an audience of peers with disabilities, however, may not be able to respond effectively to these requests.

- is often selected as a method of speaking, because of the audience advantage, and without regard to a learner's skill repertoire.

- *in sum, with this method of speaking, many of the speaker advantages of 'saying words' are lost and only part of the audience advantage is retained. In other words, it may be somewhat more difficult for a child or adult to learn to make requests, more effortful to make them, and their repertoire may be limited to requests, and when these requests are conveyed, only children and adults without disabilities will be able to understand and respond to them.*

- requires very specific teaching procedures, including errorless prompting and rapid prompt-fading (see chapter 12, Teaching Protocol 1); if these procedures are used *as they are described*, without additions or modifications, and data indicate that this method is ineffective for a specific child or adult, consider selecting a method that consider selecting **AMS 9**, **AMS 12**, or a method that includes 'signs'.

- for learners who have been using this method effectively and who have acquired a large repertoire of requests, you may want to expand their speaking repertoire to include naming or describing items, activities, persons, or places, answering questions, and participating in conversations; you can do this by gradually replacing pic-symbols with printed words and making 'visually scanning and touching printed words on a screen using a small speech-generating device (SGD) worn by the learner or attached to the learner's mobility or positioning device' (**AMS 14**) their primary or concurrent method of speaking.

Alternative Method of Speaking	AMS 13: Visually scanning and touching pic-symbols on a screen using a small speech-generating device (SGD) worn by the learner or attached to the learner's mobility or positioning device													
The Repertoires that Tend to Occur When AMS 13 is Effective														
H	S	HI	VI	HVI	Am	NAm	A	I	FM	<FM	MI	<MI	M	<M	PB	-PB
The Advantages of 'Saying Words' Retained by AMS 13														
Speaker	P	E	1S	-CD	Rq	ND	AQ	Con	Rd	RA	Audience			LA

AMS 14: Visually scanning and touching printed words on a screen using a small speech-generating device (SGD) worn by the learner or attached to the learner's mobility or positioning device

'*Visually scanning and touching printed words on a screen using a small speech-generating device (SGD) worn by the learner or attached to the learner's mobility or positioning device*' should be considered for some hearing, sighted learners who exhibit a limited repertoire of requests or no requests at all, especially those who are ambulatory and active, those who can readily match printed words to items, those with limited, but some fine motor coordination, those for whom an audience who understands and responds to signs is not available, or those who have had difficulty acquiring '*standard signs*' or '*standard, adapted, and idiosyncratic signs*'.

'*Visually scanning and touching printed words on a screen using a small speech-generating device (SGD) worn by the learner or attached to the learner's mobility or positioning device*':

- retains six of the ten speaker advantages of '*saying words*'.
- provides the advantage of portability not found in some other methods that include scanning and selecting. *This advantage cannot be overstated.*
- often results in spontaneous requests; as discussed in chapter 6, *Listener Responses, Names, and Descriptions,* this method permits learners to clearly name or describe items, activities, persons, or places, answer questions, and participate in conversations.
- some effort is involved in conveying requests, especially as more printed words are included in the device,
- requires two-step responses, even in the beginning, along with complex discriminations; printed words may require more time to make discriminations than photographs; many learners will find this method more difficult to learn than methods which include '*photographs*' or '*signs*'.
- may facilitate the emergence or re-emergence of spoken words or word approximations in children or the re-emergence of spoken words in adults. If spoken words emerge or re-emerge while touching printed words, and the words are exhibited reliably as understandable repetitions, this method should be gradually discontinued and '*saying words*' should be established as the learner's primary method of speaking; if not, '*visually scanning and touching printed words on a screen using a small speech-generating device (SGD) worn by the learner or attached to the learner's mobility or positioning device*' should be seriously considered as a permanent, primary method of speaking.
- does not permit sighted learners to read; it may, however, indicate provide some indication of comprehension if it follows exposure to printed words.
- this method retains only part of the audience advantage of '*saying words*'; in other words, a large audience of children and adults without disabilities can respond effectively to '*requests with printed words*'; an audience of peers with disabilities, however, may not be able to respond effectively to these requests.
- is often selected as a method of speaking, because of the audience advantage, and without regard to a learner's skill repertoire.
- *in sum, with this method of speaking, many of the speaker advantages of 'saying words' are lost and only part of the audience advantage is retained. In other words, it may be somewhat more difficult for a child or adult to learn to make requests, more effortful to make them, and their repertoire may be limited to requests, and when these requests are conveyed, only children and adults without disabilities will be able to understand and respond to them.*
- requires very specific teaching procedures, including errorless prompting and rapid prompt-fading (see chapter 12, Teaching Protocol 1); if these procedures are used *as they are described*, without additions or modifications, and data indicate that this method is ineffective for a specific child or adult, consider selecting **AMS 9**, **AMS 12**, or a method that includes '*signs*'.

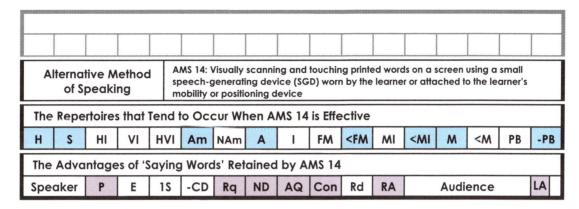

AMS 15: Visually scanning and exchanging photographs using the Picture Exchange Communication System and a PECS Binder

'Visually scanning and exchanging photographs using the Picture Exchange Communication System and a PECS binder' should be considered for some hearing, sighted learners who exhibit a limited repertoire of requests or no requests at all, especially those who are ambulatory and active, those who can readily match photographs to items, those with limited, but some fine motor coordination, those for whom an audience who understands and responds to signs is not available, or those who have had difficulty acquiring '*standard signs*' or '*standard, adapted, and idiosyncratic signs*'.

'Visually scanning and exchanging photographs using the Picture Exchange Communication System and a PECS binder':

- retains two of the ten speaker advantages of '*saying words*'.

- does not provide the advantage of portability found in some other methods that include '*signs*' and '*smaller devices*'. *This disadvantage cannot be overstated.*

- can result in spontaneous requests; as discussed in chapter 6, *Listener Responses, Names, and Descriptions,* this method does not permit learners to clearly name or describe items, activities, persons, or places, answer questions, or participate in conversations.

- some effort is involved in conveying requests, especially as more photographs are included in the binder.

- requires two-step responses, even in the beginning, along with complex discriminations; photographs, rather than pic-symbols, may result in more rapid discriminations; many learners will find this method more difficult to learn than methods which include '*signs*'.

- may facilitate the emergence or re-emergence of spoken words or word approximations in children or the re-emergence of spoken words in adults. If spoken words emerge or re-emerge while exchanging photographs, and the words are exhibited reliably as understandable repetitions, this method should be gradually discontinued and '*saying words*' should be established as the learner's primary method of speaking; if not, '*visually scanning and exchanging photographs using the Picture Exchange Communication System and a PECS binder*' should be seriously considered as a permanent, primary method of speaking.

- does not permit sighted learners to read; it may, however, indicate provide some indication of comprehension if it follows exposure to printed words.

- retains the audience advantage of '*saying words*'; in other words, a large audience of children and adults can respond effectively to '*requests with photographs*' without training.

- is often selected as a method of speaking, because of the audience advantage, and without regard to a learner's skill repertoire.

- *in sum, with this method of speaking, many of the speaker advantages of 'saying words' are lost, while the audience advantage is retained. In other words, it may be somewhat more difficult for a child or adult to learn to make requests, more effortful to make them, and their repertoire may be limited to requests, but when these requests are conveyed, children and adults with and without disabilities will have no trouble understanding and responding to them.*

- requires very specific teaching procedures, including errorless prompting and rapid prompt-fading (see chapter 12, Teaching Protocol 1); if these procedures are used *as they are described*, without additions or modifications, and data indicate that this method is ineffective for a specific child or adult, consider selecting **AMS 9**, **AMS 12**, or a method that includes '*signs*'.

- for learners who have been using this method effectively and who have acquired a large repertoire of requests, you may want to expand their speaking repertoire to include naming or describing items, activities, persons, or places, answering questions, and participating in conversations; you can do this by gradually replacing photographs with printed words and making '*visually scanning and exchanging printed words using the Picture Exchange Communication System and a PECS binder*' (**AMS 17**) their primary or concurrent method of speaking.

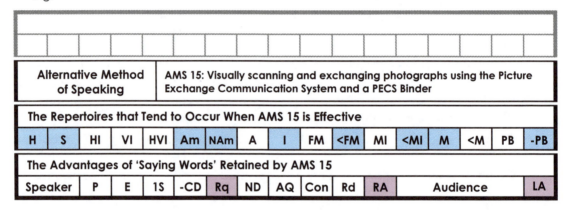

AMS 16: Visually scanning and exchanging pic-symbols using the Picture Exchange Communication System and a PECS Binder

'*Visually scanning and exchanging pic-symbols using the Picture Exchange Communication System and a PECS binder*' should be considered for some hearing, sighted learners who exhibit a limited repertoire of requests or no requests at all, especially those who are ambulatory and active, those who can readily match pic-symbols to items, those with limited, but some fine motor coordination, those for whom an audience who understands and responds to signs is not available, or those who have had difficulty acquiring '*standard signs*' or '*standard, adapted, and idiosyncratic signs*'.

'*Visually scanning and exchanging pic-symbols using the Picture Exchange Communication System and a PECS binder*':

- retains two of the ten speaker advantages of '*saying words*'.

- does not provide the advantage of portability found in other methods that include '*signs*' and '*smaller devices*'. *This disadvantage cannot be overstated.*

- can result in spontaneous requests; learners are generally taught to discriminate the more prominent pic-symbols, rather than the smaller printed words directly below them; as a result, this method does not permit learners to clearly name or describe items, activities, persons, or places, answer questions, or participate in conversations; the printed words help the audience identify the pic-symbol.

- some effort is involved in conveying requests, especially as more pic-symbols are included in the binder.

- requires two-step responses, even in the beginning, along with complex discriminations; pic-symbols may require more time to make discriminations than photographs; many learners will find this method more difficult to learn than methods which include '*photographs*' or '*signs*'.

- may facilitate the emergence or re-emergence of spoken words or word approximations in children or the re-emergence of spoken words in adults. If spoken words emerge or re-emerge while exchanging pic-symbols, and the words are exhibited reliably as understandable repetitions, this method should be gradually discontinued and 'saying words' should be established as the learner's primary method of speaking; if not, 'visually scanning and exchanging pic-symbols using the Picture Exchange Communication System and a PECS binder' should be seriously considered as a permanent, primary method of speaking.

- does not permit sighted learners to read; it may, however, indicate provide some indication of comprehension if it follows exposure to printed words.

- retains only part of the audience advantage of 'saying words'; in other words, a large audience of children and adults without disabilities can respond effectively to 'requests with pic-symbols and printed words'; an audience of peers with disabilities, however, may not be able to respond effectively to these requests.

- is often selected as a method of speaking, because of the audience advantage, and without regard to a learner's skill repertoire.

- *in sum, with this method of speaking, many of the speaker advantages of 'saying words' are lost and only part of the audience advantage is retained. In other words, it may be somewhat more difficult for a child or adult to learn to make requests, more effortful to make them, and their repertoire may be limited to requests, and when these requests are conveyed, only children and adults without disabilities will be able to understand and respond to them.*

- requires very specific teaching procedures, including errorless prompting and rapid prompt-fading (see chapter 12, Teaching Protocol 1); if these procedures are used *as they are described*, without additions or modifications, and data indicate that this method is ineffective for a specific child or adult, consider selecting **AMS 9**, **AMS 12**, **AMS 15**, or a method that includes 'signs'.

- for learners who have been using this method effectively and who have acquired a large repertoire of requests, you may want to expand their speaking repertoire to include naming or describing items, activities, persons, or places, answering questions, and participating in conversations; you can do this by gradually replacing pic-symbols with printed words and making 'visually scanning and exchanging printed words using the Picture Exchange Communication System and a PECS binder' (**AMS 17**) their primary method or concurrent method of speaking.

Alternative Method of Speaking	AMS 16: Visually scanning and exchanging pic-symbols using the Picture Exchange Communication System and a PECS Binder												
The Repertoires that Tend to Occur When AMS 16 is Effective														
H	S	HI	VI	HVI	Am	NAm	A	I	FM	<FM	MI	<MI	M	<M	PB	-PB
The Advantages of 'Saying Words' Retained by AMS 16														
Speaker	P	E	1S	-CD	Rq	ND	AQ	Con	Rd	RA	Audience		LA

AMS 17: Visually scanning and exchanging printed words using the Picture Exchange Communication System and a PECS Binder

'Visually scanning and exchanging printed words using the Picture Exchange Communication System and a PECS binder' should be considered for some hearing, sighted learners who exhibit a limited repertoire of requests or no requests at all, especially those who are ambulatory and active, those who can readily match printed words to items, those with limited, but some fine motor coordination, those for whom an audience who understands and responds to signs is not available, or those who have had difficulty acquiring *'standard signs'* or *'standard, adapted, and idiosyncratic signs'*.

'Visually scanning and exchanging printed words using the Picture Exchange Communication System and a PECS binder':

- retains five of the ten speaker advantages of 'saying words'.
- does not provide the advantage of portability found in other methods that include *'signs'* and *'smaller devices'*. *This disadvantage cannot be overstated.*
- can result in spontaneous requests; as discussed in chapter 6, *Listener Responses, Names, and Descriptions,* this method permits learners to clearly name or describe items, activities, persons, or places, answer questions, and participate in conversations.
- some effort is involved in conveying requests, especially as more printed words are included in the binder.
- requires two-step responses, even in the beginning, along with complex discriminations; printed words may require more time to make discriminations than photographs; many learners will find this method more difficult to learn than methods which include *'photographs'* or *'signs'*.
- may facilitate the emergence or re-emergence of spoken words or word approximations in children or the re-emergence of spoken words in adults. If spoken words emerge or re-emerge while exchanging printed words, and the words are exhibited reliably as understandable repetitions, this method should be gradually discontinued and *'saying words'* should be established as the learner's primary method of speaking; if not, *'visually scanning and exchanging printed words using the Picture Exchange Communication System and a PECS binder'* should be seriously considered as a permanent, primary method of speaking.
- does not permit sighted learners to read; it may, however, indicate provide some indication of comprehension if it follows exposure to printed words.
- retains only part of the audience advantage of *'saying words'*; in other words, a large audience of children and adults without disabilities can respond effectively to *'requests with printed words'*; an audience of peers with disabilities, however, may not be able to respond effectively to these requests.
- is often selected as a method of speaking, because of the audience advantage, and without regard to a learner's skill repertoire.
- *in sum, with this method of speaking, many of the speaker advantages of 'saying words' are lost and only part of the audience advantage is retained. In other words, it may be somewhat more difficult for a child or adult to learn to make requests, more effortful to make them, and their repertoire may be limited to requests, and when these requests are conveyed, only children and adults without disabilities will be able to understand and respond to them.*
- requires very specific teaching procedures, including errorless prompting and rapid prompt-fading (see chapter 12, Teaching Protocol 1); if these procedures are used *as they are described*, without additions or modifications, and data indicate that this method is ineffective for a specific child or adult, consider selecting **AMS 9**, **AMS 12**, **AMS 15**, or a method that includes *'signs'*.

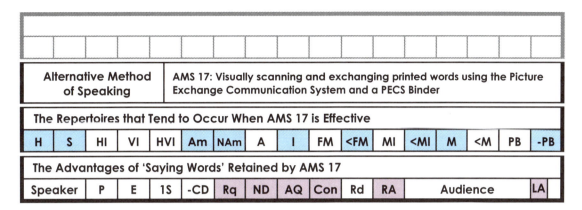

AMS 18: Scanning by touch and selecting items or miniature items attached to an object board

'Scanning by touch and selecting items or miniature items attached to an object board' is method of speaking used by children and adults with visual impairments or those with both visual and hearing impairments, who have extremely limited motor skills or who have not had the opportunity to learn a more effective method. Although an item or miniature item board can provide a learner with a schedule of daily activities, it can also permit the learner to function as an effective speaker.

'Scanning by touch and selecting items or miniature items attached to an object board':

- retains two of the ten speaker advantages of 'saying words'.
- generally results in only a very limited repertoire of requests.
- retains the audience advantage of *'saying words'*; in other words, a large audience of children and adults with and without disabilities can respond effectively to *'requests with items or miniature items'* without training.
- can often be replaced with a method that includes *'signs'*, which can greatly increase a learner's speaking repertoire.

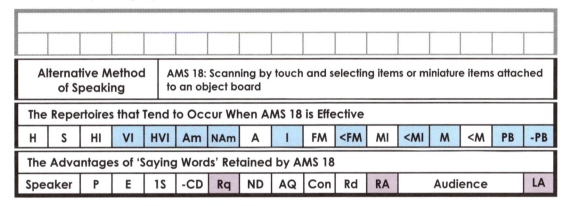

AMS 19: Visually scanning and touching photographs using a large SGD that contains 20 or fewer messages or requires another person to change templates

'Visually scanning and touching photographs using a large SGD that contains 20 or fewer messages or requires another person to change templates' should be considered a temporary method for some hearing, sighted learners who exhibit a limited repertoire of requests or no requests at all, especially those who can readily match photographs to items, those with limited, but some fine motor coordination, those for whom an audience who understands and responds to signs is not available, or those who have had difficulty acquiring *'standard signs'* or *'standard, adapted, and idiosyncratic signs'*.

'Visually scanning and touching photographs using a large SGD that contains 20 or fewer messages or requires another person to change templates':

- retains two of the ten speaker advantages of 'saying words'.
- does not provide the advantage of portability found in other methods that include '*signs*' and '*smaller devices*'. *This disadvantage cannot be overstated.*
- generally results in a limited number of requests; as discussed in chapter 6, *Listener Responses, Names, and Descriptions,* this method does not permit learners to clearly name or describe items, activities, persons, or places, answer questions, or participate in conversations.
- some effort is involved in conveying requests, especially as more photographs are included in the device.
- requires two-step responses, even in the beginning, along with complex discriminations; photographs, rather than pic-symbols, may result in more rapid discriminations; many learners will find this method more difficult to learn than methods which include '*signs*'.
- may facilitate the emergence or re-emergence of spoken words or word approximations in children or the re-emergence of spoken words in adults. If spoken words emerge or re-emerge while touching photographs, and the words are exhibited reliably as understandable repetitions, this method should be gradually discontinued and '*saying words*' should be established as the learner's primary method of speaking; if not, '*visually scanning and touching photographs using a large SGD that contains 20 or fewer messages or requires another person to change templates*' should be retained as a temporary, primary method of speaking and eventually replaced by a portable method that includes '*scanning and selecting photographs*' or by a method that includes '*signs*'.
- does not permit sighted learners to read; it may, however, indicate provide some indication of comprehension if it follows exposure to printed words.
- retains the audience advantage of '*saying words*'; in other words, a large audience of children and adults can respond effectively to '*requests with photographs*' without training.
- is often selected as a method of speaking, because of the audience advantage, and without regard to a learner's skill repertoire.
- *in sum, with this method of speaking, many of the speaker advantages of 'saying words' are lost, while the audience advantage is retained. In other words, it may be somewhat more difficult for a child or adult to learn to make requests, more effortful to make them, and their repertoire may be limited to requests, but when these requests are conveyed, children and adults with and without disabilities will have no trouble understanding and responding to them.*
- requires very specific teaching procedures, including errorless prompting and rapid prompt-fading (see chapter 12, Teaching Protocol 1); if these procedures are used *as they are described*, without additions or modifications, and data indicate that this method is ineffective for a specific child or adult, consider selecting **AMS 9**, **AMS 12**, **AMS 15**, or a method that includes '*signs*'.

Alternative Method of Speaking	AMS 19: Visually scanning and touching photographs using a large SGD that contains 20 or fewer messages or requires another person to change templates												
The Repertoires that Tend to Occur When AMS 19 is Effective													
H	S	HI	VI	HVI	Am	NAm	A	I	FM	<FM	MI	<MI	M	<M	PB	-PB
The Advantages of 'Saying Words' Retained by AMS 19													
Speaker	P	E	1S	-CD	Rq	ND	AQ	Con	Rd	RA	Audience		LA

AMS 20: Visually scanning and touching pic-symbols using a large SGD that contains 20 or fewer messages or requires another person to change templates

'Visually scanning and touching pic-symbols using a large SGD that contains 20 or fewer messages or requires another person to change templates' should be considered a temporary method for some hearing, sighted learners who exhibit a limited repertoire of requests or no requests at all, especially those who can readily match pic-symbols to items, those with limited, but some fine motor coordination, those for whom an audience who understands and responds to signs is not available, or those who have had difficulty acquiring *'standard signs'* or *'standard, adapted, and idiosyncratic signs'*.

'Visually scanning and touching photographs using a large SGD that contains 20 or fewer messages or requires another person to change templates':

- retains two of the ten speaker advantages of *'saying words'*.
- does not provide the advantage of portability found in other methods that include *'signs'* and *'smaller devices'*. *This disadvantage cannot be overstated.*
- generally results in a limited number of requests; learners are taught to discriminate the more prominent pic-symbols, rather than the smaller printed words directly below them; as a result, this method does not permit learners to clearly name or describe items, activities, persons, or places, answer questions, or participate in conversations; the printed words help the audience identify the pic-symbols.
- some effort is involved in conveying requests, especially as more pic-symbols are included in the device.
- requires two-step responses, even in the beginning, along with complex discriminations; pic-symbols may require more time to make discriminations than photographs; many learners will find this method more difficult to learn than methods which include *'photographs'* or *'signs'*.
- may facilitate the emergence or re-emergence of spoken words or word approximations in children or the re-emergence of spoken words in adults. If spoken words emerge or re-emerge while touching pic-symbols, and the words are exhibited reliably as understandable repetitions, this method should be gradually discontinued and *'saying words'* should be established as the learner's primary method of speaking; if not, *'visually scanning and touching pic-symbols using a large SGD that contains 20 or fewer messages or requires another person to change templates'* should be retained as a temporary, primary method of speaking and eventually replaced by a portable method that includes *'scanning and selecting photographs'* or by a method that includes *'signs'*.
- does not permit sighted learners to read; it may, however, indicate provide some indication of comprehension if it follows exposure to printed words.
- retains only part of the audience advantage of *'saying words'*; in other words, a large audience of children and adults without disabilities can respond effectively to *'requests with pic-symbols and printed words'*; an audience of peers with disabilities, however, may not be able to respond effectively to these requests.
- is often selected as a method of speaking, because of the audience advantage, and without regard to a learner's skill repertoire.
- *in sum, with this method of speaking, many of the speaker advantages of 'saying words' are lost and only part of the audience advantage is retained. In other words, it may be somewhat more difficult for a child or adult to learn to make requests, more effortful to make them, and their repertoire may be limited to requests, and when these requests are conveyed, only children and adults without disabilities will be able to understand and respond to them.*
- requires very specific teaching procedures, including errorless prompting and rapid prompt-fading (see chapter 12, Teaching Protocol 1); if these procedures are used *as they are described*, without additions or modifications, and data indicate that this method is ineffective for a specific child or adult, consider selecting **AMS 9, AMS 12, AMS 15**, or a method that includes *'signs'*.

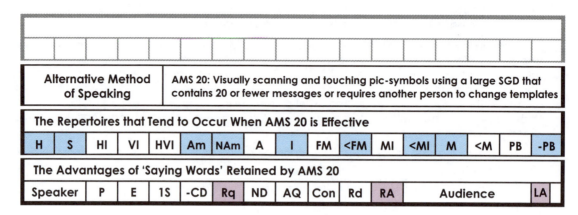

AMS 21: Visually scanning and touching printed words using a large SGD that contains 20 or fewer messages or requires another person to change templates

'*Visually scanning and touching printed words using a large SGD that contains 20 or fewer messages or requires another person to change templates*' should be considered a temporary method for some hearing, sighted learners who exhibit a limited repertoire of requests or no requests at all, especially those who can readily match printed words to items, those with limited, but some fine motor coordination, those for whom an audience who understands and responds to signs is not available, or those who have had difficulty acquiring '*standard signs*' or '*standard, adapted, and idiosyncratic signs*'.

'*Visually scanning and touching printed words using a large SGD that contains 20 or fewer messages or requires another person to change templates*':

- retains two of the ten speaker advantages of '*saying words*'.
- does not provide the advantage of portability found in other methods that include '*signs*' and '*smaller devices*'. *This disadvantage cannot be overstated.*
- generally results in a limited number of requests; as discussed in chapter 6, *Listener Responses, Names, and Descriptions,* this method, however, permits learners to clearly name or describe items, activities, persons, or places, answer questions, or participate in limited conversations.
- some effort is involved in conveying requests, especially as more printed words are included in the device.
- requires two-step responses, even in the beginning, along with complex discriminations; printed words may require more time to make discriminations than photographs; many learners will find this method more difficult to learn than methods which include '*photographs*' or '*signs*'.
- may facilitate the emergence or re-emergence of spoken words or word approximations in children or the re-emergence of spoken words in adults. If spoken words emerge or re-emerge while touching printed words, and the words are exhibited reliably as understandable repetitions, this method should be gradually discontinued and '*saying words*' should be established as the learner's primary method of speaking; if not, '*visually scanning and touching printed words using a large SGD that contains 20 or fewer messages or requires another person to change templates*' should be retained as a temporary, primary method of speaking and eventually replaced by a portable method that includes '*scanning and selecting photographs*' or by a method that includes '*signs*'.
- does not permit sighted learners to read; it may, however, indicate provide some indication of comprehension if it follows exposure to printed words.
- retains only part of the audience advantage of '*saying words*'; in other words, a large audience of children and adults without disabilities can respond effectively to '*requests with printed words*'; an audience of peers with disabilities, however, may not be able to respond effectively to these requests.

- is often selected as a method of speaking, because of the audience advantage, and without regard to a learner's skill repertoire.

- *in sum, with this method of speaking, many of the speaker advantages of 'saying words' are lost and only part of the audience advantage is retained. In other words, it may be somewhat more difficult for a child or adult to learn to make requests, more effortful to make them, and their repertoire may be limited to requests, and when these requests are conveyed, only children and adults without disabilities will be able to understand and respond to them.*

- requires very specific teaching procedures, including errorless prompting and rapid prompt-fading (see chapter 12, Teaching Protocol 1); if these procedures are used *as they are described*, without additions or modifications, and data indicate that this method is ineffective for a specific child or adult, consider selecting **AMS 9**, **AMS 12**, **AMS 15**, or a method that includes '*signs*'.

Alternative Method of Speaking	AMS 21: Visually scanning and touching printed words using a large SGD that contains 20 or fewer messages or requires another person to change templates												
The Repertoires that Tend to Occur When AMS 21 is Effective													
H	S	HI	VI	HVI	Am	NAm	A	I	FM	<FM	MI	<MI	M	<M	PB	-PB
The Advantages of 'Saying Words' Retained by AMS 21													
Speaker	P	E	1S	-CD	Rq	ND	AQ	Con	Rd	RA	Audience		LA

AMS 22: Visually scanning and selecting photographs on a large SGD by touching the screen, or by using one or two switches or eye-tracking

'*Visually scanning and selecting photographs on a large SGD by touching the screen, or by using one or two switches or eye-tracking*' should be considered for some hearing, sighted learners who exhibit a limited repertoire of requests or no requests at all, those who can readily match photographs to items, and especially those with very limited fine motor coordination or very limited motor movements.

'*Visually scanning and selecting photographs on a large SGD by touching the screen, or by using one or two switches or eye-tracking*':

- retains two of the ten speaker advantages of '*saying words*'.

- does not provide the advantage of portability found in other methods that include '*signs*' or '*smaller devices*'. *This disadvantage cannot be overstated.*

- can result spontaneous requests; as discussed in chapter 6, *Listener Responses, Names, and Descriptions*, however, this method does not permit learners to clearly name or describe items, activities, persons, or places, answer questions, or participate in conversations.

- some effort is involved in conveying requests, especially as more photographs are included in the device,

- requires two-step responses, even in the beginning, along with complex discriminations; photographs, rather than pic-symbols, may result in more rapid discriminations; many learners will find this method more difficult to learn than methods which include '*signs*';

- may facilitate the emergence or re-emergence of spoken words or word approximations in children or the re-emergence of spoken words in adults. If spoken words emerge or re-emerge while selecting photographs, and the words are exhibited reliably as understandable repetitions, this method should be gradually discontinued and '*saying words*' should be established as the learner's primary method of speaking; if not, '*visually scanning and selecting photographs on a large SGD by touching the screen, or by using one or two switches or eye-tracking*' should be seriously considered as a permanent, primary method of speaking.

- does not permit sighted learners to read; it may, however, indicate provide some indication of comprehension if it follows exposure to printed words.
- retains the audience advantage of 'saying words'; in other words, a large audience of children and adults can respond effectively to 'requests with photographs' without training.
- is often selected as a method of speaking, because of the audience advantage, and without regard to a learner's skill repertoire.
- *in sum, with this method of speaking, many of the speaker advantages of 'saying words' are lost, while the audience advantage is retained. In other words, it may be somewhat more difficult for a child or adult to learn to make requests, more effortful to make them, and their repertoire may be limited to requests, but when these requests are conveyed, children and adults with and without disabilities will have no trouble understanding and responding to them.*
- requires very specific teaching procedures, including errorless prompting and rapid prompt-fading (see chapter 12, Teaching Protocol 1); if these procedures are used *as they are described*, without additions or modifications, and data indicate that this method is ineffective for a specific child or adult, consider selecting **AMS 9**, **AMS 12**, **AMS 15** or a method that includes 'standard signs', 'adapted signs', 'idiosyncratic signs' or 'gestures'.
- for learners who have been using this method effectively and who have acquired a large repertoire of requests, you may want to expand their speaking repertoire to include naming or describing items, activities, persons, or places, answering questions, and participating in conversations; you can do this by gradually replacing photographs with printed words and making 'visually scanning and selecting printed words on a large SGD by touching the screen, or by using one or two switches or eye-tracking' (**AMS 24**) their primary or concurrent method of speaking

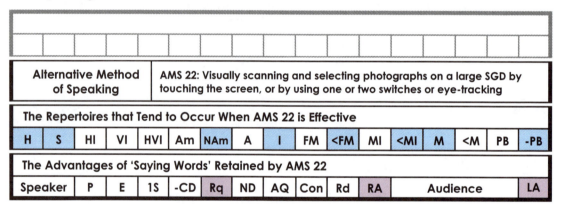

Alternative Method of Speaking	AMS 22: Visually scanning and selecting photographs on a large SGD by touching the screen, or by using one or two switches or eye-tracking													
The Repertoires that Tend to Occur When AMS 22 is Effective														
H	S	HI	VI	HVI	Am	NAm	A	I	FM	<FM	MI	<MI	M	<M	PB	-PB
The Advantages of 'Saying Words' Retained by AMS 22														
Speaker	P	E	1S	-CD	Rq	ND	AQ	Con	Rd	RA	Audience			LA

AMS 23: Visually scanning and selecting pic-symbols on a large SGD by touching the screen, or by using one or two switches or eye-tracking

'Visually scanning and selecting pic-symbols on a large SGD by touching the screen, or by using one or two switches or eye-tracking' should be considered for some hearing, sighted learners who exhibit a limited repertoire of requests or no requests at all, those who can readily match photographs to items, and especially those with very limited fine motor coordination or very limited motor movements.

'Visually scanning and selecting pic-symbols on a large SGD by touching the screen, or by using one or two switches or eye-tracking':

- retains two of the ten speaker advantages of 'saying words'.
- does not provide the advantage of portability found in other methods that include 'signs' or 'smaller devices'. *This disadvantage cannot be overstated.*
- can result in spontaneous requests; learners are generally taught to discriminate the more prominent pic-symbols, rather than the smaller printed words directly below them; as a result, this method does not permit learners to clearly name or describe items, activities, persons, or

Essential for Living   97

places, answer questions, or participate in conversations; the printed words help the audience identify the pic-symbol.

- some effort is involved in conveying requests, especially as more pic-symbols are included in the device,

- requires two-step responses, even in the beginning, along with complex discriminations; pic-symbols may require more time to make discriminations than photographs; many learners will find this method more difficult to learn than methods which include 'photographs' or 'signs'.

- may facilitate the emergence or re-emergence of spoken words or word approximations in children or the re-emergence of spoken words in adults. If spoken words emerge or re-emerge while selecting pic-symbols, and the words are exhibited reliably as understandable repetitions, this method should be gradually discontinued and 'saying words' should be established as the learner's primary method of speaking; if not, 'visually scanning and selecting pic-symbols on a large SGD by touching the screen, or by using one or two switches or eye-tracking' should be seriously considered as a permanent, primary method of speaking.

- does not permit sighted learners to read; it may, however, indicate provide some indication of comprehension if it follows exposure to printed words.

- retains only part of the audience advantage of 'saying words'; in other words, a large audience of children and adults without disabilities can respond effectively to 'requests with pic-symbols and printed words'; an audience of peers with disabilities, however, may not be able to respond effectively to these requests.

- is often selected as a method of speaking, because of the audience advantage, and without regard to a learner's skill repertoire.

- *in sum, with this method of speaking, many of the speaker advantages of 'saying words' are lost and only part of the audience advantage is retained. In other words, it may be somewhat more difficult for a child or adult to learn to make requests, more effortful to make them, and their repertoire may be limited to requests, and when these requests are conveyed, only children and adults without disabilities will be able to understand and respond to them.*

- requires very specific teaching procedures, including errorless prompting and rapid prompt-fading (see chapter 12, Teaching Protocol 1); if these procedures are used *as they are described*, without additions or modifications, and data indicate that this method is ineffective for a specific child or adult, consider selecting **AMS 9**, **AMS 12**, **AMS 15**, **AMS 22**, or a method that includes 'standard signs', 'adapted signs', 'idiosyncratic signs' or 'gestures'.

- for learners who have been using this method effectively and who have acquired a large repertoire of requests, you may want to expand their speaking repertoire to include naming or describing items, activities, persons, or places, answering questions, and participating in conversations; you can do this by gradually replacing pic-symbols with printed words and making 'visually scanning and selecting printed on a large SGD by touching the screen, or by using one or two switches or eye-tracking' (**AMS 24**) their primary or concurrent method of speaking.

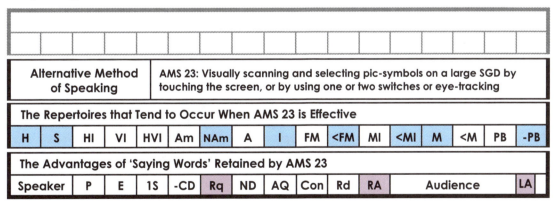

AMS 24: Visually scanning and selecting printed words on a large SGD by touching the screen, or by using one or two switches or eye-tracking

'Visually scanning and selecting printed words on a large SGD by touching the screen, or by using one or two switches or eye-tracking' should be considered for some hearing, sighted learners who exhibit a limited repertoire of requests or no requests at all, those who can readily match printed words to items, and especially those with very limited fine motor coordination or very limited motor movements.

'Visually scanning and selecting printed words on a large SGD by touching the screen, or by using one or two switches or eye-tracking':

- retains five of the ten speaker advantages of 'saying words'.
- does not provide the advantage of portability found in other methods that include '*signs*' or '*smaller devices*'. *This disadvantage cannot be overstated.*
- can result in spontaneous requests; as discussed in chapter 6, Listener Responses, Names, and Descriptions, this method permits learners to clearly name or describe items, activities, persons, or places, answer questions, and participate in conversations.
- some effort is involved in conveying requests, especially as more printed words are included in the device,
- requires two-step responses, even in the beginning, along with complex discriminations; printed words may require more time to make discriminations than photographs; many learners will find this method more difficult to learn than methods which include '*photographs*' or '*signs*'.
- may facilitate the emergence or re-emergence of spoken words or word approximations in children or the re-emergence of spoken words in adults. If spoken words emerge or re-emerge while selecting printed words, and the words are exhibited reliably as understandable repetitions, this method should be gradually discontinued and '*saying words*' should be established as the learner's primary method of speaking; if not, '*visually scanning and selecting printed words on a large SGD by touching the screen, or by using one or two switches or eye-tracking*' should be seriously considered as a permanent, primary method of speaking.
- does not permit sighted learners to read; it may, however, indicate provide some indication of comprehension if it follows exposure to printed words.
- this method retains only part of the audience advantage of '*saying words*'; in other words, a large audience of children and adults without disabilities can respond effectively to '*requests with printed words*'; an audience of peers with disabilities, however, may not be able to respond effectively to these requests.
- is often selected as a method of speaking, because of the audience advantage, and without regard to a learner's skill repertoire.
- *in sum, with this method of speaking, many of the speaker advantages of 'saying words' are lost and only part of the audience advantage is retained. In other words, it may be somewhat more difficult for a child or adult to learn to make requests, more effortful to make them, and their repertoire may be limited to requests, and when these requests are conveyed, only children and adults without disabilities will be able to understand and respond to them.*
- requires very specific teaching procedures, including errorless prompting and rapid prompt-fading (see chapter 12, Teaching Protocol 1); if these procedures are used *as they are described*, without additions or modifications, and data indicate that this method is ineffective for a specific child or adult, consider selecting **AMS 9**, **AMS 12**, **AMS 15**, **AMS 22**, or a method that includes '*standard signs*', '*adapted signs*', '*idiosyncratic signs*' or '*gestures*'.

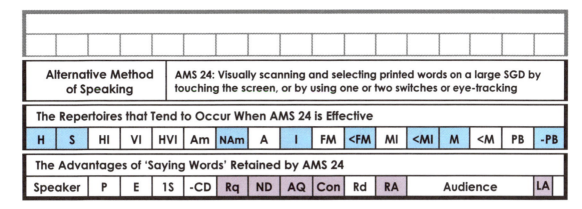

AMS 25: Typing words (Texting) with a small, electronic device

'Typing words with a small, electronic device' is used by some children and adults with hearing impairments as a secondary method of speaking. *'Typing words'* is seldom useful as a primary method for children or adults with moderate-to-severe disabilities, because it requires writing and spelling skills that result in identifiable words or word approximations. There are, however, some non-verbal adult learners who have acquired these skills and use this method effectively. *'Typing words'* can be useful as a temporary, and sometimes permanent, primary method of speaking for non-verbal children and adults who have acquired and then lost part or all of their spoken-word repertoire due to closed head injury, stroke, or other traumatic event.

'Typing words with a small, electronic device':

- retains five of the ten speaker advantages of *'saying words'*.
- requires familiarity a keyboard and a repertoire of words, which are spelled correctly or can easily be identified; does not require formal typing skills; a device with predictive text can be very helpful.
- with a small device, excellent fine motor skills and fine motor coordination are required.
- requires a considerable amount of effort to convey even simple messages.
- retains part of the audience advantage of *'saying words'*; when words are spelled correctly or can easily be identified, instructors, care providers, and peers without disabilities will understand what was *'said'*, but most peers with similar disabilities will not.

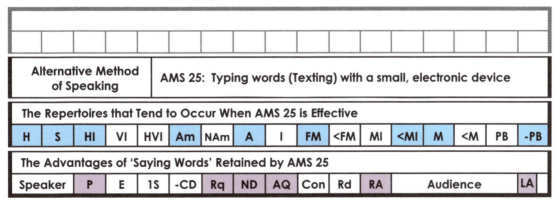

AMS 26: Typing words with a large, electronic or SGD

'Typing words with a large, electronic or SGD' is used by some children and adults with hearing impairments as a secondary method of speaking. *'Typing words'* is seldom useful as a primary method for children or adults with moderate-to-severe disabilities, because it requires writing and spelling skills that result in identifiable words or word approximations. There are, however, some non-verbal adult learners who have acquired these skills and use this method effectively. *'Typing words'* can be useful as a temporary, and sometimes permanent, primary method of speaking for non-verbal children and adults who have acquired and then lost part or all of their spoken-word repertoire due to closed head injury, stroke, or other traumatic event.

'Typing words with a large, electronic or SGD':

- retains four of the ten speaker advantages of *'saying words'*.
- requires familiarity a keyboard and a repertoire of words, which are spelled correctly or can easily be identified; does not require formal typing skills; a device with predictive text can be very helpful.
- does not provide the advantage of portability found in other methods that include *'signs'* or *'smaller devices'*. *This disadvantage cannot be overstated.*
- with a large device, some fine motor skills and fine motor coordination are still required.
- requires a considerable amount of effort to convey even simple messages.
- retains part of the audience advantage of *'saying words'*; when words are spelled correctly or can easily be identified, instructors, care providers, and peers without disabilities will understand what was 'said', but most peers with similar disabilities will not.

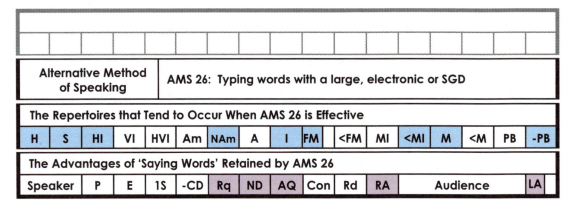

AMS 27: Typing words with a Braille Writer

'Typing words with a Braille Writer' is used by some children and adults with visual impairments as a secondary method of speaking. *'Typing words with a Braille Writer'* is seldom useful as a primary method of speaking for children or adults with moderate-to-severe disabilities, even those with visual impairments, because it requires writing and spelling skills that result in identifiable words or word approximations. There are, however, some non-verbal adult learners with visual impairments who have acquired these skills and use this method effectively.

'Typing words with a Braille Writer':

- retains four of the ten speaker advantages of *'saying words'*.
- requires familiarity a keyboard and a repertoire of words, which are spelled correctly or can easily be identified; does not require formal typing skills.
- does not provide the advantage of portability found in other methods that include *'signs'* or *'smaller devices'*. *This disadvantage cannot be overstated.*
- with a large device, some fine motor skills and fine motor coordination are required.
- requires a considerable amount of effort to convey even simple messages.
- does not retain the audience advantage of *'saying words'*; requires an audience that understands Braille.

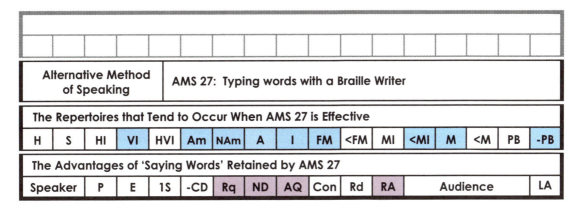

AMS 28: Typing words with a switch or eye-tracking and a large SGD

'Typing words with a switch or eye-tracking and a large SGD' is used by a small number of children and adults with very limited motor skills as a secondary method of speaking. *'Typing words'* is seldom useful as a primary method for children or adults with moderate-to-severe disabilities, because it requires writing and spelling skills that result in identifiable words or word approximations. There are, however, some non-verbal children and adults who have acquired these skills and use this method effectively. *'Typing words'* can be useful as a temporary, and sometimes permanent, primary method of speaking for non-verbal children and adults who have acquired and then lost part or all of their spoken-word repertoire due to closed head injury, stroke, or other traumatic event.

'Typing words with a switch or eye-tracking and a large SGD':

- retains four of the ten speaker advantages of *'saying words'*.
- requires familiarity a keyboard and a repertoire of words, which are spelled correctly or can easily be identified; does not require formal typing skills; a device with predictive text can be very helpful.
- with a large device, some fine motor skills and fine motor coordination are still required.
- requires a considerable amount of effort to convey even simple messages.
- retains part of the audience advantage of *'saying words'*; when words are spelled correctly or can easily be identified, instructors, care providers, and peers without disabilities will understand what was 'said', but most peers with similar disabilities will not.

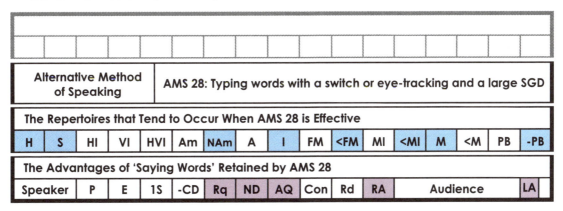

AMS 29: Scanning by listening and selecting spoken words on a large SGD by touching the screen, or by using one or two switches

'Scanning by listening and selecting spoken words on a large SGD by touching the screen, or by using one or two switches' is method of speaking used by children and adults with visual impairments and extremely limited motor skills. It is also used by some sighted learners with very limited head or eye movements. Learners need to touch the screen or exhibit a reliable motor movement that makes contact with a switch, which activates an audio scan and selects a spoken word or phrase.

'Scanning by listening and selecting spoken words on a large SGD by touching the screen, or by using one or two switches':

- retains two of the ten speaker advantages of 'saying words'.
- generally results in a limited repertoire of requests;
- retains the audience advantage of *'saying words'*; in other words, a large audience of children and adults with and without disabilities can respond effectively to these request without training.
- for some learners, the task of selecting a reliable motor movement may be quite challenging; the outcome, however, functioning as a speaker and 'making your needs and wants known', is well worth the effort.

Alternative Method of Speaking	AMS 29: Scanning by listening and selecting spoken words on a large SGD by touching the screen, or by using one or two switches													
The Repertoires that Tend to Occur When AMS 29 is Effective														
H	S	HI	VI	HVI	Am	NAm	A	I	FM	<FM	MI	<MI	M	<M	PB	-PB
The Advantages of 'Saying Words' Retained by AMS 29														
Speaker	P	E	1S	-CD	Rq	ND	AQ	Con	Rd	RA	Audience			LA

AMS 30: Scanning by touch and selecting locations on a large, adapted SGD

'Scanning by touch and selecting locations on a large, adapted SGD' is method of speaking used by children and adults with visual impairments and some fine motor coordination. The SCG will need to be adapted so that the learner can determine where his finger is without activating the device.

'Scanning by touch and selecting locations on a large, adapted SGD':

- retains two of the ten speaker advantages of 'saying words'.
- generally results in a limited repertoire of requests;
- does not provide the advantage of portability found in other methods that include *'signs'* or *'smaller devices'*. *This disadvantage cannot be overstated.*
- retains the audience advantage of *'saying words'*; in other words, a large audience of children and adults with and without disabilities can respond effectively to these requests without training.

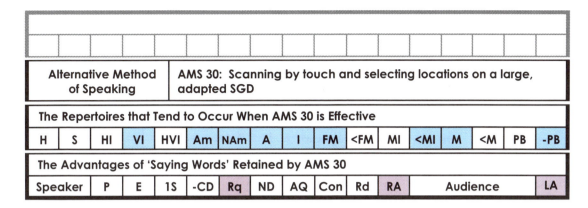

AMS 31: Visually scanning and pointing to large photographs using a binder

'*Visually scanning and pointing to large photographs using a binder*' should only be considered as a primary method speaking for learners, whose corrected visual acuity at close range is limited.

'*Visually scanning and pointing to large photographs using a binder*':

- retains two of the ten speaker advantages of '*saying words*'.
- generally results in a limited repertoire of requests;
- does not provide the advantage of portability found in some other methods that include '*signs*' and '*smaller devices*'. *This disadvantage cannot be overstated.*
- retains the audience advantage of '*saying words*'; in other words, a large audience of children and adults can respond effectively to '*requests with photographs*' without training.

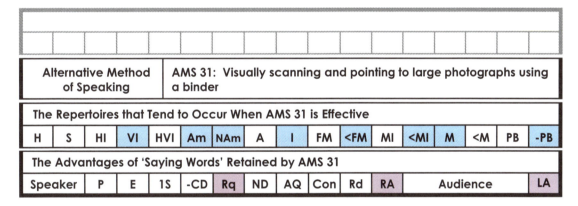

AMS 32: Visually scanning and pointing to large printed words using a binder

'*Visually scanning and pointing to large printed words using a binder*' should only be considered as a primary method speaking for learners, whose corrected visual acuity at close range is limited.

'*Visually scanning and pointing to large printed words using a binder*':

- retains four of the ten speaker advantages of '*saying words*'.
- generally results in a limited repertoire of requests; the selection of printed words may also result in a limited number of names or descriptions of items and activities, along with some answers to questions.
- does not provide the advantage of portability found in some other methods that include '*signs*' and '*smaller devices*'. *This disadvantage cannot be overstated.*
- retains part of the audience advantage of '*saying words*'; when words are spelled correctly or can easily be identified, instructors, care providers, and peers without disabilities will understand what was '*said*', but most peers with similar disabilities will not.

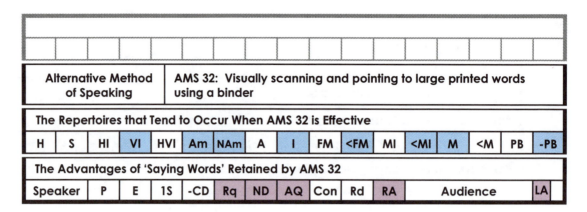

AMS 33: Visually scanning and selecting photographs presented two at a time

'*Visually scanning and selecting photographs presented two at a time*' should only be considered as a primary method speaking for learners, whose limited head, eye, and hand movements results in limited scanning skills.

'*Visually scanning and selecting photographs presented two at a time*':

- retains two of the ten speaker advantages of '*saying words*'.
- generally results in a limited repertoire of requests.
- retains the audience advantage of '*saying words*'; in other words, a large audience of children and adults can respond effectively to '*requests with photographs*' without training.

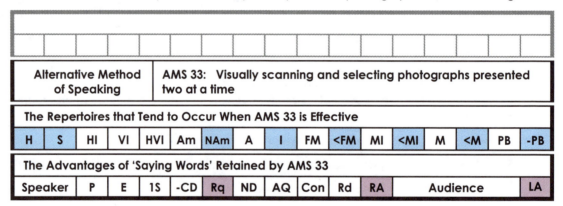

AMS 34: Visually scanning and selecting items presented two at a time

'*Visually scanning and selecting items presented two at a time*' should only be considered as a primary method speaking for learners, whose limited head, eye, and hand movements results in limited scanning skills. and who have had difficulty acquiring **AMS 33**.

'*Visually scanning and selecting items presented two at a time*':

- retains one of the ten speaker advantages of '*saying words*'.
- generally results in a very limited repertoire of requests.
- retains the audience advantage of '*saying words*'; in other words, a large audience of children and adults can respond effectively to these requests without training.

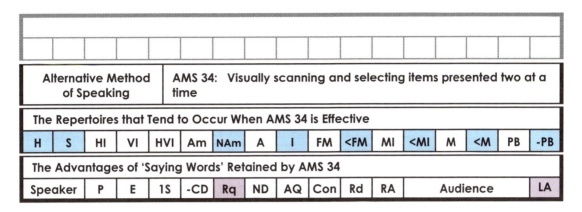

AMS 35: Scanning by touch and selecting items presented two at a time

'*Scanning by touch and selecting items presented two at a time*' should only be considered as a primary method speaking for learners with significant visual impairments, whose scanning skills are limited and who have had difficulty acquiring **AMS 18**.

'*Scanning by touch and selecting items presented two at a time*':

- retains one of the ten speaker advantages of '*saying words*'.
- generally results in a very limited repertoire of requests.
- retains the audience advantage of '*saying words*'; in other words, a large audience of children and adults can respond effectively to these requests without training.

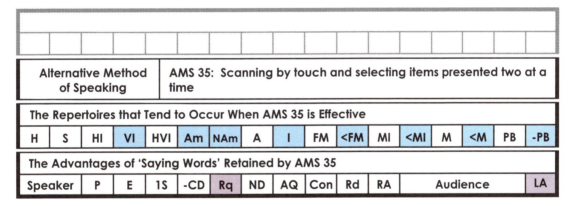

AMS 36: Looking at and selecting photographs presented one at a time

'*Looking at and selecting photographs presented one at a time*' should only be considered as a primary method speaking for learners, whose limited head, eye, and hand movements results in gazing, but no scanning skills, or who have had difficulty acquiring **AMS 33**.

'*Looking at and selecting photographs presented one at a time*':

- retains two of the ten speaker advantages of '*saying words*'.
- generally results in a limited repertoire of requests.
- retains the audience advantage of '*saying words*'; in other words, a large audience of children and adults can respond effectively to '*requests with photographs*' without training.

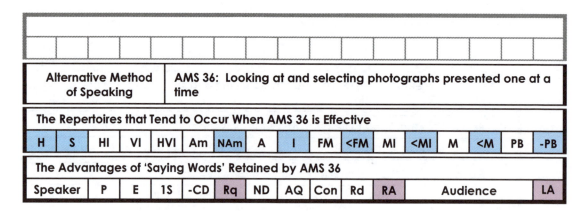

AMS 37: Looking at and selecting items presented one at a time

'*Looking at and selecting items presented one at a time*' should only be considered as a primary method speaking for learners, whose limited head, eye, and hand movements results in gazing, but no scanning skills, or who have had difficulty acquiring **AMS 33**, **34**, **or 36**.

'*Looking at and selecting items presented one at a time*':

- retains one of the ten speaker advantages of 'saying words'.
- generally results in a limited repertoire of requests.
- retains the audience advantage of '*saying words*'; in other words, a large audience of children and adults can respond effectively to these requests without training.

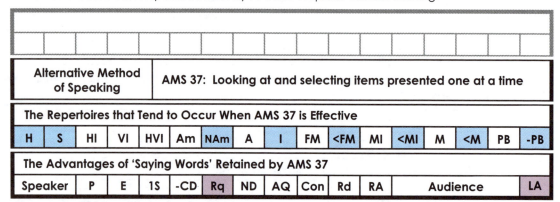

AMS 38: Touching and selecting items presented one at a time

'*Touching and selecting items presented one at a time*' should only be considered as a primary method speaking for learners with significant visual impairments, whose scanning skills are limited and who have had difficulty acquiring **AMS 18** or **AMS 35**. After touching an item, the learner selects it by maintaining the touch.

'*Touching and selecting items presented one at a time*':

- retains one of the ten speaker advantages of 'saying words'.
- generally results in a very limited repertoire of requests.
- retains the audience advantage of '*saying words*'; in other words, a large audience of children and adults can respond effectively to these requests without training.

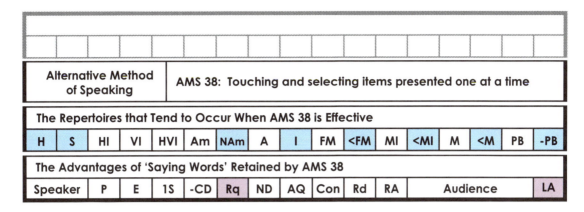

AMS 39: Scanning by listening and selecting spoken words presented two at a time

'Scanning by listening and selecting spoken words presented two at a time' is method of speaking used by children and adults with visual impairments and extremely limited motor skills or by sighted learners with very limited head or eye movements, who have had difficulty acquiring **AMS 29**. Two words or phrases are presented to the learner, who must nod or otherwise select one of the two.

'Scanning by listening and selecting spoken words presented two at a time':

- retains two of the ten speaker advantages of 'saying words'.
- generally results in a limited repertoire of requests;
- retains the audience advantage of *'saying words'*; in other words, a large audience of children and adults with and without disabilities can respond effectively to these request without training.
- for some learners, the task of selecting a reliable motor movement may be quite challenging; the outcome, however, functioning as a speaker and 'making your needs and wants known', is well worth the effort.

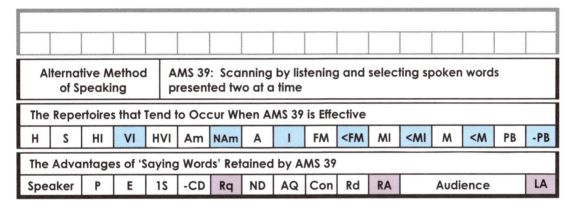

AMS 40: Listening and selecting spoken words presented one at a time

'Listening and selecting spoken words presented one at a time' is method of speaking used by children and adults with visual impairments and extremely limited motor skills or by sighted learners with very limited head or eye movements, who have had difficulty acquiring **AMS 29** or **AMS 39**. One word or phrase is presented to the learner, who must nod or make an identifiable movement within a designated number of seconds in order to select it.

'Listening and selecting spoken words presented one at a time':

- retains two of the ten speaker advantages of 'saying words'.
- generally results in a limited repertoire of requests;
- retains the audience advantage of *'saying words'*; in other words, a large audience of children and adults with and without disabilities can respond effectively to these request without training.
- for some learners, the task of selecting a reliable motor movement may be quite challenging; the outcome, however, functioning as a speaker and 'making your needs and wants known', is well worth the effort.

Alternative Method of Speaking	AMS 40: Listening and selecting spoken words presented one at a time													
The Repertoires that Tend to Occur When AMS 40 is Effective														
H	S	HI	VI	HVI	Am	NAm	A	I	FM	<FM	MI	<MI	M	<M	PB	-PB
The Advantages of 'Saying Words' Retained by AMS 40														
Speaker	P	E	1S	-CD	Rq	ND	AQ	Con	Rd	RA	Audience			LA

AMS 41: Listening to "do you want ____?" and gesturing to indicate 'yes' or 'no'

'Listening to "do you want ____?" and gesturing to indicate 'yes' or one of two switches to indicate 'yes' or 'no' is method of speaking used by children and adults, who have not had the opportunity to learn a more effective method or who have had difficulty acquiring any other method of speaking.

'Listening to "do you want ____?" and gesturing to indicate 'yes' or one of two switches to indicate 'yes' or 'no':

- retains two of the ten speaker advantages of 'saying words'.
- generally results in only a very limited repertoire of requests, which can only be made in response to very specific questions; spontaneous requests are not possible.
- retains the audience advantage of *'saying words'*; in other words, a large audience of children and adults with and without disabilities can respond effectively to these requests without training.
- should generally be replaced with a method that includes *'signs'* or *'scanning and selecting photographs'*, which permits learners to convey spontaneous requests.

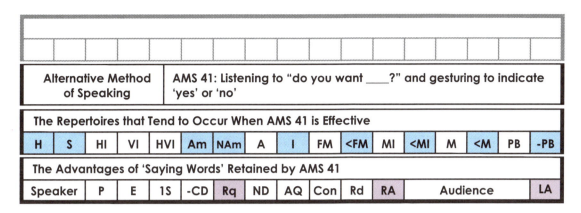

AMS 42: Listening to "do you want ___?" and activating a switch to indicate 'yes' or one of two switches to indicate 'yes' or 'no'

'Listening to "do you want ___?" and activating a switch to indicate 'yes' or one of two switches to indicate 'yes' or 'no' is method of speaking used by children and adults, who have not had the opportunity to learn a more effective method or who have had difficulty acquiring any other method of speaking.

'Listening to "do you want ___?" and activating a switch to indicate 'yes' or one of two switches to indicate 'yes' or 'no':

- retains two of the ten speaker advantages of 'saying words'.

- generally results in only a very limited repertoire of requests, which can only be made in response to very specific questions; spontaneous requests are not possible.

- retains the audience advantage of 'saying words'; in other words, a large audience of children and adults with and without disabilities can respond effectively to these requests without training.

- should generally be replaced with a method that includes 'signs' or 'scanning and selecting photographs', which permits learners to convey spontaneous requests.

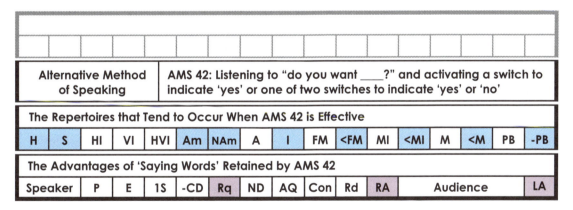

AMS 43: Reaching, pointing, gesturing, or gazing toward items or familiar locations for items

'*Reaching, pointing, gesturing, or gazing toward items or familiar locations for items*' is method of speaking used by children and adults, who have not had the opportunity to learn a more effective method or who have had difficulty acquiring any other method of speaking.

'*Reaching, pointing, gesturing, or gazing toward items or familiar locations for items*':

- retains one of the ten speaker advantages of 'saying words'.
- generally results in only a very limited repertoire of requests, which can only be made in familiar environments and in the presence of the items or activities requested.
- retains the audience advantage of '*saying words*'; in other words, a large audience of children and adults with and without disabilities can respond effectively to '*requests by leading*' without training.
- should generally be replaced with a method that includes '*signs*' or '*scanning and selecting photographs*', which permits learners to convey requests in the absence of what is being requested, and which can greatly increase a learner's speaking repertoire.

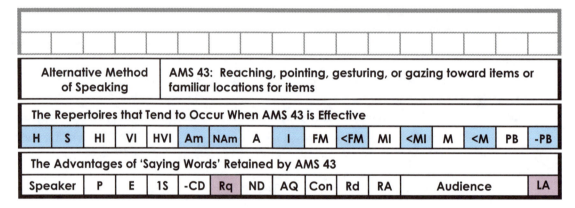

Alternative Method of Speaking	AMS 43: Reaching, pointing, gesturing, or gazing toward items or familiar locations for items												
The Repertoires that Tend to Occur When AMS 43 is Effective													
H	S	HI	VI	HVI	Am	NAm	A	I	FM	<FM	MI	<MI	M	<M	PB	-PB
The Advantages of 'Saying Words' Retained by AMS 43													
Speaker	P	E	1S	-CD	Rq	ND	AQ	Con	Rd	RA	Audience		LA

AMS 44: Leading others to items or to familiar locations for items

'*Leading others to items or to familiar locations for items*' is method of speaking used by children and adults, who have not had the opportunity to learn a more effective method or who have had difficulty acquiring any other method of speaking.

'*Leading others to items or to familiar locations for items*':

- retains one of the ten speaker advantages of 'saying words'.
- generally results in only a very limited repertoire of requests, which can only be made in familiar environments and in the presence of the items or activities requested.
- retains the audience advantage of '*saying words*'; in other words, a large audience of children and adults with and without disabilities can respond effectively to '*requests by leading*' without training.
- should generally be replaced with a method that includes '*signs*' or '*scanning and selecting photographs*', which permits learners to convey requests in the absence of what is being requested, and which can greatly increase a learner's speaking repertoire.

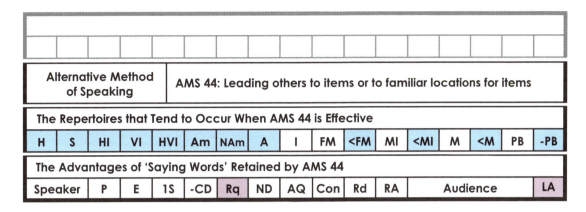

Alternative Method of Speaking	AMS 44: Leading others to items or to familiar locations for items												
The Repertoires that Tend to Occur When AMS 44 is Effective													
H	S	HI	VI	HVI	Am	NAm	A	I	FM	<FM	MI	<MI	M	<M	PB	-PB
The Advantages of 'Saying Words' Retained by AMS 44													
Speaker	P	E	1S	-CD	Rq	ND	AQ	Con	Rd	RA	Audience		LA

AMS 45: Selecting items or completing activities in the presence of another person that are typically paired with or precede preferred items or activities

'Selecting items or completing activities in the presence of another person that are typically paired with or precede preferred items or activities' is method of speaking used by children and adults, who have not had the opportunity to learn a more effective method or who have had difficulty acquiring any other method of speaking.

'Selecting items or completing activities in the presence of another person that are typically paired with or precede preferred items or activities':

- retains one of the ten speaker advantages of 'saying words'.

- generally results in only a very limited repertoire of requests, which can only be made in familiar environments and in the presence of the items or activities requested.

- retains the audience advantage of *'saying words'*; in other words, a large audience of children and adults with and without disabilities can respond effectively to these requests without training.

- should generally be replaced with a method that includes *'signs'* or *'scanning and selecting photographs'*, which permits learners to convey requests in the absence of what is being requested, and which can greatly increase a learner's speaking repertoire.

Alternative Method of Speaking	AMS 45: Selecting items or completing activities in the presence of another person that are typically paired with or precede preferred items or activities												
The Repertoires that Tend to Occur When AMS 45 is Effective													
H	S	HI	VI	HVI	Am	NAm	A	I	FM	<FM	MI	<MI	M	<M	PB	-PB
The Advantages of 'Saying Words' Retained by AMS 45													
Speaker	P	E	1S	-CD	Rq	ND	AQ	Con	Rd	RA	Audience		LA

AMS 46: Touching a photograph or printed words using a speech-generating device that contains only one message

'Touching a photograph or printed words using a speech-generating device that contains only one message' is method of speaking used by children and adults who have not had the opportunity to learn a more effective method or who have had difficulty acquiring any other method of speaking.

'Touching a photograph or printed words using a speech-generating device that contains only one message':

- retains two of the ten speaker advantages of *'saying words'*.
- generally results in only one request; can result in a limited repertoire of requests if the device is reprogrammed throughout the day in response to apparent changes in motivation.
- retains the audience advantage of *'saying words'*; in other words, a large audience of children and adults with and without disabilities can respond effectively to these requests without training.
- should almost always be replaced with a method that includes *'signs'* or *'scanning and selecting photographs'*, which permits learners to convey many requests.

Alternative Method of Speaking	AMS 46: Touching a photograph or printed words using a speech-generating device that contains only one message													
The Repertoires that Tend to Occur When AMS 46 is Effective														
H	S	HI	VI	HVI	Am	NAm	A	I	FM	<FM	MI	<MI	M	<M	PB	-PB
The Advantages of 'Saying Words' Retained by AMS 46														
Speaker	P	E	1S	-CD	Rq	ND	AQ	Con	Rd	RA	Audience			LA

Chapter 7. Speaking and Listening Skills
7a. Requests and Related Listener Responses

Requests

Requests permit a learner to respond as a speaker and to access the initial and most important outcome of communication and language -- preferred items, activities, and people when the learner wants or needs the same. As shown in Table 1, requests occur when (1) a learner indicates that he wants or needs specific items, activities, or persons, (2) says words, forms signs, selects pictures, or selects, types or writes words, and (3) gains access to specific items, activities, or persons. If the learner says a word, forms a sign, selects a picture, or selects, types or writes a word that matches the word or sign commonly used to designate that item, activity, place, or person, the request is considered 'correct' and the learner gains access to the item, activity, or person that he indicated he wanted. If not, the instructor, care provider, or parent prompts the learner to make the correct response before providing access to the item, activity, place, or person he wanted. For example, as shown in Table 1, an instructor places a cookie in front of a learner two hours after his last meal. If the learner reaches for the cookie and says or signs 'cookie', the request is correct and the care provider responds by providing access to the cookie. If the learner says or signs 'cracker', the request is incorrect and the care provider must prompt the learner to say or sign 'cookie' before providing access to the cookie. A second example involving adult children who select pictures or who select, type, or print words is also shown in Table 1.

mands reinforcers when motivating operations (MOs) related to those reinforcers occur.

contrives and captures a motivating operation.

Table 1. Requests

The learner wants or needs a specific item, activity, or person [MO] ⟶	The learner says words, forms signs, selects pictures, or selects, types or writes words [R] ⟶	The learner gains access to what or whom he wants [S^R]
An instructor places a cookie in front of a learner two hours after the last meal and the learner reaches for the cookie	The learner says or signs 'cookie'	The instructor provides access to the cookie
	The learner says or signs 'cracker'	The instructor prompts the learner to say or sign 'cookie' before providing access to the cookie
A mother sits in her adult child's favorite chair and the adult child points to the chair	The adult child selects a picture of a chair or selects, types, or prints the word 'chair'	The mother provides access to the chair
	The adult child selects a picture of a 'bed' or selects, types, or prints the word 'bed'	The mother prompts her adult child to select a picture of a 'chair' or to select, type, or print the word 'chair' before providing access to the chair

MO: a motivating operation has occurred
R: the learner exhibits a mand
S^R: learner gains access to a reinforcer

Requests should be distinguished from names or descriptions, also called labels or expressive object labels, which permit a learner to describe her or his experiences as these experiences are occurring. Names occur when the learner is directed with spoken words, signs, or printed words to produce one

tacts; not to be confused with the bi-directional naming relation described by Horne and Lowe (see references).

or more spoken words or signs, or to select one or more printed words in the presence of specific items, activities, or people, and result in praise or other forms of social approval. For example, a teacher points to a 'cookie' or a picture of a 'cookie' and says 'what's that' or 'what do you see': the learner says or signs 'cookie' or selects the word 'cookie', and the teacher responds with an expression such as 'well done' or 'that's correct'. *(non-verbal stimuli, and result in forms of generalized, conditioned reinforcement)*

Requests should also be distinguished from comments, which are names, with a minor request component, that is, a request for very brief contact with an audience. Comments permit a learner to share information or an experience with someone else. For example, the learner says 'Look, it's a big dog' or 'Mom, [it's] raining'. *(mand-tacts)*

Requests should also be distinguished from listener responses, which permit the learner to honor the requests of others. Listener responses occur when the learner is directed with spoken words, signs, or written words to point to people, items, pictures, or written words, or to complete one or more activities; these responses are also called receptive IDs and receptive commands respectively, and, again, result in praise or other forms of social approval. For example, a teacher puts a 'cookie' or a picture of a 'cookie' in an array of three or more items or pictures and says or signs 'find the cookie' or 'where's the cookie'. The learner points to the 'cookie' and the teacher responds with an expression such as 'good' or 'that's right'. In another example, a teacher places a 'plate of cookies' on a table in the kitchen and proceeds to another room where the learner is sitting on a couch. The teachers says 'please go and get the plate of cookies in the kitchen'. The learner goes to the kitchen, retrieves 'the plate of cookies', and brings it to the other room. The teacher then responds by saying 'thank you'.

Finally, requests should be distinguished from answers to questions, which permit the learner to respond to the requests of others by describing items and persons that are not present and activities that are no longer occurring. Answers to questions also permit the learner to retain an audience and to engage in conversation. Answers to questions occur when the learner is requested with spoken words, signs, printed words, or written words to respond with words, signs, or printed words that do not match the original words or signs. These responses result in praise, other forms of social approval, or requests for additional responses. For example, a care provider says or signs 'where are your shoes'. The learner says, signs, or types 'in my room' and the care provider says 'let's get them so we can go outside'. *(intraverbals)*

Related Listener Responses

Requests represent the most important function of communication and language. An equally important and closely related function is represented by Listener Responses. These related skills include:

- waiting -- after requesting a specific item, activity, or person, the learner is told to wait...the learner waits without exhibiting problem behavior or additional requests...and, gains access to the requested item, activity, or person;
- accepting removals, making transitions, sharing, and taking turns -- after preferred items or activities are removed and/or the learner is directed to a new activity, or after the learner is directed to share a preferred item or take turns with a preferred activity...the learner begins participating in the new activity or continues participating in the current activity without exhibiting problem behavior...and, gains access to forms of social approval;
- completing previously acquired tasks -- the learner is directed to complete one or more tasks...the learner does so without exhibiting problem behavior...and gains access to forms of social approval; and,
- accepting no -- after requesting a specific item, activity, or person, the learner is told 'no'...the learner continues participating in the current activity without exhibiting problem behavior...and, gains access to forms of social approval.

Other basic listener responses are included in the next chapter. The first group of Requests and Related Listener Responses are designated as *must-have skills* and make up five of what we call **The Essential 8** -- eight skills that are essential for a happy, fulfilling, and productive life as a child or as an adult.

These Must-have Requests and Related Listener Responses should always be occurring without prompts, before instruction includes Names and Descriptions or Answers to Questions. Self-injurious, aggressive, destructive, and disruptive behavior, which often occur in learners with limited requesting repertoires and poor listener responses, can often be avoided with an emphasis on these skills.

ESSENTIAL FOR LIVING
Requests and Related Listener Responses

Must-have Indications of Interest. In order for our children and adults with disabilities to learn to make requests, they must be able to indicate what interests them:

- when items and activities are made available,
- when items and activities are offered to them, and
- when items and activities are presented one at a time.

R1. Instructors, parents, and care providers begin to determine the interests of the learner

Before assessing and teaching requests, we must begin by determining the interests of the learner in specific items and activities. Some learners indicate interest in a wide variety of items and activities readily and frequently. Others indicate interest in only a few items or activities. Some learner's interests seem to be limited to one or more items they carry with them wherever they go or a repetitive movement they exhibit every few minutes throughout the day. Still others struggle to make responses that would indicate interest and to make these responses only when they are interested. Many older learners may, in the beginning, re-quire permission to indicate interest in specific items or activities.[1]

items and activities that may function as reinforcers and for which mands should be targeted

Begin by interviewing one or both parents, an instructor, or care provider who spends a considerable amount of time each day with the learner. Ask them to make a list of the learner's favorite items and activities and to prioritize this list from most to least favorite, using column **R1** of the Favorite Items and Activities Data Recording Form, a part of which is shown in Table 2 (also see the Appendix). This list should include favorite foods, drinks, toys, items of clothing, forms of entertainment, or other favorite activities. Based on your interactions and your experiences with the learner, you should also add items or activities to column **R1**, especially if parents and other instructors or care providers were only able to provide a short list. If the learner carries items with her or exhibits repetitive movements every few minutes, list these items and behaviors in the designated area of this form (see Table 2). If the learner readily accepts items and activities from instructors, care providers, and parents without resistance, and your experience with the learner suggests that this list is accurate, you can skip **R2 and R3**, score both NA (not applicable), and proceed to **R4**.

conduct an indirect preference assessment

R2. The learner indicates interest in specific items and activities made available one at a time

Begin by making each of the items and activities listed in column **R1** available *one at a time* in the learner's immediate environment without making direct contact with the learner. In other words, begin placing each of these items or provide items that are part of each of these activities in locations that, within a few seconds, will be within reach or within sensory contact of the learner. Provide the items one at a time and alternate items. If the learner indicates interest by approaching, consuming, or interacting with an item or an activity, simply permit him to do so without interacting with him or placing demands on him. As indicated in Table 2, record this indication of interest in column **R2** by drawing a circle around the numeral '1'. If the learner does not indicate interest in the item or activity within two minutes, withdraw it, and record this lack of interest by drawing a forward slash through this numeral. When each of the items and activities has been made available five times, select those in which the learner has indicated interest four or five times by placing a check mark in the box at the right side of this column. Repeat these procedures with the remainder of the items and activities in column **R1**. Then, with the checked items and activities, proceed to **R3**. Some learners may indicate interest in every item or activity, while others, including some of those who carry items with them or who exhibit repetitive movements, may not approach, consume, or interact with any of the items or activities. If either occurs, proceed to **R3**.

Begin to conduct a direct preference assessment with single stimulus engagement and without contact with another person.

---

[1] Many programs serving learners with disabilities have emphasized responding as a listener almost to the exclusion of responding as a speaker. Many of these learners have been taught, albeit inadvertently, to wait for permission to indicate 'what they want'.

Table 2.
Determining the Interests of Learners by Interviewing Others (**R1**)
and by Observing the Learner (**R2-R5**)

ESSENTIAL FOR LIVING
Favorite Items and Activities Data Recording Form

Learner: _____ Birthdate: _____ Age: _____

School, Home, Day Activity, or Residential Program: _____

Interests of the learner as indicated in a interview by persons who know the learner well	Interests of the learner as indicated by learner...							
R1: Items and activities are ranked from most favorite to least favorite All items and activities on this list go to **R2** or **R4**	**R2**: when items or activities are made available one at a time All interests that are indicated go to **R3**		**R3**: when items or activities are given one at a time When interest is indicated in four or more items or activities go to **R4**		**R4**: when items or activities are presented one at a time When interest is indicated in four or more items or activities go to **R5** or **R7**		**R5**: when items or activities are presented two or more at a time All interests that are indicated go to **R7**	
1- candy	①②③④⑤	✓	①❷③④⑤	✓	①②③④⑤	✓	①②❸④❺	✓
2- cookies	①②③❹⑤	✓	①②③④⑤	✓	①②③④⑤	✓	❶②❸④⑤	✓
3- juice	❶②③④⑤	✓	①②❸④⑤	✓	①②❸④⑤	✓	❶②③④❺	✓
4- markers	❶②③❹⑤		1 2 3 4 5		1 2 3 4 5		1 2 3 4 5	
5- puzzles	❶❷③④❺		1 2 3 4 5		1 2 3 4 5		1 2 3 4 5	
6- computer	①②③④⑤	✓	①②③④⑤	✓	①②③④⑤	✓	①②③❹⑤	✓
7- back rub	①②③❹⑤	✓	①②❸❹❺		❶②③❹❺		1 2 3 4 5	
8- yogurt	①❷③④⑤	✓	①②③④⑤	✓	①②③❹❺		1 2 3 4 5	
9- potato chips	1 2 3 4 5		1 2 3 4 5		①②③❹⑤	✓	①②③❹⑤	✓
10- DVD player	1 2 3 4 5		1 2 3 4 5		1 2 3 4 5		①❷③④⑤	✓
11-	1 2 3 4 5		1 2 3 4 5		1 2 3 4 5		1 2 3 4 5	
12-	1 2 3 4 5		1 2 3 4 5		1 2 3 4 5		1 2 3 4 5	
13-	1 2 3 4 5		1 2 3 4 5		1 2 3 4 5		1 2 3 4 5	
14-	1 2 3 4 5		1 2 3 4 5		1 2 3 4 5		1 2 3 4 5	
15-	1 2 3 4 5		1 2 3 4 5		1 2 3 4 5		1 2 3 4 5	
16-								
17-								
18-								
19-								
20-								
Items carried around by the learner or repetitive behaviors the learner exhibits frequently:								
1- a bandana which the learner wraps around her left hand and wrist								
2-								

R3. **The learner indicates interest in items and activities from R2 given one at a time**

If you skipped **R2**, also skip **R3**, and proceed to **R4**.

If you did not skip **R2**, approach the learner and immediately begin to give her each of the checked items and activities one at a time. In other words, place these items in the learner's hands or put the learner in contact with these items or activities one at a time. Remember not to place any demands on the learner. This procedure pairs the learner's preferred items and activities with the behavior of instructors, care providers, and parents, which will make it more likely that, when it is time to teach requests, the learner will readily approach these individuals and respond without resistance to prompts and other demands. Alternate items and activities, until each has been offered five times. If the learner indicates interest by consuming or interacting with an item or activity, permit the learner to do this and indicate your approval (e.g., 'cookies, good choice'). As shown in Table 2, record this indication of interest in column **R3** by drawing a circle around the numeral '1'. If the learner does not indicate interest in an item or activity within a few seconds (learners with delayed movements may require a longer period of time to respond), indicate your approval (e.g., 'I understand; you don't want the cookies.'), withdraw the item or activity, and record this lack of interest by drawing a forward slash through this numeral. When each of the items and activities has been given to the learner five times, select the items or activities in which the learner has indicated interest four or five times by placing a check mark in the box at the right side of this column.

Noncontingent stimulus-stimulus pairings of preferred items and activities with the behavior of instructors, care providers, and parents will increase the probability that these behaviors will function as reinforcers and that, when it is time to teach mands, prompts will function as establishing operations which increase, rather than decrease, the value of the items and activities, making it more likely that learners will approach, rather than avoid instructors, care providers, and parents.

For learners who did not respond to any items or activities in **R2**, and who carry items with them wherever they go, or who exhibit repetitive movements every few minutes, withdraw these items and interrupt these movements and *immediately* give them one of the first three or four items or activities on the Favorite Items and Activities Data Recording Form. If the learner begins to indicate interest in some items or activities, continue with the procedures previously described. If the learner does not begin to indicate interest in any item or activity or exhibits severe problem behavior, consult a behavior analyst or a comparable professional for assistance.

For other learners who do not respond to any items or activities, provide permission to do so by saying 'do you want this'. If the learner begins to indicate interest in some items or activities, continue with the procedures previously described.

If, as a result of any of the aforementioned procedures, the learner has indicated interest in two or fewer items or activities, interview others who know the learner well, add new items or activities to column **R1**, and continue with these procedures. As soon as the learner indicates interest in four or more items or activities, proceed to **R4**. As the learner moves on to **R4** or **R5**, continue with **R3** until the learner has indicated interest in a total of twenty items and activities.

R4. **The learner indicates interest in items and activities from R1, R2, or R3 presented one at a time**

If you skipped **R2** and **R3**, approach the learner and immediately begin to present items or activities in column **R1** on the Favorite Items and Activities Data Recording Form (see Table 2). If you completed **R3**, approach the learner and begin to present each of the items and activities that were previously given and in which she indicated interest four or five times. In other words, place each item or each item that is part of an activity near the learner so that the learner is aware of its presence and 'wait'. Remember to present these items and activities one at a time without placing any demands on the learner. If the learner indicates interest by gesturing toward an item or activity with one or more of the following movements --

- ☐ smiling
- ☐ blinking
- ☐ moving the eyes
- ☐ moving the lips
- ☐ nodding
- ☐ leaning against

☐ turning toward
☐ making a noise
☐ reaching
☐ pointing
☐ touching
☐ [a movement available to the learner] _____

-- acknowledge the selection (e.g., 'oh, you want the ball') and provide the learner with immediate access to the corresponding item or activity. If the learner has a limited repertoire of gestures, and seems hesitant to respond, prompt a gestural movement using a demonstration or hand-over-hand prompt. Wait a few seconds for the learner to respond (learners with delayed movements may require a longer period of time to respond). If the learner completes the indication of interest by accepting and consuming, or interacting with the item or activity, indicate your approval (e.g., 'you've got the markers'). Then, as shown in Table 2, record this indication of interest in column **R4** by drawing a circle around the numeral '1'. If the learner does not indicate interest in an item or activity within two minutes, indicate your approval (e.g., 'I understand; you don't want a cookie; that's fine with me.'), withdraw the item or activity, and record this lack of interest by drawing a forward slash through this numeral. When each of the items and activities has been made available five times, select those in which the learner has indicated interest four or five times by placing a check mark in the box at the right side of this column.

If, as you are working with the learner, she begins to indicate 'a new interest', add this item or activity to columns **R1** and **R4** (see Table 2). As soon as the learner indicates interest in four or more items or activities four or five times, when these items and activities are presented one at a time, you may proceed to **R5** or **R7**. In other words, you can either teach the learner to indicate interests by making choices among several items presented or encountered at the same time (**R5**) or to make requests for the items in which he has already indicated interest when they are presented one at a time (**R4**). If you decide to move on to **R7**, come back and teach **R5** at a later point in time. As the learner moves on to **R5** or **R7**, continue with **R3** and **R4** until the learner has indicated interest in a total of twenty items and activities.

Should-have Indications of Interest. In order for children and adults with moderate-to-severe disabilities to acquire a large repertoire of requests, they should be able to indicate what interests them by:

● gesturing toward items or activities presented two or more at a time, and
● leading others to specific items, or completing activities that are typically paired with or precede other specific activities.

R5. **Indicates interest in specific items or activities presented two or more at a time (makes choices)**

Many, but not all children and adults, can learn to indicate interests by making choices among several items presented or encountered at the same time. This provides learners with a distinct advantage in daily living, as several preferred items and activities are often available at the same time. *Making choices, however, is not a prerequisite for making requests.* In other words, it is not necessary for the learner to complete **R5** in order to begin **R7**. If a child or an adult learns to make requests for several items or activities without prompts, but has not completed **R2-4**, or **R5**, these skills should be added to his program.

Begin with items and activities in which the learner has already indicated interest 4 or 5 times when these same items and activities were presented one at a time (see the checked items and activities in column **R4**). If, as you are working with the learner, she begins to indicate 'a new interest', add this new item or activity to the list in columns **R1** and **R5**. For learners who carry items with them or exhibit repetitive movements, you may need to withdraw these items and interrupt these movements in order to obtain indications of interest in other items and activities.

Approach the learner and begin to present each of the items or activities two or three at a time, alternating and mixing items until each item is presented five times. In other words, place two or three items or activities, or some combination thereof, near the learner so that the learner is aware of their presence and 'wait'. Remember to alternate and mix items without placing any demands on the learner. If the learner indicates interest by gesturing toward one or other of the items or activities, acknowledge the indication (e.g., 'I see that you want the choco- Begin conducting a preference assessment with two stimuli and replacement late milk') and provide the learner with immediate access to the corresponding item or activity. If the learner completes the indication of interest by accepting and consuming or interacting with the item or activity, indicate your approval (e.g., 'enjoy your chocolate milk'). Then, record this indication of interest in column **R5** by drawing a circle around the numeral '1'. If the learner indicates lack of interest by not gesturing toward any of the items or activities, permit him to do this and indicate your approval (e.g., 'you don't want either of these; that's fine). If the learner indicates lack of interest by gesturing toward one item or activity and then not accepting, consuming, or interacting with the item, permit him to do this and indicate your approval (e.g., 'I understand; you don't want the crackers'). Then, record this lack of interest by drawing a forward slash through this numeral. When each of the items and activities has been presented five times, select the items or activities in which the learner indicated interest three or more times by placing a check mark in the box at the right side of this column (see Table 2). Then, proceed to **R7** and begin to teach requests for these items and activities. Requests for items and activities in column **R1**, but not in column **R5**, may be taught at a later time.

Many children and adults already indicate interest in specific items or activities by leading others to these items, to locations where these items are typically found, or to items that are part of these activities (e.g., taking care providers by the arm and leading them to the cabinet where the cookies are kept). If a learner does not begin to do this, prompt her to do so with items and activities in column **R5**. Some learners obtain items or complete activities that are typically paired with items or activities in which they are interested (e.g., getting the car keys and putting on a jacket). Whenever learners do this, acknowledge their indications of interest, add these new items or activities to the list in columns **R1** and **R5,** and begin to teach requests for the same. For some learners, these methods of indicating interest also function as methods of speaking (**AMS 43-44**) . These methods have significant limitations (see **AMS 43-44**), and should be replaced with other methods whenever possible.

Must-have Requests and Related Listener Responses. In order to begin functioning effectively as speakers, learners must acquire or have already acquired vocal skills or motor movements that permit the selection of a method of speaking. Then, learners must begin, as most young children do, by 'saying what they most want to say'. This insures that they will continue making the effort to 'say things'. Learners most want to request highly preferred items and activities when they want them. To make this task easier to acquire, they must begin:

- requesting items and activities that can be made frequently and immediately available, and
- requesting that certain unpleasant situations be removed or reduced in intensity.

As they learn to make these requests, they must also begin:

- waiting for the requests to be honored,
- accepting 'no' when they are not honored,
- accepting the removal or lack of availability of the items and activities they were requesting,
- sharing and taking turns obtaining preferred items and activities,
- completing required tasks or activities between opportunities to make requests, and
- makes transitions from preferred items and activities to required tasks.

Must-have requests also include:

- forcefully requesting that an intruder or a person making sexual advances go away,
- requesting 'help' in threatening or dangerous situations,
- making a generalized request for an audience, and
- making a request for a communication board, book, or device.

Must-have requests generally include just one word, one sign, or one picture.

R6. **Exhibits a reliable motor movement that permits a learner to use an alternative method of speaking which includes selecting photographs, pic-symbols, printed words, or letters**

Some learners with significant orthopedic impairments who do not exhibit spoken-word repetitions (i.e., who are aligned with Vocal Profiles 3-6), are not able to use an alternative method of speaking that includes '*forming signs*'. A reliable finger, hand, arm, leg, foot, shoulder, head, chin, facial, lip, or mouth movement that can be performed and released must be selected or acquired that permits these learners to use a method of speaking that includes pointing, touching, activating an electronic switch or device, or depressing a key, to select photographs, pic-symbols, or printed words, or type letters (**AMS9-AMS 40**).

R7. Makes requests for highly preferred snack foods, drinks, non-food items, or activities that can be made frequently and immediately available

Now that the learner has indicated interest in four or more items or activities which have been paired with an instructor, care provider, or parent and presented one at a time (**R4**) and possibly two at a time (**R5**), begin teaching requests for these same items and activities. 'Making requests' is one of **The Essential 8**. This skill permits learners to function effectively as speakers. With out this skill, they may begin to exhibit problem behavior, especially when *they want specific, preferred items and activities* and they cannot make requests for the same.

motivating operations related to specific reinforcers are strong.

Before beginning to teach children or adults to make requests, you must first select a method of speaking for each learner (see chapter 6). Once this has been accomplished, begin teaching learners to make requests for specific, highly preferred items and activities that can be made frequently and immediately available (e.g., cookies, juice, soda, tickles, hugs, movies).

If the learner's method of speaking is 'saying words', begin by teaching requests for 4-6 items or activities at the same time. If the learner's method of speaking includes 'signs', and she imitates fine motor movements, or if the learner 'selects pictures' and she matches pictures to corresponding objects, begin by teaching requests for 4-6 items or activities at the same time. For all other learners, begin by teaching requests for 2-3 items or activities. For most learners, it is not advisable to begin by teaching a request for only one item or activity at a time. Learners who acquire one spoken word, one sign, or one picture selection request, tend to perseverate on this word, sign, or picture selection, even when they want something else, making it very difficult to prompt and teach a request for a new item or activity. A protocol for teach requests is included in chapter 12.

In general, do not begin by teaching generalized requests: 'please', 'more', 'help', 'want', or 'eat'. These requests require another word, sign, or picture to have any meaning (e.g., 'want juice' or 'more tickling') and tend to interfere with the acquisition of requests for specific items and activities. Except for **R14** and **R18**, generalized requests should be taught after learners have acquired a substantial repertoire of requests for specific, preferred items and activities (**R7-8**, **R22-23**, **R27**, **R30-31**).

In general, do not begin by teaching mands for generalized, positive reinforcers.

Also, *in most circumstances, it is not advisable to begin by teaching requests for avoidance or escape from required tasks -- e.g., 'break', 'stop', or 'finished'*. These requests pair unpleasant situations with the behavior of instructors, care providers, and parents, making it more likely that, in the future, learners will withdraw from these individuals.

In most circumstances, do not begin by teaching mands for generalized, negative reinforcers

Some learners, with few to no requests, exhibit intense and frequent self-injurious, aggressive, and destructive behavior. When this occurs, it is highly advisable to enlist the services of a behavior analyst with extensive experience with these forms of problem behavior. *When these problem behaviors have resulted in escape or avoidance in the past, many behavior analysts will recommend that one of the learner's first few requests result in this same outcome*. While this may be necessary in some circumstances, we prefer to begin by reducing demands, making escape or avoidance less valuable, and teaching requests for highly preferred items and activities.

When problem behaviors are a function of avoidance or escape, many behavior analysts will recommend that "break" be one of the learner's first mands.

When you are teaching requests, circumstances will occur that will require the learner to 'wait', 'accept no', accept the withdrawal of preferred items and activities, and complete required tasks or activities between opportunities to make requests. As such, it is highly desirable to teach **R9-16**, along with **R7** and **R8**.

Continue with the procedures described in this section and those that apply from **The Essential 8** until the learner is requesting 10 items or activities without prompts (Ind). As you begin to teach requests that are part of **R22** and **R23** gradually fade the presence of the requested items and items that are part of the requested activities in **R7** and **R8**.

R8. Requests the opportunity to entertain themselves or to reduce anxiety by making stereotypic movements with highly preferred items or engaging in highly preferred stereotypic activities   produce forms of automatic positive or negative reinforcement

For learners who frequently make stereotypic movements with specific items or engage in stereotypic activities, consider teaching them to make requests for these items and activities. It is generally advisable to do this only after learners have acquired 5-6 requests in **R7**. These items and activities may include: 'a piece of yarn', 'a page from a magazine and rolled-up to form a magic wand', 'a Raggedy Ann doll', a shoestring', 'making specific finger movements', 'reciting part of the script from Dora', 'putting toy cars in a straight line', or 'rearranging items on a shelf', to name a few we have encountered. Teaching requests for these items and activities requires withdrawing access or interrupting engagement, which often results in an immediate and substantial change in motivation and one or more instances of problem behavior. Providing free and uninterrupted access to these items and activities for awhile and teaching requests for them after acquiring requests for other highly preferred items and activities, often results in only a slight change in motivation and a reduced likelihood of problem behavior.

Many professionals will recommend that access to these items be eliminated or that these activities be interrupted every time they occur. Our experience, on the other hand, suggests that access and engagement be limited to specific, well-defined situations and that requests for these items and activities be taught and honored only within these situations.

R9. Waits after making requests for each of the items and activities in R7 and R8 for gradually increasing periods of time

'Waiting' after making a request is one of **The Essential 8** and should be taught as a child or adult is learning to request each of the items and activities in **R7** and **R8**. 'Waiting' is defined as follows: after the learner exhibits a request, either of two people direct the learner to wait and the learner completes other required activities and does not exhibit problem behavior for periods of time ranging from one second to 20 minutes. Learners are expected to 'wait' as defined for ten of the items and activities from **R7** and **R8**. Many children and adults have not acquired this skill. When they are required to wait, they often exhibit problem behavior. A protocol for teaching 'waiting' is included in chapter 12.

R10. Accepts the removal of access to 10 items or activities from R7 and R8 by a person in authority

'Accepting or responding appropriately to the removal of access to preferred items or activities' is a one of **The Essential 8**. When the removal of access is exhibited by persons in authority, 'accepting' should be taught shortly after a child or adult has learned to request each of the items and activities in **R7** and **R8**. This behavior is defined as follows: after the learner makes a request for an item or activity, and spends some time interacting with that item or activity, either of two people in authority direct the learner to 'give them' or 'put away' the item or activity and the learner relinquishes access and continues to make other required responses without making requests for the removed item or activity, making requests for other items or activities, exhibiting problem behavior, or resisting or requiring prompts, even when strong motivating events occur. Learners are expected to 'accept the removal of access' as defined for 10 of the items and activities from **R7** and **R8**. Many learners have not acquired this skill. When access to preferred items or activities is removed, they often exhibit problem behavior. A protocol for teaching this skill is included in chapter 12. When the removal of access is exhibited by peers, 'responding appropriately' should be taught as part of **R46**.

R11. Completes 10 consecutive, brief, previously acquired tasks

'Completing brief, previously acquired tasks' is one of **The Essential 8** and *should be taught as learners are beginning to acquire requests* from **R7** and **R8**, a few matching and imitation skills (**M1-M3** and **Im1-2**), a few listener responses (**LR1-LR11**) and daily living skills (**DLS-EDF1-9, DLS-Slp1-2, MT1-5, DLS-AHS1-15, DLS-HS1-8**) related to learner health and safety. These previously acquired tasks should gradually be interspersed between opportunities to make requests until learners complete 10 consecutive tasks without problem behavior and without complaints. A protocol for teaching this skill is provided in chapter 12.

R12. **Shares or takes turns obtaining access to each of the items and activities in R7 and R8 with an instructor, care provider, parent, or peer**

'Sharing or taking turns' is also one of **The Essential 8** and should be taught shortly after a child or adult has learned to request each of the items and activities in **R7** and **R8**. This skill, which includes **R10** and **R9**, is defined as follows: after a learner makes a request for an item or activity and spends a few minutes receiving several items or interacting with the activity, a peer makes a request for the same item or activity and the learner provides shared or alternate access without exhibiting problem behavior. Learners are expected to 'share and take turns' as defined with respect to 10 of the items and activities from **R7** and **R8**. Please note that this skill does not require that learners make or honor requests from peers (see **R44-45**). Many children and adults have not acquired this skill. When shared or alternate access is requested, they often exhibit problem behavior. A protocol for teaching 'sharing and taking turns' is included in chapter 12.

R13. **Makes transitions from preferred items and activities to required tasks**

'Making transitions from preferred items and activities to required tasks' is one of **The Essential 8** and *should also be taught as learners are beginning to acquire a few requests* from **R7** and **R8**. This skill, which includes **R10**, accepting the removal of access to highly preferred items and activities and **R11**, completing assigned tasks, is defined as follows: after a learner requests an item or activity, and spends some time interacting with that item or activity, either of two people direct the learner to 'give them' or 'put away' the item or activity and to begin completing a new task, and the learner relinquishes access to the item or activity and completes the task without problem behavior or resistance to prompts. You should teach this skill by combining 'removals' from **R10** and tasks from **R11** that you are already teaching. Learners should be required to make transitions as defined with 10 of the items and activities from **R7** and **R8**. Many children and adults have not acquired this skill. When transitions are required, they often exhibit problem behavior. A protocol for teaching this skill is included in chapter 12.

R14. **Makes a generalized request for the removal or reduction in intensity of 1-4 situations**

Learners encounter unpleasant situations almost everyday. While they should learn to tolerate most of these situations (see **Tolerating Skills**), we should permit the removal or reduction in intensity of certain ones (and no more than four) some or most of the time. When learners have acquired at least a small repertoire of requests for access to specific items and activities (four or five of the items and activities in **R7** and **R8**), they can be taught to make a generalized request (e.g., 'stop') for the removal or reduction in intensity of 1-4 situations. They must also learn, however, to accept 'no' when this request is not honored (see **R15**). When learners are exhibiting severe forms of self-injurious, aggressive, or destructive behavior, work with a behavior analyst with extensive experience with these forms of behavior before teaching this request. When learners' requesting repertoire has been expanded (**R7, R8, R22-23, R27,** and **R30-31**), replace **R14** with specific requests for the removal or reduction in intensity of each of these situations.

R15. **'Accepts no' after making requests for items and activities that were taught and are often honored (R7, R8, and R14)**

'Accepting no after making requests that were taught and are often honored' is a one of **The Essential 8** and should be taught as a child or adult is learning to request each of the items and activities in **R7** and **R8** and each of the situations in **R14**. 'Accepting no' is defined as follows: after the learner makes a request, either of two people say something like "no, not now" or "no, you can't have that (or do that) right now", the learner continues to make other required responses, without repeating the original request, making requests for 'when' or 'later', making requests for other items or activities, exhibiting problem behavior, or resisting or requiring prompts, even when strong motivating events occur. Learners are expected to 'accept no' as defined with 10 of the items and activities from **R7**, **R8**, and **R14**. Many children and adults have not learned to 'accept no'. When they hear the word 'no', they often exhibit problem behavior. A protocol for teaching this skill is included in chapter 12.

Some learners, who have difficulty 'accepting no', tend to repeat a request for the same item or activity over and over. When this occurs, and their method of speaking includes selecting pictures or printed words, some instructors will remove access to their board, book, or electronic device. *This removal, however, prevents this skill from being taught and acquired and should always be avoided.* Sometimes our learners acquire requests inadvertently for items and activities that threaten or jeopardize their safety. We must respond "no" to these requests and expect the same performance as described earlier.

R16. **'Accepts no' after making requests for dangerous items and activities that were not taught and are never honored**

'Accepting no after making requests that were not taught and are never honored' is also one of **The Essential 8** and should be taught when learners begin to gesture or make requests for items or activities that are dangerous. 'Accepting no' is defined as follows: after the learner gestures or makes a request for an item or activity that is dangerous, either of two people say something like "no, you can't have (or do) that" and the learner returns to other activities, without repeating the original request, making requests for similar items or activities, or exhibiting problem behavior.

R17. **Makes very forceful and repeated requests for a stranger, an intruder, a person teasing, threatening, bullying, or instigating a fight, or a person making sexual advances to 'go away'**

Children and adults, especially (but not exclusively) girls and women, should be taught to make very forceful and repeated requests to 'go away' when they encounter an intruder or a person making sexual advances. This skill is of the utmost importance and should never be 'put off until later'. Teaching this skill will require extensive role-playing and practice. This request can be taught at any time, without regard to the size of the learner's requesting repertoire.

R18. **Makes a generalized request for help in a threatening or dangerous situation, by yelling "help", screaming, or otherwise making contact with an audience, calling '9-1-1', or activating a medical alert device**

All children and adults, especially those with very significant disabilities, should be taught to request 'help' in a threatening or dangerous situation (see **R17**) using all of the following methods: (1) making contact with an audience, (2) calling 9-1-1, or (3) activating a medical alert device. This skill is of the utmost importance and should never be 'put off until later'. Teaching this skill will require extensive role-playing and practice. Obviously, this request can be taught at any time, without regard to the size of the learner's requesting repertoire. Learners also need a request for 'help' in other situations that are not dangerous (see **R37**).

R19. **Makes a generalized request for an audience, followed by requests for items or activities in R7 and R8**

Now that the learner is requesting a small number of highly preferred items and activities that can be made frequently and immediately available (**R7** and **R8**), you should begin teaching the learner to make contact with an audience that is not currently attending to him and then make a request for an item or activity that was previously acquired (e.g., tapping another person on the shoulder or the arm [**AMMCA 1**], or using another alternative method of making contact with an audience, and then saying, signing, or selecting a picture for 'juice'). This skill can be taught along with **R24**. Some learners, however, will have difficulty acquiring **R24** and teaching this skill can be postponed until requests are acquired that are part of **R22** and **R23**.

This skill is often referred to as requesting attention. Our experience, however, suggests that attention comes in many forms and has many specific functions, only one of which secures an audience. Seven additional forms and functions are described in **R34**, **R35**, **R50-52**, and **R73**. It is almost never advisable to teach a generalized request for attention alone with a learner with a very limited requesting repertoire, even as part of a tactic for reducing problem behavior (e.g., Functional Communication Training). The learner will be able to make contact with another person, but will not be able to 'say' anything else to that person. It is much more functional for a learner to first acquire a repertoire of requests for items, activities, and places. Then, when contact with an audience has been made, the learner can make any of those requests (e.g., 'tapping someone's arm' and saying, signing, or selecting a picture or a word for 'juice'). *When learners are exhibiting severe forms of self-injurious, aggressive, or destructive behavior, however, it is always advisable to work with a behavior analyst with extensive experience with these forms of behavior before teaching this request.*

R20. Makes a request for a communication board, book, or device

Sometimes learners, whose method of speaking includes selecting pictures or selecting or typing words, become separated from their board, book, or device. When this begins to happen, teach them to request their board, book, or device.

R21. Politely refuses access to preferred items or activities

When children or adults have learned to request items and activities in **R7-8**, teach them to refuse access to these and other items and activities in a polite manner (e.g., "no, thank you").

Additional Must-have Requests and Related Listener Responses. With certain children and adults, you may want to select additional requests and related skills and designate these as must-have skills. This section permits you to do this.

R21a. _____

_____

R21b. _____

_____

Should-have Requests and Related Listener Responses. Once learners can request very highly preferred items and activities, we recommend that they begin learning to expand this repertoire to include:

- requesting items and activities that cannot be made available frequently or immediately,
- requesting less preferred items and activities,
- facing or looking toward an audience as they make a generalized request for that audience,
- making persistent requests when previous requests are inadvertently ignored,
- making requests for affection and companionship
- making requests with words, signs, or pictures that were previously made by gesturing, leading, or completing related activities,
- making a generalized request for 'help',
- requesting a delay in the onset of a required activity or 'a break' from that activity,
- making a generalized request for the reduction or cessation of unpleasant events,
- making a request to use the toilet,
- making requests with peers, and
- requesting that an audience notice something or someone.

They should also begin:

- honoring requests made by peers,
- thanking those who honor their requests,

and continue:

- waiting for requests to be honored,
- accepting 'no' when they are not honored,
- completing assigned tasks between opportunities to make requests, and
- accepting the removal or lack of availability of preferred items and activities.

Should-have requests include only one word, one sign, or one picture. Skills from **R33** to **R48** can be taught in any sequence. As learners are acquiring these requests, we also recommend teaching some good-to-have special requests. With learners who are able to do so, we also recommend teaching good-to-have requests that include 2-4 words, signs, or pictures.

R22. Makes requests for highly preferred foods, drinks, non-food items, or activities that can be made immediately, but not frequently, available

Now that the learner is requesting preferred items and activities that can be made frequently and immediately available and is waiting for and accepting the removal of the same (i.e., has completed **R7-10**), you should begin to increase the size of the learner's requesting repertoire. Begin by teaching requests for preferred foods, drinks, non-food items, or activities that can be made immediately, but not frequently, available (e.g., ice cream, coffee, opening a door).

R23. **Makes requests for highly preferred foods, drinks, non-food items, or activities that cannot be made either frequently or immediately available**

Requests that cannot be honored frequently or immediately (e.g., swimming, a ride in the van, a Slurpee, and trips to McDonald's) may also be acquired more slowly. As a result, they should be taught after requests that can be honored frequently and immediately, or immediately, but not frequently (i.e., after **R7** and **R22**).

R24. **Faces or looks toward an audience as the learner makes a generalized request for that audience, followed by requests for items or activities in R7-8 and R22-23**

Now that learners are requesting preferred items and activities that can be made frequently and immediately available, are waiting for and accepting the removal of the same, are making generalized requests for an audience (i.e., have completed **R7-10** and **R19**), and are beginning to expand their mand repertoire (**R22** and **R23**), you should begin to teach them to face or look toward that audience as they are making contact with them. This skill can be taught together with **R22** and **R23** or with requests already acquired in **R7** and **R8**.

This skill is often referred to as 'eye contact' and taught as a separate skill. Like many others, we have tried to prompt eye contact by physically guiding the learner's chin and found this strategy to be ineffective. We prefer teaching it in the context of making requests for highly preferred items and activities, because guiding the chin, in addition to seldom being effective, tends to increase the likelihood that the learner will try to avoid and escape the situation, whereas the opportunity to make requests, tends to increase the likelihood the learner will approach the instructor, care provider, or parent.

> guiding the chin tends to function as an abolishing operation with respect to preferred items and activities, whereas the opportunity to mand tends to function as an establishing operation with respect to those same items and activities.

R25. **Waits after making requests for each of the items and activities in R22 and R23 for gradually increasing periods of time**

'Waiting' after making a request should again be taught after a child or an adult has learned to request each of the items and activities in **R22** and **R23**. 'Waiting' is defined as it is in **R9**. Learners should be required to 'wait' as defined for each of the items and activities from **R22** and **R23**. Many learners will continue to require practice with this skill. When they are required to wait, they may again begin to exhibit problem behavior. The protocol for teaching 'waiting' is included in chapter 12.

R26. **'Accepts no' after making requests for items and activities that were taught and are often honored as part of R22 and R23**

'Accepting no after making requests that were taught and are often honored' should continue to be taught as the learner is beginning to acquire requests for items and activities in **R22** and **R23**. 'Accepting no' is defined as it is in **R15**. Learners are expected to 'accept no' after requesting each of the items and activities from **R22** and **R23**. Many children and adults will continue to require practice with this skill. When they are 'told no', after making a request, they may again begin to exhibit problem behavior. The protocol for teaching 'accepting no' is included in chapter 12.

R27. **Makes requests for less preferred foods, drinks, non-food items, activities, or places that can be made frequently and immediately available**

Now that the learner is requesting a variety of highly preferred items and activities, some of which are available infrequently and with some delay, you should continue to increase the size of the learner's requesting repertoire by teaching requests for items, activities, and places that are preferred, but less preferred than the items and activities in **R7**, **R8**, and **R22-23**. Begin with items, activities, and places that can be made frequently and immediately available. Sometimes learners appear to indicate interest in only a few items and activities. Generally, there are other preferred items, activities, and places, but we have just failed to notice them (e.g., a favorite chair, sitting in the sun, rubbing their back, singing a song to or with them, keeping their shoes off, or wearing a favorite shirt). If you pay close attention to what the learner approaches and what the learner does, you will generally notice other items and activities in which she is interested. If you cannot find any other preferred items, activities, or places, consider teaching requests from **R33-48** or **R49-70**.

R28. Says "thank you" when requests are honored

As their repertoire of requests is expanding (**R7-8**, **R22-23**, and **R27**) you should begin teaching learners to say "thank you" after their requests are honored.

R29. Completes 20 consecutive, previously acquired tasks

'Completing brief, previously acquired tasks' is first taught as part of **R11**. Expanding this repertoire to 20 consecutive tasks of slightly greater duration should occur as learners are beginning to acquire requests from **R22-23**, a few additional matching and imitation skills (**M1-M3** and **Im1-2**), a few listener responses that involve completing routine activities (**LR12-LR17**), a few additional daily living skills, and listener responses, names, and descriptions that are part of Events 1-3 (**LRND1-3**). These previously acquired tasks should be interspersed between opportunities to make requests until learners complete 20 consecutive tasks without problem behavior and without complaints. The protocol for teaching this skill is included in chapter 12.

R30. Makes requests for less preferred foods, drinks, non-food items, activities, or places that can be made immediately, but not frequently available

As you are teaching requests for less preferred items, activities, and places that can be made frequently and immediately available (**R27**), begin teaching requests for less preferred items, activities, and places that can be made immediately, but not frequently, available.

R31. Makes requests for less preferred foods, drinks, non-food items, activities, or places that cannot be made either frequently or immediately available

Also, as you are teaching requests for less preferred items, activities, and places that can be made frequently and immediately available (**R27**) or immediately, but not frequently, available (**R30**), begin teaching requests for items, activities, and places that cannot be made either frequently or immediately available.

R32. 'Accepts no' after making requests for items and activities that were taught and are often honored as part of R27 and R30-31

'Accepting no after making requests that were taught and are often honored' should continue to be taught as the child or adult is beginning to acquire requests for items and activities in **R27**, and **R30-31**. Eventually, the learner should be expected to 'accept no' after requesting 10 of these items and activities. 'Accepting no' is defined as it is in **R15**. Many children and adults will continue to require practice with this skill. When they are 'told no', after making a request, they may again begin to exhibit problem behavior. The protocol for teaching 'accepting no' is included in chapter 12.

R33. Makes a second and a third generalized request for an audience after the first or second request was ignored

As the learner begins to expand the requesting repertoire, you should anticipate that he will occasionally be ignored and will need to learn to be *persistent*. Begin contriving these situations such that the learner's request for an audience is ignored by one, and later, two persons. Then, teach the learner to make a second, and later a third, generalized request for an audience.

R34. Makes a generalized request for affection

Learners often want to request affection (e.g., 'hug') from another person, which is another form and function of what is often referred to as attention (see **R19**). If a request for affection has not been taught as a part of **R7** and **R8**, or as part of **R22-23**, or **R27**, teach it when a preference for this activity becomes apparent.

R35. Makes a generalized request for companionship

Learners often want others to 'play', 'hang out', 'talk with', or even 'work' with them (e.g., 'come here', 'play', 'sit', 'talk with me', and 'work'), which is yet another form and function of what is often referred to as attention (see **R19**). Teach a request for companionship as learners are beginning to expand their requesting repertoire (i.e., after they have completed **R7** and **R8**, and as they are completing **R22-23**, **R27**, and **R30-31**), especially when they indicate a strong preference for this activity.

R36. Makes a request for a picture schedule, printed-word schedule, or schedule board

Sometimes learners, who use a picture schedule, a printed-word schedule, or a schedule board with miniature objects, become separated from their schedule. When this begins to happen, you should teach them to request their schedule or schedule board.

R37. Makes a generalized request for 'help', followed by gestures, leading others, or completing related activities, in 6 specific situations that are not dangerous

As learners begin to expand their requesting repertoire (i.e., after they have completed **R7** and **R8**, and as they are completing **R22-23**, **R27**, and **R30-31**), they will encounter situations in which they want or need something or someone and have not acquired a request that specifies that something or someone. These are situations that are not dangerous, but in which learners:

- have not acquired a mand for something or someone,
- cannot complete a specific task,
- have made an error and cannot correct it,
- have made a 'mess' and cannot clean it up by themselves,
- have forgotten or lost an item,
- don't encounter a specific situation often,
- have encountered a sudden change in the environment, or
- have encountered something that alarms them.

In these, and other similar situations, teach learners a generalized request for 'help'. Then, if the situation does not immediately suggest the help they need, prompt them to to gesture toward items or familiar persons, lead others to the same, or complete related activities. Learners are expected to make a generalized request for 'help', followed by gestures, leading, or completing an activity as needed, in six of the aforementioned or similar situations.

Then, as soon as possible, begin replacing 'help' with requests for specific items and activities. As indicated in **R17**, learners will also need a request for 'help' when they encounter dangerous situations.

When learners exhibit severe forms of self-injurious, aggressive, or destructive behavior, work with a behavior analyst with extensive experience with these forms of behavior before teaching a request for 'help'.

R38. Makes a request to delay the onset of a required activity

Sometimes, but not often, after learners have been directed to begin an activity, we should permit them to request a brief delay in the onset of this activity. Begin to teach a request for this delay as learners are expanding their requesting repertoire (i.e., after they have completed **R7** and **R8**, and as they are completing **R22-23**, **R27**, and **R30-31**). They must also learn, however, to accept 'no' after this request (see **R40**).

When learners are exhibiting severe forms of self-injurious, aggressive, or destructive behavior, work with a behavior analyst with extensive experience with these forms of behavior before teaching this request.

R39. Makes a generalized request for a 'break' in required activities

Learners should be taught to indicate that they are '*finished*', when they complete required activities. Then they should be taught to request a brief 'break'. This same request can be taught while learners are engaged in activities of long duration. Begin to teach this request as learners are expanding their requesting repertoire (i.e., after they have completed **R7** and **R8**, and as they are completing **R22-23**, **R27**, and **R30-31**). Learners must also be taught to accept 'no' after making this request (see **R40**).

When learners are exhibiting severe forms of self-injurious, aggressive, or destructive behavior, work with a behavior analyst with extensive experience with these forms of behavior before teaching this request. Sometimes learners who are engaged in a required task, will stop working and say or sign 'finished'. Prompt them to say or sign 'break' and honor this request for a brief break (as long as it was not preceded by problem behavior). Do not teach a request for a task to be 'finished' or 'over' and do not honor this request.

R40. **'Accepts no' after making requests for a delay or 'a break' in required activities that were taught and are often honored as part of R38 and R39**

'Accepting no after making requests that were taught and are often honored' should continue to be taught shortly after a child or adult has learned to request a delay in the onset of required activities in (**R38**) or a 'break' in ongoing activities in (**R39**). 'Accepting no' is defined as it is in **R15**. Learners are expected to 'accept no' after making either of these requests. Many children and adults will continue to require practice with this skill. When they are 'told no', after making a request, they may again begin to exhibit problem behavior. The protocol for teaching 'accepting no' is included in chapter 12.

R41. **Makes specific requests for the reduction or cessation of 1-4 unpleasant situations**

As we indicated in **R14**, learners encounter unpleasant situations almost everyday. While they should learn to tolerate most of these situations (see **Tolerating Skills**), we should permit the removal or reduction in intensity of certain ones some or most of the time. In **R14**, learners were taught to make a single, generalized request (i.e., "stop") for the removal or reduction in intensity of 1-4 situations. As learners expand their requesting repertoire (**R7**, **R8**, **R22-23**, **R27**, and **R30-31**), replace **R14** with specific requests for the removal or reduction in intensity of each of these situations by prompting learners to say, sign, select a picture, or select, type or write the word 'no' and specify the situation (e.g., 'no music', 'no spaghetti', ''no mouthwash'). For many learners, this will be their first request that includes two words, two signs, or two pictures. They must also learn to 'accept no' after these requests (see **R42**). When learners are exhibiting severe forms of self-injurious, aggressive, or destructive behavior, work with a behavior analyst with extensive experience with these forms of behavior before teaching these requests.

R42. **'Accepts no' after making requests for the reduction or cessation of specific unpleasant situations or activities that were taught and are often honored as part of R41**

'Accepting no after making requests that were taught and are often honored' should continue to be taught shortly after a child or adult has learned to request 'the reduction or cessation of specific, unpleasant events' (**R41**). 'Accepting no' is defined as it is in **R15**. Learners are expected to 'accept no' after making any request that is part of **R41**. Many children and adults will continue to require practice with this skill. When they are 'told no', after making a request, they may again begin to exhibit problem behavior. The protocol for teaching 'accepting no' is included in chapter 12.

R43. **Makes a request to use the toilet, to use a catheter, to be changed, to locate a restroom, or for assistance with toileting**

Teach this request during toilet training, but try to avoid this training until learners have acquired 3-4 requests for highly preferred items and activities (**R7-8**). Begin teaching a request for the toilet as learners begin to initiate going to the bathroom. For learners who require a catheter and are learning self-catheterization, begin teaching this request as they begin to use a catheter without prompts. For learners who cannot be toilet trained or use a catheter, begin teaching this request when they indicate gesturally the need to be changed. For learners with limited requesting repertoires, who already indicate the need to be changed by gesture or facial expression, teaching them another form of this request may be redundant. Learners with complex physical conditions may require occasional or even frequent assistance with toileting.

R44. **Makes requests for 5 items or activities from R7, R8, R22-23, R27, and R30-31 from each of three peers**

As learners are expanding their requesting repertoire (i.e., after they have completed **R7** and **R8**, and as they are completing **R22-23**, **R27**, and **R30-31**), they will encounter situations in which access to preferred items and activities is controlled by peers. When this occurs, teach them to make requests for five items or activities previously acquired as part of **R7**, **R8**, **R22-23**, **R27**, and **R30-31** from each of three peers.

R45. **Honors requests from peers**

As a child or an adult is learning to make requests of peers in **R44** honoring their requests becomes equally important and should be taught. Learners should be expected to honor requests for 5 of the items and activities from **R7**, **R8**, **R22-23**, **R27**, and **R30-31**.

R46. Responds appropriately to the unauthorized removal of access to 5 preferred items or activities from R7, R8, R22-23, R27, or R30-31 by peers

When the unauthorized removal of access to preferred items and activities is exhibited by peers, 'responding appropriately' should be taught along with **R44** and **R45**. This behavior is defined as follows: after either of two peers removes access to a preferred item or activity without authorization to do so, the learner politely (1) makes one or two polite requests to retain possession of the items and activities that were removed (e.g., "please, may I have it back"), and then, if this is not successful, (2) requests help from a parent or a person in authority without exhibiting problem behavior, without resisting or requiring prompts, and when strong motivating events occur. Learners are expected to 'respond appropriately' as defined for five of the items and activities from **R7, R8, R22-23, R27,** and **R30-31**. Many children and adults have not acquired this skill. When access to preferred items or activities is removed by peers, they often exhibit problem behavior. A protocol for teaching this skill is included in chapter 12.

R47. Makes a request for assistance during menstruation

All female learners should be taught to request assistance with menstruation as soon as it begins to occur. Even learners who acquire the skills necessary to insure proper hygiene should also be taught this request, as it may be useful in circumstances when proper supplies are not available or when unexpected circumstances occur.

R48. Makes a request for lubricant for personal sexual activity

All male and female learners should be taught to request a lubricant for personal sexual activity as soon as this activity begins to occur. Lubricant will generally prevent injury and insure satisfactory completion of the activity. Observation with discretion is warranted, as this activity may begin to occur at a young age and may, without lubricant, result in self-injury.

Additional Should-have Requests and Related Listener Responses. With certain children and adults, you may want to select additional requests and related skills and designate these as should-have skills. This section permits you to do this.

R48a. _____

R48b. _____

R48c. _____

R48d. _____

R48e. _____

Good-to-have Requests and Related Listener Responses. Once learners have acquired a repertoire of must-have and should-have requests and related skills, we recommend further expanding the requesting repertoire to include 'special requests' (**R49-R70**) that are beneficial and advantageous for learners and that greatly enhance the quality of their daily experiences. For learners able to do so, we also recommend teaching requests which require 2-4 words, signs, or pictures, and which specify combinations of items, activities, people, and places (**R71-R79**). These include:

- requesting items, activities, places, or any combination thereof,
- requesting an item or an activity and a feature,
- requesting a specific person as an audience and an item, an activity, or a place
- making requests for items or activities that the learner needs, and

Makes Special Requests

R49. Makes a request for privacy and to increase personal space

A request for privacy or personal space should be taught only when older children or adults have acquired an expanded repertoire of requests for specific items and activities (**R7**, **R8**, **R22-23**, **R27**, and **R30-31**) and when interest in this preference becomes apparent.

When learners are exhibiting severe forms of self-injurious, aggressive, or destructive behavior, work with a behavior analyst with extensive experience with these forms of behavior before teaching this request.

R50. Makes a generalized request for acknowledgement

Learners often want to request acknowledgement (e.g., 'hi', 'dude', 'girl'), which is another form and function of what is often referred to as attention (see **R19**). Teach this request when learners have acquired an expanded repertoire of requests for specific items and activities (**R7**, **R8**, **R22-23**, **R27**, and **R30-31**) and when a preference for acknowledgement becomes apparent.

R51. Makes a generalized request for feedback, approval, or confirmation

Learners often want to request feedback or approval (e.g., '[is this] right'), which yet is another form and function of what is often referred to as attention (see **R19**). Teach this request when learners have acquired an expanded repertoire of requests for specific items and activities (**R7**, **R8**, **R22-23**, **R27**, and **R30-31**) and when a preference for and an interest in feedback becomes apparent, or when feedback will be helpful for the learner.

R52. Makes a request to notice something or someone

In addition to requests for an audience, learners often want an audience to notice something or someone (e.g., 'look, [it's a] train'), which is another form and function of what is often referred to as attention (see **R19**). Teach this request along with three other requests only when learners have acquired an expanded repertoire of requests for specific items and activities (**R7**, **R8**, **R22-23**, **R27**, and **R30-31**).

R53. Makes a request for others to repeat responses

Requests for others to repeat what they have said or done (e.g., 'again' or 'what?') can help children and adults acquire new skills, especially if they are beginning to make echoic or other imitative responses. Teach a request for this repetition only when learners have acquired an expanded repertoire of requests for specific items and activities (**R7**, **R8**, **R22-23**, **R27**, and **R30-31**).

R54. Makes a request for others to clarify something they have said

Many times learners encounter situations or hear, say, or feel what others have said and 'do not understand'. They need a way to request an explanation (e.g., 'I don't understand'). Teach a request for an explanation when learners have acquired an expanded repertoire of requests for specific items and activities (**R7**, **R8**, **R22-23**, **R27**, and **R30-31**). This is not a request for a detailed or lengthy explanation. Such a request would require a more extensive speaker and listener repertoire and would generally occur in the form of a 'why' question.

R55. Makes a request for protective equipment, restraint, or a self-restraint device

In some situations, learners may need to request protective equipment or help with the same. For example, some learners will require help with seat belts and other forms of adaptive equipment. As part of a behavior improvement plan, some learners are permitted, for very brief periods of time, to request forms of restraint or devices or clothing which permit self-restraint.

R56. Makes requests for others to keep items or to put items in three specific places

Often children and adults want others to keep their jacket, keys, money, or other personal belongings as they participate in other activities (e.g., 'put in your purse' or 'keep'). They may also want others to put these belongings in specific places (e.g., 'put in the drawer'). Although names for specific locations are helpful (e.g., 'put in the drawer'), learners can make these requests without them. They can specify the place (e.g., 'purse' or 'drawer') and point to the location. Teach requests for 'keep' or 'hold' and 'pocket', or 'purse' or 'drawer' (or their equivalent) when learners have acquired an expanded repertoire of requests for specific items and activities (**R7**, **R8**, **R22-23**, **R27**, and **R30-31**) and when interest becomes apparent.

R57. Makes a request for medications

Children and adults may occasionally need to remind their care providers to permit access to or administer their daily, prescribed medications. They may also want to request over-the-counter remedies by type (e.g., aspirin) or brand name (e.g., Pepto-Bismol). Teach these requests when requests that are part of **R7**, **R8**, **R22-23**, **R27**, and **R30-31** have been acquired.

R58. Makes a request to perform an activity in a preferred manner

Performing an activity in a preferred manner (i.e., 'my way') is important to many learners. Teach this request only after learners have acquired an expanded repertoire of requests for specific items and activities (**R7**, **R8**, **R22-23**, **R27**, and **R30-31**) and when interest becomes apparent.

R59. Makes a request to perform an activity without assistance

Performing an activity without assistance (i.e., 'by myself') is important to many learners. Teach this request only after learners have acquired an expanded repertoire of requests for specific items and activities (**R7**, **R8**, **R22-23**, **R27**, and **R30-31**) and when interest becomes apparent.

R60. Requests permission to access items or participate in routine activities that present some risk, that require complex discriminations, and that require supervision

Learners may want to access items like a table knife or scissors (e.g., "[can I use the] scissors"), or participate in activities like jumping on a trampoline or crossing the street (e.g., '[is it ok to] cross the street now'). These items and activities pose some risk of injury and require supervision. These requests should be taught when interest in these items and activities becomes apparent.

R61. Makes a request to return a highly preferred item to its original location or to restore a situation to its preferred condition

Learners often want others to return their belongings to their original locations.(e.g., '[put it] back'). This request should be taught only after learners have acquired an expanded repertoire of requests for specific items and activities (**R7**, **R8**, **R22-23**, **R27**, and **R30-31**) and when interest in this preference becomes apparent.

R62. Makes a request to restore the condition of a preferred item

Learners will often play or otherwise interact with an item until it is no longer working or it is broken. They will then want another person 'fix it'. This request should be taught only after learners have acquired an expanded repertoire of requests for specific items and activities (**R7**, **R8**, **R22-23**, **R27**, and **R30-31**) and when interest becomes apparent.

R63. Makes a generalized request to increase the amount of a preferred item or the duration of a preferred activity, some of which has already been received or experienced

When learners have received a small amount of a preferred item or experienced a brief duration of a preferred activity, they may want to request 'more'. Teach a request for 'more' only after learners have acquired an expanded repertoire of requests for specific items and activities (**R7**, **R8**, **R22-23**, **R27**, and **R30-31**). *Never teach this request when learners have not acquired any other request or have a very limited requesting repertoire, as it may interfere with the acquisition of requests for specific items and activities.*

R64.[2] Makes requests for the name of an item or a person

Sometimes learners who have acquired requests for items and activities, begin to point to other items and activities and indicate by gesturing that they want to know their names. When this begins to occur, teach these names.

---

[2] We were first alerted to the importance of this request by a young lady in the United Kingdom who speaks with signs and who, after acquiring a repertoire of requests, began to run about the house and the garden pointing to items and making noises as if to say "what's this called".

R65. Makes requests for others to respond more or less rapidly

Oftentimes learners want others to respond more or less rapidly. In other words, they will want to 'say', 'sign', or 'select a picture or word' for 'hurry up' or 'wait for me'. Teach requests for these preferences only when learners have acquired an expanded repertoire of requests (**R7**, **R8**, **R22-23**, **R27**, and **R30-31**) and when interest becomes apparent.

R66. Makes requests to be warmer and cooler

Learners will often feel too cold or too hot and need one or more requests which will result in being warmer or cooler. These requests come in two forms, one involving the clothing worn and the other involving changing the temperature of the environment. For example, learners can request 'a coat' or 'a tee shirt', or 'heat' or 'air conditioning'. Teach requests for these preferences only when learners have acquired an expanded repertoire of requests for specific items and activities (**R7**, **R8**, **R22-23**, **R27**, and **R30-31**) and when interest becomes apparent.

R67. Makes requests that a food or drink item be warmer and cooler

When consuming beverages, soup, macaroni and cheese, or other food items, learners will encounter occasions in which they want the item to be warmer or cooler. Teach requests for these preferences (e.g., 'cold', 'hot') only when learners have acquired an expanded repertoire of requests for specific items and activities (**R7**, **R8**, **R22-23**, **R27**, and **R30-31**) and when interest becomes apparent.

R68. 'Accepts no' after making five of the requests specified in R48-65 that were taught and are often honored

'Accepting no after making requests that were taught and are often honored' should continue to be taught as a child or adult is learning to request the items, activities, and places in **R49-67**. 'Accepting no' is defined as it is in **R15**. The learner should be expected to 'accept no' after requesting a random sample of five of these items and activities. Some children and adults will continue to require practice with this skill. When they are 'told no', after making a request, they may again begin to exhibit problem behavior. The protocol for teaching 'accepting no' is included in chapter 12.

R69. Makes a request for a special item or activity from a special person

Sometimes learners with very significant disabilities, and limited speaking repertoires, enjoy a very special item or activity with a parent, care provider, or instructor. This item or activity has never had a 'name', but both the learner and the other individual know what it is (e.g., 'singing a special song', 'making faces', or 'a hand massage'. Teach the learn to 'say', 'sign or gesture', or 'select a picture or word' for this item or activity. This request can be taught at any time, without regard to the size of the learner's requesting repertoire.

R70. Makes a generalized request for an unspecified change in the environment

Sometimes learners with very significant disabilities, and limited speaking repertoires, want some type of change in their immediate environment, but can't specify what it is. Teach the learn to 'say', 'sign', or 'gesture' for this change. When the learner makes this response or is prompted to do so, change to a new item or activity and try to determine if the learner is pleased with the change. Continue until the learner seems satisfied with the change. This request can be taught at any time, without regard to the size of the learner's requesting repertoire.

Additional Special Requests. With certain children and adults, you may want to select additional requests and related skills and designate these as should-have skills. This section permits you to do this.

R70a. _____

_____

R70b. _____

_____

R70c. _____

_____

Making Requests that Require 2-4 Words, Signs, or Pictures and which Specify Items, Activities, People, and Places

R71. **Makes requests that require 2 words, signs, or pictures and that include specific items, activities, or places for which requests were previously acquired**

After learners have acquired a large repertoire of requests for items, activities, places, and people (**R7, R8, R22-23, R27, R30-31, R33-39, R41, R43-44**, and some from **R47-70**), begin teaching requests that include two of these same items, activities, and places (e.g., juice and cookies, a Coke and a hug, ball and outside). While these requests will require two words, signs, or pictures, these requests will be ones that have already been acquired in isolation and that will result in two preferred items or activities. This should insure that a decrease in motivation related to effort will not occur.

The selection of two previously acquired responses and an increase in the amount of the reinforcer should prevent response effort from functioning as an abolishing operation with respect to preferred items and activities.

R72. **Makes requests that require 2 words, signs, or pictures and that include a specific item or activity, for which a request was previously acquired, along with a feature or a specific quantity**

After learners have acquired a large repertoire of requests (**R7, R8, R22-23, R27, R30-31, R33-39, R41, R43-44**, and some from **R47-70**), and after you have taught several requests that include two items, activities, or places (**R71**), begin teaching requests that include one item or activity with a feature or a quantity (e.g., 'strawberry ice cream', 'cheese crackers' '3 cookies', 'red Skittles', 'jump higher', or 'Coke [with] ice'). These requests require two words, signs, or pictures, one specifying the item or activity, a request for which has already been acquired, and the other specifying a feature or quantity. Since these requests permit learners to gain access to more specific items and activities, improving the quality of what they receive, and since learners are already beginning to acquire requests that require two responses, a decrease in motivation related to effort should not occur.

The selection of one previously acquired response, an increase in the quality of the reinforcer, and the learner's emerging repertoire of two-response requests should prevent response effort from functioning as an abolishing operation with respect to preferred items and activities.

Some learners will acquire requests for items with features or quantities more rapidly if you teach them to specify the item first and then the feature or the quantity (e.g., ice cream chocolate or crackers two) as you would if you were teaching them to request some other items with features (e.g., 'Coke with ice') or many activities with features (e.g., 'run faster'). Then, later, you can prompt a change in the order of the words, signs, pictures, or leave things as they are, as requests of this form are easily understood.

R73. **Makes requests that require 2 words, signs, or pictures and that include one item, activity, or place for which a request was previously acquired, along with a familiar person**

After learners have acquired a large repertoire of requests for items, activities, and places (**R7, R8, R22-23, R27, R30-31, R33-39, R41, R43-44**, and some from **R47-70**), and after you have taught several requests that include an item or an activity and a feature or quantity (**R72**), begin teaching requests that include one item or activity, along with a familiar person. In other words, teach learners to make requests to enjoy an item or participate in an activity with a specific person (e.g., 'burger [with] Mom).

R74. **Makes requests for one of three familiar persons as an audience, followed by a request that includes one item, activity, or place for which a request was previously acquired**

Once learners are making a variety of 2-word, 2-sign, or 2-picture requests that include preferred items, activities, places, and persons (**R71-73**), and they have a history of making generalized requests for an audience while facing or looking at them (**R19** and **R24**), begin teaching them to request one of three familiar persons as an audience and then make a request for a preferred item, activity, or place that was previously acquired (e.g., 'Mom, shoes' or 'Ms. Smith, movies'). This skill will permit learners to access an audience that often responds more enthusiastically and is familiar with features of their requests which they have not yet learned to specify.

R75.[3] **Makes requests that include one item, activity, or place, for which a request was previously acquired, along with a related or required item or activity**

Once learners are making a variety of 2-word, 2-sign, or 2-picture requests that include preferred items, activities, places, and persons, and also include specific persons as an audience (**R71-74**), begin teaching requests that include one item or activity from **R7**, **R8**, **R22-23**, **R27**, or **R30-31** they want and a related or required item or activity they *need* (e.g., *candy and open* [the container]). These requests specify a preferred item or activity, a request for which has already been acquired, and another related or required item or activity, which, only indirectly, benefits the learner. In order to prevent a decrease in motivation related to effort and an increase in motivation related to escaping a demand (i.e., the learner does not respond to prompts, leaves the situation, or begins to exhibit problem behavior), begin by teaching requests that include a related, rather than a required item or activity (e.g., teach *music and on* before *outside and shoes*). Then, gradually move to requests that include required items or activities (e.g., '*cake and plate*').

In order to prevent an abolishing operation with respect to preferred items and activities and an establishing operation related to escape from demands from occurring, begin by reducing the demands and, later, gradually fading-in those demands.

R76. **Makes requests that include 2 items which learners 'need' in order to complete a required activity of daily living**

Once learners are making requests for items and activities they want, along with related or required items they need (**R75**), begin teaching 'requests for two items they need'. In other words, begin teaching requests for two items that are necessary in order to complete tasks of daily living (e.g., 'soap and [a] towel' required to wash your hands, 'cleanser and [a] sponge' required to clean a sink, and 'spoons and forks' required to set a table).

R77. **Makes requests that require 3 words, signs, or pictures and that include items, activities, features and quantities, people, and places, for which requests were previously acquired**

Once learners have acquired a wide variety of requests that require two words, signs, or pictures (**R71-76**), begin to teach requests that require 3 words, signs, or pictures and that include items, activities, features and quantities, people, and places that were part of previously acquired requests (e.g., 'vanilla pudding [and a] cookie', 'jump [and] run fast').

R78. **Makes requests that require 3 words, signs, or pictures and that include items, activities, features and quantities, people, and places, for which requests were not previously acquired**

Once learners are beginning to make requests that require three words, signs, or pictures (**R77**), begin to expand this repertoire to include items, activities, features and quantities, people, and places that were not part of previously acquired requests (e.g., 'Crocs [and my] red socks ').

R79. **Makes requests that require 4 words, signs, or pictures and that include items, activities, features and quantities, people, and places, for which requests were not previously acquired**

Once the learner has acquired a wide variety of requests that require three words, signs, or pictures (**R77-78**), begin to teach 4-word, 4-sign, or 4-picture requests which include items, activities, features and quantities, people, or places that were not part of previously acquired requests (e.g., 'Mary, [may I go] outside [and] run fast', 'chocolate ice cream and three cookies').

Additional Requests that Require 2-4 Words, Signs, or Pictures, which Specify Items, Activities, People, and Places. With certain children and adults, you may want to select additional requests and designate these as good-to-have skills. This section permits you to do this.

R79a. _____

_____

R79b. _____

_____

---

[3] Beginning with R75, requesting an audience, when necessary, is assumed to occur, is not considered one of the required number of words, signs, or pictures, and is not required in order to demonstrate acquisition of a skill.

Nice-to-have Requests and Related Listener Responses. Once learners have acquired a repertoire of must-have, should-have, and good-to-have requests and related skills, we recommend that the requesting repertoire be expanded to include 'advanced requests and requests for information' which are often difficult to acquire. These requests, which will generally require five or more spoken words, signs, printed words, or typed words, will be in the form of sentences or sentence fragments, and will include:

- items, activities, and places, some with features,
- carrier phrases and connecting words,
- locations, activities with items, approximate times in relation to specific activities, and days of the week,
- 'excuse me' and 'please',
- 'where' questions,
- 'what' questions,
- 'when' questions,
- 'who' questions,
- items or activities that may provide relief or distraction from pain or discomfort, and
- activities or spoken words that may provide consolation, comfort, or reassurance when feelings of sadness or disappointment occur

Learners who make requests by selecting pictures are precluded from making 'advanced requests'. They can, however, do so by learning to select printed words or to type words.

Making Advanced Requests

R80. Makes requests that require 3 key words or signs, along with carrier phrases and connecting words or signs, and that include items, activities, features and quantities, people, and places, for which requests were previously acquired

Once learners who use spoken words, signs, printed words, or typed words have acquired requests that require 3 or 4 words or signs, and that include items, activities, features and quantities, people, and places, for which requests were previously acquired (**R77-79**), you should begin to add carrier phrases (e.g., 'I want', 'may I have', 'would you get' and connecting words (''and', 'or', 'on', 'in', and 'behind', to name a few) to their requests. These new requests will include *three key words* plus carrier phrases and connecting words (e.g., 'May I have chocolate ice cream and cookies', or 'Can you put my shoes and on the bed'). Carrier phrases help audiences distinguish requests from comments and respond accordingly. For example, a learner may walk past a plate of cookies and say "cookies". An instructor, care provider, or parent may respond by saying "yes, and they look good, don't they". If the learner was making a request and was beginning to exhibit carrier phrases, she could clarify this for her audience by saying "may I have a cookie" and increase the likelihood that her audience would respond by providing her with a cookie. Carrier phrases also make language sound more 'typical', which sometimes results in frequent and enthusiastic responses from others who might otherwise be less inclined to respond at all. Connecting words, on the other hand, often result in immediate and short-term outcomes that are favorable to learners. For example, 'and', rather than 'or', may result in gaining access to two items, rather than one ('chocolate ice cream and cookies'), and 'on', rather than 'under', may result in finding your shoes ('on the bed').

For learners who make requests by selecting pictures, however, these additions are less functional. Since selecting pictures does not permit naming or commenting, adding a carrier phrase with printed words, often called a sentence strip, does not help audiences distinguish requests from comments. It may, however, make language appear more 'typical', and result in frequent and enthusiastic responses from others, as described in the previous paragraph. And, while connecting words may have this same effect described above, we have never observed it. If, on the other hand, these learners begin to select printed words, rather than pictures, naming and describing is possible, and carrier phrases and connecting words could have all of the functions described in the previous paragraph.

R81. **Makes requests that require 3 key words or signs, along with carrier phrases and connecting words or signs, and that include items, activities, features, people, and places, for which requests were not previously acquired**

This skill is identical to **R80**, except that it includes items, activities, features and quantities, people, and places, for which requests were not previously acquired. It should be taught only after learners have acquired some requests from **R80**.

R82. **Makes requests that require 3 key words or signs, along with carrier phrases, connecting words or signs, locations, and times in relation to specific activities, and that include items, activities, features and quantities, people, and places, for which requests were previously acquired**

Now that the learner has acquired a variety of requests that require 3 key words, signs, or pictures, along with carrier phrases and connecting words or signs, and that include items, activities, features and quantities, people, and places, for which requests were not previously acquired (**R81**), you should begin to teach requests that also include locations and times in relation to specific activities (e.g., '[Could I put the] sandwich in [the] refrigerator', '[I want to get a] Coke after work', or '[May I get a] chocolate milkshake tomorrow').

R83. **Makes polite requests that require 3 or more key words or signs, along with carrier phrases, connecting words or signs, locations, times in relation to specific activities, and 'excuse me' and 'please', and that include items, activities, features and quantities, people, and places, for which requests were not previously acquired**

Now that the learner has acquired a variety of requests that require 3 key words, signs, or pictures, along with carrier phrases, connecting words or signs, locations, and times in relation to specific activities, and that include items, activities, features, people, places, for which requests were previously acquired (**R82**), you should begin teaching requests that require 3 or more key words or signs, and that also include 'excuse me' and 'please' and examples of the remaining elements required in **R82** for which requests were not previously acquired (e.g., '[Would you] please put my blue shirt in [the] washing machine', or 'Excuse me, [may I] please [get a] cheeseburger [and a] chocolate milkshake tomorrow').

Requesting Information

R84. **Makes requests for information, with 2-4 key words or signs, regarding the location of items, people, or places, some with features ['where' questions]**

Now that the learner has acquired a variety of requests that require 3 or more key words, signs, or pictures, along with carrier phrases and connecting words or signs, 'excuse me' and 'please', and that include items, activities, features and quantities, people, places, locations, and times in relation to specific activities (**R83**), you should consider teaching requests for information regarding the location of items, people, and places that require 2-4 key words or signs and that also include all of the elements of **R83** (e.g., 'where is mom', 'where are my red socks', 'where [are we going] to eat after work').

Opportunities to make these requests occur frequently in everyday living. Also, contriving these opportunities can be easily accomplished by hiding preferred items or items that are part of activities, or limiting access to specific people.

R85. **Makes requests for information, with 2-4 key words or signs, regarding the identity of items, activities, or unfamiliar persons ['what' questions]**

Now that the learner is making requests for information regarding the location of items, people, or places (**R84**), you should consider teaching requests for information regarding the identity of items, activities, and unfamiliar people that also require 2-4 key words, signs, or pictures and that include all of the elements of **R83** (e.g., 'what's that', 'what's next', 'what's your name', 'what [are we doing] after lunch', or 'what's in the blue bag').

R86. Makes requests for information, with 2-4 key words, regarding when 10 activities will occur ['when' questions]

Now that the learner is making requests for information regarding the identity of items, activities, and unfamiliar people (**R85**), you should consider teaching requests for information regarding when activities will occur that also require 2-4 key words and that include all of the elements of **R83** (e.g., 'when [are we] going shopping', 'when [is] mom [going to be] home', or 'when [is] Ms. Smith [taking] me [to] work').

R87. Makes requests for information, with 2-4 key words, regarding the identity of 10 unfamiliar persons ['who' questions]

Now that the learner is making requests for information regarding when activities will occur (**R86**), you should also consider teaching requests for information regarding the identity of specific people that also require 2-4 key words and that include all of the elements of **R83** (e.g., 'who is that', 'who [is taking] us to school', 'who [is going to the] store [with] us on Monday', or 'who will help us with dishes after dinner').

R88. Makes requests for information, with 2-4 key words, regarding the health or condition of familiar persons [a limited array of 'how' questions]

Now that the learner is making requests for information regarding the identity of specific people (**R87**), you should also consider teaching requests for information regarding the health or condition of another person that also require 2-4 key words and that include all of the elements of **R83** (e.g., 'how do you feel', 'how is grandma doing').

Other Advanced Requests

R89. Makes a request for an item or an activity that may provide relief or a distraction from each of three types of pain or discomfort

From time to time, child and adult learners will experience pain or discomfort following the occurrence of specific events (e.g., falling down or cutting their finger). If learners have acquired a name or a description for the pain or discomfort they are currently experiencing (see **LRND14**), they should be prompted to provide this name or description, followed by a request for a specific form of relief or distraction consistent with this pain or discomfort (e.g., a bandage, a cold wash cloth on the forehead, an antacid, a glass of water, or a shoulder rub). If learners have not acquired these names or descriptions, you will need to closely observe their facial expression, along with other movements of their body, to determine the source or type of pain or discomfort. Then, you will need to prompt a request for a specific form of relief or distraction from this pain or discomfort.

Teach this skill when learners have acquired a large repertoire of requests (**R7, R8, R22-23, R27, R30-31, R33-39, R41, R43-44**, and some from **R47-70**). Continue teaching this skill until the learner has acquired requests for relief or distraction from three sources or types of pain or discomfort. Although names and descriptions for these sources or types help the audience provide appropriate forms of relief or distraction, they are not required.

R90. Makes a generalized request for activities or spoken words that may provide consolation, comfort, or reassurance after the occurrence of an event that may have resulted in feelings of disappointment, sadness, or anger

From time to time, child and adult learners will also experience disappointment, sadness, or anger following the occurrence of specific events. If their facial expression and posture become consistent with feelings of disappointment, sadness, or anger when these events occur, and they begin to approach familiar persons, they should be taught a single request for one or more activities or spoken words that may provide consolation, comfort, and/or reassurance (e.g., a hug and reassuring words like "everything's going to be alright"). Other than 'hug', there are few words, signs, or pictures that easily convey this request. As a result, we suggest using the word or sign for 'sad' or 'angry'. The combination of approaching a familiar person and saying or signing 'sad' or 'angry' will convey this request. You can also use a drawing or photograph of a 'sad or angry face'. Teach this skill when learners have acquired a large repertoire of requests (**R7, R8, R22-23, R27, R30-31, R33-39, R41, R43-44**, and some from **R47-70**).

Additional Nice-to-have Requests and Related Listener Responses. With certain children and adults, you may want to se-lect additional requests and related skills and designate these as nice-to-have skills. This section permits you to do this.

R90a. _____

R90b. _____

R90c. _____

R90d. _____

R90e. _____

R90f. _____

R90g. _____

R90h. _____

R90i. _____

R90j. _____

R90k. _____

The Assessment of Requests and Related Listener Responses

Before conducting an assessment, review the procedures described in chapter 4. Then, secure a copy of the **Assessment and Record of Progress (ARP)** for each learner. and begin to conduct the assessment. Determine each learner's performance level on each of the skills in this domain, beginning with those designated as must-have requests and related skills (**R1**-**R21**) and record this level on the *ARP*. The performance levels for requests with learners aligned with Vocal Profiles 1 and 2 and learners who require an alternative method of speaking are described in Tables 3 and 4, along with sample items from the *ARP*. The performance levels for (1) waiting for requests to be honored, (2) accepting the removal of access to preferred items and activities by persons in authority and peers, (3) accepting no when requests are not honored, (4) completing 10 brief, previously acquired tasks, (5) sharing and taking turns, and (6) making transitions are described in Tables 5-10, again with sample items from the *ARP*. Continue the assessment until the learner requires prompts, exhibits inappropriate responses, or responds with problem behavior on three consecutive skills or three consecutive examples of a specific skill.

Table 3.
The Performance Levels for Requests with Learners Aligned with Vocal Profiles 1 or 2

When motivating events occur, learners request specific items, activities, or persons, or request specific information consistent with those events on three consecutive occasions...

IA	[the initial assessment of this skill has been completed]
IM	[instruction or management has begun]
-SA	without self-injurious, aggressive, or destructive behavior
-DC	without disruptive behavior or complaints
-RP	without resistance to prompts and without leaving the area
FP	with a full echoic prompt
PP	with a partial echoic prompt
MP	with a minimal echoic prompt
Ind	without prompts, without scrolling, and within two seconds
2S	in two or more settings
2P	in the presence of either of two people
<M	when motivating events have occurred, but are weak
NI	when the learner does not have sensory contact with the requested item or activity
Det	[requests are no longer occurring consistently]

R7. Requests 10 highly preferred snack foods, drinks, non-food items, or activities that can be made frequently and immediately available

1 cookies | IA | IM | -SA | -DC | -RP | FP | PP | MP | Ind | 2S | 2P | <M | Ni | Det |

Table 4
The Performance Levels for Requests With Learners who Require an Alternative Method of Speaking

When motivating events occur, learners request specific items, activities, or persons, or request specific information consistent with those events on three consecutive occasions...

IA	[the initial assessment of this skill has been completed]
IM	[instruction or management has begun]
-SA	without self-injurious, aggressive, or destructive behavior
-DC	without disruptive behavior or complaints
-RP	without resistance to prompts and without leaving the area
FP	with a full physical or full demonstration prompt
PP	with a partial physical or partial demonstration prompt
MP	with a minimal touch or minimal gestural prompt
Ind	without prompts, without scrolling, and within two seconds
2S	in two or more settings
2P	in the presence of either of two people
<M	when motivating events have occurred, but are weak
NI	when the learner does not have sensory contact with the requested item or activity
Det	[requests are no longer occurring consistently]

R7. Requests 10 highly preferred snack foods, drinks, non-food items, or activities that can be made frequently and immediately available

1 cookies | IA | IM | -SA | -DC | -RP | FP | PP | MP | Ind | 2S | 2P | <M | Ni | Det |

Table 5.
The Performance Levels for Waiting for Requests to be Honored

When directed to do so, learners wait for requests to be honored, without exhibiting problem behavior, without resisting or requiring prompts, without repeating the original request, making requests for 'when' or 'later', or making requests for other items or activities, when strong motivating events occur, in the presence of either of two persons, and continue making other required responses on three consecutive occasions...

IA	[the initial assessment of this skill has been completed]
Im	[instruction or management has begun]
1s	for 1 second
2s	for 2 seconds
5s	for 5 seconds
10s	for 10 seconds
20s	for 20 seconds
1m	for 1 minute
2m	for 2 minutes
5m	for 5 minutes
10m	for 10 minutes
20m	for 20 minutes
Det	['waiting' is no longer occurring consistently]

R9. Waits after making requests for each of the items and activities in R7 and R8 for gradually increasing periods of time

1 cookies	IA	IM	1s	2s	5s	10s	20s	1m	2m	5m	10m	20m	Det
	▓	▓	▓	▓									

Table 6.
The Performance Levels for Accepting the Removal of Access to Preferred Items and Activities by Persons in Authority or by Peers

When directed to do so, learners relinquish access and accept the removal of preferred items or activities by persons in authority by continuing to make other required responses...or...

When directed to do so, learners respond appropriately to the unauthorized removal of access to preferred items or activities by peers by politely making one or two requests to retain possession of the items or retain access to the activities that were removed (e.g., "please, May I have it back'), and then, if this is not successful, by requesting help from a person in authority on three consecutive occasions...

IA	[the initial assessment of this skill has been completed]
IM	[instruction or management has begun]
-SA	without self-injurious, aggressive, or destructive behavior
-DC	without disruptive behavior or complaints
-RP	without resistance to prompts and without leaving the area
FP	with a full physical or full demonstration prompt
PP	with a partial physical or partial demonstration prompt
MP	with a minimal touch or minimal gestural prompt
Ind	without prompts and within two seconds
2S	in two or more settings
2P	in the presence of either of two persons in authority or peers
>M	when strong motivating events have occurred
Det	[this skill is no longer occurring consistently]

R10. Accepts the removal of access to each of the 12 items or activities in R7 and R8 by persons in authority for gradually increasing periods of time

1 cookies	IA	IM	-SA	-DC	-RP	FP	PP	MP	Ind	2S	2P	>M	Det
	▓	▓	▓										

R46. Responds appropriately to the unauthorized removal of access to 5 preferred items or activities from R7, R8, R22-23, R27, or R30-31 by peers

2 coffee	IA	IM	-SA	-DC	-RP	FP	PP	MP	Ind	2S	2P	>M	Det
	▓	▓	▓										

Table 7.
The Performance Levels for 'Accepting No After Making Requests
That Were Taught and Are Often Honored'

When directed to do so, learners 'accept no after making requests that were taught and are often honored' without repeating the original request, making requests for 'when' or 'later', or making requests for other items or activities, and continue making other required responses on three consecutive occasions...

IA	[the initial assessment of this skill has been completed]
IM	[instruction or management has begun]
-SA	without self-injurious, aggressive, or destructive behavior
-DC	without disruptive behavior or complaints
2S	in two or more settings
2P	in the presence of either of two people
>M	when motivating events have occurred and are strong
Det	['accepting no' is no longer occurring consistently]

R15. 'Accepts no' after making requests for items and activities that were taught and are often honored as part of R7 and R8

2 playing in the street

IA	IM	-SA	-DC	2S	2P	>M	Det

Table 8.
The Performance Levels for 'Accepting No After Making Specific Requests
for Dangerous Items and Activities That Were Not Taught and Are Never Honored'

When directed to do so, learners 'accept no after making requests for dangerous items and activities that were not taught and are never honored' without repeating the original request, making requests for 'when' or 'later', or making requests for other items or activities, and continue making other required responses on three consecutive occasions...

IA	[the initial assessment of this skill has been completed]
IM	[instruction or management has begun]
-SA	without self-injurious, aggressive, or destructive behavior
-DC	without disruptive behavior or complaints
2S	in two or more settings
2P	in the presence of either of two people
>M	when motivating events have occurred and are strong
Det	['accepting no, never' is no longer occurring consistently]

R16. 'Accepts no' after making requests for dangerous items and activities that were not taught and are never honored

2 playing in the street

IA	IM	-SA	-DC	2S	2P	>M	Det

Table 9.
The Performance Levels for Completing 10 Consecutive Brief, Previously Acquired Tasks

When directed to do so by either of two people, and when strong motivating events occur, learners complete ___ [consecutive] brief, previously acquired task(s) between opportunities to make requests without problem behavior and without complaints on three consecutive occasions...

IA	[the initial assessment of this skill has been completed]
IM	[instruction or management has begun]
1	one brief task
2	two consecutive, brief tasks
5	five, consecutive, brief tasks
10	ten, consecutive, brief tasks
Det	[these tasks are no longer being completed consistently]

R11. Completes 10 consecutive, brief, previously acquired tasks

IA	IM	1	2	5	10	Det

Table 9. (cont.)
The Performance Levels for Completing 20 Consecutive, Previously Acquired Tasks

When directed to do so by either of two people, and when strong motivating events occur, learners complete ___ consecutive, previously acquired tasks between opportunities to make requests without problem behavior and without complaints on three consecutive occasions...

IA	[the initial assessment of this skill has been completed]
IM	[instruction or management has begun]
11	eleven consecutive, brief tasks
12	twelve consecutive, brief tasks
15	fifteen consecutive, brief tasks
20	twenty consecutive, brief tasks
Det	[these tasks are no longer being completed consistently]

R29. Completes 20 consecutive, previously acquired tasks

IA	IM	11	12	15	20	Det

Table 10.
The Performance Levels for Sharing and Taking Turns or Making Transitions

When directed to do so, learners share and take turns or make transitions on three consecutive occasions..

IA	[the initial assessment of this skill has been completed]
IM	[instruction or management has begun]
-SA	without self-injurious, aggressive, or destructive behavior
-DC	without disruptive behavior or complaints
-RP	without resistance to prompts and without leaving the area
FP	with a full physical or full demonstration prompt
PP	with a partial physical or partial demonstration prompt
MP	with a minimal touch or minimal gestural prompt
Ind	without prompts and within two seconds
2S	in two or more settings
2P	in the presence of either of two people
>M	when strong motivating events have occurred
Det	[sharing and taking turns with this item or activity or making transitions are no longer occurring consistently]

R12. Shares or takes turns obtaining access to each of the items and activities in R7 and R8 with an instructor, care provider, parent, or peer

1 cookies

IA	IM	-SA	-DC	-RP	FP	PP	MP	Ind	2S	2P	>M	Det

R13. Makes transitions from preferred items and activities to required tasks

1 from computer to washing hands

Teaching Requests and Related Listener Responses and Recording Progress

Before you begin teaching requests and related skills, make certain that the learner's primary method of speaking has been selected and confirmed. If the learner's method includes idiosyncratic signs or gestures, make certain that the signs or gestures that are required are clearly defined. Also, clearly define inappropriate responses or problem behavior. Use one of the three teaching protocols for requesting, along with the protocols for waiting, accepting no, accepting the removal of preferred items, activities, or persons, sharing and taking turns, making transitions, and completing assigned tasks between opportunities to make requests described in chapter 12. Collect data several times each week, or daily, if possible, using single-trial probes as described in chapter 4. As shown in Table 11, and described in chapter 4, record these probe data on one of the Skill Acquisition Self-graphing Data Recording Forms. These forms can be downloaded from www.behaviorchange.com. Then, as the learner reaches specific performance levels, transfer this information to the *ARP* (see Table 12). If improvement in the level of performance for any specific skill does not occur, closely follow the steps described in the teaching protocols in chapter 12 or make adjustments in these protocols.

Table 11.
Recording the Learner's Progress on Requests and Related Skills Selected for Instruction
Using First Opportunity of the Day Probe Data and Self-graphing Data Recording Forms

ESSENTIAL FOR LIVING
Skill Acquisition Self-graphing Data Recording Form
Requests with Signs: First Opportunity of the Day Probes

Request or Related Skill and Example	Day/Date and First Opportunity of the Day Probe																
	13	14	15	16	17	18	19	20	21	22	23	24	25	26	27	28	29
	S	M	T	W	T	F	S	S	M	T	W	T	F	S	S	M	T
R7. 5- Coke	Det NI <M 2P 2S Ind MP PP FP -RP -DC -SA 0	Det NI <M 2P 2S Ind MP PP FP -RP -DC (-SA) 0	Det NI <M 2P 2S Ind MP PP FP -RP (-DC) -SA 0	Det NI <M 2P 2S Ind MP PP FP -RP (-DC) -SA 0	Det NI <M 2P 2S Ind MP PP FP (-RP) -DC -SA 0	Det NI <M 2P 2S Ind MP PP FP (-RP) -DC -SA 0	Det NI <M 2P 2S Ind MP PP FP -RP -DC -SA 0	Det NI <M 2P 2S Ind MP PP FP -RP -DC -SA 0	Det NI <M 2P 2S Ind MP PP (FP) -RP -DC -SA 0	Det NI <M 2P 2S Ind MP PP (FP) -RP -DC -SA 0	Det NI <M 2P 2S Ind MP (PP) FP -RP -DC -SA 0	Det NI <M 2P 2S Ind MP PP (FP) -RP -DC -SA 0	Det NI <M 2P 2S Ind MP (PP) FP -RP -DC -SA 0	Det NI <M 2P 2S Ind MP PP FP -RP -DC -SA 0	Det NI <M 2P 2S Ind MP PP FP -RP -DC -SA 0	Det NI <M 2P 2S Ind (MP) PP FP -RP -DC -SA 0	Det NI <M 2P 2S Ind (MP) PP FP -RP -DC -SA 0

Table 12.
Transferring Data from Self-graphing Data Recording Forms
to the Assessment and Record of Progress (*ARP*)

R7. Requests 10 highly preferred snack foods, drinks, non-food items, or activities that can be made frequently and immediately available

1 cookies	IA	IM	-SA	-DC	-RP	FP	PP	MP	Ind	2S	2P	<M	Ni	Det

7b. Listener Responses, Names, and Descriptions

Listener Responses

Listener responses permit learners to do what others ask them to do. As shown in Table 1, listener responses occur when an instructor, care provider, parent, or peer directs a request toward a learner and the learner responds by pointing toward or retrieving one or more items or pictures, or completing one or more activities. The request can include spoken words, signs, or written, typed, or selected words. If the learner's response is consistent with the request, the response is considered correct or appropriate and is followed by verbal praise or other forms of approval, confirmation, or appreciation. If not, an instructor, care provider, or parent, and sometimes a peer, may prompt the learner to make the correct response before providing approval or confirmation.

Table 1.
Listener Responses

An instructor, care provider, parent, supervisor, or peer directs a request toward a learner [S^D]	The learner gestures toward, touches, or retrieves one or more items, or completes one or more activities [R]	The instructor provides verbal praise or a form of approval or confirmation [S^R]
A parent says "hold my hand"	The learner grasps and holds the parent's hand	The parents provides praise
A care provider says "put your shirt on"	The learner puts his shirt on	The care provider indicates approval
A therapist places several items on a table and says "where is the cup"	The learner gestures toward or touches the 'cup'	The therapist confirms that the selected item is a cup
A teacher places several pictures on a table and says "find the cup"	The learner points to a picture of a cup	The teacher says "that's right"
A mother signs to her son "[please get a] spoon [and a] napkin"	The son goes to the kitchen and retrieves a spoon and a napkin	Mother signs "thanks" to her son for completing the requested task
A work supervisor says "put the rags in the blue bin"	The worker gets the rags and puts them in the blue bin	The supervisor expresses her appreciation

S^D: a verbal, discriminative stimulus
R: a listener response
S^R: a social reinforcer

Listener responses come in several forms:

- **Following directions** to make responses consistent with maintaining **learner safety**,
- **Following directions** to complete **routine activities** of daily living,
- **Recognizing** items, familiar persons, places, items with features, or pictures of the same, and
- **Retrieving and relocating** items, familiar persons, or items with features, often from and to specific places or locations

Following directions occurs when learners are directed to make responses consistent with maintaining their safety -- e.g., when an instructor or care provider says "stand up" or "fasten your seat belt", and when learners are directed to perform activities of daily living -- e.g., "put your dirty socks in the laundry basket" or "wash your hands", and learners respond accordingly. *Recognizing (rec)*, on the other hand, occurs when instructors or care providers say something like "where is the spoon" or "which ones are your socks" and learners point to the spoon on the table or the socks on the floor in the laundry room. *Retrieving (ret) and relocating (rel)* are similar to recognizing, except that learners must 'get' items or familiar persons from specific places and bring them to instructors or care providers, or 'bring' items or familiar persons to new places or locations. A functional repertoire of listener responses should include all four of these forms, examples of which are provided in Table 2.

Table 2.
Commonly Occurring Listener Responses and Their Corresponding Cues

Following Directions: Learner Safety

"Stand up"
"Sit down"
"Lie down"
"Stay next to me"
"Hold my hand"

"Put your seat belt on"
"Walk with me"
"Come here"
"Wait (or Stay) here"
"Wait (or Stay) there"
"Stay in line"
"Stop (or Stop running)"

Following Directions: Routine Activities

"Put your napkin in the waste basket"
"Hold (or Carry) this box"
"Put on your shoes"
"Put away your toys"
"Put your socks in the washing machine"
"Wash your hands (or face)"

Recognizing

"Where is the flour"
"Find the mixing bowl"
"Which one is Mrs. Fredericks"

Retrieving and Relocating

"Hand me the bowl"
"Give me the bottle opener and a towel"
"Get two green glasses"
"Go to the kitchen and get two forks"
"Get two rags from under the sink"
"Put the silverware in the drawer"
"Take Mr. Smith to the woodworking area"

Names and Descriptions

Names permit learners to talk about items, familiar persons, places, and activities as they encounter them or as they are occurring in their environment. Descriptions permit learners to talk about features of items and locations (among other things). As shown in Table 3, names and descriptions (nd) occur when a learner is in sensory contact with (i.e., sees, hears, touches, smells, or tastes), but does not want, specific items, persons, places, locations, activities, or pictures of the same, and, says words, forms signs, or selects, types, or writes words. If the learner's response matches the word or sign commonly used to designate that item, person, place, location, or activity, the name or description is considered 'correct' and is followed by verbal praise or other forms of approval or confirmation. If not, an instructor, care provider, or parent, and sometimes a peer, may prompt the learner to make the correct response before providing approval or confirmation. Names and descriptions may also occur with some learners when they experience sensations of pain or discomfort, or feelings of happiness, sadness, or anger only they can feel and observe, and say words, form signs, or select, type, or write words that may correspond to what they are experiencing. Examples of names and descriptions are provided in Table 4.

public, nonverbal stimuli

private, non-verbal stimuli

Other than occasional comments (e.g., "look, it's an airplane or "it's time to go back to work"), spontaneous names or descriptions of items, familiar persons, places, locations, and activities, or photographs of the same seldom occur in everyday living. As a result, readers might conclude that naming and describing are not functional skills. Names and descriptions, however, can be transformed into following directions, recognitions, retrievals, and relocations using specific teaching procedures. In fact, teaching names and descriptions prior to listener recognitions can increase the rate of acquisition of recognitions, retrievals, and relocations. Names and descriptions can also be transformed into meaningful, rather than rote, answers to commonly occurring questions. And, names and descriptions of photographs of items, familiar persons, places, locations, and activities can help a learner use a daily picture schedule or a shopping list composed of pictures. Finally, learners' descriptions of pain and discomfort, and feelings of sadness, happiness, and anger may increase the efficiency and effectiveness of subsequent requests for information or assistance.

mand-tacts

Using the joint control procedure, stimulus control can be transferred from tacts to listener responses.

Table 3.
Names and Descriptions

A learner sees, hears, touches, smells, or tastes an item, activity, place, location, or a feature of the same, or a person or picture of the same, or a physical sensation or feeling [S^D]	⟹	The learner says words, forms signs, selects pictures, or selects, types or writes words [R]	⟹	The instructor provides verbal praise or a form of approval or confirmation [S^R]
A care provider points to a cup or a picture of a cup		A learner says the word 'cup'		The care provider provides praise and confirms that it is a 'cup'
An instructor holds a sweater in front of a learner		The learner selects, types, or prints the word 'sweater'		The instructor indicates that it is a sweater
A mother hands a learner with a visual impairment a 'large ball'		The learner says or signs 'large ball'		The mother provides her approval and confirms that it is a 'large ball'
A peer gestures toward a table		A learner reaches under the table, grasps a ball, and says 'it's under the table'		The peer says 'great, throw it back'
The learner falls cuts his knee and experiences pain		The learner 'feels pain' and says 'that hurts'		A care provider acknowledges the pain and provides a bandage

S^D: a nonverbal, discriminative stimulus
R: a speaker response
S^R: a social reinforcer

Table 4.
Examples of Names and Descriptions

- **naming an item** -- a child sees a spoon and says 'spoon' or a child with a visual impairment touches a napkin and says 'napkin',
- **naming a familiar person** -- an adult hears a familiar voice and selects a card with the word 'boss' printed on it,
- **naming a place or location** -- a child gestures toward the kitchen and signs 'kitchen', or opens a dresser drawer, points to an item, and says 'in the drawer',
- **naming an activity** -- an adult says 'washing dishes' as he or someone else is doing so,
- **describing a feature of an item** -- a child points to a big ball and writes 'big ball',
- **describing sensations** -- an adult bends forward, points to his stomach, and says 'hurts', and
- **naming feelings** -- an adult, who has accidentally spilled his favorite beverage, signs 'mad'.

Teaching Recognitions, Retrievals, Relocations, and Corresponding Names and Descriptions at the Same Time

Listener responses, in the form of recognitions, retrievals, and relocations, and corresponding names or descriptions should generally be taught at the same time. For example, as learners are taught 'to find a spoon', they should also be taught 'to provide the name'. For some learners, however, recognitions, retrievals, and relocations will need to be taught without corresponding names and descriptions. For example, *in order to name or describe, learners must function as speakers by 'saying words', or by 'writing, typing, or selecting printed words'. Learners whose only method of speaking includes selecting pictures are precluded from naming and describing, as these selections function as picture-to-item or picture-to-picture matching. If, however, pictures are exchanged for printed words, these learners can begin naming and describing. In addition, many learners with developmental disabilities who have difficulty acquiring a repertoire of* requests, also find it very difficult to acquire more than a few names or descriptions. Nonetheless, many of these same children and adults learn to respond effectively as listeners. For example, many children and adults learn to recognize their dirty socks, retrieve them from their bedroom, bring them to the laundry room, and put them in the washing machine when directed to do so without ever learning to name 'bedroom', 'socks', 'laundry room', or 'washing machine' or to describe socks as 'dirty'.

ESSENTIAL FOR LIVING
Must-have Listener Responses

Following Directions Related to Health and Safety. First and foremost, learners should be expected to *follow directions consistent with maintaining their health and safety*. These listener responses are designated as *must-have skills* and *should be given the same priority as must-have requests and some must-have tolerating skills*. These listener responses (see **LR1-11**) should be precisely defined (see **LR1-2**) and should be taught in a variety of circumstances throughout the day. For example, when being escorted off a school bus, transported from a classroom to the cafeteria, taken on a shopping trip, or taken to the park, learners should be taught to 'stand up', 'stand in line', 'move from one location to another', or 'hold the hand (or arm) of', 'come and stand next to', or 'wait next to' a care provider, an instructor, or a parent when directed to do so.

LR1. Holds and maintains contact with the hand of an instructor, care provider, or parent when directed to do so

This listener response, generally preceded by the direction "hold my hand", must be acquired in order for parents, instructors, or care providers to take children and adults to public places within the community. The required response is often not well defined. As a result, individual learners may permit their hand to be held without resistance and but may not grasp the hand of the other person. Other learners may resist their hand being held. These approximations can compromise the safety of our learners. We prefer to define the required response as 'tolerating the hand of an instructor, care provider, or parent wrapped around your hand without resistance *and* wrapping your fingers around the hand of that person when directed to do so'. 'Tolerating the hand of an instructor' may need to be taught before 'wrapping your fingers around the hand of an instructor'.   *not operationally defined*   *an operational definition*

'Interlocking arms' is often considered a more socially acceptable response form for adults. We prefer not beginning with this response form with some adults, as it may compromise their safety. With these learners, we often begin with 'holding hands' and gradually move to 'interlocking arms'. We prefer to define 'interlocking arms' as 'tolerating the arm of an instructor, care provider, or parent wrapped around yours without resistance *and* wrapping your arm around the arm of that person when directed to do so'. As with 'holding hands', 'tolerating the arm of an instructor' may need to be taught before 'wrapping your arm around the arm of an instructor'.   *an operational definition*

Learners are expected to perform this listener response as defined for gradually increasing periods of time from one second to twenty minutes (see chapter 4 and the **ARP** manual).

LR2. Moves toward and stands or sits next to an instructor, care provider, or parent when directed to do so

This listener response, often preceded by the direction 'come here', is also very important for our learners. Sometimes, as in **LR1**, the required response is not well defined. As a result, individual learners may approach, but remain at varying distances from the person who provided the direction. In some circumstances this response variation may compromise their safety. We prefer to teach this response at the same time as **LR1**, and, in the beginning, we define the required response as 'moving toward the person who directed them to do so and holding their hand'. Then, the required response becomes 'moving toward the person who provided the direction until that person is within arms length, that is, you can touch that person without moving your feet'.   *not operationally defined*   *an operational definition*

LR3.   Moves toward and stands or remains in a line when directed to do so

When a group of children or adults are about to be transported from one location to another, they are often directed to form a line. Keeping a group of learners together as they are transported helps to insure their safety. Instructors often say "everybody, get in line". As in **LR1**, the required listener response is often not well defined. As a result, individual learners may approach, but remain at varying distances from the instructor or peer who is in front of them. In a word, the line is 'all over the place'. In some circumstances this response variation could compromise learner safety.

We prefer to teach this listener response at nearly the same time as **LR1** and **LR2**, and, in the beginning, we define the required response as 'moving toward the person who provided the direction and holding a handle on a rope'. Then, gradually, the required response becomes 'moving toward the person who directed them to do so until that person or a peer already in line is within arms length, that is, you can reach out and touch their back without moving your feet'. The end of the required response in this skill is nearly the same as **LR2**, except that, if the learner is not first in the line, he must move to within arms length of a peer.

LR4.   Waits within arms length of an instructor, care provider, or parent, or waits in line when directed to do so

Once learners move next to an instructor, care provider, parent, or move toward and stand in line(**LR2** and **LR3**), they must learn to wait there. Care providers or parents often say "wait here", "wait by me" and instructors often say "wait in line". Then, either one is apt to say "hands down". The required listener response is defined as 'standing in line with their hands touching their sides when directed to do so for brief, but gradually increasing periods of time'. This response can be taught at the same time as **LR2** and **LR3** and requires maintaining the last part of the required response in **LR2** and **LR3**. Learners are expected to perform this listener response as defined for gradually increasing periods of time from one second to five minutes (see chapter 4 and the *ARP* manual).

LR5.   Stands up, sits down, folds hands, lies down, or sits up when directed to do so

Learners are often directed to "stand up" or "sit down" before performing other activities. If they are about to begin instruction at a table, they are often also directed to "fold your hands". At other times, they are directed to 'lie down' when they are tired, when they don't feel well, and when it's time to go to bed. Some learners may be directed to 'lie down' after having a seizure, while others who are bedridden or slouched in a chair, may be directed to 'sit up'. We define 'standing up' as 'standing straight with both feet on the ground', 'sitting down' as 'bottom on a chair, back straight, and legs in front', 'lying down' as 'head and rest of body, including feet, resting on a designated surface', and 'sitting up' as 'moving the head, neck, and shoulders as close to a vertical position as possible'. These listener responses should each be taught at the same time as **LR1**, **LR2**, **LR3**, and **LR4**.

LR6.   Moves from one location to another when directed to do so, while remaining next to an instructor, care provider, or parent, or while remaining in line

This listener response, defined as 'walking or moving a wheelchair, gait trainer, walker, or MOVE device from a current to a designated location, while remaining within arms length of an instructor, care provider, parent, or peer, when directed to do so', must also be acquired in order for learners to move about the community and participate in activities. Instructors, care providers, or parents often say "it's time to go" or "let's go". Some learners have difficulty acquiring this listener response, and tend, without warning, to 'plop' on the floor or the ground or 'bolt' and 'run off'. These learners, especially those who are large and difficult to move or those who run very fast, are often restricted from participating in community activities.

This listener response can be taught at the same time as **LR1**, **LR2**, **LR3**, **LR4**, and **LR5**, and may require extended practice sessions within a restricted area before venturing into the community. Learners are expected to perform this listener response as defined for gradually increasing periods of time from one minute to twenty minutes (see chapter 4 and the *ARP* manual).

Once this skill has been acquired for short distances (i.e., brief durations), directions should gradually be faded and distances gradually increased. This skill then becomes a daily living skill and learners are expected to move from a current location to a variety of other locations while remaining in line or next to an instructor, care provider, or parent.

LR7. Waits at a current location or a specific location when directed to do so

Sometimes instructors, care providers, or parents must move a short distance from learners and 'know' that they will remain in their current location. They often say "wait here", with the possible addition of "I'll be right back". The appropriate listener response is defined as 'standing in the current location with their hands touching their sides when directed to do so for brief, but gradually increasing periods of time'. Learners are expected to perform this response for gradually increasing periods of time from ten seconds to five minutes (see chapter 4 and the **ARP** manual).

This listener response can be very difficult to teach, as physical prompting requires that the person providing the direction remain with the learner and provide a prompt to wait. As a result, you must begin with a very brief period of required waiting (e.g., five seconds) [see **R8**], and, as the learner begins to wait successfully, gradually increase this periods of time to five minutes. 'Waiting at a current location' should be taught after learners have acquired **LR4**.

Sometimes instructors, care providers, or parents see a learner at a distance or receive a phone call indicating that a learner is in a specific location without adequate super-vision. When this occurs, they often say (or shout) "stay there... someone will be there soon". The appropriate listener response is defined as 'remaining in a specific location when directed to do so for gradually increasing periods of time'. Learners are expected to perform this response as defined for gradually increasing periods of time from ten seconds to five minutes (see chapter 4 and the ARP manual).

This listener response can also be very difficult to teach, because situations like this seldom occur in everyday living. Teaching this skill requires providing opportunities for guided practice when these situations do occur *and* contriving situations similar to those that might occur and again provide opportunities for guided practice until help arrives. We would suggest contriving a variety of situations and periods of time in which learners must remain where they are after being directed to do so. This skill can be taught at any time and does not require the acquisition of any other listener response.

LR8. Moves to and remains in a designated area when directed to do so

Sometimes instructors, care providers, or parents want learners to go to and remain in a designated area and 'occupy themselves'. When this occurs, they often say "go to _____ [a designated area] and play [or engage in a specific leisure activity]". This listener response is defined as 'moves to a designated area, remains in that area, and engages in an a leisure activity or acquired leisure skill for gradually increasing periods of time, when directed to do so'. Listeners are expected to move to the designated area and remain in that area for gradually increasing periods of time from 20 seconds to 20 minutes (see chapter 4 and the ARP manual).

This skill can be taught at any time and requires that learners have previously acquired one or more leisure skills (**DLS-LAH1-13** or **DLS-LAC1-12**).

LR9. Stops moving or engaging in a dangerous activity when directed to do so

Sometimes learners will run away from an instructor, care provider, or parent, or will engage in an activity that is dangerous to their health or safety. When this occurs, the individual in-charge will often say in a loud and determined voice "stop" or "stop that". The appropriate listener response is 'to immediately stop running or engaging in the specified activity and turn toward the individual who provided the direction to stop'.

This skill can also be very difficult to teach, not only because situations like this seldom occur, but because they are very difficult to contrive. We would suggest contriving a variety of situations which do not place learners at risk and 'hope' that your teaching results in generalization to dangerous situations. As is the case with **LR8**, this skill can be taught at any time and does not require the acquisition of any other listener response.

LR10. Turns toward others when her/his name is called and makes two consecutive listener responses from LR1-9

When learners are in a crowded public area or with a group of their peers, it is often necessary to secure their attention before directing them to make one of the listener responses specified in **LR1-9**. This skill is defined as 'turning toward a person who calls out your name, continuing to look toward that person as a direction is provided, and making one or two appropriate listener responses' from **LR1-9**. This skill is difficult for two reasons. First, no type of prompt insures 'looking toward another person'; you must simply repeat the direction until the learner looks toward you. Second, after 'looking', the learner is expected to make two additional listener responses.

LR11. Fastens a seat belt while in a car, a car seat, or a mobility device and remains in the seat belt for gradually increasing periods of time when directed to do so

This listener response must be acquired in order for learners to be transported safely and to safely transport themselves. Instructors, care providers, or parents often say "fasten your seat belt" and "keep your seat belt on". We define an appropriate listener response as 'fastening a seat belt while seated in the back seat of a car, a car seat, or a wheelchair, or MOVE device until the clicking sound occurs, when directed to do so, and moving (or being transported) to a specified location without unfastening or sliding out from under the seat belt'. This listener response can be taught at any time and may require an extended number of practice sessions. Learners are expected to perform this listener response as defined for gradually increasing periods of time from twenty seconds to twenty minutes (see chapter 4 and the *ARP* manual).

As you are teaching this skill, learners may also have to learn to tolerate 'sitting in the back seat of a car (see **T-Trp-01**) or in a car seat' (see **T-Trp-02**). 'Remaining in a seat belt' can also be taught (see **T-Trp-03**).

Additional Must-have Listener Responses

Following Directions Related to Health and Safety. With certain children and adults, you may want to select additional listener responses that take the form of *following directions to make responses consistent with maintaining learner safety* and designate these as *must-have skills*. This section permits you to do this.

LR11a. _____

LR11b. _____

LR11c. _____

LR11d. _____

ESSENTIAL FOR LIVING
Should-have Listener Responses

Following Directions to Complete Routine Activities. As learners are acquiring listener responses that are consistent with maintaining their safety, they should also be taught *to follow directions to complete frequently-occurring, routine activities of daily living*. These responses do not generally involve the safety of our learners, but do represent a large part of effective daily living. In fact, when directions are faded, these responses become daily living skills. We recommend teaching these *should-have* listener responses in a variety of situations throughout the day (see **LR12-17**), and, whenever possible, during commonly occurring events (see **Events 1-13**). For example, when it is time for dinner and at other appropriate times during the day, learners should be taught to 'put away your toys', 'turn off the TV', 'set the table' 'wash your hands', 'pour the milk', 'eat your dinner', and 'put your napkin in the trash can' when directed to do so.

The required listener response in each of the targeted activities in **LR12-17** should be *precisely defined for each learner* and should generally include all movements that are customarily completed by competent adults. For example: 'washing hands' could be defined as 'turning on the water, grasping the soap, scrubbing and rinsing both sides of both hands, turning off the water, drying both hands, and putting a cloth towel on the rack or disposing of a paper towel when directed to do so'. For learners with limited motor movements, this definition can be adapted to permit permanent partial assistance (see the *ARP*). For example, the definition of washing hands could be adapted to include an instructor placing the cloth towel on the towel rack. Some learners may have difficulty acquiring some of these listener responses without a detailed task analysis. If this is the case, prepare such an analysis and teach the skill first as a daily living skill and later as a listener response.

LR12. Completes five activities of dressing or personal hygiene when directed to do so

This type of listener response includes many different forms, 'washing hands', 'brushing teeth', 'putting on a shirt', or 'flushing the toilet', to name a few. Learners are expected to exhibit five forms of this listener response.

LR13. Places items in designated locations when directed to do so

This listener response, generally preceded by the direction "put [a designated item] away [or in a specified location]" is often part of a requested transition from preferred items to required tasks (**R13**), and is a listener response that should be acquired by all learners capable of doing so. This response is defined as 'putting an item in a specified location when directed to do so'. Learners are expected to exhibit this listener response with three preferred items.

LR14. 'Cleans up' after making a mess when directed to do so

Many learners resist following a direction to "clean up". An appropriate listener response is defined as 'restoring an area to its condition prior to an activity that has just concluded when directed to do so'. This response should also be acquired by all learners capable of doing so. The extent of expected restoration may depend on the age and fine motor skills of the learner.

LR15. Provides five types of help to someone when asked to do so

This listener response comes in many forms, which include 'carrying a package', 'holding an item', 'holding a door open', 'opening a container', or 'reaching for an item on a shelf when directed to do so'. Learners are expected to exhibit five forms of this listener response.

LR16. Performs five household chores or chores at work when directed to do so

This listener response also comes in many forms, 'emptying a trash can', 'putting dishes in the dishwasher', 'washing dishes', 'wiping a table', 'mopping a floor', 'folding towels', 'closing windows', or 'locking doors when directed to do so', to name a few. As with **LR12** and **LR15**, learners are expected to exhibit five forms of this listener response. Learners, who readily exhibit forms of this listener response, will come in contact with enthusiastic responses from care providers and instructors, especially when directions are faded and the the occurrence of specific situations results in these responses, which have become effective daily living skills.

LR17. Turns lights or electrical devices on or off when directed to do so

Learners are often asked to turn lights, a fan, a television, an iPod, a coffeemaker, an iron, or microwave oven 'on or off'. This listener response generally requires very little effort and is often very useful to learners and those who care for them. As with **LR12**, **LR15**, and **LR16**, learners are expected to exhibit five forms of this listener response.

Additional Should-have Listener Responses

Following Directions to Complete Routine Activities. With certain children and adults, you may want to select additional listener responses in the form of *following directions to complete routine activities of daily living* and designate these as *should-have skills*. This section permits you to do this.

LR17a. _____

LR17b. _____

LR17c. _____

LR17d. _____

LR17e. _____

ESSENTIAL FOR LIVING
Good-to-have Listener Responses, Names, and Descriptions

Recognizing, Retrieving, Relocating, Naming, Describing, and Following Directions to Complete Activities (LRND1-13). As learners are beginning to respond as effective listeners (i.e., they have acquired some of the skills in **LR1-11** and **LR12-17**), but not before then, they should be taught to *recognize* (rec) items, familiar persons, places, items with features, and, possibly, pictures of the same. They should also be taught to *retrieve* (ret) *or relocate* (rel) items, familiar persons, or items with features, often from and to specific places or locations, and to follow directions to complete additional, *routine activities of daily living* not taught in the previous section (comp). And, finally, if their method of speaking permits them to do so, teach corresponding *names and descriptions* (nd). These listener responses, names, and descriptions, designated as *good-to-have*, should be taught in the context of 13 routine events (**LRND1-13**), which learners experience every day, or at least, several times each week. For example, children may experience 'breakfast', 'getting ready for school', 'snack time', or 'going to the toilet', while adults may experience 'going shopping', 'preparing for physical therapy', 'getting ready for work', or 'break time'. During 'breakfast', a learner may hear someone say "where are the napkins" and be expected to point to them, "hand me a spoon" or "get a rag from under the sink" and be expected to go and get one, "bring the milk with you" and be expected to bring it from one place to another, "wipe your mouth" and be expected to do so. Table 5 provides a description of six groups of these routine events, when instruction with each group of events should begin, and the types of listener and speaker responses that should be taught as part of each group of events. As shown in Table 5, the number of types of listener and speaker responses that are part of each group of events are initially limited (Events 1-3, The First Time Around: LRND1-3.1 and Events 4-6, The First Time Around: LRND4-6.1) and then gradually increased (Events 1-3, The Second Time Around: LRND1-3.2 and Events 4-6, The Second Time Around: LRND4-6.2) so that, if learners have difficulty acquiring some of these types of responses, their repertoires will extend across more events.

Table 5.
Six Groups of Routine Events that Provide the Naturally Recurring Context
for Teaching Listener Responses, Names, and Descriptions

Group of Routine Events	When Instruction with Each Group of Events Should Begin	The Types of Listener Responses, Names, and Descriptions within Each Group
Events 1-3, The First Time Around: LRND1-3.1	Most of the skills in 'LR1-17' have been acquired	Preferred items, along with other items and activities
Events 4-6, The First Time Around: LRND4-6.1	After skills in 'Events 1-3: The First Time Around' have been acquired	Some preferred items, other items, activities, familiar persons, and places
Events 1-3, The Second Time Around: LRND1-3.2	After skills in 'Events 4-6: The First Time Around' have been acquired	Preferred items, other items, and activities + familiar persons, and places
Events 7-13: LRND7-13	After skills in 'Events 1-3: The Second Time Around' have been acquired	Items, activities, familiar persons, places, locations, two items at a time, two or more of the same item, items with one or two features, and items and familiar persons from and to specific places
Events 1-3, The Third Time Around: LRND1-3.3	After skills in 'Events 7-8' have been acquired	Same as Events 7-13
Events 4-6, The Second Time Around: LRND4-6.2	After skills in 'Events 1-3: The Third Time Around' have been acquired	Same as Events 7-13

Some of these listener responses eventually become daily living skills. For example, 'bringing the milk with you' may begin as a listener skill, but may eventually become something a learner does during breakfast without being directed to do so.

An additional group of events (**LRND14-15**) which occur when learners experience pain or discomfort, or feelings of happiness, sadness, or anger, and are taught 'to indicate the presence of these private experiences', cannot generally be taught until learners have acquired listener responses, names, and descriptions that are part of at least 10 events.

Events 1-3, The First Time (LRND1-3.1). Begin by selecting three events for each learner, which include preferred items for which requests were previously acquired. Then, select (1) three items that are typically part of each of these events and that learners are often required to recognize (rec), retrieve or relocate (ret/rel), and name (nd), and (2) one activity for each event that learners are often required to describe (nd) and complete (comp) when directed to do so. For example, as shown in Table 5, if 'Breakfast' is selected as Event 1, 2, or 3 for a specific learner, you should begin teaching that learner to (1) recognize, retrieve or relocate, and name 'Cheerios, Wheaties, and milk', along with 'a bowl, a napkin, and a spoon', (2) describe 'wiping [his] mouth', and (3) complete this activity when directed to do so.

Table 5.
Listener and Speaker Responses for Events 1-3: The First Time Around (LRND1-3.1)
Sample Event -- Breakfast
Introduced after Most of the Listener Responses in LR1-17 have been Acquired

Preferred Item		Preferred Item		Item	
Cheerios or Wheaties	rec	milk	rec	a bowl	rec
	ret/rel		ret/rel		ret/rel
	nd		nd		nd

Item		Item		Activity	
a napkin	rec	a spoon	rec	wiping my mouth	comp
	ret/rel		ret/rel		
	nd		nd		nd

When these events are first introduced, recognizing (rec), retrieving (ret), relocating (rel), and naming (nd), should be limited to a few items and should not include familiar persons, places, locations, more than one item at a time, two or more of a specific item, or items with features. Recognizing and naming should not include photographs (rec-p or nd-p), as this may limit learners' understanding of their environment. Also, describing and completing (nd and comp) should be limited to one activity per event. These first few events should never include recognizing, naming, or describing one's own physical sensations or feelings, as these private events require special teaching procedures.

Events 4-6: The First Time Around (LRND4-6.1). When learners have acquired most of the speaking and listening skills that are part of Events 1, 2, and 3: The First Time Around, select three new events. Each of these events should include the same components as Events 1, 2, and 3, along with (1) recognitions, retrievals, relocations, and names of two familiar persons, (2) recognitions and names of two places, and (3) a description and the completion of two activities. For example, as shown in Table 6, if 'Getting Ready to Go Home' is selected as Event 4, 5, or 6 for a specific learner, you may want to begin by teaching that learner to recognize, retrieve or relocate, and name 'her iPod and Uno cards', along with 'her purse, lunch box, back pack, and 'jacket'. You may also want her to teach her to recognize and name 'her instructor or supervisor', 'a friend', 'her locker or cubby', and 'the cafeteria', and, finally, to describe 'wiping the table' or 'throwing the trash away' and to complete these activities when directed to do so. Listener and speaker responding may also include recognizing and naming photographs (rec-p and nd-p) of these items, familiar persons, and places.

Events 1-3: The Second Time Around (LRND1-3.2). When learners have acquired most of the speaking and listening skills that are part of Events 4, 5, and 6: The First Time Around, add (1) recognitions and names of two places, (2) recognitions, retrievals, relocations, and names of one additional item and two familiar persons, and (3) the description and completion of one additional activity to Events 1-3, such that these events now include the same types of speaking and listening skills as Events 4-6: The First Time Around. For example, as shown in Table 7, you may want to expand your learner's listener and speaker repertoire during 'breakfast' to include recognizing and naming the 'cafeteria and kitchen', and recognizing, retrieving, relocating, and naming 'a teacher or friend', and describing and completing 'cleaning the table'. Listener and speaker responding may also include recognizing and naming photographs (rec-p and nd-p) of these items, persons, and places.

Table 6.
Listener and Speaker Responses for Events 4-6: The First Time Around (LRND4-6.1)
Sample Event -- Getting Ready to Go Home
Introduced after Listener and Speaker Responses have been Acquired
for Events 1-3: The First Time Around (LRND1-3.1)

Preferred Item		Preferred Item		Item	
your iPod	rec / ret/rel / rec-p / nd / nd-p	your Uno cards	rec / ret/rel / rec-p / nd / nd-p	your purse or wallet	rec / ret/rel / rec-p / nd / nd-p
Item		Item		Activity	
your lunch box	rec / ret/rel / rec-p / nd / nd-p	your back pack	rec / ret/rel / rec-p / nd / nd-p	throwing the trash away	comp / nd
Item		Activity		Familiar Person	
your jacket	rec / ret/rel / rec-p / nd / nd-p	wiping the table	comp / nd	Mr. Harris	rec / ret/rel / rec-p / nd / nd-p
Familiar Person		Place		Place	
John	rec / ret/rel / rec-p / nd / nd-p	classroom	rec / rec-p / nd / nd-p	your locker	rec / rec-p / nd / nd-p

Table 7.
Listener and Speaker Responses for Events 1-3: The Second Time Around (LRND1-3.2)
Sample Event -- Breakfast
Introduced after Listener and Speaker Responses have been Acquired
for Events 4-6: The First Time Around (LRND4-6.1)

Preferred Item		Preferred Item		Item	
Cheerios or Wheaties	rec / ret/rel / rec-p / nd / nd-p	milk	rec / ret/rel / rec-p / nd / nd-p	a bowl	rec / ret/rel / rec-p / nd / nd-p
Item		Item		Activity	
a napkin	rec / ret/rel / rec-p / nd / nd-p	a spoon	rec / ret/rel / rec-p / nd / nd-p	wiping your mouth	comp / nd
Item		Activity		Familiar Person	
juice	rec / ret/rel / rec-p / nd / nd-p	cleaning the table	comp / nd	Mrs. Ellis	rec / ret/rel / rec-p / nd / nd-p
Familiar Person		Place		Place	
Kristin	rec / ret/rel / rec-p / nd / nd-p	cafeteria	rec / rec-p / nd / nd-p	kitchen	rec / rec-p / nd / nd-p

Events 7-13 (LRND7-13). When learners have acquired most of the speaking and listening skills that are part of Events 1-3: The Second Time Around, select a few new events, which do not include items for which requests were previously acquired, but which do include (1) recognitions, retrievals, relocations, and names of six items and two familiar persons, two items at a time, two or more of the same item, and one or two items with one or two features, (2) descriptions and completions of two activities, (3) recognitions and names of two places and two locations, and (4) retrievals and relocations of items and familiar persons from and to places and locations.

Table 8.
Listener and Speaker Responses for Events 7-13 (LRND7-13)
Sample Event -- Unloading the Dishwasher
Introduced after Listener and Speaker Responses have been Acquired
for Events 1-3: The Second Time (LRND1-3.2)

Item		Item		Item	
plates	rec	cups	rec	glasses	rec
	ret/rel		ret/rel		ret/rel
	rec-p		rec-p		rec-p
	nd		nd		nd
	nd-p		nd-p		nd-p
Item		**Item**		**Activity**	
forks	rec	spoons	rec	stacking the saucers	comp
	ret/rel		ret/rel		
	rec-p		rec-p		
	nd		nd		nd
	nd-p		nd-p		
Item		**Activity**		**Familiar Person**	
plates	rec	putting the silverware away	comp	Jerry	rec
	ret/rel				ret/rel
	rec-p				rec-p
	nd		nd		nd
	nd-p				nd-p
Familiar Person		**Place**		**Place**	
Mrs. Thompson	rec	kitchen	rec	office	rec
	ret/rel				
	rec-p		rec-p		rec-p
	nd		nd		nd
	nd-p		nd-p		nd-p
Location		**Location**		**2 Items**	
on the counter	rec	in the cupboard	rec	cups and saucers	rec
					ret/rel
	rec-p		rec-p		rec-p
	nd		nd		nd
	nd-p		nd-p		nd-p
2 or More of the Same Item		**One Item with a Feature**		**One Item with 2 Features**	
4 cups	rec	red glasses	rec	large, blue plates	rec
	ret/rel		ret/rel		ret/rel
	rec-p		rec-p		rec-p
	nd		nd		nd
	nd-p		nd-p		nd-p
2 Items with a Feature		**2 Items with 2 Features**		**Items to a Place/Location**	
glass mugs and serving spoons	rec	large, mixing spoons and small, plastic glasses	rec	cups in the cupboard	rel
	ret/rel		ret/rel		
	rec-p		rec-p		
	nd		nd		
	nd-p		nd-p		
Items from a Place/Location		**Person from a Place/Location**		**Person to a Place/Location**	
spoons from the dishwasher	ret	teacher from the laundry room	ret	supervisor to the kitchen	rel

For example, as shown in Table 8, if 'Unloading the Dishwasher' is selected as one of Events 7-13 for a specific learner, you may want him to recognize, retrieve or relocate, and name 'cups', 'glasses', 'forks', 'spoons', 'plates', 'familiar persons', 'cups and saucers', '4 cups', 'the red glasses', 'the large, blue plates', 'glass mugs and serving spoons', 'large, mixing spoons and small, plastic glasses', to describe and complete the activities known as 'putting the silverware away' and 'stacking the saucers', to recognize and name 'the kitchen', 'the office', 'on the counter', and 'in the cupboard', 'to retrieve 'spoons from the dishwasher' and 'the teacher from the laundry room', and to relocate 'cups to the cupboard' and 'the supervisor to the kitchen'. Listener and speaker responding may also include recognizing, naming, and describing photographs (rec-p and nd-p) of items, familiar persons, and places.

Events 1-3: The Third Time Around (LRND1-3.3). When learners have acquired most of the speaking and listening skills that are part of Events 7 and 8, add (1) recognitions and names of two locations, (2) recognitions, retrievals, relocations, names, and descriptions of two items at a time, two or more of the same item, and one or two items with one or two features, and (3) retrievals and relocations of items and familiar persons from and to specific places and locations to Events 1-3. Now these events will include the same type of speaking and listening skills as Events 7-8.

For example, as shown in Table 9, you may want to expand your learner's speaker and listener repertoire during 'Breakfast' to include recognizing and naming 'next to the refrigerator' and 'in the sink', recognizing, retrieving, relocating, naming, and describing 'a spoon and a bowl', '3 napkins', 'cereal spoons', and '2% chocolate milk', 'blue bowls and Honey Nut Cheerios', 'red placemats and blue napkins, 'retrieving 'a bowl from the cupboard and the teacher from the classroom', and 'relocating a glass to the dishwasher and a supervisor to the cafeteria'. Listener and speaker responding may also include recognizing and naming photographs (rec-p and nd-p) of items, familiar persons, and places. Also, continue selecting and teaching listener and speaker responses as part of Events 9-13.

Events 4-6: The Second Time Around (LRND4-6.2). When learners have acquired most of the speaking and listening skills that are part of Events 1-3: The Third Time, add (1) recognitions and names of two locations, (2) recognitions, retrievals, relocations, names, and descriptions of two items at a time, two or more of the same item, and one or two items with one or two features, and (3) retrievals and relocations of items and familiar persons from and to specific places and locations to Events 4-6.

Now Events 4-6 will include the same type of speaking and listening skills as Events 7-13. For example, as shown in Table 10, you may want to expand your learner's listener and speaker repertoire during 'Getting Ready to Go Home' to include recognizing and naming 'in front of the bench' and 'in the restroom', recognizing, retrieving, relocating, naming, and describing 'her lunch box and back pack', '2 drawing pads', along with her 'blue hat', 'brown, heavy jacket', 'pink sneakers and smelly socks', 'yellow raincoat and large, blue umbrella', relocating 'her backpack next to the door and the teacher to the bus ramp', and retrieving 'her wallet from her locker and the supervisor from the office'. Listener and speaker responding may also include recognizing and naming photographs (rec-p and nd-p) of items, familiar persons, and places. Also, continue selecting and teaching listener and speaker responses as part of Events 9-13.

Table 9.
Listener and Speaker Responses for Events 1-3: The Third Time Around (LRND1-3.3)
Sample Event -- Breakfast
Introduced after Listener and Speaker Responses have been Acquired
for Events 7-8 (LRND7-8)

Preferred Item		Preferred Item		Item	
Cheerios or Wheaties	rec / ret/rel / rec-p / nd / nd-p	milk	rec / ret/rel / rec-p / nd / nd-p	a bowl	rec / ret/rel / rec-p / nd / nd-p
Item		**Item**		**Activity**	
a napkin	rec / ret/rel / rec-p / nd / nd-p	a spoon	rec / ret/rel / rec-p / nd / nd-p	wiping your mouth	comp / nd
Item		**Activity**		**Familiar Person**	
juice	rec / ret/rel / rec-p / nd / nd-p	cleaning the table	comp / nd	Mrs. Ellis	rec / ret/rel / rec-p / nd / nd-p
Familiar Person		**Place**		**Place**	
Kristin	rec / ret/rel / rec-p / nd / nd-p	cafeteria	rec / rec-p / nd / nd-p	kitchen	rec / rec-p / nd / nd-p
Location		**Location**		**2 Items**	
next to the refrigerator	rec / rec-p / nd / nd-p	in the sink	rec / rec-p / nd / nd-p	a spoon and a bowl	rec / ret/rel / rec-p / nd / nd-p
2 or More of the Same Item		**One Item with a Feature**		**One Item with 2 Features**	
3 napkins	rec / ret/rel / rec-p / nd / nd-p	cereal spoons	rec / ret/rel / rec-p / nd / nd-p	2% chocolate milk	rec / ret/rel / rec-p / nd / nd-p
2 Items with a Feature		**2 Items with 2 Features**		**Items to a Place/Location**	
blue bowls and Honey Nut Cheerios	rec / ret/rel / rec-p / nd / nd-p	red, paper placemats and blue, cloth napkins	rec / ret/rel / rec-p / nd / nd-p	the glass in the dishwasher	rel
Items from a Place/Location		**Person from a Place/Location**		**Person to a Place/Location**	
a bowl from the cupboard	ret	teacher from the classroom	ret	supervisor to the cafeteria	rel

Table 10.
Listener and Speaker Responses for Events 4-6: The Second Time Around (LRND4-6.2)
Sample Event -- Getting Ready to Go Home
Introduced after Listener and Speaker Responses have been Acquired
for Events 1-3: The Third Time Around (LRND1-3.3)

Preferred Item		Preferred Item		Item	
your iPod	rec ret/rel rec-p nd nd-p	your Uno cards	rec ret/rel rec-p nd nd-p	your purse or wallet	rec ret/rel rec-p nd nd-p
Item		Item		Activity	
your lunch box	rec ret/rel rec-p nd nd-p	your back pack	rec ret/rel rec-p nd nd-p	throwing away the trash	comp nd
Item		Activity		Familiar Person	
your jacket	rec ret/rel rec-p nd nd-p	wiping the table	comp nd	Mr. Harris	rec ret/rel rec-p nd nd-p
Familiar Person		Place		Place	
John	rec ret/rel rec-p nd nd-p	classroom	rec rec-p nd nd-p	your locker	rec rec-p nd nd-p
Location		Location		2 Items	
next to the bench	rec rec-p nd nd-p	in the restroom	rec rec-p nd nd-p	lunchbox and back pack	rec ret/rel rec-p nd nd-p
2 or More of the Same Item		One Item with a Feature		One Item with 2 Features	
2 drawing pads	rec ret/rel rec-p nd nd-p	blue hat	rec ret/rel rec-p nd nd-p	brown, heavy jacket	rec ret/rel rec-p nd nd-p
2 Items with a Feature		2 Items with 2 Features		Items to a Place/Location	
white sneakers and smelly socks	rec ret/rel rec-p nd nd-p	a yellow raincoat and a large, blue umbrella	rec ret/rel rec-p nd nd-p	back pack next to the door	rel
Items from a Place/Location		Person from a Place/Location		Person to a Place/Location	
wallet from your locker	ret	supervisor from the office	ret	teacher to the bus ramp	rel

ESSENTIAL FOR LIVING
Nice-to-have Listener Responses, Names, and Descriptions

Recognizing and Naming or Describing Physical Sensations or Emotions. After children or adults have acquired a substantial repertoire of listener and speaker responses as part of Events 1-10, consider teaching them 'to indicate the presence of their own pain or discomfort and the location thereof' and 'to indicate the presence of feelings of happiness, sadness, or anger, and the situation that may have resulted in these feelings'. *[to respond as a listener and to tact their own private physical sensations and feelings and public events that may have resulted in those feelings.]*

Event 14 (LRND14). When there is some observable indication that learners may be experiencing pain or discomfort, which we will call Event 14, teach some of them to point to 'where it hurts' when asked to do so and others to describe the sensation 'it hurts' and provide the name for the part of their body to which this description applies. For example, when a learner with a limited naming repertoire has fallen, teach her to approach a care provider, wait for that person to say "where does it hurt", and point to her knee. With a learner with an extensive naming repertoire, teach her to say, sign, write, type, or select words such as "knee hurts". Consider teaching other learners with extensive speaking repertoires to name or describe 'a headache', 'a stomach ache', 'a sinus (or migraine) headache', 'stomach cramps', 'girl pain (i.e., menstrual cramps)', 'constipation', or other forms of chronic pain or discomfort.

In some situations, there are observable conditions or behaviors which strongly suggest that learners are experiencing pain or discomfort and may suggest the location thereof. *[public accompaniment or collateral behaviors]* For example, a body temperature of 102 degrees suggests discomfort, while cuts, bruises, wincing, or rubbing part of the body suggest pain. In many other situations, however, no such conditions or behaviors occur, making it very difficult for learners to recognize or describe pain or discomfort and for parents or care providers to respond effectively to the needs of their learners.

As shown in Table 11, Event 14 should include targeted *recognitions* of locations of pain and discomfort -- 'head', 'tummy', and 'throat', and, for some learners, corresponding *names or descriptions* -- 'headache', 'tummy ache', and 'throat hurts'. Event 14 should also include targeted or previously acquired requests for items or activities that might provide relief or distraction (see **R89** -- 'lozenges', 'a warm or cool washcloth', 'a pillow or blanket', 'ice', 'a cold or hot drink', or 'a pain reliever in liquid or tablet form').

Event 14 generally occurs infrequently. Situations cannot be easily contrived, nor occurrences predicted. As a result, when events do occur, all non-essential activities should be suspended and learners should be taught to recognize and describe their own pain and discomfort.

Table 11.
Listener Responses, Names, and Requests for Event 14:
Indicating the Presence and Location of Pain or Discomfort (LRND14)
Introduced after Listener and Speaker Responses have been Acquired for 10 Events

Pain and Location		Pain and Location		Pain and Location	
head hurts or headache	rec	stomach or tummy hurts [stomach or tummy ache]	rec	throat hurts or throat is sore	rec
	nd		nd		nd
Pain and Location		**Pain and Location**		**Pain and Location**	
arm hurts	rec	leg hurts	rec	foot hurts or foot is sore	rec
	nd		nd		nd
Preferred Item or Activity		**Preferred Item or Activity**		**Preferred Item or Activity**	
a pillow	req	throat lozenges	req	ice or a warm wash cloth	req
Preferred Item or Activity		**Preferred Item or Activity**		**Preferred Item or Activity**	
aspirin	req	lying down	req	a cold or a hot drink	req

Event 15 (LRND15). When there is an indication that learners may be experiencing specific feelings, teach some learners to nod 'yes or no' when asked "are you sad" and "are you sad because (of a specific situation)" and others to name or describe their feelings and the situation. For example, when a learner with a limited naming repertoire discovers that there is no ice cream in the freezer, teach him to approach someone, wait for that person to say "are you sad" and nod 'yes or no'. If he indicated 'yes', teach him to wait again until that person says "is that because there is no ice cream" and nod 'yes". Teach learners with extensive naming repertoires to say, sign, write, type, or select the words 'I'm sad [because] there's no ice cream'. Also, teach these learners to describe other feelings and situations, such as, 'I'm frustrated [because] I can't do this'.

As shown in Table 12, Event 15 should include situations which often result in feelings of sadness, happiness, or anger -- 'the termination of a preferred activity', 'the cancellation of a scheduled activity', 'the appearance or availability of a preferred item, activity, familiar person, or place', 'the end of an unpleasant task', 'the removal of a preferred item or activity by another person', or 'an aggressive act by another person', to name a few. Event 15 should also include targeted or previously acquired requests for items, activities, persons, or places that might provide relief or distraction from feelings of sadness or anger (see **R90** -- 'my tunes and my headphones', 'Aunt Phyllis', 'Alice, my friend', 'the park') or additional feelings of happiness (see **R90** -- 'ice cream').

Event 15 may also occur infrequently and occurrences cannot be easily contrived or predicted. As a result, when events occur, all other non-essential activities should be temporarily suspended and learners should be taught to recognize and describe their own feelings of sadness, happiness, and anger.

Table 12.
Listener and Speaker Responses for Event 15:
Indicating the Presence of Feelings of Sadness, Happiness, or Anger (LRND15)
Introduced after Listener and Speaker Responses have been Acquired for 10 Events

Situation and Feeling		Situation and Feeling		Situation and Feeling	
we can't watch the rest of the movie now...	rec	karaoke has been cancelled...	rec	my supervisor brought cookies for snack...	rec
	nd		nd		nd
sad		sad		happy	
Situation and Feeling		Situation and Feeling		Situation and Feeling	
my laundry is finished...	rec	she took my iPod...	rec	he kicked me...	rec
	nd		nd		nd
happy		angry		angry	
Preferred Item or Activity		Preferred Person or Place		Preferred Person or Place	
my tunes and my headphones	req	Aunt Phyllis	req	the park	req
Preferred Item or Activity		Preferred Person or Place		Preferred Person or Place	
ice cream	req	My friend (Alice)	req	the mall	req

Events 14 and 15. Recognitions, names, and descriptions that are part of Events 14 and 15 are particularly functional as they provide learners with a way to express themselves in demanding situations without exhibiting problem behavior. They also permit learners to follow-up with requests for information or assistance from others that they could not easily secure with generalized requests alone. For example, after recognizing or describing 'knee hurts', after describing 'girl pain', or after recognizing or describing 'sad' or 'angry', learners who request 'help' can receive the specific assistance they need.

Understandably, many care providers and parents are anxious to teach these skills, so that they can be more sensitive and respond more effectively to the needs of their children or adults. They must be patient, however, as meaningful recognitions and descriptions of these events are often difficult to teach.

Despite the manner in which it is often portrayed, teaching these skills to children and adults with developmental disabilities is extremely difficult. Many of our learners never acquire either skill. Instructors often begin by bringing learners in contact with other children or adults engaged in specific activities or pictures of the same and teach them to recognize, name, or describe what they see. For example, they often point to someone or a picture of someone bent over, grabbing their stomach, say "do you think this person's stomach hurts", and prompt learners to nod 'yes'. Or, they say "what is the matter with this person" and prompt learners to say "stomach ache". When they see someone or a picture of someone crying, they often say "do you think she is sad" and prompt learners to nod 'yes'. Or, they say "how is this person feeling" and prompt learners to say "sad". With this approach, many children and adults with moderate-to-severe disabilities learn to recognize or name the activities of other people using words often used to describe pain, discomfort, or specific emotions. For example, they learn to recognize or describe a person grasping their stomach as 'a stomach ache' or crying as 'sad'. These same children and adults seldom learn to recognize 'a stomach ache' when they are experiencing this sensation or 'sadness' when they are experiencing these feelings. They also seldom express what we often describe as empathy.

The Assessment of Listener Responses, Names, and Descriptions

Before conducting an assessment, review the procedures described in chapter 4. Then, secure a copy of the *Assessment and Record of Progress (ARP)* for each learner. and begin to conduct the assessment. Determine each learner's performance level on each of the *must-have* (LR1-11) and *should-have* (LR12-17) listener responses or required examples thereof and record this level on the *ARP*. The performance levels for these listener responses, each of which require following directions and completing required activities (e.g., 'stands up' and 'turns toward someone when their name is called'), are described in Table 13, along with examples from the *ARP*. Some of these listener responses require that learners make a response and continue making that response for gradually increasing periods of time. Performance levels for these listener responses are described in Table 14, along with examples from the *ARP*.

Then, using the guidelines described earlier in this chapter, begin to assess *good-to-have listener responses, names, and descriptions* by selecting three events (LRND1-3) that occur in the daily experiences of each learner. Also select specific listener and speaker responses -- recognitions, retrievals, relocations, names, and descriptions -- that could be part of these events. Sample events, along with sample listener and speaker responses, were provided earlier in this chapter. Then, determine the performance level of each learner on the recognitions, retrievals, relocations, and names that you have selected to be are part of these events and record this level on the *ARP*. The performance levels for these responses are described in Table 15, along with examples from the *ARP*. As much as possible, assess these performance levels while the event is taking place. Continue to select events, along with listener and speaker responses, and present opportunities for learners to make those responses until they require full physical or demonstration prompts with three consecutive responses, or exhibit problem behavior on these occasions. When this occurs, discontinue the assessment of responses in this domain.

Table 13.
Performance Levels for Most Listener Responses that Require
Following Directions and Completing a Required Activity (LR1-11 and LR12-17)

When directed to do so, learners follow directions and complete a required activity on three consecutive occasions...

IA	[the initial assessment of this listener response has been completed]
IM	[instruction or management has begun]
-SA	without self-injurious, aggressive, or destructive behavior
-DC	without disruptive behavior or complaining
-RP	without resistance to prompts and without elopement
FP	with a full physical or full demonstration prompt
PP	with a partial physical or a partial demonstration prompt
MP	with a minimal touch or a minimal gestural prompt
Ind	without prompts and within two seconds
2S	in two or more situations
2P	in the presence of either of two people
Det	[this listener response is no longer occurring consistently]

LR5. Stands up, sits down, folds hands, lies down, or sits up when directed to do so

1 stands up	IA	IM	-SA	-DC	-RP	FP	PP	MP	Ind	2S	2P	Det

Essential for Living 163

Table 14.
Performance Levels for Some Listener Responses that Require Following Directions
and Continuing to Respond for Periods of Time (LR1-11 and LR12-17)

When directed to do so, learners follow a specific direction, make a specific response, and continue making that response without exhibiting problem behavior, without resisting or requiring prompts, in two or more situations, and in the presence of either of two persons on three consecutive occasions for...

- **IA**   [the initial assessment of this listener response has been completed]
- **IM**   [instruction or management has begun]
- **___s**   ___ seconds [this targeted period of time is set by the instructor or care provider]
- **___m**   ___ minutes [this targeted period of time is set by the instructor or care provider]
- **Det**   [this listener response is no longer occurring consistently]

LR1. Holds and maintains contact with the hand of an instructor, care provider, or parent when directed to do so

IA	IM	1s	2s	5s	10s	20s	1m	2m	5m	10m	20m	Det

Table 15.
Performance Levels for Recognitions, Retrievals, Relocations, Names, and Descriptions
that are Part of Events 1-15 (LRND1-15)

When directed to do so, learners (1) 'point toward', 'go and get', 'bring with them', 'name', or 'describe' items or familiar persons, (2) point to or name specific places or locations, specific parts of their body, physical sensations, or specific feelings, or (3) complete routine activities on three consecutive occasions...

- **IA**   [the initial assessment of this listener response has been completed]
- **IM**   [instruction or management has begun]
- **-SA**   without self-injurious, aggressive, or destructive behavior
- **-DC**   without disruptive behavior or complaining
- **-RP**   without resistance to prompts and without elopement
- **FP**   with a full physical, full demonstration, or full echoic prompt
- **PP**   with a partial physical, partial demonstration, or partial echoic prompt
- **MP**   with a minimal touch, minimal gestural, or minimal echoic prompt
- **Ind**   without prompts and without hesitation
- **2E**   with two or more examples of each item [does not apply to activities, persons, places, or locations
- **2p**   In the presence of either of two people
- **Det**   [this listener or speaker response is no longer occurring consistently]

Event 1: 'Breakfast' (LRND1.1)											
Preferred Item					Cheerios (Wheaties)						
rec	IA	IM	-SA	-DC	-RP	FP	PP	MP	Ind	2E	2P	Det
ret/rel	IA	IM	-SA	-DC	-RP	FP	PP	MP	Ind	2E	2P	Det
rec-p	IA	IM	-SA	-DC	-RP	FP	PP	MP	Ind	2E	2P	Det
nd	IA	IM	-SA	-DC	-RP	FP	PP	MP	Ind	2E	2P	Det
nd-p	IA	IM	-SA	-DC	-RP	FP	PP	MP	Ind	2E	2P	Det
Item					bowl						
rec	IA	IM	-SA	-DC	-RP	FP	PP	MP	Ind	2E	2P	Det
ret/rel	IA	IM	-SA	-DC	-RP	FP	PP	MP	Ind	2E	2P	Det
rec-p	IA	IM	-SA	-DC	-RP	FP	PP	MP	Ind	2E	2P	Det
nd	IA	IM	-SA	-DC	-RP	FP	PP	MP	Ind	2E	2P	Det
nd-p	IA	IM	-SA	-DC	-RP	FP	PP	MP	Ind	2E	2P	Det

Event 4: 'Getting Ready to Go Home' (LRND4.2)										
Location					in the restroom					
rec	IA	IM	-SA	-DC	-RP	FP	PP	MP	Ind	2P	Det
ret/rel	IA	IM	-SA	-DC	-RP	FP	PP	MP	Ind	2P	Det
rec-p	IA	IM	-SA	-DC	-RP	FP	PP	MP	Ind	2P	Det
nd	IA	IM	-SA	-DC	-RP	FP	PP	MP	Ind	2P	Det
nd-p	IA	IM	-SA	-DC	-RP	FP	PP	MP	Ind	2P	Det
Activity					throwing the trash away					
comp	IA	IM	-SA	-DC	-RP	FP	PP	MP	Ind	2P	Det
nd	IA	IM	-SA	-DC	-RP	FP	PP	MP	Ind	2P	Det

Table 15. (cont.)
Performance Levels for Recognitions, Retrievals, Relocations, Names, and Descriptions
that are Part of Events 1-15 (LRND1-15)

Event 7: 'Unloading the Dishwasher' (LRND7)											
2 items					plates and forks						
rec	IA	IM	-SA	-DC	-RP	FP	PP	MP	Ind	2E	2P	Det
ret/rel	IA	IM	-SA	-DC	-RP	FP	PP	MP	Ind	2E	2P	Det
rec-p	IA	IM	-SA	-DC	-RP	FP	PP	MP	Ind	2E	2P	Det
nd	IA	IM	-SA	-DC	-RP	FP	PP	MP	Ind	2E	2P	Det
nd-p	IA	IM	-SA	-DC	-RP	FP	PP	MP	Ind	2E	2P	Det

Event 14: 'Indicating the Presence and Location of Pain or Discomfort' (LRND14)											
Pain and Location					throat sore						
rec	IA	IM	-SA	-DC	-RP	FP	PP	MP	Ind		2P	Det
nd	IA	IM	-SA	-DC	-RP	FP	PP	MP	Ind		2P	Det
Preferred Item or Activity					ice chips						
req	IA	IM	-SA	-DC	-RP	FP	PP	MP	Ind		2P	Det

Teaching Listener Responses, Names, and Descriptions and Recording Progress

Before you begin teaching listener responses that include following directions related to learner safety and routine activities (see **LR1-17**), make certain to *precisely define each desired listener response* (see the examples provided in **LR1-2**). In the beginning, these listener responses should be taught *in the situations* in which they are expected to occur. Listener and speaker responses that are part of selected events (see **LRND1-15**), recognitions, retrievals, relocations, names, and descriptions, should generally be taught *during those events*. Sometimes it is difficult to provide more than a few teaching opportunities during a situation or event. When this happens, you should provide additional opportunities just before the event or situation occurs. As events and situations unfold, opportunities to teach non-targeted listener and speaker responses may occur. You should consider teaching these listener and speaker responses, as well.   *natural environment teaching*

Use the teaching protocols that are included in chapter 12. These protocols include errorless prompting and interspersing opportunities to make targeted listener and speaker responses between opportunities to make requests. In many language programs, recognitions are taught using the vocal cues "point to" or "touch". With learners with limited speaking and listening repertoires, this is not an advisable practice, as these cues almost never occur in everyday situations. We prefer "where is", "find the", "where did you put", and variations thereof, which commonly occur in daily interactions.

In everyday situations and selected events, learners will encounter directions, along with items, activities, places, and locations that vary slightly in form from those for which listener and speaker responses were taught. For example, learners may hear "Wait here" and later "Wait right here", and still later "Wait right there". They may also encounter many types of cups and spoons and many items that are 'blue'. In order to insure that listener and speaker responses continue to occur in these situations, it is important to vary the form of directions and the forms of items, activities, places, and locations as early as the second or third week of instruction.

Collect data several times each week, or even daily, if possible, using first opportunity of the day probes described in chapter 4. Then, record these data on one of the *Skill Acquisition Self-graphing Data Recording Forms* as shown in Table 16 and described in chapter 4. These data sheets can be downloaded from www.behaviorchange.com. When learners do not make progress on specific skills, make adjustments in the teaching procedures. As learners reach specific performance levels, transfer this information to the *ARP* as shown in Table 17 and described in chapter 4.

Table 16.
Recording the Learner's Progress on Listener Responses, Names, or Descriptions Selected for Instruction
Using Single-trial Probe Data and Probe Data Sheets

ESSENTIAL FOR LIVING
Skill Acquisition Self-graphing Data Recording Form
Recognitions, Retrievals, Relocations, Names, and Descriptions
First Opportunity of the Day Probes

Event 1. Breakfast	Day/Date and First Opportunity of the Day Probe																
	13	14	15	16	17	18	19	20	21	22	23	24	25	26	27	28	29
	S	M	T	W	T	F	S	S	M	T	W	T	F	S	S	M	T
Item: **Bowl** rec	Det 2P 2E Ind MP PP FP -RP -DC -SA 0	Det 2P 2E Ind MP PP (FP) -RP -DC -SA 0	Det 2P 2E Ind MP PP (FP) -RP -DC -SA 0	Det 2P 2E Ind MP PP (FP) -RP -DC -SA 0	Det 2P 2E Ind (MP) PP FP -RP -DC -SA 0	Det 2P 2E Ind MP (PP) FP -RP -DC -SA 0	Det 2P 2E Ind MP PP FP -RP -DC -SA 0	Det 2P 2E Ind MP PP FP -RP -DC -SA 0	Det 2P 2E Ind MP (PP) FP -RP -DC -SA 0	Det 2P 2E (Ind) MP PP FP -RP -DC -SA 0	Det 2P 2E (Ind) MP PP FP -RP -DC -SA 0	Det 2P 2E (Ind) MP PP FP -RP -DC -SA 0	Det 2P (2E) Ind MP PP FP -RP -DC -SA 0	Det 2P 2E Ind MP PP FP -RP -DC -SA 0	Det 2P 2E Ind MP PP FP -RP -DC -SA 0	Det 2P (2E) Ind MP PP FP -RP -DC -SA 0	Det 2P (2E) Ind MP PP FP -RP -DC -SA 0

Table 17.
Transferring Data from Self-graphing Data Recording Forms
to the Assessment and Record of Progress (*ARP*)

Event 1: 'Breakfast' (LRND1.1)											
Item					bowl							
rec	IA	IM	-SA	-DC	-RP	FP	PP	MP	Ind	2E	2P	Det
ret/rel	IA	IM	-SA	-DC	-RP	FP	PP	MP	Ind	2E	2P	Det
rec-p	IA	IM	-SA	-DC	-RP	FP	PP	MP	Ind	2E	2P	Det

If improvement in the level of performance for any specific skill does not occur, make adjustments in the teaching procedures.

7c. Answers to Questions and Conversations

Answers to Questions

Answers to questions permit learners to respond to the requests of others for information. As shown in Table 1, answers to questions occur when an instructor, care provider, parent, or peer directs a request for information toward a learner and the learner provides information. Requests and answers may occur in the same or different forms, that is, using the same or different methods of speaking (see Table 1). Answers to questions cannot occur, however, if a learner's method of speaking includes selecting pic-symbols, drawings, or photographs, as these selections cannot be distinguished from listener responses (see the previous section of this chapter).

Table 1.
Answers to Questions   Intraverbals

An instructor, care provider, parent, or peer directs a request for information toward a learner [S^D]	⟶	The learner provides the requested information [R]	⟶	The instructor provides a form of approval or confirmation, makes another request, or waits for the learner to make a request [S^R]
A father says "What do you want to drink?"		The learner, his son, says "milk"		The father says "great; I'll go and get the milk"
An instructor says "Where are your socks and shoes?"		The learner signs "on [the] bed"		The instructor says "go and get them and we'll take a ride in the van"
A care provider says "What are you going to get at the grocery store?"		The learner selects the printed word 'milk' from his PECS book		The care provider says "Don't forget to get bread, too"
A police officer says "What is your phone number"		The learner types the phone number or points to this information on his ID card		The office says "Thank you"
A peer says "When did you watch the movie"		The learner says "after lunch"		The peer says "Was it a good movie"

S^D: a verbal discriminative stimulus
R: a speaker response
S^R: a social reinforcer

Answering questions and eventually participating in conversations is something all parents, instructors, and care providers would like their children and adults to do. *Answering questions, however, is the most difficult speaker behavior for learners with moderate-to-severe disabilities to acquire.* As a result, instructors, care providers, and parents must consider the following issues when teaching this skill:

(1) learners should acquire a large repertoire of requests, along with a repertoire of names and descriptions, that are part of commonly occurring events (see the previous section of this chapter), so that their answers to questions can be based on these repertoires and can be more meaningful to them and those with whom they are speaking;   *a large repertoire of mands and tacts*

(2) answers to questions should be taught within commonly occurring events, as suggested for names and listener responses in the previous section of this chapter, so that more guided practice is available, answers are more meaningful, and, at least the beginnings of conversation, are more likely to occur.   *intraverbal responses should be taught in familiar contexts*

(3) learners should be exposed to questions that commonly occur in everyday conversations, rather than questions that are likely to occur only during academic instruction or language training, so that generalization will not be required in order for them to respond effectively to questions they encounter in daily living;   *functional exemplars* / *stimulus generalization*

(4) learners should be exposed initially to types of questions which require simpler answers (e.g., 'do', 'can', and 'what' questions) and gradually exposed to types which tend to require more complex answers (e.g., 'which', 'where', 'who', and 'when' questions); *intraverbal responses with fewer components*

(5) learners should be expected initially to provide answers that include only 1-3 words or signs and gradually expected to increase the length of answers to include 5 or more words or signs *intraverbal responses with a brief mean length of utterance*

(6) learners should be exposed initially to situations in which factors, other than the question, at least in part, control the answer (see Situations 1, 2, and 3 later in this section), and gradually exposed to situations in which the answer is controlled entirely by the question (see Situations 4 and 5); *answers to questions that are initially multipli-controlled responses and eventually 'pure' intraverbals*

(7) learners should be exposed initially to questions which require few to no complex discriminations, and gradually exposed to questions that require more of these discriminations; and, *conditional discriminations*

As you continue with this section, you should have access to a copy of the *Assessment and Record of Progress (ARP)* for each learner. Using the same 13 events selected in the previous section of this chapter, the names and descriptions selected and taught for each event, and the guidelines described in this section, begin to select answers to specific questions that could occur frequently during each event. Sample questions and answers are provided in blue script later in this section. Then, along with requests, names, and descriptions learners have already acquired as part of each event, record these selections in the *Assessment and Record of Progress (ARP)*. Also record each learner's performance with respect to the criteria specified in the *ARP*.

A repertoire of requests, names, and descriptions. Acquiring a substantial repertoire of answers to questions that are meaningful for learners and those around them, requires the prior acquisition of a large and fluent repertoire of requests, names, and descriptions. With these repertoires, answers or parts of answers to many questions can be prompted by pointing to items and features of items, activities, familiar persons, places, locations, and photographs of the same (see Listener Responses, Names, and Descriptions), along with numerals (see Numeration) and clocks and calendars (see Schedules, Lists, and Time). Then, these prompts can gradually be faded and learners' responses will be meaningful to them and to the those who asked the questions. For example, before beginning to teach a learner to answer the question 'Where is your jacket', a care provider should point to places or locations where the learner has been known to leave his jacket and determine if the learner can provide names for these places or locations rapidly and without hesitation. If so, the care provider should ask the question and direct the learner to look in these places. If the learner finds the jacket in the closet, *providing tact prompts* *the tact-to-intraverbal transfer procedure can effect a transfer of stimulus control from tacts to intraverbals.* *fluently*

the care provider should point to the closet and wait for the learner to say, sign, or write, type, Braille write, or select the word "closet" or prompt him to do so. At other times, when the jacket is on the 'floor' or elsewhere and the question is asked, the same procedure should be used. Then, on subsequent occasions, the question can be asked, pointing to the current location of the jacket can be gradually faded, and the learner can respond with "closet" or "floor" or the current location of the jacket. And, in each of these situations, the learner's answer will be meaningful to him and to the care provider who asked the question. This teaching procedure is described in greater detail in chapter 12.

If the learner has a limited repertoire of requests and names, and this repertoire does not include 'closet' or 'floor', these answers must be prompted using spoken words or signs. For example, when an instructor says to a learner "Where is your jacket", she must prompt 'closet', 'floor' or another appropriate response by saying words or forming signs (some people recommend text prompts, but we find them quite cumbersome and difficult to fade). Answers that are prompted in this manner, will not be paired with any of our learners' experiences and will tend to have little or no meaning for them. Learners will simply respond with either "closet" or "floor" or both, because these words come after "Where is your jacket", much like, '4' comes after '3' or 'go round and round' comes after 'the wheels on the bus'. These answers, which are often described as 'scripted' or 'rote', will also have no meaning for those who asked the questions.

Answers to questions regarding personal information are not based on names or descriptions. For example, answers to questions such as 'what's your name', 'how old are you', 'where do you live or what's your address', 'what's your telephone number', 'are you allergic to any medications', 'what's your blood type' are based on information learners acquire through spoken-word or sign prompts. With the exception of the response to 'how old are you', these answers tend not to vary in form and may become scripted or rote. Since these answers may have a direct bearing on learners' safety, and since rote responses tend to be fluent and reliable, rote responses to these questions are highly desirable.

Some answers or parts of answers to questions are not based on names or descriptions and cannot be taught by pointing to items, activities, familiar persons, places, locations, numerals, clocks, or calendars. These responses are based on concepts or on relationships between learners and various aspects of the environment and must be prompted with spoken words or signs. Examples include -- 'outside', 'in the morning', 'may I have', 'try', 'when', 'put away', 'tomorrow', 'yes', 'stay here', 'want', 'no', 'right now', 'more', 'later', 'the same one', 'before', 'after', or 'again'. On some occasions, these responses may affect the manner in which an audience responds.

Some intraverbal responses cannot be transferred from tacts.

On some occasions, these responses may be autoclitic

Within events. Answers to questions should be taught within groups of frequently-occurring events, specifically **Events 1-3**, **4-6**, **7-13**, and **14-15** described in *Listener Responses, Names, and Descriptions* (**LRND1-3, LRND4-6, LRND7-13,** and **LRND14-15**), but only after learners have acquired requests, names, or descriptions of items, activities, places, familiar persons, and locations that are part of each group of events. These answers will be practiced more frequently, will be more meaningful to both speakers and listeners, and are more likely to be part of conversations.

Questions encountered in daily living. Our learners should be taught to answer questions that occur in everyday conversations, rather than those that sometimes occur during language training or academic lessons. For example, 'what's in your lunchbox' and 'where is your wallet' are questions that commonly occur in conversations, whereas 'what do you wear on your head' or 'where do you put dirty laundry' are questions that often occur during academic instruction or language training. Other examples of both types of questions are listed in Table 2.

Questions that often occur during academic instruction and language training are appropriate for young learners in a developmental curriculum, such as *The VB-MAPP*. With continued developmental progression, some of these learners will begin to answer similar questions which occur during further academic instruction and everyday conversations. In other words, generalization across questions will occur. Most of our learners with limited communication repertoires, however, will not experience this generalization and will require questions, from the beginning, that commonly occur in everyday conversations.

Table 2.
Questions that Often Occur in Everyday Conversations
or during Academic Instruction and Language Training

Questions that Often Occur in Everyday Conversations	Questions that Often Occur during Academic Instruction and Language Training
'Do you want cereal'	'What do you eat cereal with'
'Can you finish setting the table'	'Can you name some silverware'
'What do you want to drink'	'What do you drink from'
'What are you drawing'	'What do you draw with'

Types of questions. Some types of questions require more complex responses than others. As a result, care providers and instructors must first consider the type of questions our learners can be expected to answer. Types of questions are shown in Table 3.

Table 3.
Types of Questions

First Word of the Question	Content of a Typical Answer
Do [Does]	yes or no
Can [Could, Will, Would]	yes or no
What	a request, a name, or a description of an Item, an activity, a place, and possibly a person
Which	a request or the name of one or more Items, activities, places, or persons from a larger group which are available
Where	the name of a place or a location
Who [Whom]	the name of a person, their position, or their title
When	a request or an indication of the time of day or the occurrence of one event relative to another

Begin by targeting answers to 'do' and 'can' questions, and gradually proceed to 'what', 'which', 'where', 'who' questions, and 'when' questions. Answers to some 'when' questions, especially those specifying a time of day or a day of the week, and answers to some 'what' and 'where' questions that require detailed descriptions of items, activities, or locations require complex responses and may be difficult for many of our learners to acquire. Answers to 'how' and 'why' questions are extremely difficult for almost all of our learners to acquire, are generally less functional for them, and are not included in this instrument.

Length of answers. In addition to types of questions we must also consider the length of answers we can realistically expect our learners to provide. Our experience suggests that, of those who acquire a repertoire of answers to questions, responses of 1-3 words or signs are common. A few learners, however, will exceed this expectation and provide some answers which include 4-10 words or signs.

Required situations. Answering questions is required in several distinctly different situations: two in which motivating events partially control the answer, two in which items, activities, people, places, locations, or pictures of the same present in the learner's immediate environment partially control the answer, one in which part of the question controls the answer, and two in which the entire question and only the question controls the answer. These situations are described in Table 4, along with guidelines for introducing questions and answers in these situations and samples of each.

Table 4.
Situations in which Answering Questions is Typically Required

Situation 1- In addition to the questions themselves, answers to questions in Situation 1 are controlled by motivating events, include responses previously acquired as requests, and occur in the presence of requested items, activities, or people. For example, if a sighted child or adult has learned to 'request cookies', she sees a plate of cookies and a pitcher of juice on a table and her friend, Ms. Miller, sitting at the table, and she indicates by gesture that she may want cookies, she can be taught to provide answers to specific questions.

Answers to questions in Situation 1 are multiply-controlled operants, specifically responses that are part mand and part intraverbal and occur in the presence of requested items, activities, or people.

Q. "Do you want a cookie (juice)" A. "yes (no)"
Q. "What do you want" A. "cookie (juice)"
Q. "Do you want juice or a cookie" A. "cookie (juice)"
Q. "Which one do you want" A. "cookie (juice)"
Q. "Where should we sit" A. "[at the] table"
Q. "With whom do you want to sit" A. "Ms. Miller"
Q. "Could you pass the cookies (juice)" A. "yes"

Answers to questions should generally be taught in Situation 1 first *and should only be taught when requests for these items, activities, and people have already been acquired and are occurring frequently and without hesitation.*

Situation 2- In addition to the questions themselves, answers to questions in Situation 2 are controlled by motivating events, include responses previously acquired as requests, and occur in the absence of requested items, activities, or people. For example, if a sighted adult is sitting with his friend Tom in the family room, when he takes your arm and leads you to the kitchen, where no food is in sight, he can be taught to provide answers to specific questions.

Answers to questions in Situation 2 are multiply-controlled operants, specifically responses that are part mand and part intraverbal and occur in the absence of requested items, activities, or people.

Q. "Do you want cheese crackers" A. "yes (no)"
Q. "What do you want [to eat]" A. "chips"
Q. "Do you want cheese crackers or chips" A. "cheese crackers (no)"
Q. "What do you want with your chips" A. "orange juice (Coke)"
Q. "Where should we have our snack" A. "family room"
Q. "With whom should we have our snack" A. "Tom"
Q. "Can you carry the cheese crackers (chips)" A. "yes"

Answers to questions in Situation 2 should be taught after answers to questions are occurring in Situation 1 *and should only be taught when requests for these items, activities, and people have already been acquired and are occurring frequently and without hesitation.*

Table 4. (cont.)
Situations in which Answering Questions is Typically Required

Situation 3- In addition to the questions themselves, answers to questions in Situation 3 are controlled by the presence of items, activities, people, places, and locations, which were previously acquired as names or descriptions. These answers are not controlled by motivating events. For example, if an adult with a visual impairment is just leaving with a group of peers and Ms. Parker, a care provider on a shopping trip, and, while holding Ms. Parker's arm, reaches into his pocket and touches coins and his wallet, he can be taught to provide answers to specific questions.

Answers to questions in Situation 3 are multiply-controlled operants, specifically responses that are part tact and part intraverbal.

Q. "Where is your wallet" A. "in my pocket"
Q. "Do you have three quarters" A. "yes, I do"
Q. "Who is going with you" A. "Ms. Parker"

Answers to questions in Situation 3 should be taught after answers to questions are occurring in Situations 1 and 2 *and should only be taught when names or descriptions of these items, activities, people, places, or locations have been already been acquired and are occurring frequently and without hesitation.*

Situation 4- Answers to questions in Situation 4 are controlled entirely by the questions and include responses which were previously acquired as names or descriptions. These answers are not controlled by motivating events or by the presence of items, activities, people, places, or locations. For example, if a sighted child, who uses signs as her primary method of speaking, just returns from having lunch at McDonald's with her parents, she can be taught to provide answers to specific questions.

Answers to questions in Situation 4 are 'pure' intraverbal responses previously acquired as tacts.

Q. "Where did you go [for lunch]" A. "McDonald's"
Q. "What did you have to eat" A. "Two cheeseburgers and fries"
Q. "Who went with you" A. "Mom and dad"

Situation 5- Answers to questions in Situation 5 are controlled entirely by the questions and include responses acquired as chains through spoken-word or sign prompts. For example, if a sighted child is asked to provide personal information in an urgent or emergency situation, he can be taught to do so.

Answers to questions in Situation 5 are 'pure', chained, intraverbal responses

Q. "What is your name" A. "_____"
Q. "What is your address" or
"Where do you live" A. "_____"
Q. "What is your phone number" A. "_____"
Q. "Are you allergic to any medications" A. "no (yes [and points to ID card)"
Q. "What is your blood type" A. "_____"

Situation 6- Answers to questions in Situation 6 are controlled entirely by the questions and include responses only part of which were previously acquired as names or descriptions. Part of these answers are based on concepts or on relationships between the learner and various aspects of the environment and must be prompted with spoken words or signs. Some of these responses may affect the manner in which an audience responds. For example, if a sighted adult arrives at her place of employment on Monday and is asked by peers about her activities over the weekend, she can be taught to do so.

Answers to questions in Situation 6 are 'pure' intraverbal responses only part of which were previously acquired as tacts. Part of some of these intraverbal responses are autoclitic.

Q. "Who came to visit you" A. "my Aunt Barbara"
Q. "What did you with Aunt Barbara" A. "shopping and [out to] lunch"
Q. "When did you go out to lunch" A. "on Saturday after shopping"
Q. "Where did you eat lunch" A. "at McDonald's next to the mall"
Q. "What time" A. "12:30"
Q. "What did you get at the mall" A. "new shoes"

Complex discriminations. An instructor, beginning to teach a learner to answer questions, may introduce the question "what do you want" and teach the learner to respond by specifying 'candy', 'crackers', 'cookies and juice', or other preferred items or activities, for which the learner has already acquired requests. In order to make this task 'easier to do', the instructor may begin by asking the question in exactly the same manner each time. Since the words and sequence of words in the question do not vary, the learner does not need to listen carefully to each word or make discriminations with respect to those words. The learner must simply listen to all or some recognizable parts of the question -- for example, 'what...want' or even 'what...', and specify 'candy', 'crackers', 'cookies and juice', or other preferred items or activities. [make a simple discrimination]

Then, quickly, the instructor must begin to expose the learner to questions such as 'which one do you want' and 'when do you want your crackers'. These variations require complex discriminations in order to properly answer the questions. Suppose, for example, that only two of the learner's preferred items are available, 'cookies' and 'juice', and the instructor holds up a 'small plate of cookies' and a 'carton of juice' and says "which one do you want". The learner must now listen carefully to each word and make a discrimination between 'what' and 'which one'. If the learner specifies "cookies" or "juice", he has made the appropriate discrimination. If, on the other hand, the learner specifies "cookies and juice" or "candy", he has failed to make this discrimination. Suppose further that the learner requests "candy" and the instructor says "when do you want candy". The learner must now distinguish 'when' from 'what' and 'which one'. If the learner specifies "after lunch" or an approximate time, he has made the appropriate discrimination. If, on the other hand, the learner specifies "cookies", or "candy", he has failed to discriminate 'when' from 'what' and 'which one'. [verbal conditional discriminations]

Later, the instructor will expose the learner to questions such as 'what comes next on your schedule' and 'where are your socks', which require more complex discriminations. The learner must now distinguish 'what comes next' and 'where' from 'when', 'what', and 'which one', and 'schedule' from 'socks'. If the instructor changes the second question slightly to 'where are my socks', the learner, must also distinguish 'my' from 'your'. As more complex discriminations are required, answers become very difficult for most of our learners to acquire.

Begin teaching answers to questions which do not require any complex discriminations and gradually introduce questions which require 1 or 2, and later, 3 or 4. Table 5 provides a list of sample questions and the estimated number of complex discriminations required to answer each question. This number will also be a function of each learner's history with respect to these questions. Of those learners who acquire a repertoire of answers to questions, most will be limited to answering questions which require no more than 4 complex discriminations.

Table 5.
The Estimated Number of Complex Discriminations
Required to Answer Sample Questions

Sample Questions	The Estimated Number of Complex Discriminations That May be Required to Answer These Questions
'Do you need help'	0 or 1
'Do you want cereal'	0 or 1
'Did you brush your teeth'	0 or 1
'What do you want'	0, 1, or 2
'What do you need'	0, 1, or 2
'Who is that'	1 or 2
'Which one do you want'	1 or 2
'What do you want to drink'	1 or 2
'Will you help me'	1 or 2
'Which one do you want to drink'	1, 2, or 3
'Where are you going'	1, 2, or 3
'What are you drawing'	1, 2, or 3
'What is your name'	1, 2, or 3
'Where is your mom'	2 or 3
'When do you have a break'	2 or 3
'When do you go to bed'	2 or 3
'Why are you sad'	2 or 3

Table 5. (cont.)
The Estimated Number of Complex Discriminations
Required to Answer Sample Questions

Sample Questions	The Estimated Number of Complex Discriminations That May be Required to Answer These Questions
'What is your phone number'	2 or 3
'Where do you live'	2 or 3
'How are you feeling'	2 or 3
'Where is your sweater'	2 or 3
'What is your last name'	2, 3, or 4
'What is your brother's name'	2, 3, or 4
'Where did you put your sweater'	3 or 4
'When do you want your cigar'	3 or 4
'What are you going to watch'	3 or 4
'Who is driving you to the mall'	3 or 4
'When are you going to get your hair done'	3 or 4
'When is mom coming home'	3 or 4
'What did you have for lunch'	3 or 4
'Where did you have lunch'	3 or 4
'Could you get Angela a cookie'	3 or 4
'Did you finish setting the table'	3 or 4
'When is your doctor's appointment'	3 or 4
'What do you want to eat with your juice'	3, 4, or 5
'What night are we going grocery shopping'	3, 4, or 5
'Where is your blue and pink blouse'	4 or 5
'What kind of sandwich would you like for lunch'	4 or 5
'Where does Mrs. Ellis keep the bus schedule'	4 or 5
'How much money do you need for bus fare and a soda'	4 or 5
'Which one of your friends is going to the movies with you'	4 or 5
'Where is the jacket you wore yesterday'	4 or 5
'When does the last train for home leave the station'	4 or 5

A summary. After reading this section, it should be evident that teaching children and adults with limited speaking repertoires to answer questions is no easy task. The following list summarizes the factors that must be taken into account when teaching this skill:

(1) teaching repertoires of requests and names;
(2) teaching answers to questions within commonly occurring events;
(3) targeting questions which commonly occur in everyday conversations;
(4) selecting types of questions so that the complexity of answers is limited;
(5) expecting answers with a reasonable range in length;
(6) teaching answers to questions in six types of situations in which they are required; and
(7) limiting and then gradually introducing questions that require complex discriminations.

The first three factors should be taken into consideration whenever you are teaching our learners to answer questions. The remaining four factors are especially important when first introducing answers to questions into specific events and require controlling the complexity of both questions and answers.

When learners have acquired requests, names or descriptions, and listener responses for items and activities within **Events 1-3** (see *Listener Responses, Names, and Descriptions*: **LRND1-3.3**), you can begin to teach answers to questions, but these questions and answers should be limited to and should include only:

- ☐ Can, Do, What, and Which questions;
- ☐ One and two-word or one and two-sign answers;
- ☐ Situations 1 and 2; and,
- ☐ 1 or 2 complex discriminations.

When learners have acquired requests, names or descriptions, and listener responses for items, activities, places, and familiar persons within **Events 4-6 (LRND4-6.2)**, you can teach answers to new questions, but these questions and answers should be limited to and should include only:

- ☐ Can, Do, What, Which, Where, and Who questions;
- ☐ One and two-word answers;
- ☐ Situations 1, 2, and 3; and,
- ☐ 1, 2, or 3 complex discriminations.

When learners have acquired requests, names or descriptions, and listener responses for items, activities, places, familiar persons, features, multiple items, and locations within **Events 7-13 and 14-15** (**LRND7-13** and **14-15**), you can teach answers to new questions, and these questions and answers may include:

- ☐ Can, Do, What, Which, Where, Who, and When questions;
- ☐ One, two, three, or four-word answers;
- ☐ Situations 1, 2, 3, 4, 5, and 6; and,
- ☐ 1, 2, 3, or 4 complex discriminations.

As we conclude this section, it is important to remember that 'answers to any questions at all' may be well beyond a reasonable expectation for many learners with moderate-to-severe disabilities. Acquiring a modest repertoire of meaningful answers to questions is, however, a reasonable expectation for some of our learners. This repertoire does provide two basic advantages for these learners: (1) they can respond to the requests of others by providing information, and (2) they can participate in conversations. For these reasons, most answers to questions should be considered *good-to-have skills*, and should never be taught before *should-have*, *must-have*, or *good-to-have* requests, listener responses, daily living skills, tolerating skills, or names and descriptions.

ESSENTIAL FOR LIVING
Good-to-have Answers to Questions

Events 1-3: The First Time Around (AQ1-3.1). When learners have acquired most of the requesting, naming, and describing skills that part of Events 1, 2, and 3: The First Time Around, begin teaching answers to 4-6 questions during these events. For example, as shown in Table 6, if 'Breakfast' is selected as Event 1, 2, or 3 for a specific learner, and this child or adult has learned to request 'Cheerios or Wheaties', to name 'a spoon', 'a bowl', and 'a napkin', and to describe 'wiping my mouth', you can teach that learner to provide answers to questions during that event, which include words or signs for these items and this activity. Begin teaching answers to questions when these items are present or these activities are occurring, and gradually do so when neither is the case. Use Teaching Protocol 10 described in chapter 12.

Table 6.
Answers to Questions for Events 1-3: The First Time Around (AQ1-3.1)
Sample Event -- Breakfast
Introduced after Requests and Names that are Part of these Events have been Acquired
(see Table 5 in *Listener Responses, Names, and Descriptions*)

Questions should first occur when specific items are present in the environment or specific activities are occurring and later when neither is the case...	
Q. "Do you want Cheerios (Wheaties)"	A. "yes (no)"
Q. "What do you want"	A. "Cheerios (Wheaties)"
Q. "Which one do you want"	A. "Cheerios (Wheaties)"
Q. "Which cereal do you want"	A. "Cheerios (Wheaties)"
Q. "What do you need"	A. "spoon (bowl)"
Q. "What do you need to do"	A. "wipe my mouth"

Events 4-6: The First Time Around (AQ4-6.1). When learners have acquired answers to questions within Events 1-3: The First Time Around, along with most of the requesting, naming, and describing skills that are part of Events 4-6: The First Time Around, begin teaching answers to 6-8 questions during these events. For example, as shown in Table 7, if 'Getting Ready to Go Home' is selected as Event 4, 5, or 6 for a specific learner, and this child or adult has learned to request their 'iPod and Uno Cards', to name their 'purse (or wallet)', 'lunch box', 'back pack', 'jacket', or 'an instructor (or supervisor)', 'a friend, 'the classroom (or cafeteria)', and their 'locker (or cubby)', and to describe 'throwing the trash away' and 'wiping the table',

you can teach that learner to provide answers to 6-8 questions during that event, which include words or signs for these items, activities, places, and familiar persons. Begin teaching answers to questions when these items, familiar persons, or places are part of the immediate environment, or these activities are occurring, and gradually do so when none of these is the case. Again, use Teaching Protocol 10 described in chapter 12.

Table 7.
Answers to Questions for Events 4-6: The First Time Around (AQ4-6.1)
Sample Event -- Getting Ready to Go Home
Introduced after Names that are Part of these Events have been Acquired
and after Answers to Questions in Events 1-3: The First Time Around (AQ1-3.1)
have also been Acquired

Questions should first occur when specific items, familiar persons, and places are part of the immediate environment, and when specific activities are occurring, and gradually when none of these is the case...	
Q. "Do you want to take home your iPod (Uno Cards)"	A. "yes"
Q. "What do you want to take home"	A. "iPod (Uno Cards)"
Q. "Which one do you want to take home"	A. "iPod (Uno Cards)"
Q. "What do you need to take home"	A. "jacket (hat)"
Q. "Where is your back pack"	A. "locker (cubby)"
Q. "Where is your jacket"	A. "classroom (cafeteria)"
Q. "Who is that"	A. "[my] supervisor"
Q. "What's his name"	A. "Mr. Harris"

Events 1-3: The Second Time Around (AQ1-3.2). When learners have acquired answers to questions within Events 4-6: The First Time, along with most of the naming and describing skills that are part of Events 1-3: The Second Time, begin teaching answers to an additional 3-5 questions during these events. For example, as shown in Table 8, if 'Breakfast' is selected as Event 1, 2, or 3 for a specific learner, and this child or adult has learned to name 'a teacher (or supervisor)', 'a friend', 'the cafeteria (or kitchen)', and 'the classroom (or work area)', and to describe 'cleaning up', you can teach that learner to provide answers to 3-5 additional questions during that event, which include words or signs for these familiar persons and places, and for this additional activity. Begin teaching answers to questions when these familiar persons or places are part of the immediate environment, and later when they are not. Again, use Teaching Protocol 10 described in chapter 12.

Table 8.
Answers to Questions for Events 1-3: The Second Time Around (AQ1-3.2)
Sample Event -- Breakfast
Introduced after Additional Names that are Part of these Events have been Acquired
and after Answers to Questions in Events 4-6: The First Time Around (AQ4-6.1)
have also been Acquired

Questions should first occur when specific items, familiar persons, and places are part of the immediate environment, and when specific activities are occurring, and gradually when none of these is the case...	
Q. "Do you want Cheerios (Wheaties)"	A. "yes (no)"
Q. "What do you want"	A. "Cheerios (Wheaties)"
Q. "Which one do you want"	A. "Cheerios (Wheaties)"
Q. "Which cereal do you want"	A. "Cheerios (Wheaties)"
Q. "What do you need"	A. "spoon (bowl)"
Q. "What do you need to do"	A. "wipe my mouth"
Q. "Where do you want to eat breakfast"	A. "kitchen (dining room)"
Q. "Whom do you want to sit with"	A. "Mrs. Ellis (Kristin)"
Q. "Who is going to eat with us"	A. "Mrs. Ellis (Kristin)"
Q. "Where is Kristin (Mrs. Ellis)"	A. "classroom (cafeteria)"
Q. "Which cereal does Kristin like"	A. "Cheerios (Wheaties)"

Events 7-13 (AQ7-13). When learners have acquired answers to questions within Events 1-3: The Second Time Around, along with most of naming and describing skills that are part of Events 7-8, begin teaching answers to 10-12 questions within these events. For example, as shown in Table 9, if 'Unloading the Dishwasher' is selected as one of Events 7-8 for a specific learner, and this child or adult has learned to (1) name 'cups, glasses, forks, spoons, and plates', 'a friend', 'a supervisor', and 'the kitchen', 'the office', (2) describe 'stacking the plates' and 'putting the dishes away', (3) describe the location of items as 'next to the dishwasher' or 'on the shelf', and (4) describe 'cups and saucers', 'large cups', 'small, green glasses', you can teach that learner to answer 10-12 questions during that event, which include words or signs for these items, activities, familiar persons, places, locations, two items at a time, and items with one or two features. Begin teaching answers to questions when these familiar items, activities, familiar persons, places, or locations are part of the immediate environment, and later when they are not. As naming and describing skills are acquired for Events 9-13, begin teaching answers to questions within these events. Again, use Teaching Protocol 10 described in chapter 12.

Table 9.
Answers to Questions for Events 7-13 (AQ7-13)
Sample Event -- Unloading the Dishwasher
Introduced after Names and Descriptions that are Part of these Events have been Acquired
and after Answers to Questions in Events 1-3: The Second Time (AQ1-3.2)
have also been Acquired

Questions should first occur when specific items, familiar persons, places, and locations are part of the immediate environment, and when specific activities are occurring, and gradually when none of these is the case...

Q. "Can you unload the dishwasher"	A. "yes"
Q. "Will you help me unload the dishwasher"	A. "yes"
Q. "What are you going to unload first"	A. "glasses"
Q. "What should we unload next"	A. "cups"
Q. "Where do the cups go"	A. "cupboard"
Q. "Where do you put the knives, forks, and spoons"	A. "drawer"
Q. "What are you trying to reach"	A. "forks and spoons"
Q. "Who is going to help you"	A. "Mrs. Thompson (Jerry)"
Q. "Which glasses go on the top shelf"	A. "large (small) red (green) glasses"
Q. "When are you going to the store"	A. "after we put the dishes away"
Q. "Where are you going to put the large items"	A. "on the counter"

Events 1-3: The Third Time Around (AQ1-3.3). When learners have acquired answers to questions within Events 7-8, along with most of the naming or describing skills that are part of Events 1-3: The Third Time Around, begin teaching answers to an additional 3-5 questions within these events. For example, as shown in Table 10, if 'Breakfast' is selected as Event 1, 2, or 3 for a specific learner, and this child or adult has learned to describe 'in the dishwasher', 'next to the trash can', 'spoon and bowl', 'napkin and glass', 'cereal spoons', 'small bowls', and '2% chocolate milk', you can teach that learner to answer 3-5 additional questions during that event, which include words or signs for these locations, pairs of items, and items with one or two features. Begin teaching answers to questions when these items and locations are part of the immediate environment, and later when they are not. As indicated earlier, use use Teaching Protocol 10 described in chapter 12.

Events 4-6: The Second Time Around (AQ4-6.2). When learners have acquired answers to questions within Events 1-3: The Third Time Around, along with most of the naming or describing skills that are part of Events 4-6: the Second Time Around, begin teaching answers to an additional 3-5 questions within these events. For example, as shown in Table 11, if 'Getting Ready to Go Home' is selected as Event 4, 5, or 6 for a specific learner, and this child or adult has learned to describe 'next to the restroom', 'in front of the bench', 'lunch box and back pack', 'blue jacket', and 'big, yellow hat', you can teach that learner to answer 3-5 additional questions during that event, which include words or signs for these items and locations. Begin teaching answers to questions when these items and locations are part of the immediate environment, and later when they are not. And, as indicated earlier, use Teaching Protocol 10 described in chapter 12.

Table 10.
Answers to Questions for Events 1-3: The Third Time Around (AQ1-3.3)
Sample Event -- Breakfast
Introduced after Additional Names and Descriptions
that are Part of these Events have been Acquired
and after Answers to Questions in Events 7-8 (AQ7-8)
have also been Acquired

Questions should first occur when specific items, familiar persons, places, and locations are part of the immediate environment, and when specific activities are occurring, and gradually when none of these is the case...

Q. "Do you want Cheerios (Wheaties)"   A. "yes (no)"
Q. "What do you want"   A. "Cheerios (Wheaties)"
Q. "Which one do you want"   A. "Cheerios (Wheaties)"
Q. "Which cereal do you want"   A. "Cheerios (Wheaties)"
Q. "What do you need"   A. "spoon"
Q. "What do you need"   A. "bowl"
Q. "What do you need"   A. "napkin"

Q. "Where do you want to eat breakfast"   A. "kitchen (dining room)"
Q. "Whom do you want to sit with"   A. "Mrs. Ellis (Kristin)"
Q. "Who is going to eat with us"   A. "Mrs. Ellis (Kristin)"
Q. "Where is Kristin (Mrs. Ellis)"   A. "classroom (cafeteria)"
Q. "Which cereal does Kristin like"   A. "Cheerios (Wheaties)"

Q. "What do you need"   A. "spoon and a bowl"
Q. "What do you need now"   A. "cereal spoons"
Q. "What do you want to drink"   A. "2% chocolate milk"
Q. "Where are you going to put the dirty dishes"   A. "in the dishwasher"
Q. "Where is the teacher"   A. "in the classroom"
Q. "When are you going to the classroom"   A. "after I wipe my mouth"
Q. "Who is going to help you with the dishes"   A. "Kristin and Mrs. Ellis"

Table 11.
Answers to Questions for Events 4-6: The Second Time Around (AQ4-6.2)
Sample Event -- Getting Ready to Go Home
Introduced after Names and Descriptions that are Part of these Events have been Acquired
and after Answers to Questions in Events 1-3: The Third Time (AQ1-3.3)
have also been Acquired

Questions should first occur when specific items, familiar persons, and places are part of the immediate environment, and when specific activities are occurring, and gradually when none of these is the case...

Q. "Do you want to take home your iPod (Uno Cards)"   A. "yes"
Q. "What do you want to take home"   A. "iPod (Uno Cards)"
Q. "Which one do you want to take home"   A. "iPod (Uno Cards)"
Q. "What do you need to take home"   A. "jacket (hat)"
Q. "Where is your back pack"   A. "locker (cubby)"
Q. "Where is your jacket"   A. "classroom (cafeteria)"
Q. "Who is that"   A. "[my] supervisor"
Q. "What's his name"   A. "Mr. Harris"

Q. "What do you need to take home"   A. lunch box and back pack
Q. "What are you looking for"   A. [my] big, yellow hat
Q. "Where did you leave your back pack"   A. [in the] cafeteria
Q. "Who is riding the bus with you"   A. John
Q. "What are you going to do now"   A. wash [my] hands
Q. "When are you going to get on the bus"   A. after I throw away the trash

ESSENTIAL FOR LIVING
Nice-to-have Answers to Questions

Answering Questions Regarding Physical Sensations or Emotions. After learners have acquired a substantial repertoire of listener and speaker responses as part of Events 1-10, consider teaching them 'to answer questions regarding (1) their own pain or discomfort and the location thereof' and (2) the presence of feelings of happiness, sadness, or anger, and the situations that may have resulted in these feelings'. These answers to questions may be very difficult to acquire, and, as a result, are designated as *nice-to-have*.

to make intraverbal responses to questions regarding their own private physical sensations and feelings and the public events that may have resulted in those feelings

Event 14 (AQ14). When learners have acquired answers to questions within Events 1-10, along with most of the naming or describing skills that are part of Event 14, you can begin to teach answers to questions within this event. For example, as shown in Table 12, when a child or an adult has learned to describe 'headache', 'arm hurts', or 'leg hurts, and to request 'a blanket', 'or the opportunity to 'lie down', you can teach that learner to answer questions during that event, which include words or signs for these descriptions of pain or discomfort and their location, along with preferred items or activities that may provide relief or a distraction. Begin by teaching learners to answer questions when it is likely that they are experiencing sensations of pain and discomfort (see *Listener Responses, Names, and Descriptions:* **LRND14**). Later, teach answers to questions when pain and discomfort are no longer occurring.

Table 12.
Answers to Questions for Event 14: Pain or Discomfort (AQ14)
Introduced after Names and Descriptions that are Part of this Event have been Acquired
and after Answers to Questions in Events 1-10 (AQ1-10) have also been Acquired

Questions should first occur when it is likely that learners are experiencing sensations of pain and discomfort and later when it is likely that these sensations are no longer occurring...	
Q. "Does your arm (leg) (stomach) hurt"	A. "yes (no)"
Q. "Where does it hurt"	A. "chest (arm) (throat)"
Q. "Are you feeling sick"	A. "yes, my stomach hurts"
Q. "How are you feeling"	A. "[I have a] headache"
Q. "What do you want (to do)"	A. "throat lozenges (lie down)"
Q. "What did you do when you had that headache"	A. "[take an] aspirin (Tylenol)"

Event 15 (AQ15). When learners have acquired answers to questions within Events 1-10, along with most of the naming or describing skills that are part of Event 15, you can begin to teach answers to questions within this event. For example, as shown in Table 13, when a child or an adult has learned to describe 'I'm sad -- we can't watch the rest of the movie', 'I'm happy -- my supervisor brought cookies for snack', 'I'm angry -- she took my iPod', and 'I'm angry -- he kicked me', you can teach that learner to answer questions during that event, which include words or signs for these descriptions of feelings and situations that may have resulted in those feelings, along with descriptions of preferred items or activities that may provide relief or distraction. Begin by teaching learners to provide answers to questions when it is likely that they are experiencing feelings of sadness, happiness, or anger (see *Listener Responses, Names, and Descriptions:* **LRND15**). Later, teach answers to questions when these feelings and the situations that may have caused them are no longer occurring.

Table 13.
Answers to Questions for Event 15: Feelings of Sadness, Happiness, and Anger (AQ15)
Introduced after Names and Descriptions that are Part of this Event have been Acquired
and after Answers to Questions in Events 1-10 (AQ1-10) have also been Acquired

Questions should first occur when learners are experiencing specific situations and it is likely that they are also experiencing feelings of sadness, happiness, or anger and later when these situations and these feelings are no longer occurring...	
Q. "Are you happy (sad) (angry)"	A. "yes (no)"
Q. "How do you feel"	A. "happy (sad) (angry)"
Q. "What do you want (to do)"	A. "a hug (lie down)"
Q. "What do you think you should do"	A. "get my iPod and calm down"
Q. "Why are you sad"	A. "karaoke has been cancelled"
Q. "Why were you angry"	A. "he kicked me"

The Assessment of Answers to Questions

Before conducting an assessment, review the procedures described in chapter 4. Then, secure a copy of the *Assessment and Record of Progress (ARP)* for each learner and begin to conduct the assessment. Wait until learners have acquired requests, names, and descriptions for Events 1-3: The First Time. Then, using the guidelines described in this section, select specific questions for this event (see Table 14) that could be answered with words or signs previously learned as requests, names, or descriptions. Then, insert these questions into each event on the *ARP* (see Table 14) and determine each learner's performance level. Repeat these procedures for Events 4-6: the First Time Around, Events 1-3: The Second Time Around, Events 7-13, Events 1-3: the Third Time Around, Events 4-6: The Second Time Around, and Events 14 and 15.

Table 14.
Performance Levels for Answers to Questions
that are Part of Events 1-15 (AQ1-15)

During selected events, learners provide answer to questions that are part of these events on three consecutive occasions...

- **IA** [the initial assessment of this speaker response has been completed]
- **IM** [instruction or management has begun]

- **FP** when there is contact with a specific item or activity
- **PP** when there is brief contact with a specific item or activity
- **MP** when there is very brief contact with a specific item or activity
- **Ind** without prompts and without hesitation
- **2E** with two or more variations of each question
- **2P** in the presence of either of two people

- **Det** [this speaker response is no longer occurring consistently]

Events 1-3: The First Time Around (AQ1-3.1)

Event 1: Breakfast (AQ1.1)

Q. "What do you want"								
A. "Cheerios (Wheaties)"	IA	IM	FP	PP	MP	Ind	2E	2P	Det
Q. "What do you need"								
A. "spoon (napkin)"	IA	IM	FP	PP	MP	Ind	2E	2P	Det

Events 4-6: The First Time Around (AQ4-6.1)

Event 4: Getting Ready to Go Home (AQ4.1)

Q. "Where is your back pack"								
A. "Locker (Cubby)"	IA	IM	FP	PP	MP	Ind	2E	2P	Det
Q. "Who is that"								
A. "[My] Supervisor"	IA	IM	FP	PP	MP	Ind	2E	2P	Det

Events 7-13 (AQ7-13)

Event 7: Unloading the Dishwasher (AQ7)

Q. "What are you trying to reach"								
A. "Forks and spoons"	IA	IM	FP	PP	MP	Ind	2E	2P	Det
Q. "Where are you going to put the large items"								
A. "On the counter"	IA	IM	FP	PP	MP	Ind	2E	2P	Det

Table 14 (cont.).
Performance Levels for Answers to Questions
that are Part of Events 1-15 (AQ1-15)

Events 1-3: The Third Time Around (AQ1-3.3)

Event 1: Breakfast (AQ1.3)

	IA	IM	FP	PP	MP	Ind	2E	2P	Det
Q. "Who is going to eat with us"									
A. "Mrs. Ellis (Kristin)"	IA	IM	FP	PP	MP	Ind	2E	2P	Det
Q. "Where is Kristin (Mrs. Ellis)"									
A. "Classroom (Cafeteria)"	IA	IM	FP	PP	MP	Ind	2E	2P	Det

Event 14: 'Indicating the Presence and Location of Pain or Discomfort' (AQ14)

	IA	IM	FP	PP	MP	Ind	2E	2P	Det
Q. "Does your stomach (head) hurt"									
A. "yes (no)"	IA	IM	FP	PP	MP	Ind	2E	2P	Det
Q. "How do you feel"									
A. "I have a stomach (head) ache"	IA	IM	FP	PP	MP	Ind	2E	2P	Det
Q. "What do you want to do"									
A. "lie down (take an aspirin)"	IA	IM	FP	PP	MP	Ind	2E	2P	Det

Teaching Answers to Questions

Answers to questions should almost always be taught as part of and during selected events (see in the natural environment **Events 1-15**). Sometimes it is difficult to provide more than a few teaching opportunities during an event. When this happens, you should provide additional opportunities just before or after the event. As events unfold and situations change, opportunities to teach non-targeted answers may occur and should be pursued.

Answers should almost always be composed of words and signs that were first acquired as requests, names, or descriptions, and should be taught using Teaching Protocol 10 included in chapter 12. In other words, answers should be prompted by pointing to items, activities, familiar persons, places, locations, numerals, clocks, and calendars for which requests, names, or descriptions were previously acquired (see the previous section, *Listener Responses, Names, and Descriptions*). As described earlier in this section, some language programs recommend prompting answers by saying words, forming signs, or by writing, typing, or selecting printed words without regard to a repertoire of requests, names, or descriptions. These prompts often result in rote responses with little or no meaning for learners or their audience.

As indicated earlier in this section, some answers or parts thereof, cannot be based on names or descriptions and cannot be taught by pointing to items, activities, familiar persons, places, locations, numerals, clocks, or calendars. These responses, which must be prompted with spoken words or signs, include 'outside', 'in the morning', 'try', 'after I finish', 'put away', 'tomorrow', 'ready', 'yes', 'stay here', 'want', 'no', 'right now', 'later', 'not yet', 'before', 'after', and 'again'. These responses can be added to answers when learners have acquired all of the speaking and listening skills that are part of each event.

In everyday situations and selected events, learners will encounter questions that vary slightly in form from those for which answers were taught. For example, learners may hear "Which one do you want" and later "Which one would you like". In order to insure that answers to questions continue to occur in these situations, it is important to vary the form of questions and prompt errorlessly as early as the second or third week of instruction.

Collect data several times each week, or even daily, if possible, using first opportunity of the day probes described in chapter 4. Then, record these data on one of the *Skill Acquisition Self-graphing Data Recording Forms* as shown in Table 15 and described in chapter 4. These data sheets can also be downloaded from www.behaviorchange.com. When learners do not make progress on specific skills, make adjustments in the teaching procedures. As learners reach specific performance levels, transfer this information to the *ARP* as shown in Table 16 and described in chapter 4.

Essential for Living 181

Table 15.
Recording the Learner's Progress on Answers to Questions Selected for Instruction
Using Single-trial Probe Data and Probe Data Sheets

ESSENTIAL FOR LIVING
Skill Acquisition Self-graphing Data Recording Form
Answers to Questions
First Opportunity of the Day Probes

Event 1. Breakfast (AQ1.1)	Day/Date and First Opportunity of the Day Probe																
	13	14	15	16	17	18	19	20	21	22	23	24	25	26	27	28	29
	S	M	T	W	T	F	S	S	M	T	W	T	F	S	S	M	T
Q. "What do you want" A. "Cheerios (Wheaties)"	Det 2P 2E Ind MP PP FP 0	Det 2P 2E Ind MP **PP** FP 0	Det 2P 2E Ind MP (PP) FP 0	Det 2P 2E Ind (MP) PP FP 0	Det 2P 2E (Ind) MP PP FP 0	Det 2P 2E (Ind) MP PP FP 0	Det 2P 2E Ind MP PP FP 0	Det 2P 2E Ind MP PP FP 0	Det 2P (2E) (Ind) MP PP FP 0	Det 2P (2E) Ind MP PP FP 0	Det 2P (2E) Ind MP PP FP 0	Det 2P (2E) Ind MP PP FP 0	Det (2P) 2E Ind MP PP FP 0	Det 2P 2E Ind MP PP FP 0	Det 2P 2E Ind MP PP FP 0	Det (2P) 2E Ind MP PP FP 0	Det 2P 2E Ind MP PP FP 0

Table 16.
Transferring Data from Self-graphing Data Recording Forms
to the Assessment and Record of Progress (ARP)

Event 1: 'Breakfast' (AQ1.1)								
Q. "What do you want"								
A. "Cheerios (Wheaties)"	IA	IM	FP	PP	MP	Ind	2E	2P	Det

Conversations

Conversations are composed of two or more exchanges of primarily but, not exclusively, speaker responses between learners and instructors, care providers, parents, and peers. Specifically, these exchanges include requests and answers to questions interspersed mands, intraverbals, and with occasional listener responses. Most of these answers are based on previously occasional listener responses. acquired requests, names, and descriptions. Conversations should always occur in the context of Events 1-13, which are an integral part of this instrument. Learners should be taught to participate in conversations during these events *only after answers to questions that are part of each event have been acquired*. Conversations are designated as *good-to-have skills and* should never be taught before *should-have, must-have,* or *good-to-have* requests, listener responses, daily living skills, or tolerating skills. Conversations concerning Events 14 and 15 are beyond the scope of this instrument.

ESSENTIAL FOR LIVING
Good-to-have Conversations

As shown in Table 17, introduce conversations into specific events (e.g., Events 1-3, The First Time Around), with two exchanges between one learner and one instructor, care provider, or parent. One of these exchanges should include a request by the learner.

Table 17.
Conversations during Events 1-3: The First Time Around (C1-3.1)
with Two Exchanges Between One Learner and A Care Provider
Sample Event -- Breakfast: Introduced after Answers to Questions
that are Part of these Events have been Acquired (see Table 6)

Marianne (a young adult learner with moderate disabilities) is just sitting down to eat breakfast at the kitchen table, when her care provider enters the room...		
Marianne:	"[May I have] Cheerios"	*request*
Care Provider:	[retrieves Cheerios]	
Care Provider:	"What else do you need"	
Marianne:	"A napkin"	*answer to a question*
Care Provider:	[retrieves a napkin]	

Then, as events include more speaking and listening skills, gradually increase the number of exchanges to four, making certain that every other exchange includes a learner request (see Table 18). Later, gradually increase the number of exchanges to six and include fewer learner requests (see Table 19). Then, begin to include a peer in the conversations, and gradually fade the instructor, care provider, or parent from some of these conversations (see Tables 20-21). And, finally, during these conversations, teach learners to make requests for information (see **R84-88**). The number of expected exchanges for each event is specified in Table 22 and the *ARP*.

Table 18.
Conversations during Events 1-3: The Second Time Around (C1-3.2)
with Four Exchanges Between One Learner and A Care Provider
Sample Event -- Breakfast
Introduced after Answers to Questions that are Part
of these Events have been Acquired (see Table 8)

Marianne (a young adult learner with moderate disabilities) is just sitting down to eat breakfast at the kitchen table, when her care provider enters the room and places a box of Cheerios and a box of Wheaties on the table...

Care Provider:	"Marianne, which one do you want"	
Marianne:	"Cheerios"	*answer to a question*
Marianne:	"[May I have] napkin"	*request*
Care Provider:	"Certainly" [retrieves a napkin]	
Care Provider:	"Who is going to eat with you"	
Marianne:	"Kristin"	*answer to a question*
Marianne:	"[May I have] juice"	*request*
Care Provider:	[hands her a juice box]	

Table 19.
Conversations during Events 1-3: The Third Time Around (C1-3.3)
with Six Exchanges Between One Adult Learner and A Care Provider
Sample Event -- Breakfast
Introduced after Answers to Questions that are Part
of these Events have been Acquired (see Table 10)

Marianne (a young adult learner with moderate disabilities) is getting ready to eat her breakfast, and her roommate Kristin is just joining her, when their care provider says...

Care Provider:	"Marianne, what do you need"	
Marianne:	"Napkins and cereal spoons"	*answer to a question*
Care Provider:	[retrieves a napkin and a cereal spoon]	
Care Provider:	"Marianne, could you get the chocolate milk for Kristin"	
Marianne:	"sure" [retrieves the chocolate milk]	*listener response*
Care Provider:	"By the way, where is Kristin"	
Marianne:	"In the laundry room"	*answer to a question*
Marianne:	"[Could we have some] juice "	*request*
Care Provider:	"certainly" [retrieves juice]	
Care Provider:	"Do you need anything else"	
Marianne:	"No [thank you]"	*answer to a question*
Care Provider:	"Make certain that you clean up when you and Kristin are finished"	
Marianne:	"O.K."	*answer to a question*
Marianne:	[cleans up when she and Kristin are finished eating breakfast]	*listener response*

Essential for Living

Table 20.
Conversations during Events 1-3: The Third Time Around (C1-3.3)
with Six Exchanges Between One Adult Learner, A Peer, and A Care Provider
Sample Event -- Breakfast
Introduced after Answers to Questions that are Part
of these Events have been Acquired (see Table 10)

Marianne and Kristin (young adult learners with moderate disabilities) are just sitting down to eat breakfast at the kitchen table, when their care provider enters the room and places a box of Cheerios and a box of Wheaties on the table...

Care Provider:	"Marianne, which one do you want"	
Marianne:	"Cheerios"	*answer to a question*
Kristin:	"May I have Wheaties"	*request*
Care Provider:	"Certainly, ladies" [hands the cereals to them]	
Care Provider:	"Marianne, could you get bowls...and Kristin, could you get cereal spoons"	
Marianne/Kristin:	[retrieve bowls and cereal spoons]	*listener responses*
Care Provider:	"Where are the napkins"	
Kristin:	"Next to the dishwasher"	*answer to a question*
Marianne:	"I'll get them"	*answer to a question*
Marianne:	[retrieves napkins]	*listener response*
Care Provider:	"What else do you ladies need"	
Kristin:	"2% Chocolate milk"	*answer to a question*
Marianne:	[retrieves the chocolate milk]	*listener response*
Marianne:	"Could you get me a juice box"	*request*
Care Provider:	[retrieves a juice box]	
Care Provider:	"Ladies, don't forget to clean up"	
Marianne:	"I'll clean up"	*answer to a question*
Kristin:	"Great, I'll help you"	*answer to a question*

Table 21.
Conversations during Events 1-3: The Third Time Around (C1-3.3)
with Six Exchanges Between Two Adult Learners
Sample Event -- Breakfast
Introduced after Answers to Questions that are Part
of these Events have been Acquired (see Table 10)

Marianne and Kristin (young adult learners with moderate disabilities) are just sitting down to eat breakfast at the kitchen table...

Marianne:	"Do you want Wheaties"	*request*
Kristin:	"Yes"	*answer to a question*
Kristin:	"Which cereal do you want"	*request*
Marianne:	"Cheerios"	*answer to a question*
Marianne:	"You get the cereal spoons and the napkins and I'll get the bowls and the milk"	*requests*
Marianne/Kristin:	[retrieve only napkins, bowls, and milk]	*listener responses*
Kristin:	"Where are the cereal spoons"	
Marianne:	"Next to the dishwasher"	*answer to a question*
Marianne:	[retrieves cereal spoons]	*listener response*
Marianne:	"What else do we need"	
Kristin:	"2% Chocolate milk and juice"	*answer to a question*
Marianne:	[retrieves the chocolate milk and the juice]	*listener response*
Kristin:	"Are you doing o.k."	*request*
Marianne:	"yes...are you o.k."	*request/answer*
Kristin:	"I'm fine"	*answer to a question*

The Assessment of Conversations

Before conducting an assessment, review the procedures described in chapter 4. Then, secure a copy of the *Assessment and Record of Progress (ARP)* for each learner and begin to conduct the assessment. When learners have acquired answers to questions for each event (e.g., AQ1.1 -- Event 1: The First Time Around), arrange conversations as described in this section and determine the extent to which each learner can participate according to the performance levels described in Table 22.

Table 22.
Performance Levels for Participating in Conversations
that are Part of Events 1-13 (C1-13)

During selected events, learners alternately answer questions, make requests, or respond as a listener without prompts and without hesitation during ___ conversational exchanges that are part of Events 1-13 on three consecutive occasions...

    IA   [the initial assessment of this speaker response has been completed]
    IM [instruction or management has begun]

    2E with two consecutive exchanges
    3E with three consecutive exchanges
    4E with four consecutive exchanges
    5E with five consecutive exchanges
    6E with six consecutive exchanges
    2T in the presence of either of two instructors, care providers, supervisors, or parents
    2F in the presence of either of two friends or peers

    Det [these listener or speaker responses are no longer occurring consistently]

Events 1-3: The First Time Around (C1-3.1)

Event 1 -- Breakfast (C1.1)	IA	IM	2E	2T	2F	Det
Event 2 -- Snack Time (C2.1)	IA	IM	2E	2T	2F	Det
Event 3 -- Getting Ready for Bed (C3.1)	IA	IM	2E	2T	2F	Det

Events 4-6: The First Time Around (C4-6.1)

Event 4 -- Getting Ready to Go Home (C4.1)	IA	IM	2E	3E	4E	2T	2F	Det
Event 5 -- Setting the Table (C5.1)	IA	IM	2E	3E	4E	2T	2F	Det
Event 6 -- Laying Out My Clothes for Tomorrow (C6.1)	IA	IM	2E	3E	4E	2T	2F	Det

Events 7-13 (C7-13)

Event 7 -- Unloading the Dishwasher (C7)	IA	IM	2E	3E	4E	5E	6E	2T	2F	Det
Event 8 -- Doing My Laundry (C8)	IA	IM	2E	3E	4E	5E	6E	2T	2F	Det
Event 9 -- Cleaning My Room (C9)	IA	IM	2E	3E	4E	5E	6E	2T	2F	Det

Events 1-3: The Third Time Around (C1-3.3)

Event 1 -- Breakfast (C1.3)	IA	IM	2E	3E	4E	5E	6E	2T	2F	Det
Event 2 -- Snack Time (C2.3)	IA	IM	2E	3E	4E	5E	6E	2T	2F	Det
Event 3 -- Getting Ready for Bed (C3.3)	IA	IM	2E	3E	4E	5E	6E	2T	2F	Det

Teaching Learners to Participate in Conversations

As previously described, teach learners to participate in conversations during selected events, beginning with with one learner and one instructor, care provider, supervisor, or parent and two exchanges, one of which includes a request. Then, while increasing the number of exchanges, decrease the number that include requests. Later, add a second learner as a participant and gradually remove non-learner participants from *some* of the conversations.

Collect data several times each week, or even daily, if possible, using first opportunity of the day probes described in chapter 4. Remember, a probe includes several responses, that is, one or more requests, answers to questions, or listener responses that are part of targeted exchanges within conversations during specific events. Record these data on one of the *Skill Acquisition Self-graphing Data Recording Forms* shown in Table 23 and described in chapter 4. These probe data sheets can also be downloaded from www.behaviorchange.com. When learners do not make progress on specific skills, make adjustments in the teaching procedures. As learners reach specific performance levels, transfer this information to the *ARP* as shown in Table 24 and described in chapter 4.

Table 23.
Recording the Learner's Progress on Participating in Conversations
Using Single-trial Probe Data and Probe Data Sheets

ESSENTIAL FOR LIVING
Skill Acquisition Self-graphing Data Recording Form
Conversational Exchanges
First Opportunity of the Day Probes

Event 1-3: The Second Time Around (C1-3.2)	Day/Date and First Opportunity of the Day Probe															
	S	M	T	W	T	F	S	S	M	T	W	T	F	S	S	M	T
Event 1. Breakfast (C1.2)	Det 2F 2T ~~6E~~ ~~5E~~ 4E 3E 2E 0	Det 2F 2T ~~6E~~ ~~5E~~ 4E 3E 2E 0	Det 2F 2T ~~6E~~ ~~5E~~ 4E 3E 2E 0	Det 2F 2T ~~6E~~ ~~5E~~ 4E 3E 2E 0	Det 2F 2T ~~6E~~ ~~5E~~ 4E 3E 2E 0	Det 2F 2T ~~6E~~ ~~5E~~ 4E 3E 2E 0	Det 2F 2T ~~6E~~ ~~5E~~ 4E 3E 2E 0	Det 2F 2T ~~6E~~ ~~5E~~ 4E 3E 2E 0	Det 2F 2T ~~6E~~ ~~5E~~ 4E 3E 2E 0	Det 2F 2T ~~6E~~ ~~5E~~ 4E 3E 2E 0	Det 2F 2T ~~6E~~ ~~5E~~ 4E 3E 2E 0	Det 2F 2T ~~6E~~ ~~5E~~ 4E 3E 2E 0	Det 2F 2T ~~6E~~ ~~5E~~ 4E 3E 2E 0	Det 2F 2T ~~6E~~ ~~5E~~ 4E 3E 2E 0	Det 2F 2T ~~6E~~ ~~5E~~ 4E 3E 2E 0	Det 2F 2T ~~6E~~ ~~5E~~ 4E 3E 2E 0

Table 24.
Transferring Data from Self-graphing Data Recording Forms
to the Assessment and Record of Progress (*ARP*)

Events 1-3: The Second Time Around (C1-3.2)								
Event 1 -- Breakfast (C1.2)	IA	IM	2E	3E	4E	2T	2F	Det
Event 2 -- Snack Time (C2.2)	IA	IM	2E	3E	4E	2T	2F	Det
Event 3 -- Getting Ready for Bed (C3.2)	IA	IM	2E	3E	4E	2T	2F	Det

Chapter 8. Doing Skills

8a. Daily Living and Related Skills

Daily Living Skills

Daily living skills are among the most functional of all skills. 'Washing our hands', 'brushing our teeth', 'going to the toilet', 'changing a sanitary napkin', 'taking medication', 'eating meals', 'doing laundry', 'putting a coat on', and 'mopping a floor' are examples of daily living skills that occupy a significant portion of our lives. These skills permit children and adults with moderate-to-severe disabilities to achieve a measure of independence. As shown in Table 1, daily living skills occur when children or adults (1) encounter situations that require specific responses, (2) exhibit part or all of those responses, and (3) either receive a form of social approval or experience completion of a task.

Table 1. Daily Living Skills

The learner encounters a situation that requires a specific response [S^D]	→	The learner exhibits part or all of that response [R]	→	The learner receives a form of social approval or experiences completion of a task [S^R]
An instructor says "It's time to get ready for lunch"		The learner performs 10 steps of 'washing her hands' and her hands are clean		An instructor says "Now you're ready for lunch"
		The learner sits down at the table		An instructor says "Your hands are dirty and points to the sink
The learner notices that his dirty laundry hamper is full		The learner begins to complete 14 interrupted steps of doing his laundry by sorting his clothes into dark and light items		The learner looks at his clean laundry and sees that he has completed this task
		The learner sits down and begins to watch TV		A care provider says "you won't have time to do your laundry tomorrow"
A bowl of cereal is placed in front of the learner		The learner picks up a spoon and begins to eat		The parent smiles and nods
		The learner waits and looks toward the parent for help		The parent points toward the spoon

S^D: a discriminative stimulus
R: the learner exhibits a daily living skill
S^R: the learner gains access to a reinforcer

Daily living skills should be distinguished from listener responses and tolerating skills. For example, 'permitting someone to wash your hands without exhibiting problem behavior' is a tolerating skill, 'washing your hands when directed to do so' is a listening skill, and 'washing your hands before a meal' is a daily living skill. Skills such as 'washing your hands' may begin as tolerating skills, evolve into listening skills, and, when directions are faded, become daily living skills. Sometimes the difference between a tolerating skill and a corresponding daily living skill may be difficult to distinguish. For example, the only difference between 'tolerating a sippy cup' and 'consuming liquids from a sippy cup' may be that, in the daily living skill, the learner, not a care provider, is holding and tipping the cup.

Some daily living skills are composed of a single response, such as, *drinks from a cup or glass* or *indicates the need to use a restroom*, while others are composed of multiple responses or steps (**MR**), such as *washes your hands, brushes your teeth,* or *puts on a pullover shirt or blouse*. These responses or steps are defined by a procedure known as a *task analysis*.

Some daily living skills require a repertoire of fine motor, tool or component skills, such as *squeezing* and *squeezing toothpaste onto a toothbrush*, while others require complex discriminations that can only be taught within the situation or context in which the skill is expected to occur, such as, *washing your hands before a meal or when they are dirty*. Some daily living skills also include critical responses, such as *opening the tube of toothpaste and squeezing the toothpaste onto the toothbrush*, or *turning on the cold water, turning on the hot water, and adjusting the water temperature to warm*, that must be completed in a *specific sequence* in order for '*brushing your teeth*' to be completed or '*washing your hands*' or '*taking a shower*' to be completed in a safe manner. And, all daily living skills include a critical outcome (**CO**), such as '*clean teeth*', '*clean hands*', or '*a clean body*', which must be achieved in order for the task to be considered completed.

Children and adults with moderate-to-severe disabilities generally do not acquire daily living skills without very specific prompting, prompt-fading, and chaining procedures. These skills, however, are often not emphasized in classrooms, or in day activity, residential, or vocational programs. Without a repertoire of basic, daily living skills, our children and adults will not experience a level of independence they deserve and will require the frequent and ongoing assistance of care providers and parents. As a result, these skills are a central part of this assessment and curriculum and are designated as *must-have, should-have* and *good-to-have* skills.

errorless prompting, prompt-fading, and forward, backward, and total task chaining

Related Skills

In addition to skills and activities generally categorized as Daily Living Skills, this section also includes:

- leisure skills -- when specific, preferred activities are available...the learner participates in these activities for substantial periods of time...and, experiences enjoyment derived from this participation; and,

- vocational skills -- when materials that are part of specific tasks or activities are present in a day activity or work environment...the learner performs the task or completes the activity without complaining or exhibiting problem behavior...and, experiences enjoyment derived from performing the task or completing the activity or gains access to forms of social approval.

These skills permit learners to 'occupy themselves' in enjoyable, meaningful, and productive ways.

ESSENTIAL FOR LIVING
Daily Living and Related Skills

Must-have Daily Living Skills Related to Health and Safety. In order for children and adults to remain safe and healthy, they must learn to perform some very specific daily living skills. These skills include (1) eating, drinking, and feeding, (2) going to sleep at appropriate times and sleeping for specific periods of time, (3) avoiding harmful items, substances, and situations, and (4) performing other activities related to health and safety. These skills are designated as *must-have* daily living skills.

Eating, Drinking, and Feeding -- These skills are often taught at the same time as T-EDF1-11.

DLS-EDF1.	Consumes thick or thickened liquids orally
DLS-EDF2.	Consumes three thin liquids orally, including water
DLS-EDF3.	Consumes three soft foods
DLS-EDF4.	Chews three soft foods
DLS-EDF5.	Munches on three crunchy foods
DLS-EDF6.	Chews three crunchy foods
DLS-EDF7.	Chews three chewy foods
DLS-EDF8.	Drinks with a sippy cup
DLS-EDF9.	Drinks from a cup or glass
DLS-EDF9a.	_____
DLS-EDF9b.	_____
DLS-EDF9c.	_____
DLS-EDF9d.	_____

Sleeping -- These skills are often taught at the same time as T-Slp1-5

DLS-Slp1.		Goes to sleep at bedtime
DLS-Slp2.		Sleeps through the night until morning
DLS-Slp2a.		_____
DLS-Slp2b.		_____

Mobility and Transportation

DLS-MT1.	MR	Transported from/to a bed, the toilet, a gait trainer, a walker, a wheelchair, or a MOVE device with a hoist
DLS-MT2.	MR	Transports self from a bed or chair to the toilet with a return
DLS-MT3.	MR	Transports self from a bed or chair to a wheelchair or a MOVE device with a return
DLS-MT4.	MR	Transports self from a bed or chair to a walker or gait trainer with a return
DLS-MT5.		Transported in a wheelchair
DLS-MT5a.	MR	_____
DLS-MT5b.		_____

Avoiding Harmful Items, Substances, and Situations

DLS-AHS1.		Does not pick up knives, scissors, and razors without supervision or training
DLS-AHS2.		Does not take medications without supervision or training
DLS-AHS3.		Does not use cleaning fluids without supervision or training
DLS-AHS4.		Does not touch insecticides
DLS-AHS5.		Does not walk after dark without a companion
DLS-AHS6.		Does not walk on wet floors
DLS-AHS7.		Does not turn on hot water before cold water
DLS-AHS8.		Does not enter pools, hot tubs, lakes, or rivers without supervision
DLS-AHS9.		Does not touch matches or lighters
DLS-AHS10.		Does not plug in or touch an iron
DLS-AHS11.		Does not pick up car keys
DLS-AHS12.		Does not put harmful, non-nutritive items in their mouth
DLS-AHS13.		Does not put anything in their eyes, ears, nose, rectum, urethra, or vagina
DLS-AHS14.		Does not run into the street or cross the street without supervision
DLS-AHS15.		Does not talk to, walk with, get in a car with, or open the door to a stranger
DLS-AHS15a.		_____
DLS-AHS15b.		_____
DLS-AHS15c.		_____

Other Activities Related to Health and Safety

DLS-HS1.	MR	Performs required exercises or therapeutic activities
DLS-HS2.	MR	Looks both ways, waits for traffic to clear, and crosses the street quickly
DLS-HS3.	MR	Wears external clothing appropriate to weather conditions
DLS-HS4.		Fastens and remains in a seat belt for the duration of specific trips
DLS-HS5.		Attends medical appointments (see also T-ORM1-11)
DLS-HS6.		Attends dental appointments (see also T-ORD1-5)
DLS-HS7.		Attends therapy appointments (see also T-SIT1-6)
DLS-HS8.	MR	Engages in safe, personal, sexual behavior in an appropriate setting
DLS-HS8a.		_____
DLS-HS8b.		_____
DLS-HS8c.	MR	_____
DLS-HS8d.	MR	_____

Should-have Daily Living and Related Skills. In order for children, and especially adults, to achieve some level of independence, they must begin to exhibit additional daily living skills. Many of these skills are designated as *should-have* daily living skills.

Eating, Drinking, and Feeding

DLS-EDF10.	Drinks from a can or bottle
DLS-EDF11.	Consumes required foods and drinks
DLS-EDF12.	Opens a can or bottle
DLS-EDF13.	Drinks from a carton or juice box
DLS-EDF14.	Opens a carton
DLS-EDF15.	Drinks with a straw
DLS-EDF16.	Feeds self three finger foods
DLS-EDF17.	Feeds self sandwiches
DLS-EDF18.	Wipes mouth and hands with a napkin
DLS-EDF19.	Takes bites from apples and peaches
DLS-EDF20.	Feeds self with a teaspoon or an adapted teaspoon
DLS-EDF21.	Feeds self cereal
DLS-EDF22.	Feeds self soup
DLS-EDF23.	Feeds self with a fork or an adapted fork
DLS-EDF24.	Feeds self meat, chicken, or fish, and potatoes or rice
DLS-EDF25.	Feeds self three cooked vegetables
DLS-EDF26.	Consumes an ice cream cone
DLS-EDF27.	Peels and eats oranges and grapefruits
DLS-EDF28.	Eats meals that are nutritionally balanced

DLS-EDF28a. _____

DLS-EDF28b. _____

DLS-EDF28c. _____

DLS-EDF28d. _____

DLS-EDF28e. _____

DLS-EDF28f. _____

Medical Procedures and Medication Administration

DLS-MM1.		Administers own liquid medication with an oral syringe
DLS-MM2.		Administers own liquid medication with a spoon
DLS-MM3.		Administers own pills or vitamins using a one-day pill sorter
DLS-MM4.		Administers own pills or vitamins using a weekly pill sorter
DLS-MM5.	MR	Washes a cut or a scrape and applies antiseptic and a bandage
DLS-MM6.		Uses an inhaler or nose spray
DLS-MM7.		Applies lip balm
DLS-MM8.	MR	Pricks finger and tests own blood
DLS-MM9.	MR	Gives own insulin injection

DLS-MM9a. _____

DLS-MM9b. _____

DLS-MM9c. MR _____

DLS-MM9d. MR _____

DLS-MM9e. _____

DLS-MM9f. _____

DLS-MM9f. _____

Sleeping

DLS-Slp3.	MR	Puts on pajamas
DLS-Slp4.		Goes to bed at a designated time
DLS-Slp5.		Remains in own bed throughout the night
DLS-Slp6.		Sleeps through the night without wetting the bed
DLS-Slp6a.	MR	_____
DLS-Slp6b.		_____
DLS-Slp6c.		_____

Mobility and Transportation

DLS-MT6.	MR	Walks with a walker
DLS-MT7.	MR	Walks with a white cane
DLS-MT8.	MR	Walks with a gait trainer
DLS-MT9.		Walks without a walker or gait trainer
DLS-MT10.	MR	Operates a manual wheelchair
DLS-MT11.	MR	Operates an electric wheelchair
DLS-MT12.		Transported in a MOVE device
DLS-MT13.	MR	Operates a MOVE device
DLS-MT14.		Transported to 5 locations by a wheelchair or MOVE device
DLS-MT15.		Transports self to 5 locations by walking, or operating a wheelchair or MOVE device
DLS-MT16.	MR	Rides a train, bus, or taxi to 5 specific locations
DLS-MT16a.	MR	_____
DLS-MT16b.	MR	_____
DLS-MT16c.		_____
DLS-MT16d.		_____

Avoiding Harmful Items, Substances, and Situations

DLS-AHS16.		Does not use a stove, oven, or microwave without supervision
DLS-AHS17.		Does not touch or turn on a fan or space heater without supervision or training
DLS-AHS18.		Consuming uncooked meat and poultry
DLS-AHS19.		Consuming foods or drinks beyond the expiration date
DLS-AHS19a.		_____
DLS-AHS19b.		_____
DLS-AHS19c.		_____

Toileting

DLS-Toil1.		Indicates when diaper, pull up, adult diaper, or underwear are soiled
DLS-Toil2.		Indicates the need to use a restroom
DLS-Toil3.		Indicates the need to use a catheter or to empty a colostomy or ileostomy bag
DLS-Toil4.	MR	Uses and manages a catheter or a colostomy or ileostomy bag
DLS-Toil5.		Urinates and defecates in a potty chair
DLS-Toil6.		Urinates and defecates on the toilet
DLS-Toil7.		Uses a urinal (for males)
DLS-Toil8.	MR	Completes a series of toileting steps at scheduled intervals which includes urinating and defecating on the toilet, using toilet paper, and flushing the toilet
DLS-Toil9.	MR	Completes a series of toileting steps which includes initiating, urinating and defecating on the toilet, using toilet paper, and flushing the toilet
DLS-Toil10.	MR	Completes a series of toileting steps during the middle of the night, which includes initiating, urinating and defecating on the toilet, using toilet paper, and flushing the toilet

Toileting (cont.)

DLS-Toil11.	MR	Locates, enters, and uses the appropriate public restroom
DLS-Toil11a.		_____
DLS-Toil11b.		_____
DLS-Toil11c.		_____

Bathing and Personal Hygiene

DLS-BPH1.	MR	Washes hands
DLS-BPH2.	MR	Washes face
DLS-BPH3.	MR	Washes hair
DLS-BPH4.	MR	Takes a shower or bath
DLS-BPH5.	MR	Cleans and clips nails
DLS-BPH6.	MR	Cleans ears
DLS-BPH7.	MR	Shaves face or legs and underarms
DLS-BPH8.	MR	Applies and changes a sanitary napkin or tampon during menstruation
DLS-BPH9.	MR	Brushes teeth and flosses twice per day
DLS-BPH10.	MR	Cleans braces or a mouthguard
DLS-BPH11.		Uses mouthwash
DLS-BPH12.		Combs or brushes hair
DLS-BPH13.	MR	Uses hair cream, gel, or hair spray
DLS-BPH14.		Curls or straightens hair
DLS-BPH15.	MR	Applies make-up
DLS-BPH16.		Sneezes into hands or sleeve
DLS-BPH17.	MR	Blows nose and disposes of handkerchief or tissue appropriately
DLS-BPH18.		Uses hand sanitizer
DLS-BPH19.		Applies deodorant
DLS-BPH20.		Applies cologne or perfume
DLS-BPH21.		Cleans glasses or inserts contact lenses
DLS-BPH21a.	MR	_____
DLS-BPH21b.	MR	_____
DLS-BPH21c.	MR	_____
DLS-BPH21d.	MR	_____
DLS-BPH21e.		_____
DLS-BPH21f.		_____
DLS-BPH21g.		_____

Dressing

DLS-D1.	MR	Extends parts of the body toward someone who is removing or putting on his/her clothes
DLS-D2.	MR	Removes a pullover shirt or blouse
DLS-D3.	MR	Removes a shirt with snaps, a zipper, or velcro
DLS-D4.	MR	Removes a shirt with buttons
DLS-D5.	MR	Removes a belt
DLS-D6.	MR	Removes shoes with laces
DLS-D7.	MR	Removes shoes with velcro
DLS-D8.		Removes slip-on shoes
DLS-D9.		Removes boots
DLS-D10.	MR	Removes pull-on pants, shorts, or a skirt
DLS-D11.	MR	Removes zippered pants, shorts, or a skirt
DLS-D12.	MR	Removes socks, stockings, or leggings
DLS-D13.	MR	Removes underpants or panties

Dressing (cont.)

ID		Description
DLS-D14.	MR	Removes a bra
DLS-D15.	MR	Removes a pullover sweater
DLS-D16.	MR	Removes a sweater, coat, or jacket with snaps, a zipper, or velcro
DLS-D17.	MR	Removes a sweater, coat, or jacket with buttons
DLS-D18.		Removes a hat or cap
DLS-D19.		Removes gloves or mittens
DLS-D20.	MR	Puts on underpants or panties
DLS-D21.	MR	Puts on a bra
DLS-D22.	MR	Puts on a pullover shirt or blouse
DLS-D23.	MR	Puts on a shirt or blouse with snaps, a zipper, or velcro
DLS-D24.	MR	Puts on a shirt or blouse with buttons
DLS-D25.	MR	Puts on socks, stockings, or leggings
DLS-D26.	MR	Puts on pull-on pants, shorts, or a skirt
DLS-D27.	MR	Puts on zippered pants, shorts, or a skirt
DLS-D28.	MR	Puts on a belt
DLS-D29.		Puts on shoes
DLS-D30.		Puts on boots
DLS-D31.	MR	Ties shoes with laces
DLS-D32.	MR	Fastens shoes with velcro
DLS-D33.	MR	Puts on a pullover sweater
DLS-D34.	MR	Puts on a sweater, coat, or jacket with snaps, a zipper, or velcro
DLS-D35.	MR	Puts on a sweater, coat, or jacket with buttons
DLS-D36.		Puts on a hat or cap
DLS-D37.		Puts on gloves or mittens
DLS-D38.		Selects clothing appropriate for four types of weather
DLS-D39.		Selects and coordinates clothing according to style, color, and situation
DLS-D39a.	MR	_____
DLS-D39b.	MR	_____
DLS-D39c.	MR	_____
DLS-D39d.		_____
DLS-D39e.		_____
DLS-D39f.	MR	_____
DLS-D39g.		_____

Leisure Activities at Home

ID		Description
DLS-LAH1.		Plays with specific toys or games
DLS-LAH2.		Puts puzzles together
DLS-LAH3.	MR	Plays card games
DLS-LAH4.	MR	Plays video games
DLS-LAH5.		Watches movies or videos
DLS-LAH6.		Colors, draws, or paints pictures
DLS-LAH7.		Shapes Play Doh or clay
DLS-LAH8.	MR	Cuts and pastes paper
DLS-LAH9.		Puts away items that are part of leisure activities
DLS-LAH10.	MR	Takes care of a lawn or garden
DLS-LAH11.	MR	Operates a digital music player or accesses music on the internet
DLS-LAH12.		Looks at books or magazines
DLS-LAH13.		Knits, crochets, or makes macrame items
DLS-LAH13a.	MR	_____
DLS-LAH13b.	MR	_____

Leisure Activities at Home (cont.)

DLS-LAH13c. _____

DLS-LAH13d. _____

DLS-LAH13e. _____

School, Instruction, and Therapy

DLS-SIT1.		Attends a school or therapy program
DLS-SIT2.		Participates in 1:1 guidance, instruction, and therapy
DLS-SIT3.		Completes single-response tasks during 1:1 instruction and therapy
DLS-SIT4.		Completes 2 consecutive, single-response tasks during 1:1 instruction and therapy
DLS-SIT5.		Completes 3 consecutive, single-response tasks during 1:1 instruction and therapy
DLS-SIT6.		Completes 5 consecutive, single-response tasks during 1:1 instruction and therapy
DLS-SIT7.		Completes 10 consecutive, single-response tasks during 1:1 instruction and therapy
DLS-SIT8.		Completes 20 consecutive, single-response tasks during 1:1 instruction and therapy
DLS-SIT9.	MR	Completes two-response tasks during 1:1 instruction and therapy
DLS-SIT10.	MR	Completes three-response tasks during 1:1 instruction and therapy
DLS-SIT11.	MR	Completes five-response tasks during 1:1 instruction and therapy
DLS-SIT12.	MR	Completes two-response tasks while working alone
DLS-SIT13.	MR	Completes three-response tasks while working alone
DLS-SIT14.	MR	Completes five-response tasks while working alone
DLS-SIT15.		Returns to tasks after significant interruptions
DLS-SIT16.		Participates in instruction with 2-4 peers (also see R8-12 and R14)
DLS-SIT17.		Completes single-response tasks during instruction with 2-4 peers
DLS-SIT18.	MR	Completes two-response tasks during instruction with 2-4 peers
DLS-SIT19.	MR	Completes three-response tasks during instruction with 2-4 peers
DLS-SIT20.	MR	Completes five-response tasks during instruction with 2-4 peers
DLS-SIT21.		Participates in instruction with 5 or more peers
DLS-SIT22.		Completes single-response tasks during instruction with 5 or more peers
DLS-SIT23.	MR	Completes two-response tasks during instruction with 5 or more peers
DLS-SIT24.	MR	Completes three-response tasks during instruction with 5 or more peers
DLS-SIT25.	MR	Completes five-response tasks during instruction with 5 or more peers

DLS-SIT25a. _____

DLS-SIT25b. _____

DLS-SIT25c. _____

DLS-SIT25d. _____

DLS-SIT25e. _____

DLS-SIT25f. _____

Day Activity Skills

DLS-DAS1.	Attends a day activity or day training program
DLS-DAS2.	Participates in a day activity or day training program
DLS-DAS3.	Participates in one form of arts and crafts
DLS-DAS4.	Participates in three forms of arts and crafts with clean-up
DLS-DAS5.	Participates in three games or recreational activities
DLS-DAS6.	Participates in a pottery, macrame, cooking, or similar class

DLS-DAS6a. _____

DLS-DAS6b. _____

DLS-DAS6c. _____

DLS-DAS6d. _____

Vocational Skills

DLS-V1.		Attends a sheltered work program
DLS-V2.		Participates in a sheltered work program
DLS-V3.		Participates in supported employment
DLS-V4.		Maintains a job in competitive employment
DLS-V5.		Completes a single-response assembly or packaging task
DLS-V6.		Completes 2 or more single-response assembly or packaging tasks
DLS-V7.	MR	Completes 2 or more two-response assembly or packaging tasks
DLS-V8.	MR	Completes 2 or more assembly or packaging tasks that require three or more responses
DLS-V9.		Completes 2 or more single-response tasks that include envelopes, stamps, or stickers
DLS-V10.	MR	Completes 2 or more two-response tasks that include envelopes, stamps, or stickers
DLS-V11.	MR	Completes 2 or more tasks that include envelopes, stamps, or stickers, and that require three or more responses
DLS-V12.		Completes 2 or more single-response tasks that include inventory control or display
DLS-V13.	MR	Completes 2 or more two-response tasks that include inventory control or display
DLS-V14.	MR	Completes 2 or more tasks that include inventory control or display, and that require three or more responses
DLS-V15.		Completes 2 or more single-response tasks that include folding, cutting, using a stapler, using a hole punch, or glue
DLS-V16.	MR	Completes 2 or more two-response tasks that include folding, cutting, using a stapler, using a hole punch, or glue
DLS-V17.	MR	Completes 2 or more tasks that include folding, cutting, using a stapler, using a hole punch, or glue, and that require three or more responses
DLS-V18.		Completes 2 or more single-response tasks that include washing, cleaning, or laundry
DLS-V19.	MR	Completes 2 or more two-response tasks that include washing, cleaning, or laundry
DLS-V20.	MR	Completes 2 or more tasks that include washing, cleaning, or laundry, and that require three or more responses
DLS-V21.		Completes 2 or more single-response tasks that include waste management or recycling
DLS-V22.	MR	Completes 2 or more two-response tasks that include waste management or recycling
DLS-V23.	MR	Completes 2 or more tasks that include waste management or recycling, and that require three or more responses
DLS-V24.		Completes 2 or more single-response tasks that include property maintenance
DLS-V25.	MR	Completes 2 or more two-response tasks that include property maintenance
DLS-V26.	MR	Completes 2 or more tasks that include property maintenance, and that require three or more responses
DLS-V27.		Completes 2 or more single-response tasks that include food preparation or clean-up
DLS-V28.	MR	Completes 2 or more two-response tasks that include food preparation or clean-up
DLS-V29.	MR	Completes 2 or more tasks that include food preparation or clean-up, and that require three or more responses
DLS-V30.		Completes 2 or more single-response tasks that include operating a machine
DLS-V31.	MR	Completes 2 or more two-response tasks that include operating a machine
DLS-V32.	MR	Completes 2 or more tasks that include operating a machine, and that require three or more responses
DLS-V33.	MR	Assists others as they perform tasks including, but not limited to, servers in a restaurant, persons providing child care, custodians, stock or shipping clerks, property managers, persons working in laundry or dry cleaners, persons working in waste management or recycling, persons operating machinery, persons performing inspections or quality control, persons managing property, or retail clerks
DLS-V34.		Works continuously for 5 minutes

Vocational Skills (cont.)

DLS-V35.		Works continuously for 10 minutes
DLS-V36.		Works for 20 minutes with one or two pauses of less than one minute
DLS-V37.		Works continuously for one hour with one or two pauses of 1-2 minutes
DLS-V38.		Returns to work after significant interruptions
DLS-V39.		completes a single-response task that includes _____
DLS-V40.		completes a single-response task that includes _____
DLS-V41.		completes a single-response task that includes _____
DLS-V42.	MR	completes a two-response task that includes _____
DLS-V43.	MR	completes a two-response task that includes _____
DLS-V44.	MR	completes a two-response task that includes _____
DLS-V45.	MR	completes a task that includes _____, and that requires three or more responses
DLS-V46.	MR	completes a task that includes _____, and that requires three or more responses
DLS-V47.	MR	completes a task that includes _____, and that requires three or more responses

Good-to-have Daily Living Skills. In the quest for some level of independence for our learners, other daily living skills are also important. These skills permit learners to participate in routine activities at home and in the community, and are designated as *good-to-have* daily living skills.

Other Routine, Daily Activities

DLS-RDA1.		Puts coat, jacket, gloves, and hat in closet
DLS-RDA2.	MR	Makes own bed
DLS-RDA3.		Places dirty clothes or cloth napkins in the hamper
DLS-RDA4.		Takes out the trash
DLS-RDA5.	MR	Cleans own room
DLS-RDA6.	MR	Retrieves dishes, glasses, cups, utensils, and napkins, and sets the table
DLS-RDA7.	MR	Places clean dishes and silverware in the appropriate locations in a drawer or cupboard
DLS-RDA8.		Retrieves the mail
DLS-RDA9.	MR	Takes house key and lunch money to work
DLS-RDA9a.	MR	_____
DLS-RDA9b.	MR	_____
DLS-RDA9c.	MR	_____
DLS-RDA9d.	MR	_____
DLS-RDA9e.	MR	_____
DLS-RDA9f.		_____
DLS-RDA9g.		_____
DLS-RDA9h.		_____
DLS-RDA9i.		_____
DLS-RDA9j.		_____
DLS-RDA9k.		_____

Leisure Activities in the Community

DLS-LAC1.	MR	Watches movies at a movie theatre
DLS-LAC2.	MR	Attends plays or concerts
DLS-LAC3.	MR	Goes to museums
DLS-LAC4.	MR	Goes bowling
DLS-LAC5.	MR	Goes to a swimming pool or to the beach
DLS-LAC6.	MR	Attends dances, parties, or other social gatherings
DLS-LAC7.	MR	Eats a meal at a fast food restaurant
DLS-LAC8.	MR	Eats a meal at a restaurant
DLS-LAC9.	MR	Goes shopping
DLS-LAC10.	MR	Attends sporting events
DLS-LAC11.	MR	Goes to a park
DLS-LAC12.	MR	Participates in Special Olympics
DLS-LAC12a.	MR	_____
DLS-LAC12b.	MR	_____
DLS-LAC12c.	MR	_____
DLS-LAC12d.	MR	_____
DLS-LAC12e.	MR	_____
DLS-LAC12f.	MR	_____
DLS-LAC12g.	MR	_____
DLS-LAC12h.	MR	_____
DLS-LAC12i.	MR	_____
DLS-LAC12j.	MR	_____

Laundry

DLS-L1.		Sort dirty laundry into dark and light colors
DLS-L2.		Indicates which clothes are clean and which are dirty
DLS-L3.	MR	Washes loads of light-colored clothes
DLS-L4.	MR	Washes loads of white clothes
DLS-L5.	MR	Washes loads of dark-colored clothes
DLS-L6.	MR	Washes loads of clothes made of fabrics requiring special treatment
DLS-L7.	MR	Washes clothes by hand
DLS-L8.	MR	Hangs up clothes which should not go in the dryer
DLS-L9.	MR	Puts loads of clothes in the dryer and operates the dryer
DLS-L10.	MR	Removes clothes from the dryer and folds towels, socks, underwear, pants, shirts, blouses, and sweaters, and puts them in the proper closet or drawer
DLS-L11.	MR	Irons pants
DLS-L12.	MR	Irons shirts
DLS-L13.	MR	Puts clean clothes in specific places in a dresser drawer or cabinet
DLS-L14.	MR	Puts clean towels and sheets in a linen closet or cabinet
DLS-L14a.	MR	_____
DLS-L14b.	MR	_____
DLS-L14c.	MR	_____
DLS-L14d.	___	_____
DLS-L14e.	___	_____
DLS-L14f.	___	_____
DLS-L14g.	___	_____

Cleaning

DLS-C1.		Scrapes and rinses off dirty dishes
DLS-C2.	MR	Washes and dries dishes
DLS-C3.		Places dirty dishes in a dishwasher
DLS-C4.		Wipes off dinner table
DLS-C5.		Places paper towels and napkins in waste basket
DLS-C6.		Wipes counter tops and tables
DLS-C7.	MR	Sweeps floors, sidewalk, and porch
DLS-C8.	MR	Scrubs floors by hand
DLS-C9.	MR	Mops floors
DLS-C10.		Shakes rugs
DLS-C11.	MR	Cleans rugs and carpet with a vacuum cleaner
DLS-C12.	MR	Washes windows and mirrors
DLS-C13.	MR	Cleans sink
DLS-C14.	MR	Cleans tub and shower
DLS-C15.	MR	Cleans toilet bowl
DLS-C16.		Replaces towels, toilet paper, and soap in bathrooms
DLS-C16a.	MR	_____
DLS-C16b.	MR	_____
DLS-C16c.	MR	_____
DLS-C16d.	MR	_____
DLS-C16e.	MR	_____
DLS-C16f.		_____
DLS-C16g.		_____
DLS-C16h.		_____
DLS-C16i.		_____
DLS-C16j.		_____
DLS-C16k.		_____

Using a Telephone

DLS-TC1.	MR	Calls 911 and provides relevant information in simulated emergencies
DLS-TC2.		Uses a phone to call friends and family
DLS-TC3.		Answers the telephone appropriately
DLS-TC4.		Summons a requested person to telephone
DLS-TC5.		Dials a telephone number written on a piece of paper
DLS-TC6.		Introduces self to receiving party
DLS-TC7.		Hangs up after answering a simulated prank call or a call from a solicitor
DLS-TC7a.	MR	_____
DLS-TC7b.	___	_____
DLS-TC7c.	___	_____

Preparing Food

DLS-PF1.	MR	Opens and closes food containers which require twisting and turning
DLS-PF2.	MR	Opens and closes food containers which require prying to open and snapping on to close
DLS-PF3.	MR	Opens pop top cans
DLS-PF4.		Opens or closes bags with twisting or sliding seals
DLS-PF5.		Opens or closes cartons

Preparing Food (cont.)

DLS-PF6.		Prepares powdered hot and cold drinks or adds sweeteners or creamers to beverages
DLS-PF7.		Pours liquid from a pitcher to a cup or glass
DLS-PF8.	MR	Fixes a bowl of cereal
DLS-PF9.	MR	Makes a pot of coffee
DLS-PF10.	MR	Fixes a glass of iced tea
DLS-PF11.	MR	Fixes a cup of coffee or tea
DLS-PF12.	MR	Fixes a smoothie using a blender
DLS-PF13.	MR	Makes toast and jam with a dull knife
DLS-PF14.	MR	Makes a sandwich with a dull knife
DLS-PF15.	MR	Makes and packs a sack lunch with a sandwich, chips, and a piece of fruit
DLS-PF16.		Fixes a bowl of ice cream or sherbet
DLS-PF17.	MR	Makes prepared noodles
DLS-PF18.	MR	Makes macaroni and cheese
DLS-PF19.	MR	Makes soup using can opener
DLS-PF20.	MR	Makes scrambled eggs
DLS-PF21.	MR	Makes waffles or pancakes
DLS-PF22.	MR	Bakes cookies using prepared mix and an oven
DLS-PF23.		Uses a microwave to reheat food
DLS-PF24.	MR	Uses a microwave to make dinners, mashed potatoes, or make popcorn
DLS-PF25.	MR	Makes hot dogs on a grill
DLS-PF25a.	MR	_____
DLS-PF25b.	MR	_____
DLS-PF25c.	MR	_____
DLS-PF25d.	MR	_____
DLS-PF25e.		_____
DLS-PF25f.		_____
DLS-PF25g.		_____
DLS-PF25h.		_____
DLS-PF25i.		_____
DLS-PF25j.		_____
DLS-PF25k.		_____

The Assessment of Daily Living Skills

Before conducting an assessment, review the procedures described in chapter 4. Then, secure a copy of the **Assessment and Record of Progress (ARP)** for each learner, and begin to conduct the assessment. Determine each learner's performance level on single-response skills and estimate each learner's performance level on multiple-response skills (**MR**) that are immediately functional for that learner. Other skills can be assessed over a 1-2 year period of time. Begin the assessment with skills that include eating, drinking, and feeding (**EDF**), along with sleeping (**Slp**), and other *must-have* skills, and record performance levels on the *ARP*. The performance levels for single-response and multiple-response (**MR**) daily living skills are described in Table 2, along with sample items from the *ARP*. Note that performance levels include _**m**, which occurs when learners exhibit all of the responses that are part of multiple-response skills without prompts and within fluently a targeted period of time, **PPA**, which occurs when learners, because of physical limitations, cannot perform a specific skill or one or more responses that are part of that skill without assistance, **APD**, which occurs when learners require an environmental adaptation or prosthetic device to perform part or all the skill, and **CO**, which occurs when the critical outcome of a skill has occurred (see the next section). Continue the assessment until the learner requires prompts, exhibits inappropriate responses, or responds with problem behavior on three consecutive skills within each skill category.

Table 2.
Performance Levels for Daily Living Skills

Performance Levels for Single-response Daily Living Skills

When they encounter situations that require specific responses, learners exhibit single-response daily living skills on three consecutive occasions...

IA	[the initial assessment of this skill has been completed]
IM	[instruction or management has begun]
-SA	without self-injurious, aggressive, or destructive behavior
-DC	without disruptive behavior or complaints
-RP	without resistance to prompts and without leaving the area
FP	with a full physical or full demonstration prompt
PP	with a partial physical or partial demonstration prompt
MP	with a minimal touch or minimal gestural prompt
Ind	without prompts and within two seconds
PPA	[performance of this task requires permanent partial assistance]
APD	[performance of this task requires an environmental adaptation or prosthetic device]
CO	[the critical outcome of this skill has occurred]
2S	in two or more settings
2P	in the presence of either of two people
Det	[this daily living skill or its critical outcome are no longer occurring consistently]

Performance Levels for Multiple-response Daily Living Skills

When they encounter situations that require specific responses, learners exhibit......[some or all of the responses (steps) of a multiple-response daily living skill]... on three consecutive occasions without exhibiting problem behavior, without complaining, and without resisting or requiring prompts

IA	[the initial assessment of this skill has been completed]
IM	[instruction or management has begun]
1st	one response (step) without prompts
1/4	one fourth of the responses (steps) that are part of the skill without prompts
1/2	one half of the responses (steps) that are part of the skill without prompts
3/4	three fourths of the responses (steps) that are part of the skill without prompts
Ind	all of the responses (steps) that are part of the skill without prompts
_m	all of the responses (steps) that are part of the skill without prompts and within _ minutes
PPA	[some or all of the responses (steps) that are part of this skill require permanent partial assistance]
APD	[some or all of the responses (steps) that are part of this skill require an environmental adaptation or prosthetic device]
CO	the critical outcome of this skill has occurred
2S	[the skill and the critical outcome have occurred in two or more settings]
2P	[the skill and the critical outcome have occurred in the presence of either of two people]
Det	[some or all of the responses (steps) that are part of this skill or its critical outcome are no longer occurring consistently]

Drinking and eating

    DLS-EDF9.   Drinks from a cup or glass   **CO**: drinking a beverage from a full cup or glass without spilling until the beverage is gone

IA	IM	-SA	-DC	-RP	FP	PP	MP	Ind	PPA	APD	CO	2S	2P	Det

Bathing and personal hygiene

    DLS-BPH1.   Washes hands   **MR**   **CO**: clean hands

IA	IM	1st	1/4	1/2	3/4	Ind	2m	PPA	APD	CO	2S	2P	Det

Teaching Daily Living Skills and Recording Progress

Before you begin teaching daily living skills, *identify the critical outcome of each skill* (see Table 3). Remember, the critical outcome is the outcome which must be achieved in order for the task to be considered completed. For example, as shown in Table 2, the critical outcome of *drinking from a cup or glass* is drinking a beverage from a full cup or glass without spilling until the beverage is gone and the critical outcome of *washing hands* is clean hands.

Also, *conduct a task analysis on each multiple-response skill* as shown in Table 3. This is done by dividing the skill into a sequence of specific responses (steps), keeping in mind that some, critical responses must be completed in a specific sequence. For example, as shown in Table 3, response 1, turning on the cold water must come before response 2, turning on the hot water, to avoid injury to learners. Response 6, scrubbing palms of hands, however, could occur either before or after response 7, scrubbing backs of hands.

Use one of four teaching protocols included in chapter 12. These protocols include chaining (forward, backward, and total task chaining), along with errorless, non-vocal prompting, and prompt-fading. Collect data 2-3 times per week, or daily, if possible, using first opportunity of the day probes des-cribed in chapter 4. Then, record these data on one of the *Skills Acquisition Self-graphing Data Recording Forms* shown in Table 4 and described in chapter 4. These probe data sheets can be downloaded from www.behaviorchange.com. For multiple-response skills, note that horizontal lines and ovals indicate specific responses and the total number of responses exhibited without prompts, respectively. Also note that ovals with gray fill indicate that the skill will require permanent partial assistance (**PPA**) or an environmental adaption or prosthetic device (**APD**), and the specific responses that will require this assistance or adaptation. As learners reach specific levels, transfer this information to the *ARP* as shown in Table 5 and described in chapter 4. When learners do not make progress on specific skills or responses, make certain that you follow the steps exactly as they are described in the teaching protocols in chapter 12, and, as necessary, make adjustments in those protocols. Also, consider making environmental adaptations to a skill or response, or using prosthetic devices (**APD**). For example, if an adult is learning 'to wash a load of white clothes', and has had great difficulty learning to set the water temperature and the wash cycle, you might place stickers on the dials at the appropriate settings. Or, if an adult cannot seem to remember to take his house key and lunch money to work, you might place a container just big enough to hold both items on a shelf next to the front door. In some cases, specific skills or responses require movements the learner appears to be incapable of making. When this occurs, consider an environmental adaptation or prosthetic device. If none seems to be available, indicate that the skill or response requires permanent assistance from another person (**PPA**).

Table 3.
Conducting a Task Analysis on Multiple-response Daily Living Skills

Bathing and Personal Hygiene		
DLS-BPH1.	**MR**	Washes hands
1		Turn on the cold water
2		Turn on the hot water
3		Adjust the water temperature **PPA**
4		Wet hands
5		Apply liquid soap or rub bar soap on hands **PPA**
6		Scrub palms and backs of hands and around finger nails
7		Rinse hands
8		Turn off hot water
9		Turn off cold water
10		Get paper or cloth towel
11		Dry hands
Critical Outcome (**CO**)		clean hands

Table 4.
Recording the Learner's Progress on Single-response Daily Living Skills
Using Single-trial Probe Data and Probe Data Sheets

ESSENTIAL FOR LIVING
Skill Acquisition Self-graphing Data Recording Form
Single-response Daily Living Skills
First Opportunity of the Day Probes

Daily Living Skill	Day/Date and First Opportunity of the Day Probe
DLS-EDF9. Drinks from a cup or glass	S M T W T F S S M T W T F S S M T (columns) Det / 2P / 2S / CO / APD / PPA / Ind / MP / PP / FP / -RP / -DC / -SA / 0

Recording the Learner's Progress on Multiple-response Daily Living Skills
Using Single-trial Probe Data and Probe Data Sheets

ESSENTIAL FOR LIVING
Skill Acquisition Self-graphing Data Recording Form
Multiple-response Daily Living Skills
First Opportunity of the Day Probes

Daily Living Skill	Day/Date and First Opportunity of the Day Probe
DLS-BPH1. Washes hands **MR** 11 responses **CO**: clean hands	S M T W T F S S M T W T F S S M T (columns) Det / 2P / 2S / CO / APD / PPA / _m 12 11 10 9 8 7 6 5 4 3 2 1 0

Table 5.
Transferring Data from Self-graphing Data Recording Forms
to the Assessment and Record of Progress (*ARP*)

Drinking and eating

    DLS-EDF9.   Drinks from a cup or glass   **CO**: drinking a beverage from a full cup or glass without spilling until the beverage is gone

IA	IM	-SA	-DC	-RP	FP	PP	MP	Ind	PPA	APD	CO	2S	2P	Det

Bathing and personal hygiene

    DLS-BPH1.   **MR**   Washes hands   **CO**: clean hands

IA	IM	1st	1/4	1/2	3/4	Ind	2m	PPA	APD	CO	2S	2P	Det

8b. Functional Academic Skills

8b1. Responding to Text as a Listener and Reading. Reading, as the term is generally used by educators, includes transforming text (i.e., printed words or words written in Braille) into your method of speaking and then responding in a way that suggests comprehension. More specifically, reading includes 'seeing words, letters, or letter combinations, or touching braille letters or letter combinations and performing three activities:

transducing

textual behavior or intraverbal reading

1. saying sounds and blending sound combinations into words, saying words, or forming signs that correspond to these words,

2. saying, writing, typing, or Braille writing a response that suggests comprehension of what was read, and

intraverbal responses

3. selecting or retrieving an item, activity, person, or a picture, or performing an activity that corresponds to these words, suggesting some understanding of the words.

listener responses

The first activity is generally described as 'reading' and includes either phonetic reading, 'saying sounds that correspond to text and combining those sounds into words', or sight-word reading, 'saying words or forming signs that correspond to text'. For example, in phonetic reading, a learner 'sees the letters or letter combinations or touches the Braille letters or letter combinations in the word cookie', says the sounds that correspond to those letters or letter combinations and combines those sounds into the word 'c-oo-k-ie'. Whereas, in sight-word reading, a learner 'sees the word cookie' or 'feels the Braille letters that are part of cookie' and says or signs 'cookie'.

textual behavior or intraverbal reading

In order to participate in the first activity of reading, a learner's primary, concurrent, back-up, or secondary method of speaking must be 'saying words', or must include 'forming standard signs' (**AMS 2**). Learners who function as speakers primarily by 'selecting pictures or printed words' or by 'writing, typing words, or Braille writing' are precluded from performing this activity.

The second activity is generally referred to as 'reading comprehension', but can also be described as 'responding to text as a speaker'. In most, but not all situations, the learner begins by performing the first activity. Then, the learner is presented with a spoken-word or signed question from another person or a written-word question in a book or examination. Finally, the learner responds by saying, signing, writing, typing (texting), or Braille writing an 'answer to the question'. For example, a learner reads a menu in a restaurant, after which her friend asks "what kind of pancakes do they have", to which she responds "buttermilk, strawberry, and blueberry". This activity requires an extensive repertoire of 'naming' and 'answering questions' as part of everyday experiences.

intraverbal response

The third activity can be described as 'responding to text as a listener'. In this activity *a learner sees words or touches Braille letters and selects an item or a picture, or performs a corresponding task*. This activity indicates some 'understanding' of the text. For example, a learner sees the word or touches the Braille letters for 'Cheerios' on a grocery shopping list and retrieves a box of Cheerios from the store shelf, or sees the word or touches the Braille letters for 'Women' or 'Men' and enters the appropriate restroom. Learners who function as speakers primarily by 'selecting pictures or printed words' or by 'writing, typing words, or Braille writing' can perform this activity.

It is important to note that 'responding to text as a listener' can be accomplished without learning to 'read'. For example, after children or adults have seen the word or touched the Braille letters for 'Cheerios', 'Women', or 'Men', they can be taught to retrieve the box of Cheerios or enter the appropriate restroom without saying the words or forming the corresponding signs. This retrieval or this task can be accomplished by matching text with items, activities, people, places, or locations, that is, matching the printed word or the Braille letters for 'Cheerios' with a box of Cheerios and the location of those boxes in the grocery store, or matching the printed words or the Braille letters for 'Women' or 'Men' on or next to a restroom door with walking through or away from the door.

arbitrary matching

'Reading comprehension' and 'responding to text as a listener', are very important skills. In fact, without one or the other, 'reading' is largely meaningless to both the learner and those around her. For example, if a learner 'reads' the dessert section of a restaurant menu, her friend says "how many flavors of ice cream do they have", and the learner responds by saying "chocolate", 'reading has occurred, but 'comprehension' has not. Or, if a learner 'reads' a sign inside the front door of a restaurant that says 'Please Wait to be Seated', but then immediately proceeds to a table, 'reading has occurred', but 'responding effectively *to text as a listener'* has not. When *'reading'* occurs without either *'comprehension'* or *'effective listener responding'*, we often refer to it as *'word calling'*.

A small number of young children with moderate disabilities learn to *'read'*. Most of these children become sight-word readers with a limited reading repertoire. Only a few acquire phonetic skills beyond the initial consonant and vowel sounds in some words. While most of these children exhibit very limited *'reading comprehension'*, they often learn to *'respond effectively to text as a listener'*.

A small, but distinctive group of children with autism acquire a large repertoire of sight words, even though the remainder of their spoken-word repertoire is limited to a few requests. These learners are often referred to as *'hyperlexic'*. In most instances, even though these children appear to be *'reading'*, they are actually *'word calling'*.

For many young children with moderate-to-severe developmental disabilities, *'reading'*, that is, learning to perform the first activity, is not an appropriate goal (for that matter, neither is *'naming the letters of the alphabet or the letter sounds)*. With a limited repertoire of requests for preferred items and activities, few-if-any names for items found in their environment, and few-to-no answers to questions, these children seldom function as speakers. If reading were introduced, both *'reading'* and *'reading comprehension'* would be required. That is, we would be requiring these children to respond effectively to text as speakers, when they seldom function as speakers during their everyday experiences. In other words, if children do not respond to questions like "What did you get at the mall", it is unlikely they will respond to questions like "What did Angela get at the mall" after reading a story that includes this information.

> Children who are not functioning as speakers during their daily experiences, especially with respect to responses that are primarily intraverbal, cannot be expected to make intraverbal responses to text.

Some older children and adults acquire a limited number of functional sight-words, but the vast majority of children and adults with moderate-to-severe disabilities never acquire even a small *'reading'* repertoire. With or without a repertoire of sight words, some of these children and adults can learn to *'respond to text in a functional and effective manner'*. *'Reading'* and *'responding to text as a listener'* should not be considered must-have or should have skills and should never be taught before must-have or should have requests, listening skills, or doing skills. At best, these skills are good-to-have and are designated accordingly in this domain.

ESSENTIAL FOR LIVING
Responses to Text as a Listener and Reading Skills

Good-to-have Responses to Text as a Listener. For learners with moderate-to-severe developmental disabilities, *'responding effectively to text as a listener'* is often more functional than *'reading'* the text itself. Listener responses can result in increased safety, increased participation in community activities, increased access to preferred items and activities, and an overall increase in the level of independent functioning. As a result, these skills are designated as *good-to-have*. It is important to remember that 'text' means 'printed words or Braille letters' and that *'responding effectively to text as a listener'* does not require *'reading'*.

- **RTL1.** Approaches and enters the appropriate restroom when designated by the text 'Women' and 'Men', 'Ladies' and 'Gentlemen', the female and male stick figures, the international symbols for female and male, Braille letters, and one other text or symbol variation
- **RTL2.** Responds appropriately to public safety, street, and emergency signs that include text or Braille letters, such as, 'Walk' and 'Don't Walk', 'Fire Escape', 'Wet Floor', and others
- **RTL3.** Recognizes common food and non-food items that do not pose a risk to safety, such as, 'tomato soup' and 'chicken noodle soup', 'Cheerios' and 'Rice Krispies', 'Ramen Noodles: Chicken' and 'Ramen Noodles: Beef', 'Equal' and 'Coffee Mate', 'Skim Milk, Gallon' or Skim Milk, Half-gallon', 'Orange Juice with Pulp' or 'Orange Juice without Pulp', 'Crest toothpaste' or 'Colgate toothpaste', 'tall kitchen bags' or 'large trash bags', and others
- **RTL4.** Recognizes common food and non-food items that represent some risk to safety, including 'ant and roach spray', 'furniture polish', 'Mr. Clean' or 'Windex', 'vinegar' or 'vegetable oil', 'Tabasco Sauce', and others, and does not open these containers or use these items without permission
- **RTL5.** Recognizes common non-food items that contain dangerous chemicals, including 'toilet bowl cleaner', 'bleach', 'Drano', 'charcoal lighter fluid', and others, and does not open these containers or ask permission to do so

RTL6.	Responds appropriately to other signs throughout the community that include text or Braille letters, such as, 'push' and 'pull', 'entrance' and 'exit', 'open' and 'closed', 'do not touch', 'please wait to be seated', and others
RTL7.	Participates in events or activities that are included in printed-word or Braille schedules
RTL8.	Completes daily living skills by following a printed-word or Braille list of steps necessary to complete each skill, for example, '12 steps of brushing your teeth', '14 steps of getting dressed', and others
RTL9.	Completes specific steps of daily living skills by responding to printed-word or Braille reminders posted in familiar places, for example, 'wash your hands with soap and warm water', 'put your tooth-brush on your shelf', 'put your towel in the hamper', and others
RTL10.	Completes routine tasks by responding to hand-written or Braille reminders from a familiar person, for example, 'take five dollars to work', 'take your bus pass', 'put a sweater and cap in your book bag', 'use mouthwash', 'take out the trash', and others
RTL11.	Selects items from restaurant menus that include printed-words or Braille letters, such as, 'blueberry waffles', 'scrambled eggs and bacon with toast', 'cheeseburger and french fries', and others
RTL12.	Retrieves items on printed-word and Braille grocery and other shopping lists, such as, '12-pack of Diet Coke', 'two gallons of 2% milk', 'large box of Cheerios', and others
RTL13.	Locates the days of the week, dates, and the months of the year on printed-word or Braille calendars
RTL14.	Follows each step in simple, printed-word or Braille recipes, such as, 'mix the flour and water', 'add one teaspoon of salt', 'turn oven to 350 degrees', 'put in the oven for 20 minutes', and others

Additional Good-to-have Responses to Text as a Listener. With certain children and adults, you may want to select additional responses to text as a listener and designate these as good-to-have skills. This section permits you to do this.

RTL14a. _____

RTL14b. _____

RTL14c. _____

RTL14d. _____

RTL14e. _____

Good-to-have Reading Skills. For most learners with moderate-to-severe developmental disabilities, a reading repertoire will be very difficult to acquire. If acquired, however, this repertoire can be transformed into 'responding effectively to text as a listener' using specific teaching procedures.

Rdg1.	Reads the text 'Women' and 'Men', 'Ladies' and 'Gentlemen', the corresponding stick figures and international symbols, Braille letters, and one other text or symbol variation
Rdg2.	Reads public safety, street, and emergency signs that include text or Braille letters, such as, 'Walk' and 'Don't Walk', 'Fire Escape', 'Wet Floor', and others
Rdg3.	Reads the essential text on containers of common food and non-food items that do not pose a risk to safety, such as, 'tomato soup' and 'chicken noodle soup', 'Cheerios' and 'Rice Krispies', 'Ramen Noodles: Chicken' and 'Ramen Noodles: Beef', 'Equal' and 'Coffee-mate', 'Skim Milk, Gallon' or Skim Milk, Half-gallon', 'Orange Juice with Pulp' or 'Orange Juice without Pulp', 'Crest toothpaste' or 'Colgate toothpaste', 'tall kitchen bags' or 'large trash bags', and others
Rdg4.	Reads the essential text on containers of common food and non-food items that represent some risk to safety, including 'ant and roach spray', 'furniture polish', 'Mr. Clean' or 'Windex', 'vinegar' or 'vegetable oil', 'Tabasco Sauce', and others

Rdg5. Reads the essential text on containers of common non-food items that contain dangerous chemicals, including 'toilet bowl cleaner', 'bleach', 'Drano', 'charcoal lighter fluid', and others

Rdg6. Reads other signs throughout the community that include text or Braille letters, such as, 'push' and 'pull', 'entrance' and 'exit', 'open' and 'closed', 'do not touch', 'please wait to be seated', and others

Rdg7. Reads words that designate events or activities that are included in printed-word or Braille schedules

Rdg8. Reads printed-word or Braille lists of steps necessary to complete daily living skills, for example, '12 steps of brushing your teeth', '14 steps of getting dressed', and others

Rdg9. Reads printed-word or Braille reminders regarding the completion of specific steps of daily living skills posted in familiar places, for example, 'wash your hands with soap and warm water', 'put your towel in the hamper', and others

Rdg10. Reads hand-written or Braille reminders from a familiar person to complete routine tasks, for example, 'take five dollars to work', 'take your bus pass', 'put a sweater in your book bag', 'use mouthwash', 'take out the trash', and others

Rdg11. Reads text (printed words or Braille letters) that is included in restaurant menus, such as, 'blueberry waffles', 'scrambled eggs and bacon with toast', 'cheeseburger and french fries', and others

Rdg12. Reads text (printed words or Braille letters) that is included in grocery and other shopping lists, for example, '12-pack of Diet Coke', 'two gallons of 2% milk', 'large box of Cheerios', 'picture hangers', and others

Rdg13. Reads the days of the week, dates, and the months of the year, including abbreviations, on printed-word or Braille calendars

Rdg14. Reads text from simple, printed-word or Braille recipes, for example, 'mix the flour and water', 'add one teaspoon of salt', 'turn oven to 350 degrees', 'put in the oven for 20 minutes', and others

Additional Good-to-have Reading Skills. With certain children and adults, you may want to select additional reading skills and designate these as good-to-have skills. This section permits you to do this.

Rdg14a. _____

Rdg14b. _____

Rdg14c. _____

Rdg14d. _____

Rdg14e. _____

The Assessment of Responding to Text as a Listener and Reading

Before conducting an assessment, review the procedures described in chapter 4. Then, secure a copy of the *Assessment and Record of Progress (ARP)* for each learner and begin to conduct the assessment. Determine each learner's performance level on each of the skills designated as good-to-have responding to text as a listener (**RTL1-14**) and record this level on the *ARP*. If a learner's primary or secondary method of speaking is *'saying words'* or *'forming standard signs'* (**AMS 2**), determine that learner's performance level on each of the skills designated as good-to-have reading skills (**Rdg1-14**) and record this level on the *ARP*. The performance levels for these skills are described in Table 1, along with sample items from the *ARP*. Select and assess a few functional examples of each skill (see Table 1) and continue the assessment until the learner requires prompts, exhibits inappropriate responses, or responds with problem behavior on three consecutive examples of responding to text as a listener or reading.

Table 1.
The Performance Levels for Reading and Responding to Text as a Listener

When one or more printed words is presented or encountered, learners read or make an appropriate listener response on three consecutive occasions...

IA	[the initial assessment of this skill has been completed]
IM	[instruction or management has begun]
-SA	without self-injurious, aggressive, or destructive behavior
-DC	without disruptive behavior or complaints
-RP	without resistance to prompts and without leaving the area
FP	with a full physical, full demonstration, or full echoic prompt
PP	with a partial physical, partial demonstration, or partial echoic prompts
MP	with a minimal touch, minimal gestural, or minimal echoic prompt
Ind	without prompts, without scrolling, and without hesitation
Det	[the skill is no longer occurring consistently]

RTL2. Responds appropriately to public safety, street, and emergency signs...

	IA	IM	-SA	-DC	-RP	FP	PP	MP	Ind	Det
1 Walk and Don't Walk	IA	IM	-SA	-DC	-RP	FP	PP	MP	Ind	Det
2 Fire Escape	IA	IM	-SA	-DC	-RP	FP	PP	MP	Ind	Det

Rdg2. Reads public safety, street, and emergency signs...

	IA	IM	-SA	-DC	-RP	FP	PP	MP	Ind	Det
1 Walk and Don't Walk	IA	IM	-SA	-DC	-RP	FP	PP	MP	Ind	Det
2 Fire Escape	IA	IM	-SA	-DC	-RP	FP	PP	MP	Ind	Det

Teaching Responding to Text as a Listener and Reading

If a learner's primary or secondary method of speaking is 'saying words' or 'forming standard signs' (**AMS 2**), begin teaching reading and responding to the same text as a listener (**Rdg1** and **RTL1**). If a learner uses any other method of speaking, begin teaching responding to text as a listener (**RTL1**). Collect data 2-3 days per week, or daily, if possible, using single-trial probes described in chapter 4. As shown in Table 2, and described in chapter 4, record these probe data on one of the *Skill Acquisition Self-graphing Data Recording Forms*. These forms can be downloaded from www.behaviorchange.com. Then, as the learner reaches specific performance levels, transfer these data to the *ARP* (see Table 3). If improvement in the level of performance for any specific skill does not occur, revise the teaching procedures.

Table 2.
Recording the Learner's Progress on Skills Selected for Instruction
Using Single-trial Probe Data and Probe Data Sheets

ESSENTIAL FOR LIVING
Skill Acquisition Probe Data Sheet
Responding to Text as a Listener: First Opportunity of the Day Probes

Responding to Text as a Listener	Day/Date and First Opportunity of the Day Probe														
	S	M	T	W	T	F	S	S	M	T	W	T	F	S	S	M	T
RTL2. 1- Walk and Don't Walk	Det Ind MP PP FP -RP -DC -SA 0	Det Ind MP (PP) FP -RP -DC -SA 0	Det Ind MP MP PP FP -RP -DC -SA 0	Det Ind MP PP FP -RP -DC -SA 0	Det Ind MP PP FP -RP -DC -SA 0	Det Ind MP PP FP -RP -DC -SA 0	Det Ind MP PP FP -RP -DC -SA 0	Det Ind MP PP FP -RP -DC -SA 0	Det Ind MP PP FP -RP -DC -SA 0	Det Ind MP PP FP -RP -DC -SA 0	Det Ind MP PP FP -RP -DC -SA 0	Det Ind MP PP FP -RP -DC -SA 0	Det Ind MP PP FP -RP -DC -SA 0	Det Ind MP PP FP -RP -DC -SA 0	Det Ind MP PP FP -RP -DC -SA 0	Det Ind MP PP FP -RP -DC -SA 0

Table 3.
Transferring Data from Probe Data Sheets to the Assessment and Record of Progress (*ARP*)

RTL2. Responds appropriately to public safety, street, and emergency signs...

	IA	IM	-SA	-DC	-RP	FP	PP	MP	Ind	Det
1 Walk and Don't Walk	IA	IM	-SA	-DC	-RP	FP	PP	MP	Ind	Det

8b2. Schedules, Lists, and Time. Personal, daily schedules and task lists help some learners with moderate-to-severe disabilities (1) participate in a sequence of events or activities, (2) make transitions from one event or activity to another, (3) retrieve items on shopping trips, (4) complete errands, or (5) complete routine tasks, in the absence of close supervision, with less anxiety, and with fewer instances of problem behavior. Prior to the introduction of schedules and lists, learners should be exposed to specific items and events, begin to participate in specific activities, complete routine tasks, and complete at least some of the steps of complex routine tasks that will eventually appear on schedules and lists. If this exposure or instruction does not occur, neither schedules nor lists will help learners respond more consistently.

discriminative or contingency-specifying stimuli

If items that are part of these activities, tasks, or events have not begun to control learners' responses with respect to participating in activities and events and beginning to complete tasks, stimulus control cannot be transferred from items to schedules or lists.

For sighted learners, personal, daily schedules are composed of photographs, drawings, or pic-symbols, designating events and activities and the order in which they are slated to occur. For children or adults with visual impairments, these schedules are composed of miniature items or symbols (e.g., a miniature bowl to designate 'breakfast'). Schedules are generally arranged vertically, when they are composed of three or more activities or events, with the activity or event that is slated to occur first at the top of the list. Sometimes, schedules with only two activities or events are arranged horizontally (e.g., First-Then Cards), with the activity or event slated to occur first on the left. Events and activities that could be part of a child's morning schedule are included in Table 1.

Table 1.
A Personal Daily Morning Schedule

Put Away Jacket, Lunch Box, and Back Pack
Breakfast
Bathroom and Wash Hands
Functional Academic Skills
Music
Snack
Bathroom and Wash Hands
Daily Living Skills
Bathroom and Wash Hands
Lunch

For sighted learners, personal tasks lists are again composed of photographs, drawings, or pic-symbols designating (1) items to retrieve on a shopping trip, (2) errands to run, (3) routine tasks to perform, or (4) steps to perform that are part of complex routine tasks and the order in which these steps should occur. For individuals with visual impairments, these lists are again composed of miniature items or symbols (e.g., a miniature towel or a piece of terry cloth to designate 'dry body'). Items, activities, tasks, and steps that could be part of four task lists are included in Table 2.

Table 2.
Personal Task Lists

Grocery Store	**Errands**	**Routine Tasks**	**Complex Routine Tasks**
Tomato juice	Haircuts	Sweep out garage	*Taking a Shower.....*
Bread	Cleaners	Dirty clothes in hamper	Turn on the Cold Water
Milk	Propane tank filled	Turn coffee pot off	Turn on the Hot Water
Frozen lima beans	Car washed	Take garbage out	Adjust Water to Warm
Tomato Soup		Put towels in the dryer	Wash Chest and Shoulders
Tortillas			Wash Arms and Underarms
Oranges			Wash Back
Sour Cream			Wash Genital Areas
Lettuce			Wash Legs and Feet
Salad Dressing			Rinse Entire Body
			Shampoo Hair and Rinse
			Turn off Hot Water
			Turn off Cold Water
			Dry Body

Schedules and personal tasks lists that include only printed words are included in the first section of this chapter (*Reading and Responding to Text as a Listener*).

Some children and adults with moderate-to-severe disabilities can learn to begin participating in events or activities that are slated to occur at specific times later that same day when these times are added to their schedule, displayed on a clock, or announced to them. Others can learn to begin participating in events or activities that are slated to occur in several days or weeks and that are posted on a calendar.

Schedules and Lists: Responding as a listener. Responding to personal, daily schedules and task lists often includes both a listener and a speaker response and appears to require 'naming'. For example, after completing an activity, children or adults may look at their schedule and see a photograph, drawing, or pic-symbol of a spoon designating 'snack or break time', or touch their schedule and feel a miniature spoon. Then, they may respond by saying or signing "snack" or "break" and beginning to enjoy either activity. Or they may look at the first few photographs, drawings, or pic-symbols or touch and maintain contact with the first few miniature items or symbols in a task list for 'washing their hands', say "cold water [first], [then] hot water" and turn on the cold water.

Closer examination, however, reveals that children and adults can learn to respond effectively to personal, daily schedules and lists as listeners and that speaker responses are not required. For example, learners may simply look at their schedule and point to a photograph, drawing, or pic-symbol or touch their schedule and maintain contact with a miniature item or symbol designating the next activity or event, and begin enjoying 'a snack or a break'. Or, they may point to the photographs, drawings, or pic-symbols or touch and maintain contact with the miniature items or symbols designating 'the errands they are supposed to run' and begin to do so without saying, signing, or naming anything (i.e., without responding as a speaker).

And, if, for sighted learners, the items, events, activities, or steps of the task are depicted with photographs (rather than drawings or pic-symbols), and, for learners who are visually impaired, with miniature items or iconic symbols, these learners can often be taught to match the photographs, miniature items, or symbols with the corresponding items, events, activities, and steps. Then, if a specific teaching procedure is used, responding effectively to these photographs, miniature items or symbols as a listener (i.e., seeing the photographs or touching and maintaining contact with the miniature items or symbols and beginning to participate in events or activities, or beginning to complete tasks or steps of tasks) should begin to occur quickly.

if sighted and visually impaired learners have acquired the arbitrary matching of photographs and symbols, respectively, to corresponding items with which they bear some resemblance, the transfer of stimulus control from items to photographs, miniature items or symbols, with respect to participating in events and activities or beginning to complete tasks or steps of tasks, should begin to occur quickly.

Often learners are expected to respond to inquiries regarding the sequence of events and activities on their schedule or items, activities, or steps on one of their task lists. For example, a care provider, peer, or instructor may say "What [or show me what] comes next on your schedule", "What [or show me what] comes *after* snack", "What's next [or show me what's next] on our shopping list", or "What do you do [or show me what you do] *before* you turn on the hot water". Children and adults can learn to respond to these inquiries as listeners by pointing to photographs or touching and maintaining contact with miniatures or symbols. In order to minimize the discriminations required to respond effectively to these inquiries, we strongly recommend a schedule or list with a vertical format, even when there are only two events, activities, or steps.

It is important to remember that schedules have a dark side. If they are used everyday and variations in the events and activities, and sequences thereof, do not occur, learners can become dependent on them and find it very difficult to respond effectively without them. In fact, sudden changes in a schedule, or leaving home without a learner's schedule, may result in severe problem behavior. To avoid this situation, introduce variations and 'blank' spaces in the schedule. Then, gradually remove the schedule for several hours and later one or more days. Then, use a schedule intermittently or not at all.

In general, learners should be taught to complete steps of routine tasks without the use of lists (see chapter 8, *Daily Living and Related Skills*). There are, however, specific neurological conditions or environmental situations which may require the use of lists for a brief, or possibly, an indefinite period of time.

Schedules and Lists: Responding as a Speaker. Even though responding effectively to schedules and lists, and to inquiries regarding which items, events, activities, or steps occur before or after others, requires only a listener response, some learners with moderate-to-severe disabilities also acquire one or more related speaker responses. Specifically, these children and adults learn to *name or describe* events, activities, or steps, along with corresponding photographs, miniature items, or symbols that are part of their schedule or their task lists. In order to acquire this repertoire, a learner's primary, concurrent, back-up, or secondary method of speaking must be '*saying words*', or must include '*forming standard signs*', '*selecting printed words*', *or* '*writing or typing words*'. As indicated in chapter 6 (*Listener Responses, Names, and Descriptions*), learners who function as speakers by '*selecting pictures*' are precluded from *naming or describing*.

Naming or describing photographs, miniature items, or symbols on schedules or lists does provide a potential advantage for some learners. It permits them to respond as speakers to inquiries about the inclusion or the sequence of activities or events on their schedule or items, activities, or steps on their lists by answering questions without looking at or touching and maintaining contact with their schedule or lists. This can be accomplished by transferring names and descriptions to answers to questions using a special teaching procedure described in chapter 12.

tacts can be transferred to 'pure' intraverbal responses using the tact-to-intraverbal stimulus control transfer procedure.

Time: Responding as a Listener. When starting times are added to personal daily schedules or announced to learners, or when days, dates, and starting times of activities or events are posted on a calendar, and learners are expected to respond as listeners in a timely manner (i.e., begin participating in activities or events on their scheduled days and dates, and at their scheduled starting times), they must also acquire several speaker responses. First, they must learn to 'tell time', that is, name times on a clock or watch to the nearest quarter hour. For example, they must see '10:15' on an analog or digital clock or watch or touch '10:15' on an analog tactile watch and say or sign "10:15" (see Table 3).

tact times on a clock or watch

Table 3.
Analog and Digital Displays of Time

Analog   Digital

Then, they must learn to 'read a calendar', that is, read the days of the week and the months of the year. For example, they must see 'Monday' or touch 'Monday in braille' and say or sign "Monday". They must also see 'March' or touch 'March in braille' and say or sign "March". They must also learn to name 'today' and 'tomorrow'. After these speaker responses have been acquired, they must also learn to respond to clocks and calendars as effective listeners. For example, when they are required to begin participating in an event or activity scheduled to occur at a specific time later that same day, they must (1) name the event or activity on their schedule and its day, date, or starting time' or 'repeat the name and starting time when it is announced to them, (2) repeat the name and starting time to themselves many times, (3) indicate to themselves when that time is approaching, and, (4) when that time occurs, say the name and time to themselves and begin participating in the event or activity. Or, when they are slated to participate in an event or activity that occurs several days or weeks from that day and is posted on a calendar, they must learn to (1) name the event or activity and locate it on the calendar, (2) name and locate today and tomorrow, (3) cross off days as they occur, (4) indicate when the event or activity occurs tomorrow and begin to make necessary preparations, and (5) indicate when the event or activity occurs today and begin participating.

read intraverbally the days of the week and months of the year

tact 'today' and 'tomorrow'

Responding effectively as a listener to events and activities scheduled to occur on specific days and dates, and at specific times, using a clock, watch, or calendar requires multiple speaker responses and multiple complex discriminations. As a result, most learners with moderate-to-severe disabilities, have considerable difficulty acquiring these skills.

many tacts, textual or intraverbal reading responses, echoics, self-echoics, and many verbal conditional discriminations.

For these learners, we recommend the use of personal, daily schedules, which require only matching and responding as a listener. For many of these learners, we also recommend prosthetic adaptations to clocks, watches, and calen-

arbitrary match-to-sample and listener responses.

dars. For example, learners can arrive at specific locations or begin specific activities at scheduled times by using watches or apps with one or more preset alarms or talking watches. They can also take medications on specific days by using preset pill organizers and reminders.

While schedules and lists, along with clocks, calendars, and prosthetic adaptations, are not necessary, they are beneficial and advantageous for many of our learners and are designated as good-to-have and nice-to-have skills. None of the skills in this domain are must-have or should-have skills and none should be taught before must-have or should-have requests, listener responses, daily living skills, or tolerating skills.

ESSENTIAL FOR LIVING
Schedules, Lists, and Time

Good-to-Have Schedules and Lists. Some of the skills in this domain include responding to schedules and lists as a listener. These skills can be acquired by many of our learners and are designated as *good-to-have skills*.

SLT1. **Participates in events and activities slated to occur later that same day using a personal, daily, picture or tactile schedule**

Many children and some adults find that personal, daily schedules permit them to begin participating in events and activities slated to occur later that same day with less anxiety and far less problem behavior. These schedules, which are generally composed of photographs, miniature items, or symbols, also help learners begin to participate in these events and activities in an orderly, that is, a sequential manner. These schedules are used by children and adults who have not learned to 'tell time', that is, 'name times on a clock or watch to at least the nearest quarter hour' (**SLT11**). Responding to schedules and announcements of events and activities slated to occur at specific times (**SLT12-14**) requires this naming repertoire.

In order for these schedules to be effective, bi-directional matching of photographs, miniature items, or symbols and items or activities is necessary (**M7-11**). Prior to using schedules, teach at least some examples of these matching skills. The remainder can be taught along with the schedule. You will notice that some learners will be able to name the photographs and the items, events, or activities, although using a picture or tactile schedule requires only matching skills and listener responses.

Children and adults are expected to learn to respond as listeners without prompts, including spoken-word prompts, and without problem behavior. In fact, using spoken-word prompts, even in the beginning, is not advisable (Wheeler et al., 1987).

using vocal-verbal prompts to teach non-vocal skills is generally not advisable.

One of the drawbacks of personal, daily schedules is the tendency for some learners to exhibit obsessive compulsive behavior with respect to them. In other words, some of our learners will insist on having a schedule for all of their daily activities and will not respond unless a task or activity is on the schedule. To avoid this dependence, changes and variations from day to day should be inserted in a schedule *from the beginning*.

Responding to schedules should not be taught as a matter of course. Many learners with moderate-to-severe disabilities will not require this skill. They will respond to daily routines without the need for a picture or tactile schedule.

SLT2. **Completes activities and obtains items using picture or tactile lists of errands or shopping lists**

Many older children and adults find lists composed of photographs, miniature items, or symbols helpful as they run errands or go shopping. These lists require the same matching skills as SLT1 (**M7-11**). A list of errands may, but need not, suggest a sequence in which specific tasks are to be completed. A shopping list, however, seldom suggests such a sequence. As with schedules, you will notice that some learners will be able to name the photographs, miniature items, or symbols, and/or the items or activities, although using a picture or tactile list requires only matching skills and listener responses.

Children and adults are again expected to learn to respond as listeners without prompts, including spoken-word prompts, and without problem behavior.

SLT3. Completes routine tasks using picture or tactile lists

Many older children and adults find reminder lists composed of photographs, miniature items, or symbols helpful helpful as they complete routine tasks of daily living, such as 'putting their dirty clothes in a hamper', 'hanging up their coat', or 'turning off the coffee pot'. These lists require the same matching skills as SLT1 (**M5-M8**) and will only be helpful if learners have already been taught skills on the lists. As with schedules, you will notice that some learners will be able to name the photographs, miniature items, or symbols, and/or the tasks, although using a picture or tactile list requires only matching skills and listener responses.

Children and adults are again expected to learn to respond as listeners without prompts, including spoken-word prompts, and without problem behavior.

SLT4. Begins sequences of steps that are part of complex routine tasks using picture or tactile lists

Many older children and adults will find lists composed of photographs, miniature items, or symbols helpful helpful as they begin a sequence of steps in a more complex task -- e.g., 'brushing their teeth' or 'taking a shower' (see Table 2). These lists require the same matching skills as SLT1 (**M5-M8**) and will only be helpful if learners have already been taught at least some of the steps on the task lists. As with schedules, you will notice that some learners will be able to name the photographs, miniature items, or symbols, and/or the tasks, although using a picture or tactile list requires only matching skills and listener responses.

Children and adults are again expected to learn to respond as listeners without prompts, including spoken-word prompts, and without problem behavior.

SLT5. Responds to inquiries by indicating the sequence of events or activities on a personal, daily, picture or tactile schedule

Many of our learners can be taught to respond as listeners to inquiries regarding the sequence of events or activities on a personal, daily schedule. In other words, they can be taught to answer questions regarding the sequence of events and activities by pointing to pictures or touching and maintaining contact with miniature items or symbols. For example, they can be taught to answer questions like 'what comes next' or 'what comes after music' by pointing to "recess" or "snack" on their schedule. Answers to questions regarding the inclusion of events or activities on their schedule or more complex questions regarding the sequence of events or activities (**SLT10**) requires speaker responses and skills **SLT6-9**.

SLT6. Names events and activities on personal, daily schedules

Some learners can be taught to name the photographs, miniature items, or symbols designating events and activities on personal, daily schedules. While this skill is not necessary in order to respond effectively to schedules, it will permit learners to respond as speakers to inquiries regarding the content of their schedule or the sequence of events or activities in the presence, and possibly later in the absence, of their schedule. In other words, this skill will permit them to answer questions like 'Do you have music today' or 'What comes after snack' by saying or signing "yes" or "music" while looking at or maintaining contact with their schedule. Later, it may also permit them to answer these questions when they do not have their schedule with them.

make tact-intraverbal responses and later 'pure' intraverbal responses regarding events and activities on their schedule.

SLT7. Names activities and items on picture or tactile lists of errands or shopping lists

Some learners can be taught to name the photographs, miniature items, or symbols designating activities and items on lists of errands or shopping lists. While this skill is not necessary in order to respond effectively to these lists, it will permit learners to respond as speakers to inquiries regarding the content of their lists or the sequence of activities in the presence, and possibly later in the absence, of their schedule. In other words, this skill will permit them to answer questions such as 'Where are you going after the cleaners' or 'Are we going to get Cheerios' by saying or signing "the grocery store" or "yes, Honey Nut Cheerios" while looking at or maintaining contact with their list. Later, it may also permit them to answer these questions when they do not have their list with them.

SLT8. Names routine tasks on picture or tactile lists

Some learners can be taught to name the photographs, miniature items, or symbols designating activities and items on lists of routine tasks. While this skill is not necessary in order to respond effectively to these lists, it will permit learners to respond as speakers to inquiries regarding the content of their lists in the presence, and possibly later in the absence, of these lists. In other words, this skill will permit them to answer questions like 'Did you remember to take out the trash' or 'What was the other thing I asked you to do' by saying or signing "not yet" or "put the dirty dishes in the dishwasher" while looking at or maintaining contact with their list. Later, it may also permit them to answer these questions when they do not have their list with them.

SLT9. Names sequences of steps that are part of complex routine tasks on picture or tactile lists

Some learners can be taught to name the photographs, miniature items, or symbols designating steps that are part of complex routing tasks. While this skill is not necessary in order to respond effectively to these lists of steps, it will permit learners to respond as speakers to inquiries regarding the sequence of steps in the presence, and possibly later in the absence, of their lists. In other words, this skill will permit them to answer questions like 'Do you turn the hot water on first' or 'After you finish drying your hands with a paper towel, what do you do with it' by saying or signing "no, you turn on the cold water first" or "throw it in the trash" while looking at or maintaining contact with their list. Later, it may also permit them to answer these questions when they do not have one of their lists with them.

SLT10. Responds to inquiries by answering questions regarding the inclusion or sequence of events, activities, items, tasks, or steps of complex tasks on picture or tactile lists

Some learners can be taught to respond as speakers to inquiries regarding the inclusion or the sequence of events, activities, items, tasks, or steps that are part of complex tasks on picture or tactile lists. In other words, they can be taught to answer questions like those described in **SLT6-9** in the presence, and possibly later in the absence, of their schedules and lists. In order to provide these answers, however, learners will need to acquire those skills (**SLT6-9**) and will also require a specific teaching protocol included in chapter 12.

the tact-to-intraverbal stimulus control transfer procedure with an interim transfer from tact to tact-intraverbal.

Nice-to-have Time Skills. Some of the skills in this domain include responding effectively as a listener to events and activities scheduled to occur on specific days and dates, and at specific times. These responses, which require the use of using a clock, watch, or calendar, can only be acquired by some of our learners and are designated as *nice-to-have skills*.

SLT11. Names times on an analog or digital clock or watch to the nearest quarter hour

In order to respond effectively as listeners to events and activities with specific starting times later that same day (**SLT12**), children and adults must learn to 'tell time'. In other words, in order for learners to begin participating in events or activities when they are scheduled to occur, they must first learn to 'name times on an analog or digital clock or watch to the nearest quarter hour'. Sighted learners will generally find it easier to name times on a digital display, which avoids many of the discriminations required by an analog display, including the alternative names for 8:45 (45 minutes after eight or fifteen minutes before nine) and determining by the position of the little hand whether it is 12:30 or 1:30. Learners with visual impairments must use a tactile watch, which includes an analog display. Children and adults are expected to learn to name times on the hour, half-past the hour, and 15 and 45 minutes after the hour without prompts and without problem behavior.

This skill should not be taught until learners have acquired a substantial repertoire of names and descriptions (see *Listener Responses, Names, and Descriptions*: **LRND12-13**).

SLT12. Participates in events and activities slated to occur at specific times later that same day using a clock or watch

Learners who can 'name times on a clock or watch to the nearest quarter hour' (**S11**) can be taught to respond effectively as listeners to events and activities with specific starting times later that same day. These events and activities may be part of a picture or tactile schedule or may simply be announced to them. Prior to teaching these listener responses, teach at least some examples of the names of times that will be necessary. The remainder can be taught along with the listener responses.

This skill will also require that learners exhibit echoic or motor imitation responses and self-echoic or self-imitation responses, and will require a specific teaching procedure [the joint control procedure]. Children and adults are expected to learn to respond as listeners without prompts and without problem behavior.

SLT13. Participates in events and activities slated to occur at specific times later that same day using a clock or watch with a prosthetic adaptation or an phone app

Children and adults, who have not learned to 'tell time' (**SLT11**) or respond to a clock or watch as a listener (**SLT12**), can arrive at specific locations or begin specific activities at scheduled times by using watches or apps with one or more preset alarms, or talking watches. Learners are expected to learn to keep these devices with them and to respond without prompts and without problem behavior.

SLT14. Responds to inquiries regarding the starting time of events and activities slated to occur later that same day

Some learners who can 'name times on a clock or watch to the nearest quarter hour' (**SLT11**) and respond effectively as listeners to events and activities with specific starting times later that same day (**SLT12**) can also be taught to respond effectively as speakers to inquiries regarding the starting times of these events and activities in the presence, and possibly later in the absence, of schedules. In other words, they can be taught to answer questions like 'What time does music class start' by saying or signing "9:30" when they are looking at or touching and maintaining contact with their schedule or when they do not have their schedule with them.

This skill will also require two specific teaching procedures [the joint control procedure and the tact-to-intraverbal stimulus control transfer procedure]. Children and adults are expected to learn to respond to these inquiries as speakers without prompts and without problem behavior.

SLT15. Participates in events and activities that are slated to occur several days or weeks from now and that are posted on a calendar

With children and adults who have learned to name times on a clock or watch (**S11**), and participate in a timely manner in events and activities with specific starting times (**S12**), you may want to teach them to respond in a similar manner to events and activities scheduled to occur on specific days and dates. In other words, you may want them to respond as listeners to events and activities posted on a calendar. For example, you may want them to 'point to the day when the next spaghetti supper occurs' or 'show me what's going on next Tuesday'.

This skill requires that learners read and respond as a listener to the days of the week, dates, and months of the year (**RTL13, Rdg13**) and that they name events and activities that are often posted on the calendar. They are expected to learn to read and respond as listeners to events and activities posted on the calendar without prompts and without problem behavior.

SLT16. Takes medication using a pill reminder

Children and adults, especially those who have not learned to read and respond as a listener to the days of the week, dates, and months of the year on a calendar, can learn to take their medications each day by opening a pill reminder (see Table 4), that is, responding to the pill reminder as a listener.

This skill is easier to acquire if learners can read and respond effectively as listeners to the days of the week (and abbreviations thereof). All that is required, however, is to scan from left to right and recognize the first compartment that contains pills.

Table 4.
A Pill Reminder

Sun	Mon	Tue	Wed	Thu	Fri	Sat

SLT17. Responds to inquiries regarding the day and date of events and activities that are posted on a calendar

Some learners can also be taught to respond effectively as speakers to inquiries regarding (1) the next day on which a specific, recurring event is scheduled to occur or (2) the events or activities which are slated to occur on specific days in the presence, and possibly later in the absence, of a calendar. In other words, they can be taught to answer questions like 'When does the next spaghetti supper occur' by saying or signing "next Friday" or "Friday, March 21" or 'What's going on next Tuesday' by saying or signing "Karaoke" when they are looking at or touching and maintaining contact with a calendar or, possibly, when they do not have a calendar with them.

This skill also requires that learners read and respond as a listener to the days of the week, dates, and months of the year (**RTL13, Rdg13**) and that they name events and activities that are often posted on the calendar. This skill also requires the use of two specific teaching procedures. [the joint control procedure and the tact-to-intraverbal stimulus control transfer procedure]

The Assessment of Schedules, Lists, and Time

Before conducting an assessment, review the procedures described in chapter 4. Then, secure a copy of the *Assessment and Record of Progress (ARP)* for each learner and begin to conduct the assessment. Determine each learner's performance level on each of the skills designated as good-to-have schedules and lists (**SLT1-10**) and **SLT17** and record this level on the *ARP*. If a learner's primary or secondary method of speaking is 'saying words' or 'forming standard signs' (**AMS 2**), determine that learner's performance level on each of the skills designated as nice-to-have time skills (**SLT11-16**), except **SLT17**, and record this level on the *ARP*. The performance levels for these skills are described in Table 5, along with sample items from the *ARP*. Select and assess a few functional examples of each skill and continue the assessment until the learner requires prompts, exhibits inappropriate responses, or responds with problem behavior on three consecutive examples of schedules, lists, and time.

Table 5.
The Performance Levels for Schedules, Lists, and Time

In the presence of a picture or tactile schedule or list, a clock or watch, or a calendar, learners begin to participate in an event or activity, respond to inquiries by pointing, or name an event or activity...or...in the presence or absence of a picture or tactile schedule or list, a clock or watch, or a calendar, respond to inquiries by answering questions on three consecutive occasions...

IA	[the initial assessment of this skill has been completed]
IM	[instruction or management has begun]
-SA	without self-injurious, aggressive, or destructive behavior
-DC	without disruptive behavior or complaints
-RP	without resistance to prompts and without leaving the area
FP	with a full physical, full demonstration, or full echoic prompt
PP	with a partial physical, partial demonstration, or partial echoic prompt
MP	with a minimal touch, minimal gestural, or minimal echoic prompt
Ind	without prompts and without hesitation
Det	[the skill is no longer occurring consistently]

Table 5. (cont.)
The Performance Levels for Schedules, Lists, and Time

SLT1. Participates in events and activities slated to occur later that same day using a personal, daily, picture or tactile schedule

IA	IM	-SA	-DC	-RP	FP	PP	MP	Ind	Det

SLT15. Participates in events and activities that are slated to occur several days or weeks from now and that are posted on a calendar

IA	IM	-SA	-DC	-RP	FP	PP	MP	Ind	Det

Teaching Schedules, Lists, and Time

If a learner's primary or secondary method of speaking is 'saying words' or 'forming standard signs' (**AMS 2**), begin teaching each of the skills designated as nice-to-have time skills (**SLT11-16**), except **SLT17**. If a learner uses any other method of speaking, begin teaching each of the skills designated as good-to-have schedules and lists (**SLT1-10**) and **SLT17**. Collect data 2-3 days per week, or daily, if possible, using single-trial probes also described in chapter 4. As shown in Table 6, and described in chapter 4, record these probe data on one of the *Skill Acquisition Self-graphing Data Recording Forms*. These forms can be downloaded from www.behaviorchange.com. Then, as the learner reaches specific performance levels, transfer this information to the *ARP* (see Table 7). If improvement in the level of performance for any specific skill does not occur, make adjustments in the teaching procedures.

Table 6.
Recording the Learner's Progress on Skills Selected for Instruction
Using Single-trial Probe Data and Probe Data Sheets

ESSENTIAL FOR LIVING
Skill Acquisition Probe Data Sheet
Schedules, Lists, and Time: First Opportunity of the Day Probes

Schedules, Lists, and Time	Day/Date and First Opportunity of the Day Probe																
	13	14	15	16	17	18	19	20	21	22	23	24	25	26	27	28	29
	S	M	T	W	T	F	S	S	M	T	W	T	F	S	S	M	T
SLT1. Participates in events and activities slated to occur later that same day using a personal, daily, picture or tactile schedule	Det Ind MP PP FP -RP -DC -SA 0	Det Ind MP PP FP -RP -DC -SA 0	Det Ind MP PP FP -RP -DC -SA 0	Det Ind MP PP FP -RP -DC -SA 0	Det Ind MP PP FP -RP -DC -SA 0	Det Ind MP PP FP -RP -DC -SA 0	Det Ind MP PP FP -RP -DC -SA 0	Det Ind MP PP FP -RP -DC -SA 0	Det Ind MP PP FP -RP -DC -SA 0	Det Ind MP PP FP -RP -DC -SA 0	Det Ind MP PP FP -RP -DC -SA 0	Det Ind MP PP FP -RP -DC -SA 0	Det Ind MP PP FP -RP -DC -SA 0	Det Ind MP PP FP -RP -DC -SA 0	Det Ind MP PP FP -RP -DC -SA 0	Det Ind MP PP FP -RP -DC -SA 0	Det Ind MP PP FP -RP -DC -SA 0

Table 7.
Transferring Data from Probe Data Sheets to the Assessment and Record of Progress (*ARP*)

SLT1. Participates in events and activities slated to occur later that same day using a personal, daily, picture or tactile schedule

IA	IM	-SA	-DC	-RP	FP	PP	MP	Ind	Det

8b3. Math Skills. Counting, the most fundamental and functional of all skills with numbers, permits children and adults to complete many tasks of daily living. For example, learners can retrieve three forks or empty two waste bas-kets when directed to do so. They can also make four sandwiches, one for themselves and three for their housemates. And, they can put six quarters in a vending machine to purchase a beverage or a snack. Counting also permits adults to complete some vocational tasks. For example, learners can count and place four bolts and four nuts in a plastic bag or place three 'fragile stickers' on a carton.

Measuring quantities and making purchases which include counting or using numbers, also permit learners to complete many daily living and vocational tasks. For example, learners can measure 1/2 cup of milk and pour it into a mixing bowl as part of preparing pancakes. They can purchase a loaf of bread and a half-gallon of milk with money or a debit or credit card. They can also accumulate the amount of purchases while grocery shopping using a calculator.

Counting. Counting often, but not always, includes a listener response that is enabled by two speaker responses. [a listener response, mediated by two verbal responses] For example, adult learners in a vocational setting are assigned a job which requires counting and placing eight rubber washers in plastic bags. The learners hear their supervisor say '8', see or feel him sign '8', or see '8' written on an instruction sheet and begin (1) counting by saying or signing each number and simultaneously collecting rubber washers one at a time until they reach '8', or (2) counting by naming each numeral on a number line and simultaneously placing one washer next to each numeral until they reach '8'. The first of these skills can be described as 'counting items' and requires that 'counting and collecting' occur, in that sequence, for each number. The second can be described as 'counting items using a number line' and requires that 'naming and placing' occur, in that sequence, for each number. When discussing 'counting', teachers often refer to this sequence as establishing '1:1 correspondence'. Both skills also require that learners 'keep 8 in mind', that is, occasionally say, sign, or 'think 8' as [a covert verbal response] they are counting for-ward so that they know when to stop, that is, they stop counting when 'the 8 they have in mind' or the 'numeral 8 they see' matches 'the 8 they have just said or signed'.

Many of our learners have difficulty acquiring either of these two counting skills. Some can 'count and col-lect', while others can 'name and place', but many, who can do so, continue 'counting and collecting' or 'counting and placing' beyond '8'. This can be remedied by teaching these learners to begin with '8' and stop when they hear themselves say '1', see or feel themselves sign '1', or 'see the numeral 1'. This strategy permits learners to count as speakers, but requires counting numbers or naming numerals backward and continues to require 1:1 correspondence.

Many of our children and adults have been taught 'rote counting' forward from 1-10 or 1-20. Some have struggled with this skill, often omitting or juxtaposing the numbers. This may occur because saying or signing '4' is supposed to occur after learners hear, see, or feel themselves say or sign '3', with no other concrete item or event they can experience as they count. Other learners who have acquired and exhibit this skill correctly and without hesitation, find it very difficult to slow down and say or sign one number per item or stop when they say or sign the requested number. In view of these difficulties, and the few situations in which 'rote counting' is a functional skill, we strongly recommend that children and adults, who have not yet learned to count, be taught to do so by 'counting and collecting' or 'naming and placing', rather than by 'rote counting'.

Counting can also be accomplished with only listener and matching responses. For example, adult learners hear, see, or feel the number '8' and, after pointing to '8' on a number line, begin placing a washer next to each numeral beginning with '8' and concluding with '1' without saying or signing numbers or naming numerals. Counting in this manner no longer requires speaker responses, but continues to require 1:1 corres-pondence.

Another type of counting requires only a matching response. For example, adult learners, provided with 'an inset counting jig' set to '8', place a washer in each inset until all insets have a washer in them. Counting in this manner no longer requires listener responses to the number '8', but may continue to require 1:1 correspondence. This requirement, however, can be virtually eliminated if the jig is constructed specifically for this task such that the inset is large enough to contain only one washer.

Measuring. Measuring quantities, along with counting, often includes both a listener and a speaker res-ponse and appears to require naming units and fractions thereof. For example, young adult learners hear their instructor say '1/2 cup of water', see or feel him sign '1/2 cup of water', or see '1/2 cup of water' written in a recipe and say or sign '1/2 cup of water', repeat what they just said or signed several times until they find a familiar measuring cup, and pour water into the cup until it reaches the '1/2 cup mark'. Closer examination, however, reveals that measuring quantities, like counting, can also be accomplished with listener and matching responses, and does not require naming. For example, adult learners hear, see, or feel '1/2 cup of water' and, after pointing to '1/2 cup of water' on a measuring cup or feeling raised characters or a raised mark, begin filling it with water to the '1/2 cup' mark without saying, signing, or naming anything.

Purchasing. Making purchases often requires both listener and speaker responses and may include counting amounts of money, using debit and credit cards, writing personal checks, or using a calculator. These skills are often quite complex and much too difficult for most of our learners to acquire. There are, however, parts of these skills that some of our learners can not only accomplish, but perform quite well. For example, many of our children and adults can learn to operate a vending machine using dollar bills, coins, or a debit or credit card. Others can learn to select the 'next dollar amount' for combinations of common grocery items, give the clerk that amount, and wait for the change. These skills require only counting and matching skills. Some of our adults could learn to complete all of these steps, while others could achieve 'partial participation' (**PPA**), that is, learn to complete some or all of these steps.

require conditional discriminations and verbal conditional discriminations

Other adults can learn to assist with grocery shopping and staying within a budget by using a calculator to accumulate the total amount of purchases. For example they can (1) select needed items, (2) select and press the keys on the calculator that match the price of each item, (3) press the '+' key, and (4) alert care providers when the budgeted amount is about to be exceeded. Again, some of our adults could acquire all of these steps, while others could achieve partial participation.

Many children and adults learn to count and some acquire a limited number of additional measuring and purchasing skills. Some learners, however, with very severe disabilities, never acquire a single skill that includes counting, measuring, and purchasing. *Counting, measuring, or purchasing should not be considered must-have or should have skills and should never be taught before must-have or should have requests, listening skills, or doing skills. At best, these skills are good-to-have and are designated accordingly in this domain.*

ESSENTIAL FOR LIVING
Math Skills

Good-to-have Math Skills. For learners with moderate-to-severe disabilities, 'counting', 'measuring', and 'purchasing' are quite functional and result in increased participation in activities at home and within the community, and an overall increase in the level of independent functioning. As a result, these skills are designated as *good-to-have*. Some skills require a speaker response and are designated as such (**Spk**), while others include multiple steps or responses and require a task analysis (**MR**).

Mth1.		Counts a specified number of items from 1-10 using an inset counting jig
Mth2.	Spk	Counts a specified number of items from 1-10 using a number line and backward counting
Mth3.	Spk	Counts a specified number of items from 1-10 using only backward counting
Mth4.	Spk	Counts a specified number of items from 1-10 using a number line and forward counting
Mth5.	Spk	Counts a specified number of items from 1-10 using only forward counting
Mth6.	Spk	Adds a specified number from 1-10 to an existing set of items (e.g., '4 more') using only forward counting
Mth7.	Spk	Removes a specified number from 1-10 from an existing set of items (e.g., '3 less') using only forward counting
Mth8.		Measures amounts of liquids or powders by matching numbers in a recipe and identical numbers on measuring spoons and cups
Mth9.		Measures quantities of liquids and powders by listening to spoken-word directions
Mth10.	MR	Makes purchases using a debit or credit card
Mth11.		Makes purchases with dollar bills using a vending machine
Mth12.		Makes purchases with coins using a vending machine

Mth13.		MR	Selects the 'next dollar amount' for a set of items after viewing the items or pictures of the items
Mth14.		MR	Makes purchases by viewing a set of items, selecting a correct 'next dollar amount', and waiting for the change
Mth15.		MR	Accumulates amounts of selected items during a shopping trip using an adding machine
Mth16.		MR	Accumulates amounts of selected items during a shopping trip using an a calculator and alerting someone when a budgeted amount is about to be exceeded

Additional Good-to-have Math Skills. With some children and adults, you may want to select additional counting, measuring, and purchasing skills and designate these as good-to-have skills. This section permits you to do this.

Mth16a.		_____
Mth16b.		_____
Mth16c.	Spk	_____
Mth16d.	Spk	_____
Mth16e.		_____
Mth16f.	MR	_____
Mth16g.	MR	_____

The Assessment of Math Skills

Before conducting an assessment, review the procedures described in chapter 4. Then, secure a copy of the *Assessment and Record of Progress (ARP)* for each learner and begin to conduct the assessment. Determine each learner's performance level on each of the skills designated as good-to-have Math skills (**Mth1-16**) and record this level on the *ARP*. Some skills require a speaker response (**Spk**), while others include multiple steps or responses (**MR**) and require a task analysis. The performance levels for all Math skills are described in Table 1, along with sample items from the *ARP*. Select and assess a few examples of each skill and continue the assessment until the learner requires prompts, exhibits inappropriate responses, or responds with problem behavior on three consecutive examples of counting, measuring, or purchasing.

Table 1.
The Performance Levels for Math Skills

Performance Levels for Single-response Math Skills

When they encounter situations that require specific responses, learners exhibit single-response Math skills on three consecutive occasions...

IA	[the initial assessment of this skill has been completed]
IM	[instruction or management has begun]
-SA	without self-injurious, aggressive, or destructive behavior
-DC	without disruptive behavior or complaints
-RP	without resistance to prompts and without leaving the area
FP	with a full physical, full demonstration, or full echoic prompt
PP	with a partial physical, partial demonstration, or partial echoic prompt
MP	with a minimal touch, minimal gestural, or minimal echoic prompt
Ind	without prompts and within two seconds
PPA	[this skill requires permanent partial assistance]
APD	[this skill requires an environmental adaptation or prosthetic device]
Det	[this Math skill is no longer occurring consistently]

Mth5. Counts a specified number of items from 1-10 using only forward counting   **Spk** | IA | IM | -SA | -DC | -RP | FP | PP | MP | Ind | PPA | APD | Det |

Table 1. (cont.)
The Performance Levels for Math Skills

Performance Levels for Multiple-response Skills that Include Math

When they encounter situations that require specific responses, learners exhibit... [some or all of the responses (steps) of a multiple-response skill that includes Math] without exhibiting problem behavior, without complaining, and without resisting or requiring prompts on three consecutive occasions...

IA	[the initial assessment of this skill has been completed]
IM	[instruction or management has begun]
1st	one response (step) without prompts
1/4	one fourth of the responses (steps) that are part of the skill without prompts
1/2	one half of the responses (steps) that are part of the skill without prompts
3/4	three fourths of the responses (steps) that are part of the skill without prompts
Ind	all of the responses (steps) that are part of the skill without prompts
_m	all of the responses (steps) that are part of the skill without prompts and within _ minutes
PPA	[some or all of the responses (steps) that are part of this skill require permanent partial assistance]
APD	[some or all of the responses (steps) that are part of this skill require an environmental adaptation or prosthetic device]
Det	[this Math skill is no longer occurring consistently]

Mth10. Makes purchases using a debit or credit card **MR**

IA	IM	1st	1/4	1/2	3/4	Ind	_m	PPA	APD	Det

Teaching Math Skills

If a learner's primary or secondary method of speaking is 'saying words' or 'forming standard signs' (**AMS 1**), begin teaching 'counting skills' that require a speaker response (**Mth3** or **Mth5-7**). If these skills are not easily acquired, or a learner uses another alternative method of speaking (**AMS 2-AMS 46**), teach counting skills that require only listener responses and matching (**Mth1-2** or **Mth4**). Then, teach 'measuring and purchasing skills' in this domain, which require only listener responses and matching. A task analysis should be conducted with those purchasing skills which include multiple responses (**MR**) (see *Daily Living and Related Skills*). Collect data several times each week, or daily, if possible, using single-trial probes described in chapter 4. As shown in Table 2, and described in chapter 4, record these probe data on one of the *Skill Acquisition Self-graphing Data Recording Forms*. These single and multiple-response probe data sheets can be downloaded from www.behaviorchange.com. Then, as the learner reaches specific performance levels, transfer this information to the *ARP* (see Table 3). If improvement in the level of performance for any specific skill does not occur, make adjustments in the teaching procedures.

Table 2.
Recording the Learner's Progress on Single-response Math Skills
Using Single-trial Probe Data and Probe Data Sheets

ESSENTIAL FOR LIVING
Skill Acquisition Self-graphing Data Recording Form
Single-response Math Skills: First Opportunity of the Day Probes

Math Skill	Day/Date and First Opportunity of the Day Probe															
	S	M	T	W	T	F	S	S	M	T	W	T	F	S	S	M	T
Mth5. Spk Counts a specified number of items from 1-10 using only forward counting	Det APD PPA Ind MP PP FP -RP -DC -SA 0	Det APD PPA Ind MP PP FP -RP -DC -SA 0	Det APD PPA Ind MP PP FP -RP -DC -SA 0	Det APD PPA Ind MP PP FP -RP -DC -SA 0	Det APD PPA Ind MP PP FP -RP -DC -SA 0	Det APD PPA Ind MP PP FP -RP -DC -SA 0	Det APD PPA Ind MP PP FP -RP -DC -SA 0	Det APD PPA Ind MP PP FP -RP -DC -SA 0	Det APD PPA Ind MP PP FP -RP -DC -SA 0	Det APD PPA Ind MP PP FP -RP -DC -SA 0	Det APD PPA Ind MP PP FP -RP -DC -SA 0	Det APD PPA Ind MP PP FP -RP -DC -SA 0	Det APD PPA Ind MP PP FP -RP -DC -SA 0	Det APD PPA Ind MP PP FP -RP -DC -SA 0	Det APD PPA Ind MP PP FP -RP -DC -SA 0	Det APD PPA Ind MP PP FP -RP -DC -SA 0

Table 2. (cont.)
Recording the Learner's Progress on Multiple-response Skills that Include Math
Using Single-trial Probe Data and Probe Data Sheets

ESSENTIAL FOR LIVING
Skill Acquisition Self-graphing Data Recording Form
Multiple-response Skills that Include Math
First Opportunity of the Day Probes

Math Skill	Day/Date and First Opportunity of the Day Probe															
	S	M	T	W	T	F	S	S	M	T	W	T	F	S	S	M	T
Mth10. Makes purchases using a debit or credit card **MR**	Det APD PPA _m 12 11 10 9 8 7 6 5 4 3 2 1 0	Det APD (PPA) _m 12 11 10 9 8 7 6 (5) 4 3 2 1 (0)	Det APD (PPA) _m 12 11 10 9 8 7 (6) 5 4 3 2 (1) 0	Det APD (PPA) _m 12 11 10 9 8 7 (6) 5 4 3 2 (1) 0	Det APD PPA _m 12 11 10 9 8 7 6 5 4 3 2 1 0	Det APD PPA _m 12 11 10 9 8 7 6 5 4 3 2 1 0	Det APD PPA _m 12 11 10 9 8 7 6 5 4 3 2 1 0	Det APD PPA _m 12 11 10 9 8 7 6 5 4 3 2 1 0	Det APD PPA _m 12 11 10 9 8 7 6 5 4 3 2 1 0	Det APD PPA _m 12 11 10 9 8 7 6 5 4 3 2 1 0	Det APD PPA _m 12 11 10 9 8 7 6 5 4 3 2 1 0	Det APD PPA _m 12 11 10 9 8 7 6 5 4 3 2 1 0	Det APD PPA _m 12 11 10 9 8 7 6 5 4 3 2 1 0	Det APD PPA _m 12 11 10 9 8 7 6 5 4 3 2 1 0	Det APD PPA _m 12 11 10 9 8 7 6 5 4 3 2 1 0	Det APD PPA _m 12 11 10 9 8 7 6 5 4 3 2 1 0

Table 3.
Transferring Data from Self-graphing Data Recording Forms
to the Assessment and Record of Progress (ARP)

Mth5. **Spk** Counts a specified number of items from 1-10 using only forward counting
| IA | IM | -SA | -DC | -RP | FP | PP | MP | Ind | PPA | APD | Det |

Mth10. Makes purchases using a debit or credit card
| IA | IM | 1st | 1/4 | 1/2 | 3/4 | Ind | _m | PPA | APD | Det |

8b4. Writing or Typing Skills. As described in chapter 6, most of us communicate by 'saying words', 'writing words', and 'typing words'. 'Saying words' is our primary method of speaking, as we use it frequently to converse with others, while 'writing words, typing words, and texting' are secondary methods, which we use less frequently to convey messages to those who are not within the sound of our voice and to produce permanent records of 'what we have said'.

Children and adults with moderate-to-severe disabilities, especially those with limited to no spoken-word repertoires (i.e., those aligned with *Vocal Profiles 2-6*), often have difficulty acquiring and maintaining a primary method of speaking and learning to function effectively as a speaker with those in their immediate environment. And, those who have a larger repertoire of spoken words often have difficulty expanding this repertoire beyond very familiar topics. As a result, for our learners, acquiring and maintaining a secondary method of speaking is seldom functional.

With some learners, however, whose primary method of speaking includes *'visually scanning and selecting pic-symbols, drawings, or photographs'* or *'touching and maintaining contact with miniature items or symbols'*, a secondary method may be functional. If these learners have acquired a substantial repertoire of requests, a secondary method of speaking that includes *'selecting printed words'* or *'selecting words written in Braille'*, may permit them to expand their speaking repertoire by naming and describing items, activities, people, places, and locations, and may eventually permit them to function as more effective listeners, or answer questions concerning items, activities, people, and places they have learned to name or describe (see chapter 6). *'Writing words', 'typing words'*, or *'Braille writing'* could permit these learners to expand their speaking repertoire even further. These methods, however, which require *'spelling'* or *'some spelling skills and an electronic device with predictive text'*, are quite effortful and very difficult to acquire. Only a very small number of these learners can expand their speaking repertoire in this manner.

Most instructors and care providers are inclined to teach child and adult learners to *'copy'* and later *'write, type, or Braille write their name'* and later, *'their address and phone number'*. While (1) learners' interest in the task, (2) emergency situations, (3) job application forms, and (4) legal documents are often mentioned as part of the rationale for teaching these skills, only the first two make the case for designating these skills as functional. For almost all of our learners, additional *writing, typing,* or *Braille writing* skills are extremely difficult to acquire and are only occasionally functional in their daily lives.

Writing, typing, and Braille writing are *good-to-have* and *nice-to-have* skills, which should never be taught before *must-have or should-have requests or listener skills, or must-have tolerating or daily living skills*. *'Copying text'* (i.e., letters of the alphabet), which is included in chapter 8, *should be accorded no greater priority*.

ESSENTIAL FOR LIVING
Writing or Typing Skills

Good-to-have Writing or Typing Skills. For children and adults with moderate-to-severe disabilities, some *'writing', 'typing',* and *'Braille writing'* skills provide personal satisfaction. They may also provide a second method of speaking in an emergency situation in case their primary method temporarily 'fails' them. It is important to remember that *'writing'* generally means *'manuscript, rather than cursive'*.

WT1.	Writes, types, or Braille writes their first name when asked to do so
WT2.	Writes, types, or Braille writes their first and last name when asked to do so
WT3.	Writes, types, or Braille writes their street address, city, state, and zip (postal) code when asked to do so
WT4.	Writes, types, or Braille writes their home and mobile phone number with the words *'home or parents'* or *'mobile or cell'* next to each number when asked to do so
WT5.	Writes or Braille writes phrases such as 'hi', 'sincerely', 'all my love', or 'I love you' when signing greeting cards
WT6.	Writes or Braille writes phrases such as 'happy birthday', and 'get well soon' when making greeting cards

Additional Good-to-have Writing or Typing Skills. With certain children and adults, you may want to select additional *'writing', 'typing',* and *'Braille writing'* skills and designate these as good-to-have skills. This section permits you to do this.

WT6a. _____

WT6b. _____

Nice-to-have Writing or Typing Skills. *'Writing'*, *'typing'*, or *'Braille writing'* skills permit some learners to participate more actively in frequently occurring activities (**WT7-9**). These skills also permit a relatively few number of learners to expand their requesting, naming, and describing repertoires and to answer questions based on these repertoires (**WT10-12**).

- **WT7.** Writes, types, or Braille writes words that often appear on shopping lists
- **WT8.** Writes, types, or Braille writes words that correspond to preferred items and activities that are often posted on a calendar
- **WT9.** Writes, types, or Braille writes words that correspond to activities that are often included in a personal, daily schedule
- **WT10.** Writes, types, or Braille writes words that are part of requests for preferred items, activities, people, and places
- **WT11.** Writes, types, or Braille writes words that are part of names and descriptions of familiar items, activities, people, places, and locations
- **WT12.** Writes, types, or Braille writes words that are part of answers to questions regarding familiar items, activities, people, and places

Additional Nice-to-have Writing or Typing Skills. With certain children and adults, you may want to select additional *'writing'*, *'typing'*, and *'Braille writing'* skills and designate these as nice-to-have skills. This section permits you to do this.

- **WT12a.** _____
- **WT12b.** _____
- **WT12c.** _____
- **WT12d.** _____

The Assessment of Writing or Typing Skills

Before conducting an assessment, review the procedures described in chapter 4. Then, obtain a copy of the *Assessment and Record of Progress (ARP)* for each learner and begin to conduct the assessment. Determine each learner's performance level on each of the skills designated as good-to-have writing or typing (**WT1-WT6**) and record this level on the *ARP*. Then, if a learner exhibits some of these skills with little to no prompt, proceed to the nice-to-have skills (**WT7-WT12**). The performance levels for these skills are described in Table 1, along with sample items from the *ARP*. Select and assess a few functional examples of each skill and continue the assessment until the learner requires prompts, exhibits inappropriate responses, or responds with problem behavior on three consecutive examples of writing, typing, or Braille writing.

Table 1.
The Performance Levels for Writing or Typing

When directed to do so or when appropriate situations occur, learners *'write'*, *'type'*, or *'Braille write'* specific words on three consecutive occasions...

IA	[the initial assessment of this skill has been completed]
IM	[instruction or management has begun]
-SA	without self-injurious, aggressive, or destructive behavior
-DC	without disruptive behavior or complaints
-RP	without resistance to prompts and without leaving the area
FP	with a full physical or full demonstration prompt
PP	with a partial physical or partial demonstration prompt
MP	with a minimal physical or minimal gestural prompt
Ind	without prompts and without hesitation
Det	[the skill is no longer occurring consistently]

Table 1. (cont.)
The Performance Levels for Writing or Typing

WT1. Writes, types, or Braille writes their first name when asked to do so

Braille writes first name	IA	IM	-SA	-DC	-RP	FP	PP	MP	Ind	Det

WT7. Writes, types, or Braille writes words that often appear on shopping lists

Writes 'chocolate milk'	IA	IM	-SA	-DC	-RP	FP	PP	MP	Ind	Det

Teaching Writing or Typing Skills

Begin teaching 'writing', 'typing', or 'Braille writing'. Collect data 2-3 days per week, or daily, if possible, using single-trial probes described in chapter 4. As shown in Table 2, and described in chapter 4, record these probe data on one of the *Skill Acquisition Self-graphing Data Recording Forms*. These data sheets can be downloaded from www.behaviorchange.com. Then, as the learner reaches specific performance levels, transfer this information to the *ARP* (see Table 3). If improvement in the level of performance for any specific skill does not occur, as shown in Table 2, make adjustment in the teaching procedures.

Table 2.
Recording the Learner's Progress on Skills Selected for Instruction
Using Single-trial Probe Data and Probe Data Sheets

ESSENTIAL FOR LIVING
Skill Acquisition Probe Data Sheet
Writing, Typing, or Braille Writing: First Opportunity of the Day Probes

Writing or Typing	Day/Date and First Opportunity of the Day Probe																
	13	14	15	16	17	18	19	20	21	22	23	24	25	26	27	28	29
	S	M	T	W	T	F	S	S	M	T	W	T	F	S	S	M	T
WT1. Braille writes first name	Det Ind MP PP FP -RP -DC -SA 0	Det Ind MP PP FP -RP -DC -SA 0	Det Ind MP PP FP -RP -DC -SA 0	Det Ind MP PP FP -RP -DC -SA 0	Det Ind MP PP FP -RP -DC -SA 0	Det Ind MP PP FP -RP -DC -SA 0	Det Ind MP PP FP -RP -DC -SA 0	Det Ind MP PP FP -RP -DC -SA 0	Det Ind MP PP FP -RP -DC -SA 0	Det Ind MP PP FP -RP -DC -SA 0	Det Ind MP PP FP -RP -DC -SA 0	Det Ind MP PP FP -RP -DC -SA 0	Det Ind MP PP FP -RP -DC -SA 0	Det Ind MP PP FP -RP -DC -SA 0	Det Ind MP PP FP -RP -DC -SA 0	Det Ind MP PP FP -RP -DC -SA 0	Det Ind MP PP FP -RP -DC -SA 0

Table 3.
Transferring Data from Probe Data Sheets to the Assessment and Record of Progress (*ARP*)

WT1. Writes, types, or Braille writes their first name when asked to do so

Braille writes first name	IA	IM	-SA	-DC	-RP	FP	PP	MP	Ind	Det

Chapter 9. Tolerating Skills and Eggshells

Most of the skills in this instrument involve physically interacting with items, activities, or persons. Some, however, involve tolerating situations, rather than interacting with anyone or anything. These skills are functional for many of our child and adult learners, especially those with complex medical conditions, adaptive equipment, limited skill repertoires, autism, or severe problem behavior.

Some of these situations are required for the learner's health and safety (e.g., pureed foods, a hearing aide, a seat belt, AFOs, or a helmet). Others are part of everyday life and are impossible to avoid (e.g., a vacuum cleaner, socks, lights off, or hearing the word 'no'). Others can be avoided for periods of time (e.g., a blood pressure cuff, needles and the drawing of blood, and a dental examination), but must eventually be confronted in order to insure proper medical and dental care. Still others could be avoided, but doing so would result in substantial disruptions in the lives of family members, fellow students, fellow workers, roommates, instructors, and care providers (e.g., changes in a picture schedule, driving past a fire station, or a video playing on a monitor in a store). And, still others, if avoided, would interfere with or interrupt the acquisition of functional skills (e.g., a bus, an apron, or background music). When exposed to specific situations, some of our learners 'cry', 'scream', 'leave the immediate environment', or 'exhibit problem behavior'. In other words, they *do not tolerate* one or other of these situations. *Learning to tolerate situations is one of the* **Essential 8,** *is defined as not exhibiting any of these behaviors when exposed to specific situations,* and should be taught as soon as these behaviors begin to occur.

If learners exhibit moderate or severe problem behavior when exposed to specific situations, instructors, parents, and care providers tend to avoid these situations in the future, and, as a result, avoid the problem behavior. This previously unnamed phenomenon is quite common and quite disruptive to the lives of our learners, their peers, their parents, their instructors, their care providers, and those around them. We refer to this phenomenon as **Eggshells** and the avoidance of these situations as **Walking on Eggshells**.

Eggshells can also be defined in plain language as *'places you don't go, things you don't come near, words you don't say, and things you don't do, for fear of what will happen'*. As a child becomes older and eventually becomes an adult, a life with many situations which the learner does not tolerate or many eggshells is a very restricted life. Failure to learn to tolerate these situations restricts the places a learner can go, the items a learner can access, the activities in which a learner can participate, and the people with whom a learner can interact. On the other hand, a life with a substantial repertoire of tolerating skills and few to no eggshells results in few of these restrictions, and, as a result, a much fuller, richer, and happier life.

This domain provides a list of situations which many children and adults have difficulty learning to tolerate. While some of these situations will not apply to your learner, most of those that do should be considered *must-have* or *should-have* skills. If a specific situation applies to your learner, but is not listed below, add it to your learner's list. No skills in this domain are designated as *good-to-have* or *nice-to-have*.

Learners can be exposed frequently to most of the situations listed in this domain and taught to tolerate the same. Learners cannot, however, be exposed to some occasional, routine medical and dental procedures (e.g., a needle and an injection or drilling as part of a tooth restoration) frequently or outside of a physician's or dentist's office. Tolerating skills can only be acquired with repeated, albeit occasional, exposure to these situations and settings. Learners can, however, be exposed to parts of other routine medical and dental procedures (e.g., a stethoscope or an explorer and a mirror used in dental examinations) frequently and outside of a physician's or dentist's office.

ESSENTIAL FOR LIVING
Functional Tolerating Skills

Must-have Tolerating Skills Related to Health and Safety. Many children and adults have not learned to tolerate specific, unpleasant situations which have an immediate impact on their health and safety (e.g., 'being fed through a gastrostomy tube', 'being physically prompted or guided', 'receiving liquid medication from an oral syringe', 'having their face washed', 'range of motion exercises', or 'wearing ankle-foot orthotics [AFOs]'). These situations *'must'* be included in their instructional, habilitation, or support plan.

    Basic Human Interaction -- Tolerating these situations is essential for effective parenting, instruction, and habilitation, and must always be emphasized, even at a very young age. These skills are often taught at the same time as R1-R5.

T-BHI1.	**The sight, sound, or scent of an unfamiliar person**
T-BHI2.	**In the same room with an unfamiliar person**

Basic Human Interaction (cont.)

T-BHI3.	In close physical proximity to an unfamiliar person
T-BHI4.	Demonstration prompts
T-BHI5.	Touch, physical guidance, or physical prompts
T-BHI5a.	_____
T-BHI5b.	_____
T-BHI5c.	_____

Eating, Drinking, and Feeding -- These skills are often taught at the same time as DLS-EDF1-9.

T-EDF1.	A gastrostomy or nasogastric tube
T-EDF2.	A feeding pump
T-EDF3.	Thickened liquids
T-EDF4.	Liquids
T-EDF5.	Baby food
T-EDF6.	Pureed foods
T-EDF7.	Soft foods
T-EDF8.	Mashed foods
T-EDF9.	An adapted spoon
T-EDF10.	An adapted cup, bowl, or plate
T-EDF11.	Solid foods
T-EDF11a.	_____
T-EDF11b.	_____
T-EDF11c.	_____
T-EDF11d.	_____

Daily Medical Procedures and Medication Administration

T-DM1.	Medication hidden in food
T-DM2.	Liquid medication from an oral syringe
T-DM3.	Liquid medication from a spoon
T-DM4.	Pills or vitamins
T-DM5.	Oxygen from a nasal tube
T-DM6.	An inhaler
T-DM7.	Testing blood by pricking a finger
T-DM8.	Insulin injection
T-DM9.	Ventilation and suction
T-DM9a.	_____
T-DM9b.	_____
T-DM9c.	_____
T-DM9d.	_____

Sleeping -- These skills are often taught at the same time as DLS-Slp1-2.

T-Slp1.	Parents' bed
T-Slp2.	A crib
T-Slp3.	Own bed
T-Slp4.	Pajamas
T-Slp5.	Lights off
T-Slp5a.	_____
T-Slp5b.	_____

Toileting

T-Toil1.	**Someone changing your diaper**
T-Toil2.	**Potty chair or adapted toilet**
T-Toil3.	**Toilet**
T-Toil4.	**Catheter**
T-Toil5.	**A colostomy or ileostomy bag**
T-Toil5a.	_____
T-Toil5b.	_____
T-Toil5c.	_____
T-Toil5d.	_____

Positioning and Range of Motion -- Some of our learners with very limited gross and fine motor movements must learn to tolerate various positions, along with range of motion exercises. This will decrease the probability of pressure sores and muscle atrophy and may increase the probability of acquiring additional gross and fine motor movements.

T-PRM1.	**A bed chair**
T-PRM2.	**A side lyer**
T-PRM3.	**A corner chair**
T-PRM4.	**A prone or supine stander**
T-PRM5.	**An adapted chair**
T-PRM6.	**Range of motion exercises**
T-PRM6a.	_____
T-PRM6b.	_____
T-PRM6c.	_____
T-PRM6d.	_____
T-PRM6e.	_____

Prosthetic, Therapeutic, and Adapted Equipment -- Some of our learners with very limited gross and fine motor movements must learn to tolerate prosthetic, therapeutic, or adapted equipment. This equipment may improve their vision or hearing, or increase their mobility.

T-PTA1.	**Glasses or contact lenses**
T-PTA2.	**A hearing aide or cochlear implant**
T-PTA3.	**A wheelchair**
T-PTA4.	**A gait trainer**
T-PTA5.	**A walker**
T-PTA6.	**A seat belt**
T-PTA7.	**A MOVE device**
T-PTA8.	**A helmet**
T-PTA9.	**AFOs**
T-PTA10.	**Splints**
T-PTA11.	**Braces**
T-PTA11a.	_____
T-PTA11b.	_____
T-PTA11c.	_____
T-PTA11d.	_____
T-PTA11e.	_____
T-PTA11f.	_____

Protective Equipment and Mechanical Restraints -- Some of our learners require protective equipment or mechanical restraints to protect themselves and others from injury while they are walking, sleeping, or engaged in other activities. Others require protective equipment or restraint because they exhibit severe problem behavior. Protective equipment prevents injury to the learner without restricting movement, while mechanical restraints also prevent injury, but restrict movement, generally preventing the learner from exhibiting the problem behavior. Learners for whom this applies must learn to tolerate either or both protective equipment or mechanical restraints as long as they are necessary.

T-PEMR1.	A helmet
T-PEMR2.	A face guard
T-PEMR3.	Padded arm guards
T-PEMR4.	Padded gloves or mitts
T-PEMR5.	Finger cots
T-PEMR6.	Knee or elbow pads
T-PEMR7.	A jumpsuit
T-PEMR8.	A Posey vest
T-PEMR9.	Arm splints
T-PEMR10.	A mat wrap or restraint board
T-PEMR10a.	_____
T-PEMR10b.	_____
T-PEMR10c.	_____
T-PEMR10d.	_____

Bathing and Personal Hygiene -- Some of our child and adult learners do not tolerate items and activities involved in personal care and hygiene, making it very difficult for parents, care providers, and instructors to keep them clean and for learners themselves to acquire these same skills.

T-BPH1.	Someone washing your hands
T-BPH2.	Someone washing your face
T-BPH3.	Someone washing your ears
T-BPH4.	Someone shampooing your hair
T-BPH5.	Someone brushing or combing your hair
T-BPH6.	A sponge bath
T-BPH7.	A tub bath
T-BPH8.	A hoist
T-BPH8a.	_____
T-BPH8b.	_____
T-BPH8c.	_____
T-BPH8d.	_____
T-BPH8e.	_____
T-BPH8f.	_____

Daily Dental Procedures -- Tolerating daily dental procedures *is essential for the safety and well-being* of our children and adults. Frequent exposure to these procedures permits frequent opportunities for teaching and learning.

T-DD1.	Someone brushing your teeth
T-DD1a.	_____
T-DD1b.	_____
T-DD1c.	_____

Should-have Tolerating Skills. If learners do not tolerate specific situations that they encounter frequently and that cannot be limited or easily avoided (e.g., sitting in the back seat or a car seat, wearing a bra, sleeping in their own bed, physical therapy sessions, and being required to put on socks before going to school), these situations *'should' be included* in their instructional, habilitation, or support plan.

Clothing and Accessories -- Some of our learners, including but not limited to, those with autism, have difficulty tolerating articles of clothing, making it very difficult for parents, care providers, and instructors to keep them properly attired, especially in public.

T-C1.	**Someone putting on your clothes**
T-C2.	**Underpants**
T-C3.	**Undershirts**
T-C4.	**Bras**
T-C5.	**Shirts or tops**
T-C6.	**Shorts**
T-C7.	**Jeans**
T-C8.	**Pants or slacks**
T-C9.	**Shoes**
T-C10.	**Socks**
T-C11.	**Sweaters or jumpers**
T-C12.	**Coats or jackets**
T-C13.	**Hats**
T-C14.	**Clothing made from cotton, wool, or synthetic materials**
T-C15.	**A purse or a wallet with an ID card**
T-C15a.	_____
T-C15b.	_____
T-C15c.	_____

Transportation -- Some of our learners have difficulty tolerating various aspects of transportation, making it very difficult for parents, care providers, and instructors to keep them safely seated while the vehicle is moving.

T-Trp1.	**Back seat**
T-Trp2.	**Car seat**
T-Trp3.	**Seat Belt**
T-Trp4.	**Bus or School Bus**
T-Trp5.	**Bus with peers onboard**
T-Trp6.	**Taxi or train**
T-Trp7.	**Elevator**
T-Trp8.	**Escalator**
T-Trp9.	**A trained companion or guide dog**
T-Trp9a.	_____
T-Trp9b.	_____
T-Trp9b.	_____

Sleeping -- These skills are often taught at the same time as DLS-Slp3-6.

T-Slp6.	**A baby bed**
T-Slp7.	**Own bed**
T-Slp8.	**Bed time**
T-Slp8a.	_____
T-Slp8b.	_____
T-Slp8c.	_____

Daily Dental Procedures

T-DD2.	Someone flossing between your teeth
T-DD3.	A fluoride rinse or mouthwash
T-DD4.	Braces or a mouthguard
T-DD4a.	_____
T-DD4b.	_____
T-DD4c.	_____

Bathing and Personal Hygiene

T-BPH9.	A shower at home
T-BPH10.	Deodorant
T-BPH11.	Hand or body lotion
T-BPH12.	Someone cleaning and clipping your nails
T-BPH13.	A shower in another person's home or a locker room
T-BPH13a.	_____
T-BPH13b.	_____
T-BPH13c.	_____
T-BPH13d.	_____

School, Instruction, and Therapy

Tolerating school or therapy center environments or procedures that are part of physical, occupational, or speech-language therapy, or that occur in school-based, center-based, and home-based programs are essential in order for the performance of our learners on targeted skills to improve.

T-SIT1.	Physical therapy sessions
T-SIT2.	Occupational therapy sessions
T-SIT4.	School or therapy center environments
T-SIT5.	Speech and language therapy sessions
T-SIT6.	Specific speech or language therapy procedures
T-SIT7.	1:1 instruction
T-SIT8.	Small group instruction
T-SIT9.	Specific teaching procedures
T-SIT9a.	_____
T-SIT9b.	_____
T-SIT9c.	_____
T-SIT9d.	_____
T-SIT9e.	_____
T-SIT9f.	_____

Eating, Drinking, and Feeding

T-EDF13.	Fruits
T-EDF14.	Vegetables
T-EDF15.	Chewy foods
T-EDF16.	Crunchy foods
T-EDF17.	Hot foods
T-EDF18.	Cold foods
T-EDF18a.	_____
T-EDF18b.	_____

T-EDF18c.	_____
T-EDF18d.	_____
T-EDF18e.	_____
T-EDF18f.	_____

Basic Human Interaction -- Tolerating these situations is essential for effective parenting, instruction, and habilitation and must always be emphasized, even at a very young age.

T-BHI6.	**Praise or indications of approval or correct responding**
T-BHI7.	**The word "no" or other indications of disapproval or incorrect responding**
T-BHI8.	**Praise or indications of approval or correct responding given to others**
T-BHI9.	**Indications of disapproval or incorrect responding given to others**
T-BHI10.	**Someone crying, making loud noises, or exhibiting problem behavior**
T-BHI11.	**Someone talking on the phone**
T-BHI12.	**Gentle teasing from friends or harsh teasing from others**
T-BHI12a.	_____
T-BHI12b.	_____
T-BHI12c.	_____
T-BHI12d.	_____

Basic Daily Activities -- For many learners, there are situations that are part of basic, daily activities that they have not yet learned to tolerate. Tolerating these situations is essential for effective parenting, instruction, and habilitation and must always be emphasized, even at a very young age.

T-BDA1.	**Missing items required to complete activities**
T-BDA2.	**A change in a schedule or sequence of events**
T-BDA3.	**The elimination of an event from a schedule**
T-BDA4.	**Waiting in line with peers**
T-BDA5.	**Not being first or first in line**
T-BDA6.	**Losing in a game or competition**
T-BDA7.	**Waiting for clerks to respond**
T-BDA8.	**A requested item or activity is denied while on a shopping trip**
T-BDA9.	**A requested item in a store is not available**
T-BDA10.	**A store is closed**
T-BDA10a.	_____
T-BDA10b.	_____
T-BDA10c.	_____
T-BDA10d.	_____
T-BDA10e.	_____
T-BDA10f.	_____

Toileting

T-Toil7.	**A restroom in a familiar person's home**
T-Toil8.	**A restroom in a school**
T-Toil9.	**Public restrooms**
T-Toil9a.	_____
T-Toil9b.	_____
T-Toil9c.	_____

Occasional, Routine Medical Procedures -- Tolerating occasional, routine medical procedures *is essential for the safety and well-being* of our children and adults. Infrequent exposure to these procedures limits opportunities for teaching and learning. Exposure to some aspects of some of these procedures, however, can occur outside of the physician's office.

T-ORM1.	A heart and lung examination with a stethoscope
T-ORM2.	An ear examination with an otoscope
T-ORM3.	Blood pressure measurement with a stethoscope and a cuff
T-ORM4.	A mouth and throat examination with a tongue depressor
T-ORM5.	Measurement of heart functioning with an electrocardiogram
T-ORM6.	X-rays
T-ORM7.	A cup for a urine sample
T-ORM8.	Testing blood by pricking a finger
T-ORM9.	A needle and an injection
T-ORM10.	A needle and drawing blood
T-ORM10a.	_____
T-ORM10b.	_____
T-ORM10c.	_____
T-ORM10d.	_____

Occasional, Routine Dental Procedures -- Tolerating occasional, routine dental procedures, *is also essential for the safety and well-being* of our children and adults. Infrequent exposure to these procedures limits opportunities for teaching and learning. Exposure to some aspects of some of these procedures can occur, however, outside of the dentist's office.

T-ORD1.	An examination with an explorer and a mirror
T-ORD2.	Cleaning
T-ORD3.	X-rays
T-ORD4.	Drilling and restorations (fillings)
T-ORD4a.	_____
T-ORD4b.	_____
T-ORD4a.	_____
T-ORD4b.	_____

Home and Community -- There are many other situations in the home and the community that some of our learners have difficulty tolerating. The list below includes many that have been difficult for learners with whom we have worked. If a situation or circumstance not listed below applies to your learner, add it to your learner's list.

T-HC1.	Haircuts and hair clippers
T-HC2.	Vacuum cleaners
T-HC3.	Blenders
T-HC4.	Fire alarms
T-HC5.	A loud radio, stereo, or television
T-HC6.	Background noise or music in a school cafeteria or restaurant
T-HC7.	Losing a game
T-HC8.	A 'don't walk' sign
T-HC9.	A traffic jam
T-HC10.	Making right (or left) turns while driving home
T-HC11.	Unfinished tasks, games, or other activities
T-HC11a.	_____
T-HC11b.	_____
T-HC11c.	_____

T-HC11d. _____

T-HC11e. _____

T-HC11f. _____

T-HC11g. _____

T-HC11h. _____

The Assessment of Tolerating Skills

Before conducting an assessment, review the procedures described in chapter 4. Then, secure a copy of the **Assessment and Record of Progress (ARP)** for each learner. and begin to conduct the assessment. Determine each learner's performance level on each of the skills in this domain, beginning with Basic Human Interaction (**BHI1-5**), Eating, Drinking, and Feeding(**EDF1-11**), Daily Medical Procedures and Medication Administration (**DM1-9**) and other skill sets as they may apply to each learner and record this level on the *ARP*. The performance levels for tolerating skills are described in Table 1, along with sample items from the *ARP*. Continue the assessment until the learner requires prompts, exhibits inappropriate responses, or responds with problem behavior on three consecutive skills within each skill category. At the conclusion of the assessment, you should have a list of specific situations which the learner does not tolerate (see Table 2).

Table 1.
Performance Levels for Tolerating Skills

After exposure to this situation, learners resume on-going activities for ___ (seconds/minutes) or complete ___ (1/4, 1/2, 3/4, or all of) these activities, without prompts, without self-injurious, aggressive, destructive, or disruptive behavior, without complaints, and without leaving the area on three consecutive occasions...

IA	[the initial assessment of this skill has been completed]
IM	[instruction or management has begun]
Egg	[situations are avoided because problem behavior occurs]
-Egg	[situations are no longer avoided because problem behavior occurs]
10s	for 10 seconds
1m	for 1 minute
1/4	for 5 minutes or 1/4 of the required duration of an activity
1/2	for 10 minutes or 1/2 of the required duration of an activity
3/4	for 20 minutes or 3/4 of the required duration of an activity
Ind	for 1 hour or the required duration of an activity
Det	[this tolerating skill is no longer occurring consistently]

Basic human interaction

T-BHI5. Touch, physical guidance, or physical prompts

| IA | IM | Egg | -Egg | 10s | 1m | 1/4 | 1/2 | 3/4 | Ind | Det |

Basic daily activities

T-BDA1. Missing items required to complete activities

| IA | IM | Egg | -Egg | 10s | 1m | 1/4 | 1/2 | 3/4 | Ind | Det |

Teaching Tolerating Skills and Recording Progress

Begin by ranking this list of situations which the learner does not tolerate from 'most (1) to least likely to result in severe problem behavior' using a data sheet similar to the one shown in Table 2 . Then, select one or two situations at the 'least likely' end of the list, or situations that must be addressed immediately, and use the teaching procedures described in chapter 12, Teaching Protocol 8. Any time you encounter or recall new situations that the learner does not tolerate, add them to the list.

Record the learner's performance level on the *Skill Acquisition Self-graphing Data Recording Form* shown in Table 3. These forms can be downloaded from www.behaviorchange.com. Then, as the learner reaches specific performance levels, transfer this information to the ARP (see Table 4). As tolerating improves, gradually move from 'less likely' to 'more likely' situations until the learner tolerates all targeted situations and *there are no eggshells in the learner's life.*

Table 2.
Situations that a Learner Does Not Tolerate
Ranked from Most-to-least Likely to Result in Severe Problem Behavior

Ranking (Most-to-least)	Skill Number	Situation	IM
1	T-SIT8.	Small group instruction	
2	T-Slp4.	Lights off	
3	T-EDF14.	Vegetables	
4	T-Slp6.	Own bed	
5	T-BDA5.	Not being first or first in line	
6	T-BHI5.	Touch, physical guidance, or physical prompts	X
7	T-BDA1.	Missing items required to complete activities	X

Table 3.
Recording the Learner's Progress on Tolerating Skills Selected for Instruction
Using Single-trial Probe Data and Probe Data Sheets

ESSENTIAL FOR LIVING
Skill Acquisition Self-graphing Data Recording Form
Tolerating Skills: First Opportunity of the Day Probes

Tolerating Skill	Day/Date and First Opportunity of the Day Probe																
	13	14	15	16	17	18	19	20	21	22	23	24	25	26	27	28	29
	S	M	T	W	T	F	S	S	M	T	W	T	F	S	S	M	T
T-BDA1. Missing items required to complete activities	Det Ind 3/4 1/2 1/4 1m 10s 0 -Egg Egg	Det Ind 3/4 1/2 1/4 1m 10s 0 -Egg Egg	Det Ind 3/4 1/2 1/4 1m 10s 0 -Egg Egg	Det Ind 3/4 1/2 1/4 1m 10s 0 -Egg Egg	Det Ind 3/4 1/2 1/4 1m 10s 0 -Egg Egg	Det Ind 3/4 1/2 1/4 1m 10s 0 -Egg Egg	Det Ind 3/4 1/2 1/4 1m 10s 0 -Egg Egg	Det Ind 3/4 1/2 1/4 1m 10s 0 -Egg Egg	Det Ind 3/4 1/2 1/4 1m 10s 0 -Egg Egg	Det Ind 3/4 1/2 1/4 1m 10s 0 -Egg Egg	Det Ind 3/4 1/2 1/4 1m 10s 0 -Egg Egg	Det Ind 3/4 1/2 1/4 1m 10s 0 -Egg Egg	Det Ind 3/4 1/2 1/4 1m 10s 0 -Egg Egg	Det Ind 3/4 1/2 1/4 1m 10s 0 -Egg Egg	Det Ind 3/4 1/2 1/4 1m 10s 0 -Egg Egg	Det Ind 3/4 1/2 1/4 1m 10s 0 -Egg Egg	Det Ind 3/4 1/2 1/4 1m 10s 0 -Egg Egg

Table 4.
Transferring Data from Probe Data Sheets to the Assessment and Record of Progress

Basic daily activities

T-BDA1. Missing items required to complete activities

IA	IM	Egg	-Egg	10s	1m	1/4	1/2	3/4	Ind	Det

When tolerating does not improve with respect to specific situations, make certain that you follow the steps exactly as they are described in the teaching protocol in chapter 12, and, as necessary, make adjustments in this protocol.

Chapter 10. Problem Behavior

Some of our children and adults with moderate-to-severe disabilities exhibit forms of behavior that result in short-term outcomes that present substantial problems for themselves, their immediate environment, and those around them. As shown in Table 1, these outcomes define five types of problem behavior. If these behaviors occur frequently and with high intensity, the long-term outcomes also present problems (see Table 2).

Table 1.
Types of Problem Behavior and Typical Short-term Outcomes

Self-injurious	**SIB**	physical harm to that child or adult
Aggressive	**Agg**	physical harm to another person
Destructive	**Des**	property damage or destruction
Disruptive	**Dis**	interruption in the ongoing activities of other children or adults
Repetitive	**Rep**	interruption in the ongoing activities of that child or adult

Table 2. Possible Long-term Outcomes of High Frequency or High Intensity Problem Behavior

An imminent threat to health and safety
Difficulty acquiring other skills
Limited residential and vocational options
Limited mobility within the community
Limited access to preferred items and activities
Frequent contact with non-preferred items and activities

In light of these short and long-term outcomes, problem behavior must be part of an assessment, curriculum, and teaching manual for children and adults with moderate-to-severe disabilities.

We begin by assessing the extent to which learners exhibit problem behavior and the supports that are provided because of this behavior. Extent includes the type of each problem behavior, a precise definition of the form, and an estimate of the frequency and intensity. Supports include protective equipment or mechanical restraint, crisis stabilization procedures, and psychoactive medications. Supports also include forms of self-restraint which some learners exhibit.

Then, in order to provide effective treatment, we can use one of two strategies. We can begin by estimating the function of each behavior, that is, the extent to which specific events that occur *before* and immediately *after* each behavior may be controlling or maintaining the occurrence of that behavior. This is done by conducting a functional assessment. Once this assessment is completed, the estimated functions may suggest skills or behaviors to replace the problem behaviors and specific behavioral interventions. These interventions generally include changing events that occur before the problem behavior and arranging for events that previously occurred after the problem behavior to occur after an expected or replacement skill or behavior [differential reinforcement]. In some situations, problem behaviors require interventions that are not based on a functional assessment [that include punishment]. Or, we might begin by selecting situations in which the problem behaviors typically occur and teaching skills appropriate to those situations using function-based teaching protocols, which also include procedures designed to decrease the extent to which problem behaviors occur.

Assessing the Extent of Occurrence of Problem Behavior and the Supports Provided

Begin by observing the learner in several circumstances within a school, residential, or vocational environment, noting the occurrence of behaviors that appear to present a problem for the learner or those around the learner. Briefly describe each of these behaviors. Or, if observation is not feasible, begin by interviewing 2-3 people who are familiar with the learner, noting their descriptions of specific behaviors. Your descriptions or their descriptions may include: *standing while eating, head banging, arm biting, walking on her toes, slapping the instructor, attempting to kick his mother, screaming at the top of his lungs, running out of the room, throwing toys, tearing her shirt, or flicking his fingers in front of his eyes.*

Determining the Type of Problem Behavior. If any of the observed behaviors result in the outcomes described in Table 1, these behaviors present a problem for the learner and the outcome defines the type of behavior. For example, 'standing while eating' may not result in any of the outcomes described in Table 1, and, at least for the time being, should not be considered a problem behavior. In another example, *'slapping the instructor'* may result in physical harm to that person and should be considered a problem behavior of the aggressive type.

Defining the Form of Problem Behavior. Once behaviors are determined to be a problem, the form of these behaviors must be precisely defined in order to accurately record occurrences and provide effective treatment.

The description of each problem behavior should be transformed into a precise definition of the form. This is done by noting the movements the learner makes from the start to the end of an instance or occurrence. an operational definition / the movement cycle For example:

    an instance of *'head hitting'* may be defined as...

        makes a fist with his right hand, brings his hand rapidly toward and makes contact with his head just above his right ear; or,

    an instance of *'tearing his shirt'* may be defined as...

        grasps his shirt with one or both hands and pulls it away from his body until it begins to tear.

If several instances of the same behavior occur within a few seconds, making it difficult to record each occurrence, it may be advisable to define and record episodes, rather than instances. In this case, the end of an episode will need to be defined by a specific period of time during which no instance of the problem behavior occurs. For example:

    an episode of *'face slapping'* may be defined as...

        brings either open hand rapidly toward and makes repeated contact with his face and does not make any of these movements for one minute or,

    an episode of *'running out of the room'* may be defined as...

        begins to move rapidly away from an assigned area and runs toward and out of the door into the hallway, and, after being escorted back into the room, does not make any of these movements for two minutes.

Sometimes more than one problem behavior can occur within a few seconds, in which case defining and recording episodes is also advisable. For example:

    an episode of *'head hitting and arm biting'* may be defined as:

        makes a fist with his right hand, brings his hand rapidly toward and makes contact with his head just above his right ear; and brings his teeth toward and makes contact with his right forearm and does not make any of these movements for 30 seconds.

The Use of Psychoactive Medications. The form and intensity of some problem behaviors may lead to the use of one or more psychoactive medications. As shown in Table 3, the extent to which psychoactive medication is used can be defined by the number of such medications currently taken daily by a learner and any recent increases or reductions in dosage. Changes in the number and dosage of these medications is an indication of the degree of support required by a learner with problem behavior.

Table 3.
The Extent to which Psychoactive Medication is Used

Med 3+>	Three or more psychoactive medications with some increases in dosage
Med 3+	Three or more psychoactive medications
Med 3+<	Three or more psychoactive medications with some reductions in dosage
Med 2>	Two psychoactive medications with some increases in dosage
Med 2	Two psychoactive medications
Med 2<	Two psychoactive medications with some reductions in dosage
Med 1>	One psychoactive medication with some increase in dosage
Med 1	One psychoactive medication
Med 1<	One psychoactive medication with some reductions in dosage
-Med	No psychoactive medications

Recording the Type and Form of Problem Behavior and the Use of Psychoactive Medications. As shown in Table 4, enter the form and type of each problem behavior on the first section of the *Problem Behavior Direct Observation and Interview Form*, along with the psychoactive medications and dosages taken by the learner. The entire form is shown in the Appendix and in the *Assessment and Record of Progress (ARP)*.

Table 4.
Enter the Form and Type of Each Problem Behavior
and the Extent to Which Psychoactive Medication is Used
on the *Problem Behavior Direct Observation and Interview Form*

ESSENTIAL FOR LIVING

The First Two Sections of the Problem Behavior Direct Observation and Interview Form

Learner: _____ Environment(s): _____

Date: _____ Observer or Person Interviewed: _____ Recording Period: _____

Definition of Problem Behavior(s) 1 -- **PB1**: *makes a fist with his right hand, repeatedly brings his hand rapidly toward and makes repeated contact with his head just above his right ear and does not make any of these movements for one minute*	Definition of Problem Behavior(s) 2 -- **PB2**: *raises his arm and, with an open hand, slaps others*
Instance (**Episode**) SIB (Agg) Des Dis Rep	(**Instance**) Episode SIB (**Agg**) Des Dis Rep

Medications: *Risperdal, Clonidine*

The Occurrence of Problem Behavior. Record instances or episodes of the previously defined problem behaviors for a fixed amount of time (e.g., five hours) each day. The amount of time spent recording can vary from 5 minutes (in situations which include intense self-injurious, aggressive, or destructive behavior) to 16 hours (in hospitals or large residential facilities). If more than 20 instances or episodes occur during a recording period, you should consider decreasing the length of this period. If less than 5 instances or episodes occur, you should consider increasing the length of this period.

The Intensity of Problem Behavior. The intensity with which learners exhibit specific problem behaviors varies greatly. For example, *'head hitting'* may have already resulted in serious injuries or may occur with such force that serious injuries could easily occur. On the other hand, *'head hitting'* may not have resulted in any injuries, but may occur with force that could result in minor injuries over an extended period of time. Determine the current intensity of each problem behavior by comparing the current or probable outcomes with those described in Table 5. Changes in intensity, which often indicate a degree of improvement or worsening in a problem behavior, will need to be recorded as each occurrence of problem behavior is also recorded.

Table 5.
Defining and Recording the Intensity Problem Behavior

The intensity of specific types and forms of problem behavior is defined by a more detailed description of the probable outcome of these behaviors:

Severe	**Sev**	movements of a learner that have resulted or could result in serious injuries to that learner or others requiring medical attention, and, in some cases, resulting in a permanent impairment;
Moderate	**Mod**	movements of a learner that have resulted or could result in minor injuries to that learner or others; or,
Mild	**Mild**	movements of a learner that have not resulted in injuries to that learner or others; if, however, these movements became more forceful or occurred over an extended period of time, minor or serious injuries could begin to occur

The Use of Protective Equipment and Mechanical Restraint. The form and intensity of some problem behaviors may require the use of protective equipment or mechanical restraint in order to protect the learner. Protective equipment is designed to prevent injuries, but does not limit movements learners can make. Mechanical restraints, however, while also designed to protect the learner, limit movements learners can make. A padded helmet is an example of protective equipment, while an arm split is an example of mechanical restraint. Protective equipment and mechanical restraints can be applied continuously, that is, throughout the day or contingently, that is, from the beginning to the end of episodes of problem behavior. The extent to which continuous protective equipment (**PEA**) and mechanical restraints (**MRA**) are used is defined across two dimensions: form and duration. In other words, **PEA** and **MRA** can be increased or faded in terms of appearance or length of time either is applied. The use of contingent protective equipment (**PEC**) and mechanical restraints (**MRC**) is defined by form only. In other words, **PEC** and **MRC** are applied until the learner is calm and can be increased or faded in appearance only. As shown in Table 6, the extent to which protective equipment and mechanical restraint are used can be measured along these dimensions. Changes in form or duration, which are often an indication of the degree of support required by a learner, will need to be recorded as each occurrence of problem behavior is also recorded.

Table 6.
Defining and Measuring the Extent of
Protective Equipment and Mechanical Restraint

PE>2	Protective equipment has been increased twice
PE>1	Protective equipment has been increased once
PE	Protective equipment at the time of the initial assessment: _____
	_____
PE<1	Protective equipment has been partially faded once
PE<2	Protective equipment has been partially faded twice
PE<3	Protective equipment has been partially faded three times
-PE	Protective equipment is not required
MR>2	Mechanical restraints have been increased twice
MR>1	Mechanical restraints have been increased once
MR	Mechanical restraints at the time of the initial assessment: _____
	_____
MR<1	Mechanical restraints have been partially faded once
MR<2	Mechanical restraints have been partially faded twice
MR<3	Mechanical restraints have been partially faded three times
-MR	Mechanical restraints are not required

The Use of Crisis Stabilization Procedures. The form and intensity of some problem behaviors may require the use of crisis stabilization procedures, such as PCM[1], in order to protect the learner. These procedures include physically assisted transportation and temporary immobilization. As shown in Table 7, the extent to which crisis stabilization procedures are used can be defined by the total duration of these procedures per week. Changes in the duration of these procedures, which often indicate some degree of improvement or worsening in a problem behavior, will need to be recorded as each occurrence of problem behavior is also recorded.

Table 7.
Defining and Measuring the Extent to Which
Crisis Stabilization Procedures are Used

CS>5hW	Crisis stabilization procedures are used more than 5 hours per week
CS2-5hW	Crisis stabilization procedures are used 2-5 hours per week
CS1-2hW	Crisis stabilization procedures are used 1-2 hours per week
CS30m-1hW	Crisis stabilization procedures are used 30 minutes to hour per week
CS<30mW	Crisis stabilization procedures are used less than 30 minutes per week
-CS	Crisis stabilization procedures are not required

The Extent to Which Self-restraint Occurs. Some learners exhibit what is often called 'self-restraint'. Examples include 'placing their hands under their shirt', 'placing a cap or helmet on their head', or 'carrying small toys or other items in both hands'. These activities temporarily limit movements they can make or provide a form of protection. Unlike mechanical restraint or protective equipment, learners can discontinue these activities at any time. As shown in Table 8, the extent to which self-restraint occurs is defined and measured by its form. Changes in the extent to which self-restraint occurs, which are often an indication of the degree of support required by a learner with problem behavior, will need to be recorded as each occurrence of problem behavior is also recorded.

---

[1] PCM is an abbreviation for Professional Crisis Management, a crisis stabilization and emergency restraint system that is extremely safe and effective, while maintaining the dignity of our children and adults with severe problem behavior. Training and certification in this system, which we highly recommend, is available from http://www.pcma.com.

Table 8.
Defining and Measuring the Extent
to Which Self-restraint Occurs

SR>2   Self-restraints have increased twice
SR>1   Self-restraints have increased once
SR   Self-restraints at the time of the initial assessment: _____

_____

SR<1   Self-restraints have been partially faded once
SR<2   Self-restraints have been partially faded twice
SR<3   Self-restraints have been partially faded three times
-SR   Self-restraint does not occur

Recording the Occurrence and Intensity of Problem Behavior, along with the Use of Protective Equipment, Restraint, and Crisis Stabilization Procedures. As shown in Table 9, begin to record instances or episodes of the previously defined problem behaviors for a specific amount of time each day using the *Problem Behavior Direct Observation and Interview Form*. Also record the intensity of each instance or episode as severe, moderate, or mild, according to criteria previously specified, along with the extent to which protective equipment, mechanical restraints, or crisis stabilization procedures are used. Also record the extent, if any, to which the learner exhibits self-restraint.

Table 9.
Recording the Occurrence of Problem Behaviors
on the Problem Behavior Direct Observation and Interview Form

ESSENTIAL FOR LIVING
Problem Behavior Direct Observation and Interview Form

Learner: _____ Environment(s): _____
Date: _____ Observer or Person Interviewed: _____ Recording Period: **5 hours**

Definition of Problem Behavior(s) 1 -- **PB1**: *makes a fist with his right hand, repeatedly brings his hand rapidly toward and makes repeated contact with his head just above his right ear and does not make any of these movements for one minute*

Definition of Problem Behavior(s) 2 -- **PB2**: *raises his arm and, with an open hand, slaps others*

Instance (**Episode**)   (**SIB**) Agg Des Dis Rep   (**Instance**) Episode   SIB (**Agg**) Des Dis Rep

Medications: *Risperdal, Clonidine*

Direct Observation

PB1	Intensity	MRA	MRC	PEA	PEC	CS (min)	SR
1	**Sev**-Mod-Mild			PE: sk hlmt			
2	**Sev**-Mod-Mild			PE		22	
3	Sev-Mod-**Mild**			PE			
4	**Sev**-Mod-Mild			PE		14	
5	Sev-Mod-**Mild**			PE			
6	Sev-**Mod**-Mild			PE			
7	Sev-**Mod**-Mild			PE		17	

PB2	Intensity	MRA	MRC	PEA	PEC	CS (min)	SR
1	**Sev**-Mod-Mild						X
2	**Sev**-Mod-Mild					8	X
3	**Sev**-Mod-Mild					4	X
4	**Sev**-Mod-Mild					5	X
5	Sev-Mod-Mild						
6	Sev-Mod-Mild						
7	Sev-Mod-Mild						

Interview

This behavior occurs **8-10** per day ___ per week ___ per month ___ per year
and the intensity is: ___ sev **X** mod ___ mild
The learner wears, requires, or exhibits:
MRA or **MRC**: *none*
PEA or **PEC**: *soft, karate helmet*
CS: ___ minutes per day **3** hours per week
SR: *none*

This behavior occurs **3-4** per day ___ per week ___ per month ___ per year
and the intensity is: **X** sev ___ mod ___ mild
The learner wears, requires, or exhibits:
MRA or **MRC**: *none*
PEA or **PEC**: *none*
CS: **20** minutes per day ___ hours per week
SR: *tucks his hands under his t-shirt*

Continue Recording the Occurrence of Problem Behavior. Continue recording for 6-10 days and, as shown in Table 10 with Problem Behavior 1 (**PB1**), transfer the total number of instances or episodes each day to a chart or graph. At least six days are necessary in order to obtain a general path or direction of the problem behavior that has predictive value, that is, in order to determine if instances or episodes of the problem behavior are increasing or decreasing and likely to continue doing so (Koenig, 1972; White and Haring, 1980). Most people choose non-standard, hand-drawn or computer-generated graphs. These graphs result in displays of data that are partly a function of how the hand-drawn graph was constructed or the extent to which a computer program adjusted the appearance of the graph based on new data points. We strongly recommend spending a few minutes learning to use the *Daily Standard Celeration Chart*[2] or the *Adapted Daily Standard Celeration Chart*[3], and getting comfortable with their appearance (a small section of the *Adapted Daily Standard Celeration Chart* is included in Tables 10, 11, 12, and 21).

Once this is done, most parents, instructors, and care providers find standard charts considerably more informative. As shown in Tables 11 and 12, construct a best-fit line   trend or celeration line which splits the data points and suggests the general path of the data. If this path does not indicate that the problem behavior is decreasing in frequency (see Table 11), begin developing a plan of treatment and instruction, which is described in the next section. If, on the other hand, the path indicates that the problem behaviors are beginning to decrease in frequency (see Table 12), continue recording without making any changes. Then, as shown in Table 13 with Problem Behavior 1 (**PB1**), transfer this information and these data to the *Assessment and Record of Progress* (ARP).

Table 10.
Continue to Record the Total Number of Instances or Episodes of
Problem Behavior for 6-7 Days and Transfer These Data
to the Adapted Standard Celeration Chart or a
Non-standard Hand-drawn or Computer-generated Graph

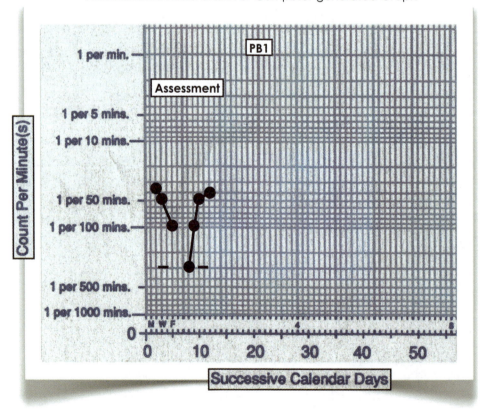

---

[2] available from http://www.behaviorresearchcompany.com.

[3] available from http://www.behaviorchange.com.

Table 10. (cont.)
Continue to Record the Total Number of Instances or Episodes of
Problem Behavior for 6-7 Days and Transfer These Data
to the Adapted Standard Celeration Chart or a
Non-standard Hand-drawn or Computer-generated Graph

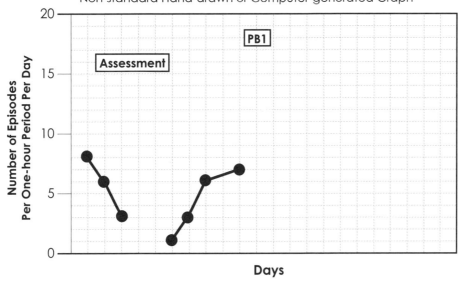

Table 11.
If the General Path of the Data Does Not Indicate that the Problem Behavior
is Decreasing in Frequency, Conduct a Functional Assessment or
Develop a Plan of Treatment and Instruction in the Context of Teaching New Skills

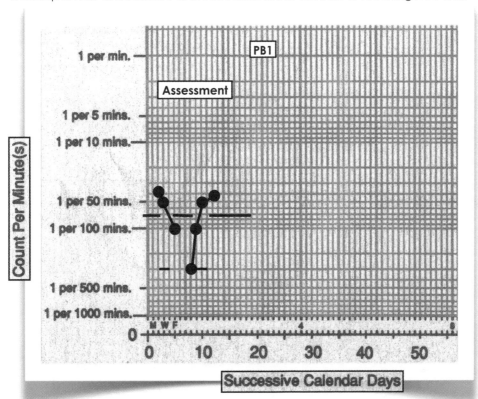

Table 12.
If the General Path of the Data Indicates that the Problem Behavior is Decreasing in Frequency, Continue Recording Without Making Any Changes

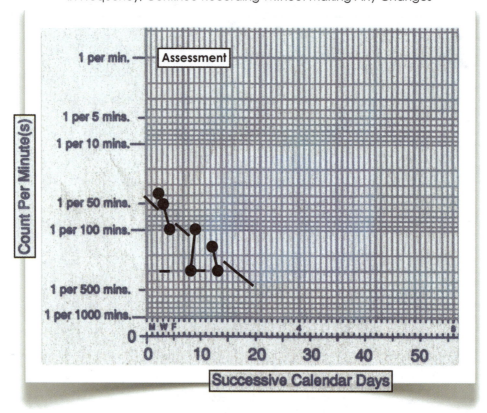

Table 13.
Transferring Information and Data from
the *Problem Behavior Direct Observation and Interview Form*
and to the Adapted Standard Celeration Chart or a
Non-standard Hand-drawn or Computer-generated Graph
to the Assessment and Record of Progress (ARP)

ESSENTIAL FOR LIVING
Assessment and Record of Progress (ARP): Problem Behavior

PB1. Makes a fist with his right hand, repeatedly and rapidly brings his hand toward and makes contact with his head just above his right ear and does not make any of these movements for one minute

IA	IM		Instance	Episode		SIB	Agg	Des	Dis	Rep
							Sev	Mod	Mild
Med3+>	Med3+	Med3+<	Med2>	Med2	Med2<	Med1>	Med1	Med1<	-Med
MRA	MRC		MR2>	MR1>	MR	MR1<	MR2<	MR3<	-MR
PEA	PEC		PE2>	PE1>	PE	PE!<	PE2<	PE3<	-PE
			CS>5hW	CS 2-5hW	CS 1-2hW	CS 30m-1hW	CS<30mW	-CS
			SR2>	SR1>	SR	SR1<	SR2<	SR3<	-SR
		>100D	50-100D	20-50D	10-20D	1-10D	<1D	<1W	<1M	<1Y

Providing Effective Treatment for Problem Behavior

The effective treatment of problem behavior can be accomplished by conducting a formal, functional assessment. The results provide an estimate of whether specific problem behaviors are a function of one or more of the following consequent events:

- attention,
- avoidance or escape from demands,
- access to tangible items and activities, or
- some sort of automatically-occurring sensory event.

In other words, the results indicate whether specific problem behaviors are followed by and maintained by one or more of these consequent events. Then, as part of behavioral treatment that is based on function, these events are withheld when problem behaviors occur and made available when designated replacement behaviors occur.

In most situations, we prefer an alternative approach that includes managing problem behavior in the context of skill development. This approach includes two components: (1) **The Essential Eight**, a set of skills which children and adults of all ages are expected to exhibit, and, in the absence of which problem behaviors tend to occur, and (2) function-based teaching protocols which include procedures designed to teach these skills and, at the same time, decrease the frequency of problem behaviors that tend to occur in their absence. These skills were initially described in chapter 1 and are presented again in Table 14, along with the likely function of problem behaviors that occur in their absence.

Continuing with our previous examples, Problem Behavior 1 (**PB1**), '*face slapping*', may occur when a learner is directed to complete assigned tasks. If these tasks are removed when he does so, this problem behavior will likely become a function of '*avoidance or escape from demands*', and possibly also a function of '*attention*'. In the absence of a teaching protocol based on these functions, the learner will continue to '*slap his face*' when he is directed to complete these tasks. Problem Behavior 2 (**PB2**), '*shirt tearing*', may occur when a learner wants specific items or activities. If he receives these items when he does so, these problem behaviors will likely become a function of '*access to tangible items or activities*', and may also become a function of '*attention*', In the absence of a teaching protocol based on these functions, the learner will continue to '*tear his shirt*' when he wants these items or activities.

Table 14.
The Essential Eight and the Likely Functions of Problem Behaviors
that May Occur in the Absence of These Skills

The Essential Eight: Eight Skills that Learners are Expected to Exhibit in Specific Situations		
One. Requesting an audience	**Two.** Waiting	**One.** Requesting preferred items and activities
One. Requesting companionship	**Three.** Accepting the removal of preferred items and activities and transitioning from preferred to non-preferred activities	
One. Requesting affection	**Four.** Sharing and taking turns	
One. Requesting feedback, approval, or confirmation	**Five.** Completing assigned tasks	
One. Requesting acknowledgment	**Six.** Accepting 'no'	
	Seven. Following directions regarding community safety	
	Eight. Tolerating physical prompts and routine activities and events	
In the absence of these skills, problem behaviors may occur, which will likely become a function of... *attention*	In the absence of these skills, problem behaviors may occur, which will likely become a function of... *avoidance or escape from demands* and, possibly *attention*	In the absence of this skill, problem behaviors may occur, which will likely become a function of... *access to tangible items or activities* and, possibly *attention*

To prevent problem behaviors from occurring, we strongly recommend teaching **The Essential Eight** as soon as possible using the teaching protocols included in chapter 12. If problem behaviors occurred during the initial assessment or begin to occur at any other time, and the path of 6-7 data points indicates that these behaviors are not decreasing in frequency, begin to assess the extent to which each of **The Essential Eight** are occurring without problem behavior. Then, select examples of one or more of these skills, which have not been acquired, and, in the absence of which, problem behaviors are occurring. Then, use function-based teaching protocols included in chapter 12 that are designed to teach these skills and reduce the frequency of problem behaviors that occur in their absence. These protocols, which are specific to each of the skills and functions depicted in Table 13, include:

(1) capturing and contriving situations in which these specific skills are expected to occur,
(2) providing prompts, and when skills occur, providing reinforcers and fading prompts, and
(3) providing consequences when problem behaviors occur that are consistent with their likely function and any other functions they may acquire.

A problem behavior such as **PB1**, '*face slapping*', may occur in the absence of completing two or more consecutive, brief, previously acquired tasks (see Table 15). If this occurs, we strongly suggest providing frequent opportunities to complete these tasks (**R11**) and using the teaching protocol which is shown in Table 16 and included in chapter 12. We also recommend collecting probe data on this skill as described in chapter 4 and recording these data on a *Skill Acquisition Self-graphing Data Recording Form* (see Table 20). These probe data sheets can be downloaded from www.behaviorchange.com.

Table 15.
Selecting Examples of One or More of *The Essential Eight*
in the Absence of Which Problem Behaviors Occur

R11. Completes 10 consecutive, brief, previously acquired tasks

IA	IM	1	2	5	10	Det

Table 16.
Completing Consecutive, Brief, Previously Acquired Tasks: A Teaching Protocol

1. Begin with brief, previously acquired tasks that require very little effort; gradually increase the number of tasks, and intersperse tasks of greater duration, and ones that require more effort
2. Direct the learner to complete the task
3. If the learner completes the task without exhibiting the problem behavior or complaints, provide praise and an opportunity to make a request
4. If the problem behavior occurs, manually interrupt it or wait until it is no longer occurring
5. Do not talk with the learner or acknowledge what he is doing
6. Return to the same task; wait with the learner until he completes the task
7. Do not provide praise or an opportunity to request a preferred item or activity
8. Return to step 1 and provide another task

1. Begin with brief tasks that require very little effort, which the learner has previously completed without prompts; use stimulus fading to increase the duration of the task and the effort required;
2. Provide a cue to complete the task
3. If the learner completes the task, provide differential reinforcement in the form of praise and an opportunity to mand
4. If problem behavior occurs, provide continuous, response interruption until the problem behavior has not occurred for 2-3 seconds
5. Withhold attention (social extinction)
6. Use escape extinction without prompts
7. Withhold reinforcement
8. Return to step 1 and provide a cue for another task

If a problem behavior such as (**PB2**), '*shirt tearing*', occurs in the absence of making requests for preferred items and activities, we suggest frequently capturing and contriving motivation for highly preferred items or activities (e.g., cookies and juice, as shown in Table 17) and teaching the learner to request the same (**R7**) using a teaching protocol described in chapter 12. A variation of this protocol, Making Requests with Signs, is also shown in Table 18. We also recommend collecting probe data on this skill.

Table 17.
Selecting Examples of One or More of *The Essential Eight*
in the Absence of Which Problem Behaviors Occur

R7. Requests 10 highly preferred snack foods, drinks, non-food items, or activities that can be made frequently and immediately available

	IA	IM	-SA	-DC	-RP	FP	PP	MP	Ind	2S	2P	<M	Det
→ 1 cookies													
→ 2 juice													

As you implement one or more of these teaching protocols, continue to collect data on the problem behaviors during the daily recording period using the direct observation section of the Problem Behavior Direct Observation and Interview Form. As indicated in the assessment section of this chapter, transfer these data to a hand-drawn or computer-generated graph, the Daily Standard Celeration Chart, or the Adapted Daily Standard Celeration Chart.

Table 18.
Making Requests with Signs: A Teaching Protocol

1. Make items and activities available that are preferred by the learner; wait for him to indicate by gesturing what he 'wants' at that moment	1. Capture or contrive a motivating operation related to a targeted mand
2. Prompt a sign that corresponds to the item or activity the learner wants; provide a demonstration prompt or a full physical prompt; gradually fade prompts	2. Prompt a sign mand using a full demonstration or a full physical prompt; gradually, fade prompts
3. If the learner forms the appropriate sign, provide access to the requested item or activity	3. If the learner forms the correct sign, provide a specific reinforcer
4. If problem behavior occurs, interrupt it or wait until it is no longer occurring;	4. If problem behavior occurs, provide continuous, response interruption until the problem behavior has not occurred for 2-3 seconds
5. Do not provide access to the requested item or activity	5. Withhold the specific reinforcer
6. Do not talk with the learner or acknowledge what he is doing	6. Withhold attention
7. Wait an additional period of time specific to each learner, ranging from 5 seconds to several minutes	7. Withhold attention and specific reinforcers for an additional period of time
8. If problem behavior does not occur, return to step 1	8. If problem behavior does not occur

Then, as previously described and shown in Tables 11 and 12, construct a best-fit line which represents the path of the data. Then, using the path of the data for the problem behaviors and the path of the targeted skills from **The Essential Eight**, make decisions whether to continue with the current treatment procedures or make a change. If the path of the last 6-7 days of data indicates that the problem behaviors are not decreasing in frequency and/or the performance levels of the expected skills are not improving, make certain that you are implementing the protocols as they are written or make an adjustment by modifying or adding one or more procedures. If, on the other hand, the path of the last 6-7 days of data indicates that the problem behaviors are decreasing in frequency and the performance levels of the expected skills are improving, continue recording without making any changes. If the path of the last 6-7 days of data is not clear or the last few data points are beginning to divert from the apparent path, continue recording for several more days. Then, examine the last 7 seven data points and estimate the path of the data. Then, make a decision consistent with this path.

For example, as shown in Table 19, after the first 7 days of treatment with Problem Behavior 1 (**PB1**), there was a slight decrease in the frequency of problem behavior (indicated by a red line). Data shown in Table 20 indicated that task completions were beginning to occur without problem behavior. These data suggested that the program should be continued without changes. After 3 more days, a review of the last 7 days (see the blue line in Table 19) indicated that the frequency of problem behavior was no longer decreasing. Also, as shown in Table 20, task completions were not continuing to increase. Based on these data, the protocols were implemented more carefully. As shown in Tables 19 and 20, this change resulted in rapid and substantial improvement.

As shown in Table 21, with Problem Behavior 2 (**PB2**), there was no change in the frequency of problem behavior (indicated by a red line) after 7 days of treatment. Even though data shown in Table 22 indicated that requests for 2 highly preferred items were beginning to occur without prompts, the problem behavior data suggested a change in the procedures within the protocol. After specific changes were made, there was a rapid decrease in the frequency of the problem behavior and an increase in the performance level of two requests, one for cookies and the other for juice.

Essential for Living 253

Table 19.
Problem Behavior 1 (**PB1**) and Completing Consecutive, Brief, Previously Acquired Tasks:
Deciding Whether to Continue Treatment Procedures or Make a Change

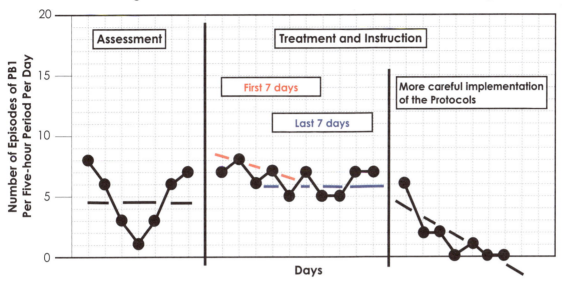

Table 20.
Problem Behavior 1 (**PB1**) and Completing Consecutive, Brief, Previously Acquired Tasks:
Deciding Whether to Continue Treatment Procedures or Make a Change

ESSENTIAL FOR LIVING
Skill Acquisition Data Recording Form

Completing Consecutive, Brief, Previously Acquired Tasks:
First Opportunity of the Day Probes

	Day/Date and First Opportunity of the Day Probe
	13 · 14 · 15 · 16 · 17 · 18 · 19 · 20 · 21 · 22 · More careful implementation of the Protocols
R11. Completes 10 consecutive, brief, previously acquired tasks	S M T W T F S S M T ...

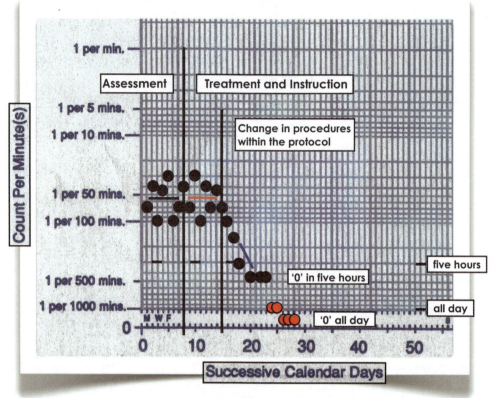

Table 21.
Problem Behavior 2 (**PB2**) and Requesting Preferred Items and Activities:
Deciding Whether to Continue Treatment Procedures or Make a Change

Table 22.
Problem Behavior 2 (**PB2**) and Requesting Preferred Items and Activities:
Deciding Whether to Continue Treatment Procedures or Make a Change

Preferred Items and Activities	Day/Date and First Opportunity of the Day Probe																			
	5	6	7	8	9	10	11	12	13	\multicolumn{9}{c	}{Change in procedures within the protocol}	24	25
	S	M	T	W	T	F	S	S	M	T	W	T	F	S	S	M	T	W	T	F	S
R6. 1- Cookies	Det NI <M 2P 2S Ind MP PP FP -NR -DC -SA 0	Det NI <M 2P 2S Ind MP PP FP -NR -DC (-SA) 0	Det NI <M 2P 2S Ind MP PP (FP) -(NR) -DC -SA 0	Det NI <M 2P 2S Ind MP (PP) FP -NR -DC -SA 0	Det NI <M 2P 2S Ind MP (PP) FP -NR -DC -SA 0	Det NI <M 2P 2S Ind MP PP (FP) -NR -DC -SA 0	Det NI <M 2P 2S Ind MP (PP) FP -NR -DC -SA 0	Det NI <M 2P 2S (Ind) MP PP FP -NR -DC -SA 0	Det NI <M 2P 2S (Ind) MP PP FP -NR -DC -SA 0	Det NI <M 2P (2S) (Ind) MP PP FP -NR -DC -SA 0	Det NI <M (2P) (2S) Ind MP PP FP -NR -DC -SA 0	Det NI <M (2P) (2S) Ind MP PP FP -NR -DC -SA 0	Det NI (<M) (2P) 2S Ind MP PP FP -NR -DC -SA 0	Det NI (<M) (2P) 2S Ind MP PP FP -NR -DC -SA 0	Det NI (<M) 2P 2S Ind MP PP FP -NR -DC -SA 0	Det NI (<M) (2P) 2S Ind MP PP FP -NR -DC -SA 0	Det NI (<M) 2P 2S Ind MP PP FP -NR -DC -SA 0	Det NI (<M) 2P 2S Ind MP PP FP -NR -DC -SA 0	Det NI <M 2P 2S Ind MP PP FP -NR -DC -SA 0	Det (NI) <M 2P 2S Ind MP PP FP -NR -DC -SA 0
R6. 2- Juice	Det NI <M 2P 2S Ind MP PP FP -NR -DC -SA 0	Det NI <M 2P 2S Ind MP PP FP (-NR) -DC -SA 0	Det NI <M 2P 2S Ind MP (PP) FP (-NR) -DC -SA 0	Det NI <M 2P 2S (Ind) MP (MP) PP FP -NR -DC -SA 0	Det NI <M 2P 2S (Ind) (MP) PP FP -NR -DC -SA 0	Det NI <M 2P 2S Ind (MP) PP FP -NR -DC -SA 0	Det NI <M 2P 2S (Ind) (MP) PP FP (-NR) -DC -SA 0	Det NI <M 2P 2S (Ind) MP PP FP -NR -DC -SA 0	Det NI <M 2P (2S) (Ind) (MP) PP FP -NR -DC -SA 0	Det NI <M 2P 2S (Ind) MP PP FP -NR -DC -SA 0	Det NI <M 2P 2S (Ind) MP PP FP -NR -DC -SA 0	Det NI <M 2P (2S) (Ind) MP (PP) FP -NR -DC -SA 0	Det NI <M (2P) 2S (Ind) MP PP FP -NR -DC -SA 0	Det NI (<M) 2P 2S Ind MP PP FP -NR -DC -SA 0	Det (NI) <M 2P 2S Ind MP PP FP -NR -DC -SA 0	Det (NI) <M 2P 2S Ind MP PP FP -NR -DC -SA 0	Det (NI) <M 2P 2S Ind MP PP FP -NR -DC -SA 0	Det NI <M 2P 2S Ind MP PP FP -NR -DC -SA 0	Det NI <M 2P 2S Ind MP PP FP -NR -DC -SA 0	Det NI <M 2P 2S Ind MP PP FP -NR -DC -SA 0

Continue using the teaching protocols until the problem behaviors have not occurred during the recording period for three consecutive days *and* the expected skills have occurred without prompts and without problem behavior for the same three days. Then, if the recording period is less than a day, extend these protocols to the entire day and, if possible, collect data for this entire period. If you are using a hand-drawn or computer-generated graph, you will need to draw a new graph, change the measure along the vertical axis, and perform a calculation on the existing data so that they are comparable with new data. If, on the other hand, you are using the Daily Standard Celeration Chart or the Adapted Daily Standard Celeration Chart, this will not be necessary. As shown in Table 21, when treatment is extended from five hours (300 minutes) per day to all day (16 hours or 1,000 minutes), these graphs will accommodate this new recording period and a new graph is not necessary (see the red data points).

As shown in Table 23, with Problem Behavior 1 (**PB1**) and Completing Consecutive, Brief, Previously Acquired Tasks (**R11**), when there are changes in the problem behaviors or in the performance level of the expected skills, record these changes on the **Assessment and Record of Progress (ARP)**. *If the problem behaviors begin to occur again or the expected skills occur inconsistently or not at all, return to the same protocols and procedures that resulted in their reduction or acquisition.*

Table 23.
When There are Changes in Problem Behaviors
or in the Performance Level of Expected Skills
Record These Changes on the ARP

ESSENTIAL FOR LIVING
Assessment and Record of Progress (ARP): Problem Behavior

PB1. Makes a fist with his right hand, repeatedly and rapidly brings his hand toward and makes contact with his head just above his right ear and does not make any of these movements for one minute

IA	IM		Instance	Episode		SIB	Agg	Des	Dis	Rep
								Sev	Mod	Mild
Med3+>	Med3+	Med3+<	Med2>	Med2	Med2<	Med1>	Med1	Med1<	-Med	
MRA	MRC		MR2>	MR1>	MR	MR1<	MR2<	MR3<	-MR	
PEA	PEC		PE2>	PE1>	PE	PE!<	PE2<	PE3<	-PE	
				CS>5hW	CS 2-5hW	CS 1-2hW	CS 30m-1hW	CS<30mW	-CS	
			SR2>	SR1>	SR	SR1<	SR2<	SR3<	-SR	
	>100D	50-100D	20-50D	10-20D	1-10D	<1D	<1W	<1M	<1Y	

R11. Completes 10 consecutive, brief, previously acquired tasks

IA	IM	1	2	5	10	Det

If this approach to the treatment of problem behavior does not result in a significant decrease in the frequency and intensity of specific problem behaviors, and a corresponding increase in the frequency and the size of the expected skill repertoires, even after several adjustments in teaching procedures, we recommend contacting a behavior analyst, who can assist with the conduct of a formal, functional assessment.

If the problem behaviors are not situation-specific, that is, they occur in many situations, and they frequently occur when the learner is alone, they may be a function of automatically-occurring sensory events. If you suspect that this is occurring, it is highly advisable to seek the assistance of a behavior analyst.

Chapter 11. Tool Skills and Component Skills

Basic gross and fine motor movements were originally described by Eric Haughton as *tool skills* (Haughton, 1980). Later, Kent Johnson and Joe Layng again described *tool skills, along with component skills* and *composite skills* (Johnson and Layng, 1992). Many of the functional communication and daily living skills in this instrument are composite skills, that is, skills that include many specific movements. For example, feeding yourself with an adapted teaspoon (**DLS-EDF-20**), removing socks from the dryer, folding them, and putting them in a drawer (**DLS-L10**), and making a request for candy (**R7**) are composite skills. Tool skills are basic motor movements, matching skills, or imitation skills, such as, '*grasping*', '*matching identical items*', and '*imitating hand movements*'. These skills are not functional in isolation, but are part of many functional daily living and communication skills. Component skills, on the other hand, tend to be part of specific composite skills. For example, '*grasping an adapted teaspoon*' is part of feeding yourself with an adapted teaspoon (**DLS-EDF-20**), '*matching pairs of socks*' is part of removing socks from the dryer, folding them, and putting them in a drawer (**DLS-L10**), and '*imitating someone make the standard sign for candy*' is part of making a request for candy (**R7**).

The acquisition of complex daily living and communication skills does not require the prior acquisition of either tool skills or component skills. If, however, some tool skills or component skills are taught until they occur without prompts and without hesitation, some of our learners will acquire composite skills with minimal or no instruction (Johnson and Layng, 1992; Binder, 1996). For example, if examples of '*matching items, activities, people, places, and locations to corresponding photographs*' or '*matching highly preferred items or activities to corresponding photographs*' are taught to some of our learners until these examples occur without prompts and without hesitation and their method of speaking includes selecting *photographs* (**AMS 9, 12, 15, 19, 22, 31, 36**), they may experience a rapid increase in the extent of their requesting repertoire with much less formal instruction.

> If, however, some tool or component skills are taught to fluency, some of our learners will acquire composite skills with minimal to no instruction.

In many early intervention programs, especially those for children with autism, basic gross and fine motor movements, along with matching and imitation skills, are emphasized from the beginning. Several of these tool skills are displayed in Table 1, along with examples of each skill often taught in these programs.

Table 1.
Tool Skills and Examples of Each Skill
Often Taught in Early intervention Programs

Tool Skill	Examples of Each Skill
grasping items	Theraputty tennis balls
matching identical items	laminated triangles square blocks
imitating motor movements with items	tapping a pencil on a table placing a spoon in a cup

Some younger learners acquire many examples of gross and fine motor movements, along with matching and imitation skills, and, after doing so, begin to experience the outcomes previously described. Many of our younger and older learners, however, even with extended practice on examples of these tool skills, do not achieve these outcomes. Instead, at best, they acquire a few examples of motor movements, matching skills, or imitation skills, such as those listed in Table 1. And, since these examples are not components of functional daily living or communication skills, they are not functional for these learners.

As a result, we recommend that examples of gross and fine motor movements, along with matching and imitation skills, are functional *from the beginning*. To ensure that this occurs, we strongly recommend waiting until the initial assessment of functional skills and problem behavior has been completed. Then, after selecting specific skills for instruction, instructors and care providers can set aside several composite skills. As shown in Table 2. they should determine if there are one or more tool skills that are part of each of these composite skills. Then, they should select corresponding component skills. For example, if **DLS-EDF-20**, '*feeding herself with an adapted teaspoon*', is indicated as a skill deficit for a specific learner during the assessment, and this skill is selected for instruction, '*grasping items*' can easily be identified as a tool skill and '*grasping an adapted teaspoon*' as a component skill. If **DLS-C12**, '*washes windows and mirrors*' is identified as a skill deficit and selected for instruction, an examination of Table 2, which includes the composite skill '*wiping a table*', suggests that '*imitating motor movements with items*' is a tool skill and '*imitating someone wiping a window with a towel*' is a component skill. Once these component skills are identified, instructors and care providers may decide to include them in a learner's instructional program prior to introducing the corresponding composite skill or while they are teaching this skill. Then, if learners acquire a few component skills, they may experience more rapid acquisition of the corresponding composite skills. At the very least, their repertoire will include part of several composite skills, which occur with demonstration prompts, which may be more easily faded than physical prompts.

Table 2.
Tool Skills and Component Skills
that are Part of Functional Composite Skills

Tool Skill	Component Skills	Functional Composite Skills
MM1. Reaching for a device or a person	reaching for the handle of a MOVE device or for a care provider's arm or hand	reaching for support while moving around or changing positions
MM2. Reaching for items	Reaching for items that are part of a snack or a meal	requesting preferred foods during a snack or a meal
MM3. Pointing toward items	Pointing to items that are part of making cookies	responding to "where's the mixing spoon" while making cookies
	Pointing to preferred items	indicating a preference for specific items
MM4. Touching a person	Touching a familiar person's hand	giving a 'high five'
MM5. Touching items	Touching a mixing spoon with an instructor	participating in making cookies by touching a mixing spoon as an instructor stirs the cookie dough
MM6. Grasping a person	Grasping a familiar person's arm or hand	leading someone to a preferred item
MM7. Grasping items	Grasping a spoon	feeding yourself with a spoon
MM8. Placing items in locations	Placing dishes, glasses, cups, utensils, and napkins at the appropriate places on the table	setting the table
MM9. Releasing your grasp of a person	Releasing a familiar person's arm or hand	letting go of someone's arm or hand after reaching a destination
MM10. Releasing your grasp of an item	Releasing clothes	putting dirty clothes in the hamper
MM11. Making and releasing contact with a switch	Activating a switch connected to a speech-generating device	requesting preferred items and activities
M1. Matching identical items	Matching pairs of socks	removing socks from the dryer, folding them, and putting them in a drawer
	Matching identical packages of cookies	stocking shelves in the grocery store
M2. Matching essential items to other items that are part of an activity	Matching a mop to a sink, liquid soap, and a bucket	mopping a floor

Table 2. (cont.)
Tool Skills and Component Skills
that are Part of Functional Composite Skills

Tool Skill	Component Skills	Functional Composite Skills
M3. Matching items to corresponding containers or locations	Matching dishes, glasses, cups, utensils, and napkins to their appropriate positions on the table	unloading the dishwasher and putting dishes, glasses, cups, utensils, and napkins in the cupboard and the drawer
	Matching your wallet and house key to your top dresser drawer	putting your wallet and house key away at night
M4. Matching containers or locations to corresponding items	Matching a specific drawer in the kitchen with dishes, glasses, cups, utensils, and napkins	retrieving dishes, glasses, cups, utensils, and napkins, and setting the table
	Matching a cookie jar with cookies'	retrieving cookies from the cookie jar
M5. Matching items with identical letters, numbers, shapes, sizes, configurations, or colors	Matching puzzle pieces with corresponding spaces	putting together a puzzle
	Matching playing cards or Uno cards	playing Go Fish, Hearts, or Uno
M6. Matching items with similar forms of the same letter or number, similar shapes, sizes, or configurations, or similar shades of color or the same color	Matching dark and light colored clothes	sorting clothes before putting them in the washing machine
	Matching various shades of blue socks	retrieving all your pairs of blue socks and selecting a dark blue pair to wear
M7. Matching items, activities, people, places, or locations to corresponding miniature items or iconic symbols	Matching preferred items, activities, people, places, or locations to corresponding miniature items or iconic symbols	scanning by touch and making requests by touching and briefly holding on to miniature items or iconic symbols
M8. Matching miniature items or iconic symbols to corresponding items, activities, people, places, or locations	Matching miniature items or iconic symbols to corresponding items, activities, people, places, and locations that a part of the learner's everyday experiences	using a tactile schedule to determine the next scheduled activity
M9. Matching identical photographs	Matching identical photographs of items, activities, places, or locations which designate a scheduled activity	using a picture schedule to locate corresponding work stations
M10. Matching items, activities, people, places, or locations to corresponding photographs	Matching preferred items, activities, people, places, or locations to corresponding photographs	visually scanning and making requests by selecting photographs of preferred items, activities, people, places, or locations
M11. Matching photographs to corresponding items, activities, people, places, or locations	Matching photographs to corresponding items, activities, people, places, or locations that a part of the learner's everyday experiences	using a picture schedule to determine the next scheduled activity and to assemble items necessary for that activity

Table 2. (cont.)
Tool Skills and Component Skills
that are Part of Functional Composite Skills

Tool Skill	Component Skills	Functional Composite Skills
M12. Matching text to corresponding items, activities, people, places, or locations	Matching printed words on a shopping list to items in a grocery store	looking at a list and retrieving items while grocery shopping
	Matching the sign MEN or WOMEN to a corresponding activity	entering the appropriate public restroom
	Matching printed words on a laminated placard on the bathroom wall to steps of brushing your teeth, washing your face, brushing your hair, and using deodorant	getting ready in the morning
	Matching printed words on a recipe to items and activities in the kitchen	assisting with cooking
	Matching text to an item or to an item that that is part of an activity	using a printed-word schedule to determine the next scheduled activity and to assemble items necessary for that activity
M13. Matching items, activities, people, places, or locations to corresponding text	Matching preferred items, activities, people, places, or locations to printed words	visually scanning and making requests by selecting printed words for preferred items, activities, people, places, or locations
Im1. Imitating motor movements	Imitating someone make the standard signs for preferred items, activities, people, places, and locations	making requests for preferred items, activities, people, places, and locations using standard signs
Im2. Imitating motor movements with items	Imitating someone placing a sponge under running water and squeeze it out	wiping a table
	Imitating someone operate a washing machine	operating a washing machine
	Imitating someone take liquid medication with an oral syringe	taking liquid medication with an oral syringe
	Imitating someone peel an orange	peeling an orange
	Imitating someone put their socks on	putting your socks on
	Imitating someone load the dishwasher	loading a dishwasher
	Imitating someone empty the trash	emptying the trash
Im3. Copying words written, typed, or Braille-written by another person	Copying words that are part of a shopping lists	making a shopping list

The tool skills in this domain are listed in the next section. Basic motor movements are designated as *should-have*, while matching and imitation skills are designated as *good-to-have and nice-to-have*. The *ARP* manual provides space for 10 component skills per tool skill. Some learners will not benefit from this many component skills.

As you will notice, the direction of the 'match' in non-identical matching skills, is specified. In other words, the skill and example specify the object with which the matching task begins. For instance, '*matching items, activities, people, places, or locations to corresponding photographs*' specifies that you begin with items, activities, people, places, or locations and match one or other of these to photographs, rather than beginning with photographs. This is necessary because, with many of our learners, examples of arbitrary matching skills that are acquired in one direction do not necessarily occur in the other without additional instruction.

acquired arbitrary matching skills do not always result in symmetry and the formation of equivalence classes.

ESSENTIAL FOR LIVING
Tool Skills and Component Skills

Should-have Basic Motor Movements. These gross and fine motor movements were originally described by Eric Haughton as the Big Six (Haughton, 1980) and, for some learners, are part of occupational or physical therapy. Teaching these movements as component skills, rather than simply as tools skills, insures that they are functional for the learner. Space is provided in the *ARP* for 10 component skills for **MM1-9** and 3 component skills for **MM10**, although some learners may not require this many examples.

- **MM1.** Reaches for a device or a person
- **MM2.** Reaches for items
- **MM3.** Points toward items
- **MM4.** Touches a person
- **MM5.** Touches items
- **MM6.** Grasps a person
- **MM7.** Grasps items
- **MM8.** Places items in locations
- **MM9.** Releases items after placing them in specific locations
- **MM10.** Releases someone's arm or hand
- **MM11.** Makes and releases contact with a switch

Additional Should-have Basic Motor Movements. With certain children and adults, you may want to select additional basic motor movements and designate these as must-have skills. This section permits you to do this.

- **MM11a.** _____
- **MM11b.** _____

Good-to-have Matching Skills. These matching skills include items, activities, people, places, locations, or photographs of the same, but do not include written words, typed words, or words written in Braille. Space is provided in the *ARP* for 10 examples of each skill, although learners may not require this many examples.

- **M1.** Matches identical items
- **M2.** Matches essential items to other items that are part of an activity
- **M3.** Matches items to corresponding containers or locations
- **M4.** Matches containers or locations to corresponding items
- **M5.** Matches items with identical letters, numbers, shapes, sizes, configurations, or colors
- **M6.** Matches items with similar forms of the same letter or number, similar shapes, sizes, or configurations, or similar shades of color or the same color
- **M7.** Matches items, activities, people, places, or locations to corresponding miniature items or iconic symbols
- **M8.** Matches miniature items or iconic symbols to corresponding activities
- **M9.** Matches identical photographs
- **M10.** Matches items, activities, people, places, or locations to corresponding photographs
- **M11.** Matches photographs to corresponding items, activities, people, places, or locations

Additional Good-to-have Matching Skills. With certain learners, you may want to select additional matching skills that do not include written words, typed words, or words written in Braille and designate these as must-have skills. This section permits you to do this.

M11a. _____

M11b. _____

Nice-to-have Matching Skills. These matching skills include items, activities, people, places, locations, *and* written words, typed words, or words written in Braille. Space is provided in the *ARP* for 10 examples of each skill, although some learners may not require this many examples.

M12.   Matches text to items, activities, people, places, or locations
M13.   Matches items, activities, people, places, or locations to text

Additional Nice-to-have Matching Skills. With certain children and adults, you may want to select additional matching skills that include written words, typed words, or words written in Braille and designate these as nice-to-have skills. This section permits you to do this.

M13a. _____

M13b. _____

Good-to-have Imitation Skills. The following imitation skills are considered good-to-have. These skills include finger, hand, and arm movements with and without items, but do not include copying written words, typed words, or words written in Braille. Space is provided in the *ARP* for 10 examples of each skill, although some learners may not require this many examples.

Im1.   Imitates motor movements
Im2.   Imitates motor movements with items

Additional Good-to-have Imitation Skills. With certain children and adults, you may want to select additional imitation skills that do not include copying written words, typed words, or words written in Braille. and designate these as good-to-have skills. This section permits you to do this.

Im2a. _____

Im2b. _____

Nice-to-have Imitation Skills. The following imitation skills are considered nice-to-have. These skills include copying letters and words written, typed, or Braille-written by another person. Space is provided in the *ARP* for 10 examples of each skill, although some learners may not require this many examples.

Im3.   Copies words written, typed, or Braille-written by another person   copying text

Additional Nice-to-have Imitation Skills. With certain children and adults, you may want to select additional imitation skills that do not include copying written words, typed words, or words written in Braille and designate these as nice-to-have skills. This section permits you to do this.

Im3a. _____

Im3b. _____

The Assessment of Tool Skills and Component Skills

After an initial assessment of functional skills and problem behavior for a specific learner has been completed, select specific skills for instruction and behaviors for management. Then consider setting aside several composite skills, determining if there are one or more appropriate tool skills, and selecting corresponding component skills for instruction. Then, list these component skills under the corresponding tool skills in the *Assessment and Record of Progress (ARP) manual*, assess the current performance level for each skill, and record these levels on the *ARP*. For example, if **DLS-RDA6,** 'retrieves dishes, glasses, cups, utensils, and napkins, and sets the table' is selected for instruction, select the tool skill **M4**, 'matches containers or other locations to corresponding items'. Then, select the component skill 'matches a specific drawer and cupboard in the kitchen with dishes, glasses, cups, utensils, and napkins', list this skill as an example of **M4**, assess the current performance level for that skill, and record this level on the *ARP* (see Tables 2 and 3).

Begin with tool skills designated as *should-have* and *good-to-have* (**MM1-11, M1-M11, Im1-2**) and corresponding component skills, as these skills are generally part of more functional composite skills, and record performance levels on the *ARP*. The performance levels for these skills are described in Table 3, along with sample skills from the *ARP*. Continue the assessment until the learner requires prompts, exhibits inappropriate responses, or responds with problem behavior on three consecutive component skills.

Table 3.
The Performance Levels for Basic Motor Movements, Matching Skills, and Imitation Skills

When directed to do so, learners make gross or fine motor movements, or when an item, photograph, symbol, text, person, place, or location is presented or encountered and learners make identical or arbitrary matches, or when a motor movement is exhibited by an instructor, parent, or care provider and learners make the same movement on three consecutive occasions...

IA	[the initial assessment of this skill has been completed]
IM	[instruction or management has begun]
-SA	without self-injurious, aggressive, or destructive behavior
-DC	without disruptive behavior or complaints
-RP	without resistance to prompts and without leaving the area
FP	with a full physical or full demonstration prompt
PP	with a partial physical or partial demonstration prompt
MP	with a minimal physical or minimal gestural prompt
Ind	without prompts, without scrolling, and without hesitation
Det	[the skill is no longer occurring consistently]

MM7. Grasps items

		IA	IM	-SA	-DC	-RP	FP	PP	MP	Ind	Det
1	stocking cap	IA	IM	-SA	-DC	-RP	FP	PP	MP	Ind	Det
2	handle on a back pack	IA	IM	-SA	-DC	-RP	FP	PP	MP	Ind	Det

MM11. Makes and releases contact with a switch

		IA	IM	-SA	-DC	-RP	FP	PP	MP	Ind	Det
1	moves the head to the left and makes and releases contact with a switch connected to a speech-generating device	IA	IM	-SA	-DC	-RP	FP	PP	MP	Ind	Det

M1. Matches identical Items

		IA	IM	-SA	-DC	-RP	FP	PP	MP	Ind	Det
1	pairs of socks	IA	IM	-SA	-DC	-RP	FP	PP	MP	Ind	Det
2	boxes of Cheerios	IA	IM	-SA	-DC	-RP	FP	PP	MP	Ind	Det

M4. Matches containers or other locations to corresponding items

		IA	IM	-SA	-DC	-RP	FP	PP	MP	Ind	Det
1	matches a specific drawer and cupboard in the kitchen with dishes, glasses, cups, utensils, and napkins	IA	IM	-SA	-DC	-RP	FP	PP	MP	Ind	Det
2	_____	IA	IM	-SA	-DC	-RP	FP	PP	MP	Ind	Det

Im2. Imitates motor movements with items

		IA	IM	-SA	-DC	-RP	FP	PP	MP	Ind	Det
1	wiping a table with a rag	IA	IM	-SA	-DC	-RP	FP	PP	MP	Ind	Det
2	turning the cap on a jar of peanut butter	IA	IM	-SA	-DC	-RP	FP	PP	MP	Ind	Det

Teaching Tool Skills and Component Skills

Component skills can be taught prior to introducing the corresponding composite skills or at the same time these skills are being taught. For example, **M1.** -- 1. 'matching pairs of socks' can be taught separately at another time during the day or at the same time as **DLS-L10**, 'removes clothes from the dryer and folds towels, socks, underwear, pants, shirts, blouses, and sweaters, and puts them in the proper closet or drawer'.

We suggest using Teaching Protocol 7, which is described in chapter 12. Collect data several times each week, or daily, if possible, using single-trial probes and the *Skill Acquisition Self-graphing Data Recording Form* described in chapter 4 and shown in Table 4. This probe data sheet for basic motor movements, matching skills, and imitation skills can be downloaded from www.behaviorchange.com.

As the learner achieves specific performance levels, transfer this information to the *ARP* (see Table 5). If improvement in the level of performance for any example of these skills does not occur, as shown in Table 4, make certain that you follow the steps exactly as they are described in Teaching Protocol 7, and, as necessary, make adjustments in this protocol.

Table 4.
Recording the Learner's Progress on Skills Selected for Instruction
Using Single-trial Probe Data and Probe Data Sheets

ESSENTIAL FOR LIVING
Skill Acquisition Probe Data Sheet
Matching: First Opportunity of the Day Probes

Matching Task and Example	Day/Date and First Opportunity of the Day Probe																
	13	14	15	16	17	18	19	20	21	22	23	24	25	26	27	28	29
	S	M	T	W	T	F	S	S	M	T	W	T	F	S	S	M	T
M1. 1- Socks	Det Ind MP PP (FP) -RP -DC -SA 0	Det Ind MP PP FP (-RP) -DC -SA 0	Det Ind MP PP FP (-RP) -DC -SA 0	Det Ind MP PP (FP) -RP -DC -SA 0	Det Ind MP PP (FP) -RP -DC -SA 0	Det Ind MP PP FP -RP -DC -SA 0	Det Ind MP (PP) FP -RP -DC -SA 0	Det Ind MP PP (FP) -RP -DC -SA 0	Det Ind MP PP (FP) -RP -DC -SA 0	Det Ind MP (PP) FP -RP -DC -SA 0	Det Ind MP (PP) FP -RP -DC -SA 0	Det Ind MP (PP) FP -RP -DC -SA 0	Det Ind MP PP (FP) -RP -DC -SA 0	Det Ind MP (PP) FP -RP -DC -SA 0	Det Ind MP PP (FP) -RP -DC -SA 0	Det Ind MP (PP) FP -RP -DC -SA 0	Det Ind MP PP FP -RP -DC -SA 0

Table 5.
Transferring Data from Probe Data Sheets to the Assessment and Record of Progress

M1. Matching Identical Items

1 socks _____ | IA | IM | -SA | -DC | -RP | FP | PP | MP | Ind | Det |

Chapter 12. Teaching Protocols

This chapter includes teaching protocols for each of the *Essential Eight* skills, along with listener responses in the form of recognitions, retrievals, and relocations, and corresponding names, descriptions, and answers to questions. These protocols include teaching procedures that have been validated in the scientific literature. It is generally advisable to follow these protocols *exactly as they are written without additions, deletions, or substitutions* until data suggest that alternative procedures may be necessary.

ESSENTIAL FOR LIVING

Teaching Protocol 1. Making Requests (**R7-8**, **R14**, **R17-21**)
[this protocol includes the echoic-to-request teaching procedure and can be used with any skill that includes making requests]

the echoic-to-mand transfer procedure

What to Do	What Not to Do
1. Make items and activities available that are highly preferred; wait for the learner to indicate by gesturing what he 'wants' at that moment; proceed to step 2 or 3	
2. For learners aligned with Vocal Profiles 1 or 2 (i.e., learners who reliably repeat spoken words) immediately provide an echoic prompt -- say the word or phrase that corresponds to the item or activity the learner wants (e.g., "cookie"); if a learner's repetitions are controlled, also provide a vocal cue to do so (e.g., "say, (pause) cookie") For learners who use an alternative method of speaking, provide an immediate full demonstration prompt or a full physical prompt of the sign, picture or word selection, or typed word until the learner makes the appropriate response; then, proceed to step 4	2. Say part of the word or phrase, or provide a partial demonstration or partial physical prompt
3. If the learner makes the appropriate response several consecutive times, begin to fade the prompts; fade echoic prompts all-at-once, fade demonstration prompts all-at-once or gradually, and fade full physical prompts gradually; proceed to step 4	
4. If the learner exhibits the appropriate word, forms the appropriate sign, selects the appropriate picture or printed word, or types the appropriate word, say the word and provide access to the requested item or activity; if a learner who uses an alternative method of speaking, says part or all of the word, provide an additional amount or duration of the item or activity; proceed to steps 1 and 3 until all prompts have been completely faded; continue returning to step1 until the learner is making 10 requests from **R7**, **R8**, **R14**, and **R17-21**	
5. If the learner makes several additional responses (scrolls), return to step 2 or 3 and provide a prompt until only the appropriate response occurs	
6. If problem behaviors occur, manually interrupt them or wait until they are no longer occurring; then, wait an additional period of time specific to each learner, ranging from 5 seconds to several minutes; if problem behaviors occur during this period of time, restart the time period and continue until these behaviors no longer occur during the entire period of time; then, proceed to step 1	6. Provide access to the requested item or activity, talk with the learner or acknowledge what he is doing, or permit him to engage in other activities

1. Capture or contrive a motivating operation (MO) related to a targeted mand
2. Prompt a vocal-verbal mand using an errorless echoic prompt; or prompt a sign or a selection mand using an errorless, full demonstration or full physical prompt; do not use partial echoic prompts; do not begin with partial demonstration or partial physical prompts; proceed to step 4
3. If the learner makes the appropriate response several consecutive times, fade an echoic prompt by time delay, a demonstration prompt by topography or time delay, or a physical prompt by topography and proceed to step 4
4. If the learner makes the appropriate response, say the word and provide access to the requested item or activity; if a learner who uses an alternative response form, exhibits the word or an approximation, provide an additional amount or duration of the item or activity; proceed to steps 1 and 3 until all prompts have been faded; continue returning to step1 until the learner is making 10 requests from **R7**, **R8**, **R14**, and **R17-21**
5. If the learner scrolls or does not make the appropriate response, return to step 2 or 3 and provide an errorless prompt
6. If problem behaviors occur, provide continuous, response interruption or social extinction until these behaviors have not occurred for a few seconds; implement a brief timeout from all preferred items and activities and all forms of attention and recycle this procedure if problem behaviors occur; then, proceed to step 1

ESSENTIAL FOR LIVING

Teaching Protocol 1a. Encouraging the Occurrence of Sounds, Spoken Words, and Repetitions [this protocol includes pairing vocalizations with highly preferred items and activities]

Stimulus-stimulus Pairing

What to Do	What Not to Do	
1. If the learner exhibits spoken words, sounds, or word approximations, provide immediate access to specific, highly preferred items and activities; if words, sounds, or word approximations seldom occur, proceed to step 2; if the learner begins exhibiting words frequently, proceed to step 4		1. If spoken words or word approximations occur, provide immediate access to specific, highly preferred items and activities; if words or word approximations seldom occur, proceed to step 2; if words are occurring frequently, proceed to step 4
2. Provide the learner with access to one or two highly preferred items or activities; at the same time, say the word or sounds that are part of the word; do this often throughout the day;	2. Withhold access to the items or activities if the learner does not say the word or sounds that are part of the word	2. Use the stimulus-stimulus pairing procedure many times throughout the day
3. If the learner exhibits a spoken word or one or more sounds that are part of a word, say the word or sound(s), and proceed to step 1		3. If a spoken word or word approximation occurs, proceed to step 1
4. When the learner approaches a preferred item or activity and says the corresponding word, say the same word; if the learner repeats the word, provide immediate access to a larger amount or longer duration of the preferred item or activity; if the learner does not repeat the word, provide immediate access to a smaller amount or shorter duration of the preferred item or activity; continue with this step until the learner exhibits these repetitions with words containing many different sounds		4. When the learner approaches a preferred item or activity and says the corresponding word, say the same word; if the learner exhibits a spoken-word echoic response, provide immediate access to a larger amount or longer duration of the preferred item or activity; if the learner does not exhibit this response, provide immediate access to a smaller amount or shorter duration of the preferred item or activity; continue with this step until the learner exhibits these spoken-word echoic responses with words containing many different sounds

ESSENTIAL FOR LIVING

Teaching Protocol 2. Waiting After Making Requests (**R9**) [this protocol can also be used with **R25**]

What to Do	What Not to Do	
1. Require the learner to wait for 1-2 seconds after making requests and complete other required activities, and gradually, but in an indistinguishable pattern, increase this period of time		1. Begin with brief periods of waiting; use a gradually increasing variable schedule of stimulus fading to increase the duration of the waiting period
2. When the learner makes a request for a preferred item or activity, direct the learner to "wait" for a specific period of time	2. Repeat the direction or indicate the required period of waiting	2. Provide one cue to 'wait' and do not indicate the requirement for reinforcement
3. If the learner waits for the required period of time and completes other required activities, provide praise and the preferred item or activity for which he was waiting; continue returning to step 1 until the learner has waited for 10 of the items and activities in **R7** and **R8** for 20 minutes		3. If the learner waits for the required period of time, provide differential reinforcement in the form of praise and the item or activity for which he was waiting; continue returning to step 1 until the learner has waited for 10 of the items and activities in **R7** and **R8** for 20 minutes
4. If problem behaviors occur, manually interrupt them or wait until they are no longer occurring; then, wait an additional period of time specific to each learner, ranging from 5 seconds to several minutes; if problem behaviors occur during this period of time, restart the time period and continue until these behaviors no longer occur during the entire period of time; then, proceed to step 2 and the same required period of waiting	4. Provide access to the item or activity for which he is waiting, talk with the learner or acknowledge what he is doing, or permit him to engage in other activities	4. If problem behaviors occur, provide continuous, response interruption or social extinction until these behaviors have not occurred for a few seconds; implement a brief timeout from all preferred items and activities and all forms of attention and recycle this procedure if problem behaviors occur, proceed to step 2 and use escape extinction

ESSENTIAL FOR LIVING

Teaching Protocol 3. Accepting the Removal of Access to Preferred Items and Activities by Persons in Authority, Sharing, Taking Turns, and Making Transitions (**R10**, **R12**, and **R13**)
[this protocol can be modified slightly and used with **R46**]

What to Do	What Not to Do	
1. When the learner is interacting with a preferred item or activity, either of two people in authority should direct him to relinquish access to this item or activity and (1) accept its removal by continuing to make other required responses (**R10**), (2) share or take turns with the item or activity (**R12**), or (3) make a transition to a required activity (**R13**); then, proceed to step 2	1. Indicate when access or sole access to the item or activity will be restored	1. Provide one cue to relinquish the item or activity and proceed to step 2
2. Provide an immediate gestural or a full physical prompt until the learner relinquishes access to the item or activity, and makes one of the appropriate responses described in step 1; then, proceed to step 4	2. Use prompts that do not result in one of the appropriate responses	2. Provide an errorless gestural or full physical prompt and proceed to step 4
3. If the learner exhibits one of the skills described in step 1 several consecutive times, begin to fade the prompts gradually and proceed to step 4		3. If the learner exhibits one of the skills described in step1 several consecutive times, fade the gestural or physical prompts by topography and proceed to step 4
4. If the learner exhibits one of the skills described in step 1, provide praise; proceed to steps 1 and 3 until all prompts have been completely faded; then, gradually provide praise less and less often; continue returning to step 1 until the learner has exhibited all three skills with 10 of the items and activities in **R7** and **R8**	4. Provide an opportunity for the learner to make a request for a different item or activity	4. If the learner exhibits one of the skills described in step1, provide praise and proceed to steps 1 and 3 until all prompts have been faded; then, gradually move praise to a VR5 schedule; continue returning to step 1 until the learner has exhibited all three skills with 10 of the items and activities in **R7** and **R8**
5. If problem behaviors occur, manually interrupt them or wait until they are no longer occurring; if the learner makes requests for the removed item or activity, makes requests for other items or activities, or resists prompts, wait until these behaviors are no longer occurring; then, wait an additional period of time specific to each learner, ranging from 5 seconds to several minutes; if the aforementioned behaviors occur during this period of time, restart the time period and continue until these behaviors no longer occur during the entire period of time; then, proceed to step 1 with the same item or activity	5. Talk with the learner, acknowledge what he is doing, permit him to engage in other activities, or provide praise or an opportunity to request the preferred item or activity	5. If problem behaviors or other inappropriate behaviors occur, provide continuous, response interruption or social extinction until these behaviors have not occurred for a few seconds; implement a brief timeout from all preferred items and activities and all forms of attention and recycle this procedure if problem behaviors occur; then, proceed to step 1 and use escape extinction

ESSENTIAL FOR LIVING

Teaching Protocol 4. Completing 10 Consecutive, Brief, Previously Acquired Tasks **(R11)**
[this protocol can also be used with **R29**]

What to Do	What Not to Do	
1. Require the learner to complete a few consecutive, brief, previously acquired tasks that require very little effort; gradually, but in an indistinguishable pattern, increase the number of consecutive tasks that are required, the duration of each task, and the effort that each task requires		1. Begin with a few brief tasks with minimal response cost, which the learner has previously completed without prompts; use a gradually increasing variable schedule of stimulus fading to increase the number of consecutive tasks required, along with the duration and response cost of each task
2. Direct the learner to complete a specific number of consecutive tasks	2. Repeat the directions	2. Direct the learner to complete a specific number of consecutive tasks, providing only one cue to do so
3. If the learner completes the required number of consecutive tasks, provide praise and an opportunity to request a preferred item or activity; proceed to step 2; then, gradually provide praise and an opportunity to make a request less and less often; continue returning to step 2 until the learner completes 20 consecutive tasks		3. If the learner completes the required number of tasks, provide reinforcement in the form of praise and an opportunity to mand; then, gradually move both to a VR5 schedule
4. If problem behavior or complaining occurs, or the learner does not complete the required number of consecutive tasks; manually interrupt the behavior or wait until it is no longer occurring; then, repeat step 2 with the same set of tasks	4. Talk with the learner, acknowledge what he is doing, permit him to engage in other activities, or provide praise or an opportunity to request a preferred item or activity	4. If problem behavior or complaining occurs, or the learner does not complete the required number of consecutive tasks, provide continuous, response interruption or social extinction until these behaviors have not occurred for a few seconds; then, repeat step 2 and use escape extinction

ESSENTIAL FOR LIVING

Teaching Protocol 5. Accepting 'No' (**R15** and **R16**)
[this protocol can also be used with **R26, R32, R40,** and **R42**]

What to Do	What Not to Do	
1. Require the learner to 'accept no' after making requests for items and activities in **R7, R8,** and **R14** that can be honored; also, require the learner to 'accept no' after making requests for potentially dangerous items and activities		1. Begin requiring the learner to 'accept no' after mands for items and activities that can be honored; also require the learner to 'accept no' after mands for potentially dangerous items and activities
2. When the learner makes a request for a specific item or activity from **R7, R8,** or **R14** or for a dangerous item and activity, say "no" and deny this request;	2. Repeat the direction or indicate when the request from **R7, R8,** or **R14** that was denied will be honored again	2. Provide one cue -- 'no' -- and do not indicate when a mand for the requested item or activity will be honored again
3. If the learner 'accepts no' by continuing to make other required responses, provide praise; then, gradually provide praise less and less often; continue returning to step 1 until the learner has accepted 'no' for 10 of the items and activities in **R7, R8,** and **R14** and for other dangerous items and activities	3. Provide an opportunity for the learner to make a request for a different item or activity	3. If the learner 'accepts no' by continuing to make other required responses, provide praise; then, gradually move praise to a VR5 schedule; continue returning to step 1 until the learner has accepted 'no' for 10 of the items and activities in **R7, R8,** and **R14** and for other dangerous items and activities
4. If problem behaviors occur, manually interrupt them or wait until they are no longer occurring; if the learner repeats the original request, makes requests for 'when' or 'later', makes requests for other items or activities, or resists prompts, wait until these behaviors are no longer occurring; then, wait an additional period of time specific to each learner, ranging from 5 seconds to several minutes; if the aforementioned behaviors occur during this period of time, restart the time period and continue until these behaviors no longer occur during the entire period of time; then, proceed to step 1 with the same item or activity	4. Talk with the learner, acknowledge what he is doing, permit him to engage in other activities, or provide praise or an opportunity to request a preferred item or activity	4. If problem behaviors or other inappropriate behaviors occur, provide continuous, response interruption or social extinction until these behaviors have not occurred for a few seconds; implement a brief timeout from all preferred items and activities and all forms of attention and recycle this procedure if problem behaviors occur; then, proceed to step 2 and use escape extinction

ESSENTIAL FOR LIVING

Teaching Protocol 6. Following Directions Related to Safety (**LR1-11**)
[this protocol or a slight modification thereof can also be used with **LR12-17** and many other listener responses]

What to Do	What Not to Do	
1. Require the learner to follow directions to make specific responses related to safety (**LR1-11**)		1. Require the learner to follow 11 directions related to safety (**R1-11**)
2. Direct the learner to make a specific response (one of the responses specified in **LR1-11**)	2. Repeat the direction	2. Provide one cue to follow a direction and make a specific response
3. Provide an immediate full demonstration prompt or a full physical prompt until the learner makes the appropriate response; then, proceed to step 5	3. Begin with partial demonstration or partial physical prompts	3. Provide an errorless, full demonstration or full physical prompt; do not begin with partial demonstration or partial physical prompts; proceed to step 5
4. If the learner exhibits the appropriate response several consecutive times, fade demonstration prompts all-at-once or gradually, or full physical prompts gradually; then, proceed to step 5		4. If the learner exhibits the appropriate response several consecutive times, fade a demonstration prompt by time delay or topography or a physical prompt by topography; then, proceed to step 5
5. If the learner follows the direction and exhibits the appropriate response, provide praise and an opportunity to request a preferred item or activity; then, gradually provide both less and less often; continue until the learner follows all 11 directions and exhibits the appropriate responses (**LR1-11**) without prompts		5. If the learner follows the direction and completes the task, provide reinforcement in the form of praise and an opportunity to mand; then, gradually move both to a VR5 schedule
6. If problem behavior or complaining occurs, or the learner does not follow the direction, manually interrupt the behavior or wait until it is no longer occurring; then, repeat step 2 with the same direction	6. Talk with the learner, acknowledge what he is doing, permit him to engage in other activities, or provide praise or an opportunity to request a preferred item or activity	6. If problem behavior or complaining occurs, or the learner does not follow the direction, provide continuous, response interruption or social extinction until these behaviors have not occurred for a few seconds; then, repeat step 2 and use escape extinction

ESSENTIAL FOR LIVING

Teaching Protocol 7. Completing Single-Response Daily Living Skills Related to Health and Safety
(**DLS-EDF1-9, DLS-Slp1-2, DLS-MT1-5, DLS-AHS1-15, DLS-HS1-8**)
Basic Motor Movements, Matching Skills, and Imitation Skills
[this protocol can be used with most single-response daily living skills and most component skills]

What to Do	What Not to Do	
1. Require the learner to begin and complete daily living skills that are composed of single responses		1. Require the learner to begin and complete single-response daily living skills
2. Select a single-response daily living skill		2. Select a single-response daily living skill
3. Arrange the setting so that it closely resembles what is typically present just before the learner is required to perform the single-response skill	3. Provide directions to begin exhibiting the skill or to make a specific response	3. Arrange stimuli in the environment that could and should become discriminative for the targeted single-response, daily living skill
4. Provide an immediate full demonstration prompt or a full physical prompt until the learner begins and completes the skill; then, proceed to step 6	4. Begin with partial demonstration or partial physical prompts	4. Provide an errorless, full demonstration or full physical prompt; do not begin with partial demonstration or partial physical prompts; proceed to step 6
5. If the learner exhibits the skill several consecutive times, fade demonstration prompts all-at-once or gradually, or full physical prompts gradually; then, proceed to step 6		5. If the learner exhibits the skill several consecutive times, fade a demonstration prompt by time delay or topography or a physical prompt by topography; then, proceed to step 6
6. If the learner exhibits the skill, provide praise and an opportunity to request a preferred item or activity; if the skill can and often is repeated many times in succession, proceed to step 3; if not, as soon as possible, return to this skill and steps 3-6 until all prompts have been completely faded and the learner exhibits the skill without hesitation; then, gradually provide praise and an opportunity to make a request less and less often		6. If the learner exhibits the skill, provide reinforcement in the form of praise and an opportunity to mand; if the skill can and often is repeated many times in succession, proceed to step 3; if not, as soon as possible, return to this skill and steps 3-6 until all prompts have been completely faded and the learner exhibits the skill at a fluent level; then, gradually move praise and an opportunity to mand to a VR5 schedule
7. If problem behaviors occur, manually interrupt them or wait until they are no longer occurring; then, repeat step 3	7. Provide access to a preferred item or activity, talk with the learner or acknowledge what he is doing, or permit him to engage in other activities	7. If problem behaviors occur, provide continuous, response interruption or social extinction until these behaviors have not occurred for a few seconds; implement a brief timeout from all preferred items and activities and all forms of attention and recycle this procedure if problem behaviors occur; then, repeat step 3 and use escape extinction

ESSENTIAL FOR LIVING

Teaching Protocol 7a. Completing Multiple-Response Daily Living Skills Related to Health and Safety (**DLS-EDF1-9**, **DLS-Slp1-2**, **DLS-MT1-5**, **DLS-AHS1-15**, **DLS-HS1-8**)
[this protocol includes teaching one response at a time beginning   Forward Chaining with the first response; it can be used with most multiple-response daily living skills]

	What to Do	What Not to Do
1.	Require the learner to complete daily living skills that are composed of multiple responses (**MR**)	
2.	Select a multiple-response daily living skill and divide this skill into a sequence of specific responses or select a sequence that has already been developed (see the Murdoch Center Program Library)	
3.	Decide which of three teaching procedures to use: (a) teach one response at a time from the begin-ning of the sequence, (b) teach one response at a time from the end of the sequence, or (c) teach all responses at the same time	
4.	If you chose procedure (a), arrange the setting so that it closely resembles what is typically present just before the learner is required to perform the skill; or, wait until the learner makes the first response and all subsequent responses in the sequence he has already learned to make	4. Provide directions to begin exhibiting the skill or to make a specific response
5.	Provide an immediate full demonstration prompt or full physical prompt until the learner makes the first response in the sequence or the first response he has not learned to make; proceed to step 7;	5. Begin with partial demonstration or partial physical prompts; use spoken-word prompts
6.	If the learner makes the appropriate response several consecutive times, fade demonstration prompts all-at-once or gradually, or full physical prompts gradually; then, proceed to step 7	
7.	If the learner makes the appropriate response, provide very brief praise and immediately guide the learner through the next response and the remainder of the responses in the sequence; then, as soon as possible, return to this skill, this response, and steps 4-6 until all prompts have been completely faded; continue until the learner makes the entire sequence of responses without prompts and without hesitation	
8.	If problem behaviors occur, manually interrupt them or wait until they are no longer occurring; then, begin again with step 4	8. Provide access to a preferred item or activity, talk with the learner or acknowledge what he is doing, or permit him to engage in other activities

1. Require the learner to complete multiple-response daily living skills
2. Select a multiple-response daily living skill and perform or select a task analysis for that skill
3. Decide whether to use forward, backward, or total task chaining
4. Use forward chaining; arrange stimuli in the environment or wait for the learner's responses to occasion stimuli that could become discriminative for responses that are part of the targeted daily living skill
5. Provide an errorless, full demonstration or full physical prompt; do not begin with partial demonstration or partial physical prompts; *do not use vocal-verbal prompts*
6. If the learner makes the appropriate response several consecutive times, fade a demonstration prompt by time delay or topography or a physical prompt by topography; then, proceed to step 7
7. If the learner makes the appropriate response, provide brief praise and guide the learner through the next response and the remainder of the responses in the sequence; then, as soon as possible, return to this skill, this response, and steps 4-6 until all prompts have been completely faded; continue until the learner exhibits the entire skill at a fluent level
8. If problem behaviors occur, provide continuous, response interruption or social extinction until these behaviors have not occurred for a few seconds; implement a brief timeout from all preferred items and activities and all forms of attention and recycle this procedure if problem behaviors occur; then, repeat step 4 and use escape extinction

ESSENTIAL FOR LIVING

Teaching Protocol 7b. Completing Multiple-Response Daily Living Skills Related to Health and Safety (**DLS-EDF1-9, DLS-Slp1-2, DLS-MT1-5, DLS-AHS1-15, DLS-HS1-8**)
[this protocol includes teaching one response at a time beginning   Backward Chaining with the last response; it can be used with most multiple-response daily living skills]

What to Do	What Not to Do	
1. Require the learner to complete daily living skills that are composed of multiple responses (**MR**)		1. Require the learner to complete multiple-response daily living skills
2. Select a multiple-response daily living skill and divide this skill into a sequence of specific responses or select a sequence that has already been developed (see the Murdoch Center Program Library)		2. Select a multiple-response daily living skill and perform or select a task analysis for that skill
3. Decide which of three teaching procedures to use: (a) teach one response at a time from the begin-ning of the sequence, (b) teach one response at a time from the end of the sequence, or (c) teach all responses at the same time		3. Decide whether to use forward, backward, or total task chaining
4. If you chose procedure (b), arrange the setting so that it closely resembles what is typically present just before the learner is required to perform the last response in the sequence or the last response in the sequence he has not learned to make, or guide the learner through the task until you reach that response	4. Provide directions to begin exhibiting the skill or to make a specific response	4. Use backward chaining; arrange stimuli in the environment, guide the learner, or wait for the learner's responses to occasion stimuli that could become discriminative for responses that are part of the targeted daily living skill
5. Provide an immediate full demonstration prompt or full physical prompt until the learner makes the last response in the sequence or the last response in the sequence he has not learned to make; proceed to step 7	5. Begin with partial demonstration or partial physical prompts; use spoken-word prompts	5. Provide an errorless, full demonstration or full physical prompt; do not begin with partial demonstration or partial physical prompts; *do not use vocal-verbal prompts*
6. If the learner makes the appropriate response several consecutive times, fade demonstration prompts all-at-once or gradually, or full physical prompts gradually; then, proceed to step 7		6. If the learner makes the appropriate response several consecutive times, fade a demonstration prompt by time delay or topography or a physical prompt by topography; then, proceed to step 7
7. If the learner makes the appropriate response, provide very brief praise and permit the learner to make the next response and the remainder of the responses in the sequence; then, as soon as possible, return to this skill, this response, and steps 4-6 until all prompts have been completely faded; continue until the learner makes the entire sequence of responses without prompts and without hesitation		7. If the learner makes the appropriate response, provide brief praise and permit the learner to make the next response and the remainder of the responses in the sequence; then, as soon as possible, return to this skill, this response, and steps 4-6 until all prompts have been completely faded; continue until the learner exhibits the entire skill at a fluent level
8. If problem behaviors occur, manually interrupt them or wait until they are no longer occurring; then, begin again with step 4	8. Provide access to a preferred item or activity, talk with the learner or acknowledge what he is doing, or permit him to engage in other activities	8. If problem behaviors occur, provide continuous, response interruption or social extinction until these behaviors have not occurred for a few seconds; implement a brief timeout from all preferred items and activities and all forms of attention and recycle this procedure if problem behaviors occur; then, repeat step 4 and use escape extinction

ESSENTIAL FOR LIVING

Teaching Protocol 7c. Completing Multiple-Response (**MR**) Daily Living Skills Related to Health and Safety (**DLS-EDF1-9, DLS-Slp1-2, DLS-MT1-5, DLS-AHS1-15, DLS-HS1-8**)
[this protocol includes *teaching all responses at the same time*; *Total Task Chaining* it can be used with most multiple-response daily living skills]

What to Do	What Not to Do	
1. Require the learner to complete daily living skills that are composed of multiple responses (**MR**)		1. Require the learner to complete multiple-response daily living skills
2. Select a multiple-response daily living skill and divide this skill into a sequence of specific responses or select a sequence that has already been developed (see the Murdoch Center Program Library)		2. Select a multiple-response daily living skill and perform or select a task analysis for that skill
3. Decide which of three teaching procedures to use: (a) teach one response at a time from the beginning of the sequence, (b) teach one response at a time from the end of the sequence, or (c) teach all responses at the same time		3. Decide whether to use forward, backward, or total task chaining
4. If you chose procedure (c), arrange the setting so that it closely resembles what is typically present just before the learner is required to perform the skill and/or wait until the learner hesitates before making a response in the sequence; then, proceed to step 5	4. Provide directions to begin exhibiting the skill or to make a specific response	4. Use total task chaining; arrange stimuli in the environment and/or wait for the learner's responses to occasion stimuli that could become discriminative for responses that are part of the targeted daily living skill
5. Provide an immediate full demonstration prompt or full physical prompt until the learner makes the first response in the sequence or the first response he has not learned to make; proceed to step 7;	5. Begin with partial demonstration or partial physical prompts; *use spoken-word prompts*	5. Provide an errorless, full demonstration or full physical prompt; do not begin with partial demonstration or partial physical prompts; *do not use vocal-verbal prompts*
6. If the learner makes the appropriate response several consecutive times, fade demonstration prompts all-at-once or gradually, or full physical prompts gradually; then, proceed to step 7		6. If the learner makes the appropriate response several consecutive times, fade a demonstration prompt by time delay or topography or a physical prompt by topography; then, proceed to step 7
7. If the learner makes the appropriate response, provide very brief praise and permit the learner to make the next response and the remainder of the responses in the sequence; then, as soon as possible, return to this skill, responses that require prompts, and steps 4-6 until all prompts with these responses have been completely faded; continue until the learner makes the entire sequence of responses without prompts and without hesitation		7. If the learner makes the appropriate response, provide brief praise and permit the learner to make the next response and the remainder of the responses in the sequence; then, as soon as possible, return to this skill, responses that require prompts, and steps 4-6 until all prompts with these responses have been completely faded; continue until the learner exhibits the entire skill at a fluent level
8. If problem behaviors occur, manually interrupt them or wait until they are no longer occurring; then, begin again with step 4	8. Provide access to a preferred item or activity, talk with the learner or acknowledge what he is doing, or permit him to engage in other activities	8. If problem behaviors occur, provide continuous, response interruption or social extinction until these behaviors have not occurred for a few seconds; implement a brief timeout from all preferred items and activities and all forms of attention and recycle this procedure if problem behaviors occur; then, repeat step 4 and use escape extinction

ESSENTIAL FOR LIVING

Teaching Protocol 8. Tolerating Situations Related to Health and Safety
(**T-BHI-5, T-EDF1-11, T-DM1-9, T-Slp1-5, T-Toil1-5, T-PRM1-6, T-PTA1-11, T-PEMR1-10, T-BPH1-8, T-DD1**)
[this protocol includes desensitization procedures and can be used with most tolerating skills]

Systematic Desensitization

What to Do	What Not to Do
1. Require the learner to tolerate targeted unpleasant situations	
2. Select a specific unpleasant situation; make a list of approximations to this situation; this list should begin with distant approximations of that would not result in anxious or problem behavior and end with the targeted unpleasant situation as it occurs in everyday living; then, proceed to step 3	
3. Expose the learner to (1) the most distant approximation on the list, (2) the most distant approximation to which he has not been exposed, or (3) the closest approximation in response to which he has remained calm; at the same time, provide the learner with a highly preferred item; then, proceed to step 4	3. Distract the learner during the exposure
4. If the learner responds to an approximation in a calm manner without problem behavior, provide praise and an opportunity to request more of the highly preferred item that was paired with this approximation; then, as soon as possible, return to step 3	
5. If the learner responds to an approximation in a calm manner without problem behavior on three consecutive exposures, return to step 3 and expose the learner to a closer approximation that is next on the list and continue in this manner until the learner has been exposed to the targeted unpleasant situation and has responded in a calm manner without problem behavior on three consecutive exposures	
6. If problem behavior occurs, discontinue the exposure and remain with the learner until he is calm; then, return to step 3 and expose the learner to a more distant approximation that is unlikely to result in problem behavior	

1. Require the learner to tolerate stimuli related to his health and safety
2. Select an aversive stimulus and construct a stimulus hierarchy
3. Use systematic desensitization: gradually expose the learner to closer approximations to the aversive stimulus, while pairing these exposures with a highly preferred item
4. If the learner remains calm and does not exhibit problem behavior, provide differential reinforcement in the form of praise and an opportunity to mand for the highly preferred item that accompanied exposure to the stimulus
5. If the learner remains calm and does not exhibit problem behavior on three consecutive exposures, return to step 3 and expose the learner to a closer approximation that is next on the list and continue in this manner until the learner has been exposed to the targeted aversive stimulus and has responded in a calm manner without problem behavior on three consecutive exposures
6. If problem behavior occurs, discontinue exposure to the current stimulus and return to a more distant approximation that is unlikely to evoke problem behavior

ESSENTIAL FOR LIVING

Teaching Protocol 9. Recognitions, Retrievals, Relocations, Names, and Descriptions (**LRND1-13**)

What to Do	What Not to Do	
1. Require the learner to make listener responses, in the form of recognitions, retrievals, and relocations of items, activities, persons, places, and locations that occur in the context of routine events. Also require the learner to make corresponding speaker responses, in the form of names and descriptions.		1. Require the learner to make receptive responses and to tact items, activities, persons, places, and locations
2. Direct a learner to... recognize an item (e.g., "Where is the towel"), retrieve an item (e.g., "Please get me a towel), relocate an item (e.g., "Put the towel in the washer), or name or describe an item (e.g., "What is that")	2. Repeat the direction	2. Provide one and only one cue to make an appropriate receptive or tact response;
3. For listener responses, provide an immediate full demonstration prompt or a full physical prompt until the learner makes the appropriate response; then, proceed to step 5 For speaker responses... For learners aligned with Vocal Profiles 1 or 2 (i.e., learners who reliably repeat spoken words), immediately provide an echoic prompt -- say the word or phrase that corresponds to the item or activity (e.g., "hat"); if a learner's repetitions are controlled, also provide a vocal cue to do so (e.g., "say, (pause) hat"); then, proceed to step 5 For learners who use an alternative method of speaking, provide an immediate full demonstration prompt or a full physical prompt of the sign, word selection, or typed word until the learner makes the appropriate response; then, proceed to step 5	3. For listener responses...use spoken-word prompts, partial demonstration prompts, or partial physical prompts For speaker responses...use partial spoken-word prompts, partial demonstration prompts, or partial physical prompts	3. For listener responses, provide an errorless, full demonstration or full physical prompt; *do not use vocal-verbal prompts* For tact responses, provide an errorless echoic prompt; or provide an errorless, full demonstration or full physical prompt of a sign, word selection, of typed word; do not use partial echoic prompts and do not begin with partial demonstration or partial physical prompts; then, proceed to step 5
4. If the learner makes the appropriate response several consecutive times, begin to fade the prompts; fade echoic prompts all-at-once, fade demonstration prompts all-at-once or gradually, and fade full physical prompts gradually; proceed to step 5		4. If the learner makes the appropriate response several consecutive times, fade an echoic prompt by time delay, a demonstration prompt by topography or time delay, or a physical prompt by topography, and proceed to step 5
5. If the learner makes the appropriate response, provide praise; proceed to steps 2 and 4 until all prompts have been completely faded; in order to build a sizable listening and speaking repertoire, continue returning to step 2 with new items, activities, persons, places, and locations		5. If the learner makes the appropriate response, provide praise; proceed to steps 2 and 4 until all prompts have been completely faded; in order to build a sizable receptive and tact repertoire, continue returning to step 2
6. If the learner makes several additional responses (scrolls), return to steps 2 and 3 and provide a prompt until only the appropriate response occurs		6. If the learner scrolls or does not make the appropriate response, return to steps 2 and 3 and provide an errorless prompt
7. If problem behaviors occur, manually interrupt them or wait until they are no longer occurring; then, wait an additional period of time specific to each learner, ranging from 5 seconds to several minutes; if problem behaviors occur during this period of time, restart the time period and continue until these behaviors no longer occur during the entire period of time; then, repeat step 2	7. Provide access to a preferred item or activity, talk with the learner or acknowledge what he is doing, or permit him to engage in other activities	7. If problem behaviors occur, provide continuous, response interruption or social extinction until these behaviors have not occurred for a few seconds; implement a brief timeout from all preferred items and activities and all forms of attention and recycle this procedure if problem behaviors occur; then, repeat step 2 and use escape extinction

ESSENTIAL FOR LIVING

Teaching Protocol 10. Answers to Questions (**AQ1-13**)

What to Do	What Not to Do	
1. Require the learner to answer questions that occur in the context of the same routine events during which names, and descriptions were previously taught.		1. Require the learner to make intraverbal responses in the same context in which tacts were previously taught
2. Ask a learner a question (e.g., "Where are your socks")	2. Repeat the question	2. Provide one and only one cue for an intraverbal response
3. Provide an immediate prompt by pointing to an item or activity for which a name or description has already been acquired; then, proceed to step 5	3. Use spoken-word prompts, partial demonstration prompts, partial physical prompts, or printed-word prompts; use many picture prompts	3. Provide an errorless prompt by pointing to an item, activity, person, place or location for which a tact was previously acquired; *do not use vocal-verbal or printed-word prompts, and use only a limited number of picture prompts*
4. If the learner makes the appropriate response several consecutive times, begin to fade the prompts gradually; then, proceed to step 5		4. If the learner makes the appropriate response several consecutive times, fade the prompt by topography; then, proceed to step 5
5. If the learner makes the appropriate response, provide praise; proceed to steps 2 and 4 until the prompt has been completely faded; in order to build a sizable speaking repertoire, continue returning to step 2 with new questions		5. If the learner makes the appropriate response, provide praise; proceed to steps 2 and 4 until the prompt has been completely faded; in order to build a sizable intraverbal repertoire, continue returning to step 2 with new questions
6. If problem behaviors occur, manually interrupt them or wait until they are no longer occurring; then, wait an additional period of time specific to each learner, ranging from 5 seconds to several minutes; if problem behaviors occur during this period of time, restart the time period and continue until these behaviors no longer occur during the entire period of time; then, repeat step 2	6. Provide access to a preferred item or activity, talk with the learner or acknowledge what he is doing, or permit him to engage in other activities	6. If problem behaviors occur, provide continuous, response interruption or social extinction until these behaviors have not occurred for a few seconds; implement a brief timeout from all preferred items and activities and all forms of attention and recycle this procedure if problem behaviors occur; then, repeat step 2 and use escape extinction

Chapter 13. References

Adams, G. L. and Engelmann, S. (1996). Research on Direct Instruction: 25 Years beyond Distar. Seattle: Educational Achievement Systems.

Adkins, T. & Axelrod, S. (2002). Topography-based versus selection-based responding: A comparison of mand acquisition in each modality. The Behavior Analyst Today, 2, 259-266.

Barrera, R. D., Lobato-Barrera, D., & Sulzer-Azaroff, B. (1980). A simultaneous treatment comparison of three expressive language training programs with a mute autistic child. Journal of Autism and Developmental Disorders, 10, 21-37.

Barrett, R.P. & Sisson, L.A. (1987). Use of the alternating treatments design as a strategy for empirically determining language training approaches with mentally retarded children. Research in Developmental Disabilities, 8, 401 – 412.

Bartman, S., & Freeman, N. (2003). Teaching language to a two-year-old with autism. Journal on Developmental Disabilities, 10(1), 47-53.

Becker, W. C. (1992). Direct Instruction: A twenty year review. In R. P. West and L. A. Hamerlynck (Eds.). Designs for excellence in education: The legacy of B. F. Skinner (pp. 71-112). Longmont, Colorado: Sopris West.

Billington, E. J., Skinner, C. H., Hutchins, H. M., & Malone, J. C. (2004). Varying problem effort and choice: Using the interspersal technique to influence choice towards more effortful assignments. Journal of Behavioral Education, 13(3), 193-207.

Binder, C. (1996). Behavioral fluency: Evolution of a new paradigm. The Behavior Analyst, 19, 163-197.

Binder, C., Haughton, E. & Van Eyk, D. (1990). Increasing endurance by building fluency: Precision Teaching attention span. Teaching Exceptional Children, 22(3), 24-27.

Bondy, A., & Frost, L. (2001). The picture exchange communication system. Behavior Modification, 25, 725-744.

Born-Miller, K. L. (2002). The use of an errorless teaching procedure to teach children with autism for whom trial-and-error teaching has failed. ProQuest Information & Learning. Dissertation Abstracts International: Section B: The Sciences and Engineering, 63(4-B), 2088.

Bowman, L. G., Fisher, W. W., Thompson, R. H., & Piazza, C. C. (1997). On the relation of mands and the function of destructive behavior. Journal of Applied Behavior Analysis, 30, 251-265.

Braam, S. J., & Poling, A. (1983). Development of intraverbal behavior in mentally retarded individuals through transfer of stimulus control procedures: Classification of verbal res-ponses. Applied Research in Mental Retardation, 4, 279-302.

Braam, S. J., & Sundberg, M. L. (1991). The effects of specific versus nonspecific reinforcement on verbal behavior. The Analysis of Verbal Behavior, 9, 19-28.

Brady, N. C., Saunders, K. J., & Spradlin, J. E. (1994). A conceptual analysis of request teaching procedures for individuals with severely limited verbal repertoires. The Analysis of Verbal Behavior, 12, 43-52.

Browder, D. M., Morris, W. W., & Snell, M. E. (1981). Using time delay to teach manual signs to a severely retarded student. Education and Training of the Mentally Retarded, 16(4), 252-258.

Brown, R. (1973). A first language: The early stages. Cambridge, MA: Harvard University Press.

Brownjohn, M. D. (1988). Acquisition of makaton symbols by a young man with severe learning difficulties. Behavioural Psychotherapy, 16(2), 85-94.

Carbone, V. J. (2001). Teaching language to children with developmental disabilities, including autism. Guided notes from ABA-Verbal Behavior workshops, from introductory to advanced levels, presented to audiences in the U.S. and many other countries.

Carbone, V. J. (2004). Teaching language to children with developmental disabilities, including autism. Guided notes from ABA-Verbal Behavior workshops, from introductory to advanced levels, presented to audiences in the U.S. and many other countries. Valley Cottage, NY: The Carbone Clinic.

Carbone, V. J., Lewis, L., Sweeney-Kerwin, E. J., Dixon, J., Louden, R., & Quinn, S. (2006). A comparison of two approaches for teaching VB functions: Total communication vs. vocal-alone. Journal of Speech-Language Pathology and Applied Behavior Analysis, 1, 181-191.

Carbone, V. J., Morgenstern, B., Zecchin-Tirri, G., & Kolberg, L. (2007). The role of the reflexive conditioned motivating operation (CMO-R) during discrete trial instruction of children with autism. Journal of Early and Intensive Behavioral Intervention, 4(4), 658-680.

Carnine, D. W. (1976). Effects of two teacher-presentation rates on off-task behavior, answering correctly, and participation. Journal of Applied Behavior Analysis, 9(2), 199-206.

Carr, E. G. (1979). Teaching autistic children to use sign language. Journal of Autism and Developmental Disorders, 9, 345-359.

Carr, E. G. (1982). Sign language. In R. Koegel, A. Rincover, & A. Egel (Eds.), Educating and understanding autistic children (pp. 142–157). San Diego, CA: College-Hill Press.

Carr, E. G., & Durand, V. M. (1985). Reducing behavior problems through functional communication training. Journal of Applied Behavior Analysis, 18, 111-126.

Carr, J. E., & Firth, A. M. (2005). The verbal behavior approach to early and intensive behavioral intervention for autism: A call for additional empirical support. Journal of Early and Intensive Behavioral Intervention, 2, 18-27.

Carroll, R. J., & Hesse, B. E. (1987). The effects of alternating mand and tact training on the acquisition of tacts. The Analysis of Verbal Behavior, 5, 55-65.

Catania, A. C. (1973a). The concept of the operant in the analysis of behavior. Behaviorism, 1, 103-116.

Catania, A. C. (1973b). The psychologies of structure, function, and development. American Psychologist, 28, 434-443.

Catania, A. C. (1979). Learning. Englewood Cliffs, NJ: Prentice-Hall.

Catania, A. C. (2007). Learning (interim 4th ed.). Cornwall-on-Hudson, NY: Sloan Publishing.

Cautilli, J. (2006). Validation of the verbal behavior package: Old wine new bottle -- A reply to Carr & Firth (2005). The Journal of Speech-Language Pathology and Applied Behavior Analysis, 1, 81-92.

Chambers, M., & Rehfeldt, R.A. (2003). Assessing the acquisition and generalization of two mand forms with adults with severe developmental disabilities. Research in Developmental Disabilities, 24(4), 265-280.

Charlop, M. H., & Haymes, L. K. (1994). Speech and language acquisition and intervention: Behavioral approaches. In J. L. Matson (Ed.), autism in children and adults: Etiology, assessment, and intervention (pp. 213–240). Pacific Grove, CA: Brooks/Cole.

Charlop-Christy, M. H., Carpenter, M., Le, L., LeBlanc, L. A., & Kellet, K. (2002). Using the picture exchange communication system (PECS) with children with autism: Assessment of PECS acquisition, speech, social-communicative behavior, and problem behavior. Journal of Applied Behavior Analysis, 35(3), 213-231.

Chomsky, N. (1957). Syntactic structures. The Hague: Mouton and Company.

Chomsky, N. (1959). A review of B. F. Skinner's Verbal Behavior. Language, 35, 26-58.

Darch, C., & Gersten, R. (1985). The effects of teacher presentation rate and praise on LD students' oral reading performance. British Journal of Educational Psychology, 55(3),295-303.

Donahoe, J. W., & Palmer, D. C. (2004). Learning and complex behavior. Richmond, MA: Ledgetop Publishing.

Dunlap, G. (1984). The influence of task variation and maintenance tasks on the learning and affect of autistic children. Journal of Experimental Child Psychology, 37(1), 41-64.

Dymond, S., O'Hora, D., Whelan, R., & O'Donovan, A. (2006). Citation analysis of Skinner's Verbal Behavior: 1984-2004. The Behavior Analyst, 29, 253-267.

Englert, C. S. (1984). Effective direct instruction practices in special education settings. Remedial & Special Education, 5(2), 38-47.

Esch, B. E., Carr, J. E., & Michael, J. (2005). Evaluating stimulus-stimulus pairing and direct reinforcement in the establishment of an echoic repertoire of children diagnosed with autism. The Analysis of Verbal Behavior, 21, 43-58.

Eshleman, J. (1991). Quantified trends in the history of verbal behavior research. The Analysis of Verbal Behavior, 9, 61-80.

Frost, L. A., & Bondy, A. S. (1994). The picture exchange communication system training manual. Cherry Hill, NJ: Pyramid Educational Consultants.

Frost, L. A., & Bondy, A. S. (1998). The picture exchange communication system. Seminars in Speech and Language, 19, 373–389.

Ganz, J. B., Simpson, R. L. (2004). Effects on communicative requesting and speech development of the picture exchange communication system in children with characteristics of autism. Journal of Autism and Developmental Disorders, 34(4), 395-409.

Granzin, A. C., & Carnine, D. W. (1977). Child performance on discrimination tasks: Effects of amount of stimulus variation. Journal of Experimental Child Psychology, 24(2), 332-342.

Green, G. (2003). The "Verbal Behavior" approach to autism: Where are the data? An invited address to the annual meeting of the Florida Association for Behavior Analysis, St. Petersburg, FL.

Green, G. (2004). The "Verbal Behavior" approach to autism: Where are the data? An invited address to the annual meeting of the Experimental Analysis of Behavior Group, London, England.

Greer, R. D., & Ross, D. (2007). Verbal behavior analysis: Inducing and expanding new verbal capabilities in children with language delays. New York, NY: Pearson Education, Inc.

Hall, G., & Sundberg, M.L. (1987). Teaching mands by manipulating conditioned establishing operations. The Analysis of Verbal Behavior, 5, 41-53.

Hart, B., & Risley, T. R. (1975). Incidental teaching of language in the preschool. Journal of Applied Behavior Analysis, 8, 411-420.

Haughton, E. C. (1972). Aims: Growing and sharing. In J. B. Jordan & L. S. Robbins (Eds.), Let's try doing something else kind of thing. Arlington, VA: Council on Exceptional Children.

Heflin, L. J., & Alberto, P. A. (2001). Establishing a behavioral context for learning for students with autism. Focus on Autism and Other Developmental Disabilities, 16(2), 93-101.

Hodges, P., & Schwethelm, B. (1984). A comparison of the effectiveness of graphic symbol and manual sign training with profoundly retarded children. Applied Psycholinguistics, 5, 223-253.

Horner, R. H., & Albin, R. W. (1988). Research on general-case procedures for learners with severe disabilities. Education and Treatment of Children, 11(4), 375-388.

Johnston, J. M., & Pennypacker, H. S. (1993). Strategies and tactics of behavioral research (second edition). Hillsdale, NJ: Lawrence Erlbaum Associates.

Kahng, S. W., Hendrickson, D. J., & Vu, C. P. (2000). Comparison of single and multiple functional communication training responses for the treatment of problem behavior. Journal of Applied Behavior Analysis, 33, 321-324.

Kates-McElrath, K., & Axelrod, S. (2006). Behavioral intervention for autism: A distinction between two behavior analytic approaches. The Behavior Analyst Today, 7, 242-252.

Kouri, T.A. (1988). Effects of simultaneous communication in a child-directed treatment approach with preschoolers with severe disabilities. Augmentative and Alternative Communication, 4, 222 – 230.

Kravits, T. R., Kamps, D. M., Kemmerer, K., Potucek, J. (2002). Brief report: Increasing communication skills for an elementary-aged student with autism using the picture exchange communication system. Journal of Autism and Developmental Disorders, 32(3), 225-230.

LaMarre, J., & Holland, J.G. (1985). The functional independence of mands and tacts. Journal of the Experimental Analysis of Behavior, 43, 5-19.

LeBlanc, L. A., Esch, J., Sidener, T. M., & Firth. A. M. (2006). Behavioral language interventions for children with autism: Comparing Applied Verbal Behavior and Naturalistic teaching approaches. The Analysis of Verbal Behavior, 22, 49-60.

Lerman, D. C., Parten, M., Addison, L. R., Vorndran, C. M., Volkert, V. M., & Kodak, T. (2005). A methodology for assessing the functions of emerging speech in children with developmental disabilities. Journal of Applied Behavior Analysis, 38, 303-316.

Lovaas, O. I. (1987). Behavioral treatment and normal educational and intellectual functioning in young autistic children. Journal of Consulting and Clinical Psychology, 55, 3–9.

Lowenkron, B. (1991). Joint control and the generalization of selection-based verbal behavior. The Analysis of Verbal Behavior, 9, 123-128.

Lowenkron, B. (2004). Meaning: A verbal behavior account. The Analysis of Verbal Behavior, 20, 121-126.

Lowenkron, B. (2006). An introduction to joint control. The Analysis of Verbal Behavior, 22, 123-127.

Luciano, M. C. (1986). Acquisition, maintenance, and generalization of productive intraverbal behavior through transfer of stimulus control procedures. Applied Research in Mental Retardation, 7, 1-20.

MacCorquodale, K. (1969). B. F. Skinner's Verbal Behavior: A retrospective appreciation. Journal of the Experimental Analysis of Behavior, 12, 831-841.

MacCorquodale, K. (1970). On Chomsky's review of Skinner's Verbal Behavior. Journal of the Experimental Analysis of Behavior, 13, 83-99.

McGreevy, P. (2002). Teaching language to children and adults with developmental disabilities, including autism. Guided notes from ABA-Verbal Behavior workshops, from introductory to advanced levels, presented to audiences in the U.S., the U.K., Canada, The United Arab Emirates, and India. Winter Park, FL: Patrick McGreevy, Ph.D., P.A. and Associates.

McGreevy, P. (2005). Teaching signs and sign language to children and adults with developmental disabilities, including autism. Guided notes from a workshop presented to audiences in the U.S. and Canada. Winter Park, FL: Patrick McGreevy, Ph.D., P.A. and Associates.

McGreevy, P. (2007). Teaching signs and sign language to children and adults with developmental disabilities, including autism. A pre-conference workshop presented to the annual meeting of the Association for Behavior Analysis, San Diego, CA.

McGreevy, P., & Sundberg, C. T. (2007). Teaching signs and sign language to children and adults with developmental disabilities, including autism. A pre-conference workshop presented to the annual meeting of the California Association for Behavior Analysis, San Francisco, CA.

Michael, J. (1982a). Distinguishing between discriminative and motivational functions of stimuli. Journal of the Experimental Analysis of Behavior, 37, 149-155.

Michael, J. (1982b). Skinner's elementary verbal relations: Some new categories. The Analysis of Verbal Behavior, 1, 1-3.

Michael, J. (1983). Evocative and repertoire-altering effects of an environmental event. The Analysis of Verbal Behavior, 2, 19-21.

Michael, J. (1984). Verbal behavior. Journal of the Experimental Analysis of Behavior, 42, 363-376.

Michael, J. (1985). Two kinds of verbal behavior plus a possible third. The Analysis of Verbal Behavior, 3, 1-4.

Michael, J. (1988). Establishing operations and the mand. The Analysis of Verbal Behavior, 6, 3-9.

Michael, J. (1993). Establishing operations. The Behavior Analyst, 16, 191-206.

Michael, J. (2000). Implications and refinements of the establishing operation concept. Journal of Applied Behavior Analysis, 33, 401-410.

Miguel. C. F., Petursdottir, A. I., & Carr, J. E. (2005). The effects of multiple-tact and receptive-discrimination training on the acquisition of intraverbal behavior. The Analysis of Verbal Behavior, 21, 27-41.

Moore, R., & Goldiamond, I. (1964). Errorless establishment of visual discrimination using fading procedures. Journal of the Experimental Analysis of Behavior, 7, 269-272.

Oah, S., & Dickinson, A. M. (1989). A review of empiricial studies of verbal behavior. The Analysis of Verbal Behavior, 7, 53-68.

Palmer, D. C. (2006). On Chomsky's appraisal of Skinner's Verbal Behavior: A half century of misunderstanding. The Behavior Analyst, 29(2), 253-267.

Partington, J. W. (2007). The assessment of basic language and learning skills: The ABLLS-R Protocol. Pleasant Hill, CA: Behavior Analysts, Inc.

Partington, J. W., & Bailey, J. S. (1993). Teaching intraverbal behavior to preschool children. The Analysis of Verbal Behavior, 11, 9-18.

Partington, J. W., & Sundberg, M. L. (1999). The assessment of basic language and learning skills: The ABLLS. Pleasant Hill, CA: Behavior Analysts, Inc.

Piaget, J. (1926). The language and thought of the child. London: Routledge and Kegan Paul, Ltd.

Pinker, S. (1994). The language instinct. New York: William Morrow and Company.

Reichle, J., Sigafoos, J., & Remington, B. (1991). Beginning an augmentative communication system with individuals who have severe disabilities. In B. Remington (Ed.), The challenge of severe mental handicaps. Chichester, NH: Wiley and Sons.

Remington, B., & Clarke, S. (1983). Acquisition of expressive signing by autistic children: An evaluation of the relative effects of simultaneous communication and sign-alone training. Journal of Applied Behavior Analysis, 16(3), 315-327.

Richman, D. M., Wacker, D. P., & Winborn, L. (2001). Response efficiency during functional communication training: Effects of effort on response allocation. Journal of Applied Behavior Analysis, 34, 73-76.

Ritseman, S. K., Malanga, P. R., Seevers, R. L., & Cooper, J. O. (1996). Immediate retelling of current events from Channel One by students with developmental disabilities and its effect on their delayed retelling. Journal of Precision Teaching, 14, 18-34.

Rogers-Warren, A., & Warren, S. (1980). Mands for verbalization: Facilitating the display of newly trained language in children. Behavior Modification, 4, 361-382.

Rowan, V. C., & Pear, J. J. (1985). A comparison of the effects of interspersal and concurrent training sequences on acquisition, retention, and generalization of picture names. Applied Research in Mental Retardation, 6(2), 127-145.

Sautter, R. A., & LeBlanc, L. A. (2006). Empirical applications of Skinner's analysis of verbal behavior with humans. The Analysis of Verbal Behavior, 22, 35-48.

Shafer, E. (1993). Teaching topography-based and selection-based verbal behavior to developmentally disabled individuals: Some considerations. The Analysis of Verbal Behavior, 11, 117-133.

Shafer, E. (1994). A review of interventions to teach a mand repertoire. The Analysis of Verbal Behavior, 12, 53-66.

Shirley, M. J., & Pennypacker, H. S. (1994). The effects of performance criteria on learning and retention of spelling words. Journal of Precision Teaching, 12, 73-86.

Sigafoos, J., Doss, S., & Reichle, J. (1989). Developing mand and tact repertoires with persons with severe developmental disabilities with graphic symbols. Research in Developmental Disabilities, 11, 165-176.

Sisson, L.A., & Barrett, R.P. (1984). An alternating treatment comparison of oral and total communication training with minimally verbal retarded children. Journal of Applied Behavior Analysis, 17, 559 – 566.

Skinner, B. F. (1938). The behavior of organisms. New York, NY: Appleton-Century-Crofts.

Skinner, B. F. (1953). Science and human behavior. New York, NY: MacMillan.

Skinner, B. F. (1957, 1992). Verbal Behavior. Acton, MA: Copley Publishing Group and the B.F. Skinner Foundation.

Skinner, B.F. (1974). About behaviorism. New York, NY: Random House.

Spradlin, J. E. (1963). Assessment of speech and language of retarded children: The Parsons language sample. Journal of Speech and Hearing Disorders Monograph, 10, 8-31.

Spradlin, J. E. (1985). Studying the effects of the audience on verbal behavior. The Analysis of Verbal Behavior, 3, 5-9.

Stafford, Mark W., Sundberg, Mark L., & Braam, Steven J. (1988). A preliminary investigation of the consequences that define the mand and the tact. The Analysis of Verbal Behavior, 6, 61-71.

Sternberg, M. L. A. (1998). American sign language dictionary. New York, NY: HarperCollins Publishers.

Sundberg, C. T., & McGreevy, P. (2007). Teaching signs and sign language to hearing children and adults with developmental disabilities including autism. A pre-conference workshop presented at the annual conference of the California Association for Behavior Analysis.

Sundberg, C. T., & Sundberg, M. L. (1990). Comparing topography-based verbal behavior with selection-based verbal behavior. The Analysis of Verbal Behavior, 8, 31-41.

Sundberg, M. L. (1980). Developing a verbal repertoire using sign language and Skinner's analysis of verbal behavior. Unpublished doctoral dissertation, Western Michigan University.

Sundberg, M. L. (1993). Selecting a response form for nonverbal persons: Facilitated communication, pointing systems, or sign language. The Analysis of Verbal Behavior, 11, 99-116.

Sundberg, M. L. (2007a). Verbal behavior. In J. O. Cooper, T. Heron, & W. L. Heward, W. L. (Eds.), Applied Behavior Analysis [2nd ed.] (p. 526-547). Upper Saddle River, NJ: Pearson Education, Inc.

Sundberg, M. L. (2007b). The Verbal Behavior Milestones Assessment and Placement Program: The VB-MAPP. A pre-conference workshop presented to the annual meeting of the Association for Behavior Analysis, San Diego, CA.

Sundberg, M. L. (in press). The Verbal Behavior Milestones Assessment and Placement Program: The VB-MAPP.

Sundberg, M. L., Loeb, M., Hale, L., & Eigenheer, P. (2001-2002). Contriving establishing operations to teach mands for information. The Analysis of Verbal Behavior, 18, 15-29.

Sundberg, M. L., & Michael, J. (2001). The benefits of Skinner's analysis of verbal behavior for children with autism. Behavior Modification, 25, 698-724.

Sundberg, M. J., Michael, J., Partington, J. W., & Sundberg, C. A. (1996). The role of automatic reinforcement in early language acquisition. The Analysis of Verbal Behavior, 13, 21-37).

Sundberg, M. L., & Partington, J. W. (1998). Teaching language to children with autism or other developmental disabilities. Pleasant Hill, CA: Behavior Analysts, Inc.

Sundberg, M. L., & Partington, J. W. (2001). QuickTips: Behavioral teaching strategies. Pleasant Hill, CA: Behavior Analysts, Inc.

Sweeney-Kerwin, E. J., Carbone, V. J., O'Brien, L., Zecchin, G., & Janecky, M. N. (2007). Transferring control of the mand to the motivating operation in children with autism. The Analysis of Verbal Behavior, 23, 89-102.

Tateyama-Sniezek, K. M. (1989). The effects of stimulus variation on the generalization performance of students with moderate retardation. Education and Training in Mental Retardation, 24(1), 89-94.

Terrace, H. S. (1963). Errorless transfer of a discrimination across two continua. Journal of the Experimental Analysis of Behavior, 6(2), 223-232.

Tincani, M. (2004). Comparing the picture exchange communication system and sign language training for children with autism. Focus on Autism and Other Developmental Disabilities, 19(3), 152-163.

Tincani, M., Crozier, S., Alazetta, L. (2006). The picture exchange communication system: Effects on manding and speech development for school-Aged children with autism. Education and Training in Developmental Disabilities, 41(2), 177-184.

Touchette, P. E. (1971). Transfer of stimulus control: measuring the moment of transfer. Journal of the Experimental Analysis of Behavior, 15, 347-354.

Tsiouri, I., & Greer, R. D. (2003). Inducing vocal verbal behavior in children with severe language delays through rapid motor imitation responding. Journal of Behavioral Education 12(3), 185-206.

Twyman, J. S. (1996). The functional independence of impure mands and tacts of abstract stimulus properties. Analysis of Verbal Behavior, 13, 1-19.

Vargas, E. A. (1982). Intraverbal behavior: The codic, duplic, and sequelic subtypes. The Analysis of Verbal Behavior, 1, 5-7.

Vargas, E. A. (1986). Intraverbal behavior. In L. J. Parrot & P. Chase (Eds.), Psychological aspects of language (p. 128-151). Springfield, IL: Thomas Publishing.

Walsh, B. F., & Lamberts, F. (1979). Errorless discrimination and picture fading as techniques for teaching sight words to TMR students. American Journal of Mental Deficiency, 83(5), 473-479.

Watkins, C. L. Pack-Teixteira, L., & Howard, J. S. (1989). Teaching intraverbal behavior to severely retarded children. The Analysis of Verbal Behavior, 7, 69-81.

Williams, G., & Greer, R. D. (1993). A comparison of verbal behavior and linguistic curricula. Behaviorology, 1, 31-46.

Winborn, L., Wacker, D. P., Richman, D. M., Asmus, J., & Geier, D. (2002). Assessment of mand selection for functional communication training packages. Journal of Applied Behavior Analysis, 35, 295-298.

Wraikat, R., Sundberg, C. T., & Michael, J. (1991). Topography-based and selection-based verbal behavior: A further comparison. The Analysis of Verbal Behavior, 9, 1-17.

Yi, J. I., Christian, L., Vittimberga, G., & Lowenkron, B. (2006). Generalized negatively reinforced manding in children with autism. The Analysis of Verbal Behavior, 22, 21-33.

Yoon, S. & Bennett, G. M. (2000). Effects of a stimulus-stimulus pairing procedure on conditioning vocal sounds as reinforcers. The Analysis of Verbal Behavior, 17, 75-88.

Yokoyama, K., Naoi, N., Yamamoto, J. (2006). Teaching verbal behavior using the picture exchange communication system (PECS) with children with autistic spectrum disorders. Japanese Journal of Special Education, 43(6), 485-503.

Appendix

The Favorite Items and Activities Data Recording Form

The process of determining a learner's favorite items and activities is described in chapter 7a. The Favorite Items and Activities Data Recording Form is also described in this chapter. A copy of this form is included in this Appendix. A copy can also be downloaded from http//:www.behaviorchange.com.

Probe Data Recording Forms

The process of collecting, recording, and displaying probe data is described in chapter 4. Probe data recording forms are skill specific and examples of each form are also described in the chapter dedicated to that skill. These forms can be downloaded from http//:www.behaviorchange.com.

The Problem Behavior Direct Observation and Interview Form

The process of collecting, recording, and displaying frequency data with respect to problem behaviors is also described in chapter 4. Defining and recording the intensity of these behaviors, recording the extent to which psychoactive medications, protective equipment, mechanical restraints, and crisis stabilization procedures are used, and recording the extent to which self-restraint occurs using the Problem Behavior Direct Observation and Interview Form are also described. A copy of this form is included in this Appendix. A copy can also be downloaded from http//:www.behaviorchange.com.

ESSENTIAL FOR LIVING
Favorite Items and Activities Data Recording Form

Learner: _____ Birthdate: _____ Age: _____

School, Home, Day Activity, or Residential Program: _____

Interests of the learner as indicated in an interview by persons who know the learner well...	Interests of the learner as indicated by learner...			
R1: Items and activities are ranked from most favorite to least favorite All items and activities on this list go to **R2** or **R4**	**R2:** when items or activities are made available one at a time All items and activities on the list or interests that are indicated go to **R3**	**R3:** when items or activities are given one at a time When interest is indicated in four or more items or activities go to **R4**	**R4:** when items or activities are presented one at a time When interest is indicated in four or more items or activities go to **R5** or **R7**	**R5:** when items or activities are presented two or more at a time All interests that are indicated go to **R7**
1-	1 2 3 4 5	1 2 3 4 5	1 2 3 4 5	1 2 3 4 5
2-	1 2 3 4 5	1 2 3 4 5	1 2 3 4 5	1 2 3 4 5
3-	1 2 3 4 5	1 2 3 4 5	1 2 3 4 5	1 2 3 4 5
4-	1 2 3 4 5	1 2 3 4 5	1 2 3 4 5	1 2 3 4 5
5-	1 2 3 4 5	1 2 3 4 5	1 2 3 4 5	1 2 3 4 5
6-	1 2 3 4 5	1 2 3 4 5	1 2 3 4 5	1 2 3 4 5
7-	1 2 3 4 5	1 2 3 4 5	1 2 3 4 5	1 2 3 4 5
8-	1 2 3 4 5	1 2 3 4 5	1 2 3 4 5	1 2 3 4 5
9-	1 2 3 4 5	1 2 3 4 5	1 2 3 4 5	1 2 3 4 5
10-	1 2 3 4 5	1 2 3 4 5	1 2 3 4 5	1 2 3 4 5
11-	1 2 3 4 5	1 2 3 4 5	1 2 3 4 5	1 2 3 4 5
12-	1 2 3 4 5	1 2 3 4 5	1 2 3 4 5	1 2 3 4 5
13-	1 2 3 4 5	1 2 3 4 5	1 2 3 4 5	1 2 3 4 5
14-	1 2 3 4 5	1 2 3 4 5	1 2 3 4 5	1 2 3 4 5
15-	1 2 3 4 5	1 2 3 4 5	1 2 3 4 5	1 2 3 4 5
16-	1 2 3 4 5	1 2 3 4 5	1 2 3 4 5	1 2 3 4 5
17-	1 2 3 4 5	1 2 3 4 5	1 2 3 4 5	1 2 3 4 5
18-	1 2 3 4 5	1 2 3 4 5	1 2 3 4 5	1 2 3 4 5
19-	1 2 3 4 5	1 2 3 4 5	1 2 3 4 5	1 2 3 4 5
20-	1 2 3 4 5	1 2 3 4 5	1 2 3 4 5	1 2 3 4 5

Items carried around by the learner or specific, repetitive behaviors the learner exhibits frequently:

1-

2-

ESSENTIAL FOR LIVING

Problem Behavior Direct Observation and Interview Form

Learner: _____ Environment(s): _____

Date: _____ Observer or Person Interviewed: _____ Counting Period: _____

Definition of Problem Behavior 1 --							Definition of Problem Behavior 2 --						
Instance	Episode		SIB	Agg	Des	Dis	Rep	Instance	Episode		SIB	Agg	Des	Dis	Rep

Medications: _____

Direct Observation

PB1	Intensity	MRA	MRC	PEA	PEC	CS (min)	SR	PB2	Intensity	MRA	MRC	PEA	PEC	CS (min)	SR
1	Sev-Mod-Mild							1	Sev-Mod-Mild						
2	Sev-Mod-Mild							2	Sev-Mod-Mild						
3	Sev-Mod-Mild							3	Sev-Mod-Mild						
4	Sev-Mod-Mild							4	Sev-Mod-Mild						
5	Sev-Mod-Mild							5	Sev-Mod-Mild						
6	Sev-Mod-Mild							6	Sev-Mod-Mild						
7	Sev-Mod-Mild							7	Sev-Mod-Mild						
8	Sev-Mod-Mild							8	Sev-Mod-Mild						
9	Sev-Mod-Mild							9	Sev-Mod-Mild						
10	Sev-Mod-Mild							10	Sev-Mod-Mild						
11	Sev-Mod-Mild							11	Sev-Mod-Mild						
12	Sev-Mod-Mild							12	Sev-Mod-Mild						
13	Sev-Mod-Mild							13	Sev-Mod-Mild						
14	Sev-Mod-Mild							14	Sev-Mod-Mild						
15	Sev-Mod-Mild							15	Sev-Mod-Mild						
16	Sev-Mod-Mild							16	Sev-Mod-Mild						
17	Sev-Mod-Mild							17	Sev-Mod-Mild						
18	Sev-Mod-Mild							18	Sev-Mod-Mild						
19	Sev-Mod-Mild							19	Sev-Mod-Mild						
20	Sev-Mod-Mild							20	Sev-Mod-Mild						

Interview

This behavior occurs ___ per day ___ per week ___ per month ___ per year and the intensity is: ___ sev ___ mod ___ mild
The learner wears, requires, or exhibits:

MRA or **MRC**: _____

PEA or **PEC**: _____

CS: ___ minutes per day ___ hours per week

SR: _____

This behavior occurs ___ per day ___ per week ___ per month ___ per year and the intensity is: ___ sev ___ mod ___ mild
The learner wears, requires, or exhibits:

MRA or **MRC**: _____

PEA or **PEC**: _____

CS: ___ minutes per day ___ hours per week

SR: _____